Born Losers

Born Losers

A HISTORY

OF FAILURE

IN AMERICA

SCOTT A. SANDAGE

Harvard University Press

Cambridge, Massachusetts, and London, England

First Harvard University Press paperback edition, 2006

Quotations from the song "I Don't Mind Failing," words and music by
Malvina Reynolds, copyright Schroder Music Co. (ASCAP). Used by permission. All rights reserved.

Quotations from "The Times They Are a-Changin'," "Subterranean
Homesick Blues," and "Love Minus Zero / No Limit" by Bob Dylan. Used
by permission of Special Rider Music.

Library of Congress Cataloging-in-Publication Data

Sandage, Scott A.
  Born losers : a history of failure in America / Scott A. Sandage.
    p. cm.
  "Born losers began as a 1995 doctoral dissertation at Rutgers University"—
P. .
  Includes bibliographical references and index.
  ISBN 0-674-01510-X (cloth: alk. paper)
  ISBN 0-674-02107-X (pbk.)
  1. Social values—United States—History—19th century. 2. Losers—
United States—History—19th century. 3. Failure (Psychology)—United
States—History—19th century. 4. Capitalism—Social aspects—United
States—History—19th century. 5. Identity (Psychology)—United States—
History—19th century. 6. Stigma (Social psychology) 7. Social status—
United States—History—19th century. I. Title: History of failure in
America. II. Title.
  HN90.M6S25 2005
  303.3'72'097309034—dc22   2004051134

To my family

and for Greg

Contents

Illustrations

Born Losers

Prologue:
Lives of Quiet Desperation

The American Dream died young and was laid to rest on a splendid afternoon in May 1862, when blooming apple trees heralded the arrival of spring. At three o'clock, a bell tolled forty-four times, once for each year of a life cut short. Dismissed from school, three hundred children marched to the funeral under the bright sun. Those with luck and pluck would grow up to transform American capitalism during the Gilded Age. But on this day the scent in the air was not wealth, but wildflowers. Violets dotted the grass outside the First Parish Church. The casket in the vestibule bore a wreath of andromeda and a blanket of flowers that perfumed the sanctuary with the sweetness of spring.[1]

Townsfolk and visiting notables crowded in to hear the eulogist admit what many had thought all along: the dearly departed had wasted his gifts. Neither a deadbeat nor a drunkard, he was the worst kind of failure: a dreamer. "He seemed born for greatness ... and I cannot help counting it a fault in him that he had no ambition," the speaker grieved. Rather than an engineer or a great general, "he was the captain of a huckleberry-party." When not picking berries, the deceased had tried his hand at a variety of occupations: teacher, surveyor, pencilmaker, housepainter, mason, farmer, gardener, and writer. Some who congregated that day in Concord, Massachusetts, thought it tactless to say such things of Henry Thoreau at his own funeral, however true Mr. Emerson's sermon about his dear friend was: Henry's quirky ambitions hardly amounted to a hill of beans.[2]

Perhaps no one present fully understood what Ralph Waldo Emerson was saying about ambition, least of all the children fidgeting and daydreaming in the pews. Someday they would rise and fall in the world the sermon presaged, where berry picking was a higher crime than bankruptcy. If a man could fail simply by not succeeding or not striving, then ambition was not an opportunity but an obligation. Following the casket to the grave, stooping here and there to collect petals that wafted from it, the children buried more than the odd little man they had seen in the woods or on the street. Part of the American Dream of success went asunder: the part that gave them any choice in the matter.

We live daily with Emerson's disappointment in Thoreau. The promise of America is that nobody is a born loser, but who has never wondered, "Am I wasting my life?" We imagine escaping the mad scramble, yet kick ourselves for lacking drive. Low ambition offends Americans even more than low achievement. How we play the game is the important thing, or so we say. Win or lose, Thoreau taunts us from the dog-eared pages and dogwooded shores of *Walden:* "The mass of men lead lives of quiet desperation." We sprint as much to outrun failure as to catch success. Failure conjures such vivid pictures of lost souls that it is hard to imagine a time, before the Civil War, when the word commonly meant "breaking in business"—going broke. How did it become a name for a deficient self, an identity in the red? Why do we manage identity the way we run a business—by investment, risk, profit, and loss? Why do we calculate failure in lost dreams as much as in lost dollars?[3]

Henry D. Thoreau, age forty-four, knew he was dying when a friend asked him to sit for this final portrait in late August 1861. (Ambrotype by E. S. Dunshee; copyright 1879 by George F. Parlow. Prints and Photographs Division, Library of Congress.)

This book tells the story of America's unsung losers: men who failed in a nation that worships success. The time is the nineteenth century, when capitalism came of age and entrepreneurship became the primary model of American identity. This was the era of self-made men and manifest destiny. The nation we know today evolved between the inaugurations of Thomas Jefferson and Theodore Roosevelt, 1801 to 1901—a century that began and ended with empire builders in the White House, icons of individualism and progress. The industrial revolution sped economic growth, the Civil War remade freedom and political growth, the rise of mass media animated cultural growth, and frontier and imperialist incursions secured territorial growth. Most of what the twenty-first-century public knows about nineteenth-century America fits somewhere into this general outline.[4]

Little collective memory remains of the *other* nineteenth century: the rough ride between the panics of 1819 and 1893. Unprecedented growth brought equally unprecedented volatility, and both spurred new thinking about economic identity and the groundings of freedom. "I am now 54 years of age," a ruined merchant wrote in 1866, begging Congress to pass a federal bankruptcy law. "Having given up the entire earnings of thirty years of business life, have I not a right to be legally released? that I may again lift up my head and feel that I have some manhood left Me?" The wives of incapacitated or despondent men also assumed heavy burdens. A Pennsylvania woman confided in 1892, "My husband is now 64 years old and . . . cannot seem to turn himself around and take care of himself. I being 42, the effort falls upon me. I took his business in hands [sic] and went West, saved what little I could." Families held sheriffs and auctioneers at bay, decade upon decade, while lawmakers, reformers, and capitalists debated how to manage debt, credit, currency, and bankruptcy in an entrepreneurial culture unable to do without them.[5]

Businessmen dominate this story because their loss of money and manhood drove legislative, commercial, and cultural solutions that redefined failure: from the lost capital of a bankruptcy to the lost chances of a wasted life. This shift from ordeal to identity expanded the constituency of failure. Women, workers, and African Americans were put on notice: ruin was no longer just for white businessmen. As the twentieth century dawned, popular magazines were enlivened by "Frank Confessions from Men and Women Who Missed Success." *The Cosmopolitan* named "The Fear of Failure" as the bane of "many a young man and woman." Correspondence schools taunted laborers to escape "the treadmill positions of life." Upon founding the National Negro Business League, Booker T. Washington urged that "more attention . . . be directed to [Negroes] who have succeeded, and less to those who have failed." By 1900, anybody could end up "a 'Nobody,'" plodding down the "many paths leading to the Land of 'Nowhere.'" Failure had become what it remains in the new millennium: the most damning incarnation of the connection between achievement and personal identity. "I feel like a failure." The expression comes so naturally that we forget it is a figure of speech: the language of business applied to the soul.[6]

Everyman's alma mater, the school of hard knocks, expelled at least as many as it graduated. If the market is an invisible hand, failure is how that hand disciplines and ejects the misfits of capitalism. A century ago, in his 1905 classic work *The Protestant Ethic and the Spirit of Capitalism*, Max Weber argued that striving for success is a compulsory virtue, even a sacred duty in American culture. "The capitalistic economy of the present day is an immense cosmos into which the individual is born, and which presents itself to him, at least as an individual, as an unalterable order of things in which he must live," Weber explained. "It forces the individual, in so far as he is involved in the system of market relationships, to conform to capitalistic rules of action." These rules include the rational pursuit of profit, the perpetual increase of capital as an end in itself, the development of an acquisitive personality, and the belief that ceaseless work is a necessity of life.[7]

With few exceptions, the only identity deemed legitimate in America is a capitalist identity; in every walk of life, investment and acquisition are the keys to moving forward and avoiding stagnation. "It is never enough that our life is an easy one—we must live on the stretch," Thoreau remarked in 1840. In a sense, Max Weber added scholarly confirmation to Thoreau's warning: solvency, esteem, and even self-respect in America depended on approaching life with a sense of perpetual ambition. Failure attached to all who were unwilling or unable to "live on the stretch." In Weber's analysis, the capitalist theology of perpetual advance required conformity in economic behavior and even in temperament. "Whoever does not adapt his manner of life to the conditions of capitalistic success," Weber concluded, "must go under, or at least cannot rise."[8]

The misfits of capitalism are the people we label born losers. The names of most of the men in this book will be unfamiliar; most hardly mattered even when they lived. People called them bankrupts, deadbeats, broken men, down-and-outers, bad risks, good-for-nothings, no-accounts, third-raters, flunkies, little men, loafers, small fries, small potatoes, old fogies, goners, flops, has-beens, ne'er-do-wells, nobodies, forgotten men. Social Darwinist William Graham Sumner coined the last term in an 1883 essay about the little guy who plodded along, never complaining or asking for help, while reformers handed out free meal tickets to lazy scum. In 1932, Franklin D. Roosevelt borrowed Sumner's phrase (and reversed its meaning) to ennoble the stubbled faces of the Great Depression: "the forgotten man at the bottom of the economic pyramid." For FDR, the forgotten man was the nice guy who finished last, a capable citizen facing oblivion without bold government reform. Cultural concerns added to the economic enormity of the Depression. Failure ravaged drunkards and loafers as a matter of course, but the fall of good men was a national emergency.[9]

American men started jumping out of windows long before the Great Crash. A hundred years earlier, in 1829, failed Bostonians reportedly "preferred death, by their own hands, to a life of misery and disgrace." In the panic of 1837, Emerson wrote in his journal, "The land stinks with suicide." Having left the pulpit for literary pursuits, he confessed that he was "glad it is not my duty to preach," because he would not have known what to say. By 1841, the magazine *Arcturus* renamed the era of the self-made man: "Ours is the age of suicide and mysterious disappearance."[10]

Nonliterary reporters were no less grim. A New York clerk noted dozens of failures in his diary and reported, "The alarming increase of suicides in this country, is . . . generally remarked upon by the news papers. Scarcely a day passes, in which there are not one or more deaths from self destruction." The scourge spread beyond commercial cities. A Virginia coroner's jury ruled that Stephen Woodson "blew his brains out!" because of "pecuniary embarrassment." In 1837, a sea captain robbed by "land-pirates" killed himself in Rochester, New York; a Louisiana merchant "terminated his existence by shooting himself—supposed to have been caused by business embarrassments and pecuniary troubles." An entire article on suicide notes appeared in Horace Greeley's *New-Yorker* magazine in 1839. U.S. District Attorney William Price described "pecuniary troubles" in a note before ending his life in Manhattan in 1846. Suicide reports belonged to the hearsay of hard times, days when the future itself seemed in jeopardy. "Nobody can foretell what course matters will take," worried a New York merchant in 1837. "Posterity may get out of it, but the sun of the present generation will never shine out."[11]

Scholarly calculations offer different but no less severe measures of hard times. Peter J. Coleman, in his history of debtor-creditor relations, estimates that "by the early nineteenth century one householder in every five would, during his working lifetime, fail outright rather than merely default on a particular debt." Peter Decker found that half to two-thirds of San Francisco merchants failed in the 1850s, and many more avoided formal bankruptcy because taking refuge in the law was considered unmanly. Likewise, Clyde Griffen and Sally Griffen judged that 30 to 60 percent of small businesses in Poughkeepsie, New York, folded within three years. All these scholars emphasize that, in addition to those who went broke or bankrupt, thousands of businessmen teetered on the brink for years.[12]

Contemporaries marshaled their own facts and figures of hard times. Harshest of all was an assessment popularized in Thoreau's *Walden:* that among all merchants, "a very large majority, even ninety-seven in a hundred, are sure to fail." He added that "probably not even the other three succeed in saving their souls, but are perchance bankrupt in a worse sense than they who fail honestly." Thoreau relished "the sweetest fact that statistics have yet revealed," but his scolding had less force than the number itself. Ninety-seven in a hundred! Having first seen print in an 1834 novel about the Manhattan business district, *The Perils of Pearl Street,* it endured as the most cited failure ratio of the century. In 1840, General Henry Dearborn (a hero of the War of 1812) affirmed it in a much published speech. Judging from his years as

collector of the Port of Boston, Dearborn thundered, "AMONG
ONE HUNDRED MERCHANTS AND TRADERS, NOT MORE THAN
THREE, in this city, ever acquire independence." As in a child's
whispering game, the number made the rounds in private diaries
and congressional reports as representing the truth not merely
about Boston but about the wider culture. Everyone from abolitionist Thomas Wentworth Higginson to proslavery apologist
George Fitzhugh cited the statistic to support one cause or another. From 1870 to 1925, Russell Conwell taught it to more than
six thousand audiences in his famous motivational talk, "Acres of
Diamonds." Letters to editors sent confirmation from city directories, probate records, and the memories of "antiquarian" merchants. In 1905, Bradstreet's credit agency finally debunked it for
Success magazine; but *System: The Magazine of Business* reinstated
it in a special issue on failure in 1908. The figure reverberated for
seventy-five years because it conveyed not the economic but the
emotional magnitude of ubiquitous failure.[13]

The men eulogized by this hyperbole were forgotten in their
day and ours. Since the publication of the first cheap editions of
The Autobiography of Benjamin Franklin in the 1840s, thousands of
self-help manuals, inspirational tracts, and learned studies have
toasted success. Books about losers have been few and far between. Stalled politically in the 1850s, Abraham Lincoln moaned,
"Men are greedy to publish the successes of [their] efforts, but
meanly shy as to publishing the failures of men. Men are ruined
by this one sided practice of concealment of blunders and failures." A popular 1881 success guide echoed, "Why should not
Failure . . . have its Plutarch as well as Success?"—and answered
that a loser's biography would be "excessively depressing as well as
uninstructive reading." In 1952, a Cold War industrialist panned
Ernest Hemingway's *The Old Man and the Sea*. "Why would anyone be interested in some old man who was a failure," he asked,
"and never amounted to anything anyway?" Scholars until recently shared this view. As late as 1975, preeminent business historian Alfred D. Chandler, Jr., commented that studying failure in

and of itself would not be a useful enterprise. As social historians revised the past "from the bottom up," many regarded business-men as strikebreakers and power brokers who deserved to lose, but usually didn't. Cultural historians, interested in middle-class consumerism, paid more attention to desire and accumulation than disgrace and dispossession as hallmarks of American life.[14]

Deadbeats tell no tales, it seems. Distinguished libraries saved the papers of history makers, but where might one look for scraps from the fallen—the dead letter office? "Those who repeatedly failed in their bids for an independent competence," historian Joyce Appleby has written, "formed a wordless substratum in a society whose speakers and writers preferred to talk about success." On the contrary: failure was so common that its refuse landed in myriad libraries, museums, and public archives. This paper trail is the hidden history of pessimism in a culture of optimism. The voices and experiences of men who failed (and of their wives and families) echo from private letters, diaries, business records, bankruptcy cases, suicide notes, political mail, credit agency reports, charity requests, and memoirs.[15]

Failure stories are everywhere, if we can bear to hear them. Writing down and calculating the moral and financial value of life stories was central to nineteenth-century culture. "Down and out" was just as much a story as "rags to riches." As these idioms imply, life stories carried different rewards and punishments. "Every man's name [is] likely in some form or other to creep into print," remarked a Boston minister in an 1842 sermon about failure, "either through the 'Dead' or 'Married' list, or the police report, or the list of passengers . . . blown up on a railroad." Journalists and bureaucrats now wrote about common people, giving everyone "an equitable chance to descend in black and white to the remotest future."[16] By midcentury, success or failure often depended on the story a man could tell about his own life—or that others could tell about him. Bureaucratic institutions such as credit-rating agencies, bankruptcy courts, and charity bureaus added their own form of discipline to that of the marketplace.

Such agencies operated by classifying people, putting them into boxes tagged "failure" or "success," "winner" or "loser." Life stories took on tangible consequences for both the financial security and social worth of an individual.

Black and white are the favorite colors of capitalism, which pays a premium for clear distinctions and bold contrasts. Failure is gray, smudging whatever it touches. However unsightly, failure pervades the cultural history of capitalism. Understanding how the pursuit of profit shaped cultural values and everyday life is now a joint venture among literary critics, historians, and sociologists. Some argue that a nineteenth-century "market revolution" recast financial, transportation, and communication infrastructures to foster and reward individual enterprise. The "culture of the market" changed how people bargained, borrowed, dunned, paid, and trusted each other. Studies of gender and masculinity have explored circumstances (like economic failure) that made masculine norms harder to achieve. Business and legal historians such as Edward Balleisen and Bruce Mann have studied bankruptcy and debtors' prison in antebellum America. Taking a broader and longer view of American culture, across the nineteenth century and into the twentieth, the question remains: how did financial circumstances evolve into everyday categories of personal identity?[17]

And why did this happen in the nineteenth century, after 250 years of Yankee enterprise? Contrary to myth, corporations and profiteers settled British America. The Virginia Company of 1607 was a bold (and initially disastrous) investment scheme, and the Massachusetts Bay Company was pious and prosperous in equal measure. Two full centuries before the rise of individualism, colonists asked how personal gain impaired commonweal; "the wrong thing was also the right thing," as Perry Miller wrote in *The New England Mind.* Moreover, debtors and idlers abounded in the colonial era, but falling in business was not so calamitous as falling from grace. Preachers hurled the twelfth Psalm at wanderers from God's path: "Help, Lord; for the godly man ceaseth; for the faithful fail from among the children of men." Yet the doctrines of original sin and predestination did outline a kind of investment scheme: the sinner risks and loses all in order to gain all in Christ.[18]

In early America, fear of failure loomed largest on Sunday. Monday morning dawned about the year 1800. By then, "failure" meant an entrepreneurial fall from grace—"a breaking in business," as Caleb Alexander's *Columbian Dictionary* duly noted. Failure was an incident, not an identity, in lexicons and common usage. In awkward but typical phrasing, the *Pennsylvania Gazette* reported in 1793, "They have not yet indeed made a failure, but they can do very little business." Early Americans "made" failures, but it took a while before failures made—or unmade—men. One man wrote of life on the Ohio frontier about 1819, "Father made, or rather caused his boys (and me as the oldest) to make a miserable failure in farming." To fail as a farmer and blame your father's ineptitude, not insects or the weather, suggested the magnitude of economic and cultural change. The market "revolution" occurred gradually, but people saw it coming. "Mercantile transactions, by the extension of commerce, are widely diffused, and every man who has anything beyond his own wants, is obliged to partake of them," the *North American Review* noted in 1820. "The agriculturalist, who employs any capital, must be extensively engaged in buying and selling; and . . . conversant with many commercial transactions and keep in view the general state of commerce." Failure was something made, not someone born—until the market revolution. What if a man could not or would not go through life "engaged in buying and selling"? The *Review* answered, "he will be a great loser."[19]

Failure. Loser. Far into the nineteenth century, the public needed instruction about market redefinitions of everyday words. "In the technical language of the commercial world," a newspaper explained in 1830, "they *fail*, or in common parlance, they *break*." An 1852 children's guide taught that to fail was "to be unable to pay one's debts." Noah Webster defined *failure* as "a breaking, or becoming insolvent" in his famed dictionary of 1828 and a posthumous 1855 volume; but the 1857 revision blamed "some weakness in a man's character, disposition, or habit." Not until the eve of the Civil War did Americans commonly label an insolvent man "a failure." A glossary in the 1861 *Merchants' and Bankers' Almanac* included failure as "the general term applied to an individual or concern that has become bankrupt." Even then, embracing events and people, it was mainly a business term.[20]

The name for "an individual . . . that has become bankrupt" was a powerful metaphor for identity in a commercial democracy. Ralph Waldo Emerson dismissed American youth as "all promising failures" in an 1844 journal entry. Nathaniel Hawthorne's *The House of the Seven Gables* (1851) claimed that everyone was "a ruin, a failure," even if some hid it better than others. Herman Melville, who knew a lot about disappointment, published a story called "The Happy Failure" in *Harper's* in 1854. Abraham Lincoln, whose vernacular ear rivaled Mark Twain's, said in 1856, "With *me*, the race of ambition has been a failure—a flat failure." Henry Thoreau was offended by a business proposition that suggested that "I had absolutely nothing to do, my life having been a complete failure hitherto." In the 1855 first edition of *Leaves of Grass,* Walt Whitman shouted "Vivas to those who have failed."[21]

Poets of the self knew a good metaphor when they saw one. To call a man "a complete failure" tallied both the economics of capitalism and the economics of selfhood; that is, the external and internal transactions that reckon how we see ourselves and how others see us. Soon a man would be nothing more nor less than his occupation. Thoreau ground this axe in an 1854 lecture called "Getting a Living," which he mailed off to the *Atlantic Monthly*—under the punning title "Life without Principle"—two months before his death. He complained that people called him "a loafer" for taking daily walks in the woods. Yet were he to spend the day as a timber speculator, denuding the landscape, he would be "esteemed an industrious and enterprising citizen."[22]

Like Max Weber after him, Thoreau wondered if his neighbors

worked to live or lived to work. "There is no more fatal blunderer than he who consumes the greater part of his life getting his living," he wrote, returning to that ominous statistic of failure. "But as it is said of the merchants that ninety-seven in a hundred fail, so the life of men generally, tried by this standard, is a failure, and bankruptcy may surely be prophesied." Thoreau denounced "this incessant business" because he deemed it a "shirking of the real business of life." All of his writings pondered the changing economics of the self; in his journal, he explained this concept as a man's higher calling "to invent something, to be somebody,—*i.e.*, to invent and get a patent for himself—so that all may see his originality." Weber would call this lifestyle "the Protestant ethic and the spirit of capitalism," but Thoreau offered his critique in plainer language: "In my opinion, the sun was made to light worthier toil than this."[23]

By the 1850s, businessmen already complained that they were too busy to read even a newspaper anymore. Less pastoral souls than Thoreau felt the unrelenting pressure of enterprise. A New York bookseller and binder looked with envy on a country cousin. "I noticed . . . the remark that you 'led a *peacefull quiet life*,'" Asa Shipman wrote in answer to an 1859 letter. Recounting his unemployment after the panic of 1837 and a fire that destroyed his bindery in 1855, Shipman's career had been anything but quiet. "I sometimes long to lead a quiet life. My whole life thus far has been one of trouble hurry or excitement."[24]

Failure troubled, hurried, and excited nineteenth-century Americans not only because more of them were going bust, even in "flush" times, but also because their attitudes toward ambition were changing. Alexis de Tocqueville averred in 1840 that "ambition is the universal feeling" in America. Like many of his adages, this was part description and part prophesy. Inheriting classical republican qualms about ambition from the founders, young men weighed it against the capitalist ethos they helped build. What Tocqueville dubbed "the most imperious of all necessities, that of not sinking in the world" we call fear of failure. Economic growth

magnified "the yearning desire to rise." Ambition grew more legitimate as occupational mobility deposed the Calvinist sense of
calling; the sin of pride made room for the virtue of striving. "The
installation of ambition as the one common good was the great
transformation of nineteenth-century American life," writes Andrew Delbanco. Ambition was the holy host in the religion of
American enterprise.[25]

Ordinary people felt this change in their daily lives. In 1835, a
Virginia schoolboy had to compose a theme on ambition. James
Holladay wrote, "Some Ambition is necessary for every man . . .
to carry and extricate himself from all the dangers & difficulties,
that he is necessarily obliged to undergo, in his general course
of life." Ambition seemed the best defense for anyone "necessarily obliged" to risk and to strive through life. "If it were not for
ambition," Holladay asserted, "we would not lead a life of energy,
or activity and of course we would not be as happy, as if we had
some ambition."[26]

The trinity sounds familiar: life, ambition, and the pursuit of
happiness. Nineteenth-century Americans swapped liberty for
ambition, adopting the striver's ethic as the best of all possible
freedoms. Even a boy could recognize entrepreneurial traits like
energy and activity as emergent, liberal virtues. But when as-
signed to define happiness, Holladay retreated to republican
cheers for the "independent" and "contented" man who avoids
debt and feels "happy, because he knows, that their [sic] are no
person's to dun or disgrace him." New and old worlds collided in
this boy's life. Were ambition and debt compulsory insurance
against failure, or could a contented cash payer keep his head
when all about were losing theirs? "A person is happy, or not
happy, according to his general way of living," the boy shrugged.[27]

Choosing between ambition and contentment tormented a
prosperous New York merchant named Chauncey W. Moore in
the days before Christmas 1842. "Every body is crying hard
times," he grumbled in his diary. Despite the passage of a federal
bankruptcy act, the depression begun by the panic of 1837 had

"not touched bottom." On Christmas Eve, thirty applicants over-
whelmed Moore's wife as she hired servants to look after their
two sons. Moore's dry-goods house was prosperous, and he resented men who were not. He turned away an aged colleague who
wanted to borrow money; right after Christmas this "neighborly
honest & good man" was broke. The old gentleman had insufficient funds to cover a small bank draft, and the payee had filed a
legal complaint. Moore felt a chill. "An honest, upright industrious & economical man conducts [business] for 40 years," he
wrote, "& at the end of that period is obliged to allow a protest on
a check of 32 dollars."[28]

Everybody knew those smug couplets about pennies saved and
earned, and self-righteous chirping always disturbed the calm after a financial storm. Franklinesque proverbs blamed failure on la-
ziness, drunkenness, greed, ignorance, extravagance, and a host of
other sins. But what to do when the market ejected "an honest,
upright industrious & economical man"? If the problem of failure
was the fall of good men, its root was a growing breach between
character and fortune, between rectitude and reward. The vicissitudes of capitalism were such that honest dealings and hard work
could earn failure. Moral maxims never seemed to fit when the
"great loser" was a hardworking chap around the corner.

The Christmas vision of his friend's ruin haunted Chauncey
Moore into the New Year and through the winter of 1843. In his
diary, he yearned to "get away & escape" after twenty years at it
yet rebuked himself for plodding "on the usual worn track." Come
spring, he had a religious conversion and copied verses from the
book of Job: "Lo, all these *things* worketh God oftentimes with
man, To bring back his soul from the pit, to be enlightened with
the light of the living." What afflicted Moore? On a single day in
April, he took in $7,500 in cash; a week later, he made $4,500 one
day and $2,500 the next. "Not quite so hurrying as yesterday—
but quite enough so," he wrote. "Do not think so favorably of the
tug of business as formerly & I almost wish for a relief." Ten years
later, a credit agency recorded Moore's annual gross of $700,000

and personal fortune of more than $125,000. The plague of profit had not abated. "I shall either have to sell more or business will not go on as formerly," Moore had written back in 1843. "There is a kind of failure to keep up to par."[29]

Chauncey Moore's diary charted a widening spectrum of contemporary worries about failure. Moore touched on economic cycles, legislative solutions, moral condemnation, religious fervor, and the bonds between a flourishing business and a respectable home. He also pondered the changing meanings of failure. First, his old neighbor went broke. Moore's own torment was less a fall than a feeling. He must always do more or "pass muster merely." Stagnation might overtake him even if financial ruin did not: "There is a kind of failure to keep up to par." Besides marking particular reversals of fortune, Moore perceived that failure measured a man's ambition and approach to life. In a culture defined by "the tug of business," failure was no longer just an affliction; it was fast becoming an identity. In 1851, a credit agency recorded that Moore's career had begun about 1830, as a junior partner, but that "M[oore] had too m[u]ch A[mbitio]n to be content" working under someone else.[30]

For all his introspection, Chauncey Moore did not escape failure. The end of his story typified the volatility of business in the nineteenth century, when men could literally be ruined overnight. Like many northern dry-goods men, Moore sold the bulk of his goods to storekeepers in southern states. When war broke out in 1861, his southern clients stopped paying their bills. Moore became one of the "Bankrupts of Sixty-One." By November 1861, Chauncey Moore was nearly a million dollars in debt. Ten years later, this once eminent merchant struggled to earn a bare living in obscurity. "He has lost nearly all the prestige & connection he may have had in the dry goods bus[iness]," a credit agency reported of Moore. "A few friends may sell [to] him for old acquaintance sake." Moore spent his last years dependent on his wife and her family. To men of his day, there was no more humiliating "failure to keep up to par."[31]

By the time Chauncey Moore died a "great loser," the nation had endured the panics of 1819, 1837, 1857, and 1873; numerous minor dips; and a civil war. Such ordeals forged new models of identity; the age of the self-made man was also the age of the broken man. "Ovid knew nothing, or at least tells us nothing of failures, as we call them. They are quite of our day, and incidental to our mercantile communities," one observer wrote in 1856. "A true man, indeed, never fails, in the proper significance of that term; but I use it now in its mercantile and American sense."[32]

This "American sense" looked upon failure as "a moral sieve" that trapped the loafer and passed the true man through. Such ideologies fixed blame squarely on individual faults, not extenuating circumstances like Chauncey Moore's. Losers and nobodies stagnated while the likes of Cornelius Vanderbilt and Phineas T. Barnum proved that any poor boy with grit and sturdy bootstraps could make good. *The Life of P. T. Barnum, Written by Himself* (1855) and Barnum's later memoir, *Struggles and Triumphs* (1869), headed a burgeoning genre of success stories and primers long before Horatio Alger mastered the art. Protagonists like Ulysses S. Grant or Thomas Edison overcame early setbacks, proving that a winner never quits. Penny-a-liners extolled Abe Lincoln as the "peculiarly typical American!" and enthused, "His life to every American boy is one of the most inspiring in all history, for it portrays the qualities necessary to make a successful man of business." But in fact Lincoln's brief stint as a storekeeper ended in bankruptcy, and he did not try, try again to succeed in business. Yet posterity repeated the lesson "A little more persistence, a little more effort, and what seemed hopeless failure may turn to glorious success. There is no failure except in no longer trying."[33]

The Civil War consecrated in blood this ideal of manhood, by redefining the connection between identity and achievement. A rail-splitter who rose from log cabin to White House rewrote the gospel of the bootstrap and called it "a new birth of freedom." Black and white men would be equally free—free to strive, that is, in what Lincoln hailed as "the race of life." The ultimate terms of

Reconstruction obliged former slaves to enter the marketplace with "nothing but freedom," just as J. P. Morgan and John D. Rockefeller were said to have done. When an 1844 success manual was republished just after the Civil War, in 1868, the author adopted a new motto: "self-made or never-made." Emancipation enacted the end logic and absolute limits of individualism: the belief that true freedom rests not on your birth status but on the identity you achieve.[34]

The American paradox of liberty and bondage fell away, but another took its place. "The great American Assumption," noted W. E. B. Du Bois, "was that wealth is mainly the result of its owner's effort and that any average worker can by thrift become a capitalist." But the postwar transformation of the corporate and industrial economy made this ideal harder than ever to attain; as a small businessman in Kansas stated frankly in 1890, "firms of large capital . . . have advantages that I cant secure." Yet "the great American Assumption" promoted the idea that men who were failures simply lacked ability, ambition, or both; what had once been said of the captives of slavery now belittled the misfits of capitalism. The new birth of freedom was an ideology of achieved identity; citizen and slave gave way to success and failure as the two faces of American freedom. That ideal depended not only on the chance of success but on the risk of failure.[35]

The American who fails is a prophet without honor in his own country. Our creed is that hard work earns prosperity and prestige. When talk turns to failure, people change the subject with an uneasy laugh and a cliché. Quitters never win. Failure builds character. And yet, everyone knows a modern Job, a salt-of-the-earth type who tries and tries but meets only disaster. We mention him with sympathy and disgust. "Poor Uncle Bud." "That brother-in-law of mine's in trouble again." The problem is not that our bootstrap creed is a bald-faced lie, although it is. The real problem is that failure hits home; we take it personally. To know a "great loser"—a father, a neighbor, a classmate—is to glimpse our own worst future. Times change, deals collapse, accidents happen.

This 1865 lithograph featured a rare depiction of poor whites, opposite a slave family kneeling before the idealized emancipator, acknowledging the promises and perils the new birth of freedom held for all downtrodden Americans. ("Emancipation," Philadelphia, 1865. Alfred Whital Stern Collection of Lincolniana, Rare Book and Special Collections Division, Library of Congress.)

Failure imperils the future even more than it taints the past. What if I never bounce back? An American with no prospects or plans, with nothing to look forward to, almost ceases to exist.

James Holladay, the schoolboy; Chauncey Moore, the merchant; and Henry Thoreau, the dreamer, were all prophets of failure. Each sensed that it not only tallied losses, it gauged ambition. Each foresaw that ambition would eventually redefine freedom in the race of life. "Let us remember not to strive upwards too long," Thoreau warned, "but sometimes drop plumb down the other way, and wallow in meanness: From the deepest pit we may see the stars, if not the sun." Always chasing the sun, the striver was on a fool's errand. If tuberculosis had spared Thoreau for just one more year, the abolitionist in him would have celebrated Emancipation Day, while the skeptic would have distrusted the new birth of freedom. As it was, Thoreau did manage to address the nation in the year of Jubilee. "Life without Principle" appeared posthumously in the October 1863 *Atlantic Monthly,* when Abraham Lincoln was preparing to journey to Gettysburg. "What is the value of any political freedom, but as a means to moral freedom?" the writer who went into the woods asked the president who came out of them. "Is it a freedom to be slaves, or a freedom to be free, of which we boast?" Only an oddball who enjoyed sauntering more than striving, berry picking more than bill counting, could see beyond emancipation to the race of life that would transform freedom for everyone—black and white, success or failure.[36]

Sweet new grass had scarcely covered the bare earth of Henry Thoreau's grave when a few weeks after the funeral his publisher issued a second edition of *Walden.* Since 1862, the book has never been out of print. Generations have found in it at least a momentary epiphany before beginning or resuming the struggle to balance ambition and contentment, to find success and evade failure. "Why should we be in such desperate haste to succeed, and in such desperate enterprises?" Thoreau asked in the final pages. "If a man does not keep pace with his companions, perhaps it is because he hears a different drummer." This benediction echoes so often in everyday speech that we forget it was an early warning about the race of life and its stakes. Thoreau's contemporaries realized only gradually that everyone was at risk, not merely bankrupts and speculators. Each summer when the days grew longer and brighter, the glare bouncing off Walden Pond made people squint at their own bobbing reflections. To see themselves clearly, the generation that buried Thoreau would have to look skyward, and stare into the sun of their own ambitions.[37]

1 Going Bust in the Age of Go-Ahead

Nineteenth-century Americans had to learn to live in a new world where the sky was always falling. No imaginary chimera induced more terror than the all-too-real beast they saw in the woodcuts of penny newspapers. Out of a bank or exchange surged a modern hydra—eyes blazing, mouths roaring, fists clenching worthless paper—a wounded Leviathan sporting a thousand silk hats. Front and center gaped a broker or two, individuals for half an instant more until devoured by the anonymous behemoth of broken men. This scene was the financial *panic*. Earlier generations had used the whimsical word *bubble* to mock speculators whose shimmering schemes burst. But after 1815 or so, commerce linked individual fortunes so perilously that few could afford to laugh. "Panic" was a Greek word for a sudden fear with no obvious cause, which the ancients blamed on pranks by the goat-god Pan. He first visited America in the spring of 1819, when an unfathomable depression ruined thousands and awakened the rest to a Great Fear. Panic returned in 1837, 1857, 1873, 1893; in between were lesser crises. People muddled through

Success and failure defined each other through the pairing (at left)
of a stout gentleman and stooped ragpicker. ("Run on the Seamen's
Savings' Bank during the Panic," *Harper's Weekly,* 31 October 1857. Author's
collection; photo by Ken Andreyo.)

"hard times" and "dull times," but a "panic" gave them chills. The
word captured a recurrent sense of collective mania and individual
anxiety during the century when aspiration became a way of life.[1]

Between 1819 and 1929, the goat-god came to America at least
once in every generation. In 1819, most citizens had never heard of
Wall Street, but the woes of urban banks and merchants re-
sounded from saltwater farms in Maine to wayside inns along
Mississippi's Natchez Trace to Shaker colonies in the Ohio River
valley (at that time the nation's western frontier). The market that
tied such outposts together fostered its own vocabulary for
achievement and identity. Words like "panic" bespoke a new
economy with new emotions and moral dilemmas. "A panic is one
of those things in nature . . . which may be felt, but can neither be
traced or followed," a Wall Streeter warned in 1841; "you may easily turn the world upside down with it." Naysayers expected a
financial and moral cloudburst to wash away their city upon a hill:
"Our new world seems to be coming to an end in common bank-

ruptcy." Unprecedented striving had built this topsy-turvy heaven
and spawned the gods and monsters beneath it; but the bogeymen
of high finance could not take all the blame for a people experimenting with enterprise and ambition as never before.[2]

The first nationwide panics struck like an eclipse over a medieval village. "Circumstances & the state of the country has [*sic*]
bewildered and disappointed the calculations of every one," New
Yorker Frederick Westbrook wrote in his diary in 1842. "The Sun
Shine of Prosperity has been succeeded by the blasts of adversity—few have escaped its wilting effects." What was the cause?
Did men "wilt" because of "circumstances" beyond their control
or by faulty "calculations"? Was the problem bad luck or bad
character, misfortune or misconduct, flaws in society or in the individual temperament? Either way, the future looked risky. Individual ambition meant that *both* success and failure would always
be just around the corner. Neither the tycoon nor the boot-
strapper ever felt quite satisfied with his gains, nor quite safe from
sudden losses. "I have been struggling to get along," Westbrook
complained, "and have found my expectations blasted." The panics revealed a fearsome paradox: men's fondest hopes laid the rails
to their deepest disappointments; restless ambition battled relentless contingency.[3]

Getting Along, Going Ahead, Gone to Smash

From Wall Street to the muddiest rural lane, failure and the fear
of it left a garrulous people at a loss for words. "You do not know
how I feel I cannot describe it," wrote a Vermonter from debtor's
prison after the panic of 1837. *"Miserable beyond Language,"* he
moaned to a friend. Describing such feelings taxed the imagination. A Virginia schoolmaster living without hope or salary diagnosed a "strange malaria" in the swampy dog days of August 1838.
"I have the tremulors, if I may be allowed to coin a new word," he
wrote in his diary, "a curious strange feeling, which is a compound
of fear, suspense, desire, anxiety and numerous other nameless ills,

producing peevishness and restlessness." Worried about wasting his life, the young man insisted, "Ambition in itself is honourable if uncontaminated by *envy* and other malignities of nature." But soon his mounting debts compelled a retraction: "I am most tired of living beyond my means. It is best to be content." Did he suffer the symptoms of ambition or contentment? "Tremulors again," he wrote in September. "It is better to be born lucky than rich. Better not be born at all, without one of these advantages."[4]

John Russell Bartlett's *Dictionary of Americanisms* missed "tremulors," but by 1848 the pioneering ethnologist transcribed great mouthfuls of caterwauling about failure. Folks often invent slang to make sense of cultural crisis, and Bartlett overheard "busted" merchants yowling that they were "flat broke" or "dead broke," "up a tree," "hand to mouth," "hard up," "hard pushed," or "hard run." They were obliged to "face the music," "go through the mill," "wind up," "wipe out," "peter out," "flunk out," "flat out," "fizzle out," or "go to smash." People really talked this way. A clerk who was denied a Christmas bonus during hard times concluded that his boss "to use a common expression 'Is dead broke.'" One credit agent quoted a tailor, "To use his own words is broke all to smash & gone to Texas"; another rated the inventors of a new steam engine: "I predict the concern will fizzle out." A diarist in western New York reported, "Rathbone's business is so extended . . . I should not be suprized if He should burst into thin air." The same man exulted at the "Failure of Hollister A Meteor of Utica," a merchant who soared too quickly, then plummeted spectacularly. One way or another, fizzlers and meteors smashed to earth.[5]

The rockets' red glare was visible as far as St. Petersburg, Russia, where Joseph Ropes tended his family's commercial interests. The Ropes dynasty began with Puritan merchants in Salem, Massachusetts. In 1839, Joseph was twenty-four and had been abroad eight years. When the patriarch, his grandfather Samuel Ropes, called him home, Joseph admitted to an uncle that he wanted no part of "the American *go-aheadism*." Joseph replied to his grandfather, "I confess I do not think myself particularly well fitted to be useful in America now. . . . I have not enough of the *go ahead* principle to Keep up with them there, while here I can perhaps even keep *ahead of them*."[6]

Back home that year, Davy Crockett's *Almanac* roared on its cover, "GO AHEAD!" and boasted that its sales had "gone ahead like a steamboat." Assessing the late panic, a steamboat explosion, and the collapse of a profanely tall building (six stories), former New York mayor and financier Philip Hone wrote in his diary, "We have become the most careless, reckless, headlong people on the face of the earth. 'Go ahead' is our maxim and password; and we do go ahead with a vengeance." By 1851, a popular magazine opined that "the American language" would overtake the King's English because the "rapid terseness" of Yankee traders created new words and meanings to suit ambitious lives: "We love quickness." Four years later, the *New-York Times* touted "go-aheadativeness" as shorthand for "the spirit of progress." Though far from home, Joseph Ropes heard the password of his age.[7]

What did it mean to go bust in the age of go-ahead? Failure grew into a national dilemma between the panics of 1819 and 1857. "Are we merely toiling at the eternal task of Sisyphus," a popular magazine asked in 1857, "or are we merely the victims of a vicious system and a more vicious practice?" Rolling the rock, day by day, was easier than facing such questions, for two reasons. First, because they ruined the innocent bystander and the blameworthy speculator alike, the panics blurred the causes of economic failure. Contemporaries vied to assign blame, morally and legally, when a man could not pay his debts. This was an old problem, but it grew more complicated as people invented new prospects, new defeats, and new ways to think about both. The second reason echoed Joseph Ropes's confession that he lacked the temperament to be an American. His reluctance to quit "the quiet life of old Europe" reflected his distaste for the pace of business and the place of ambition at home. "The *go ahead* principle" was a new ideal of achievement and identity—with a hitch. The ideal was unreachable unless a man pushed uphill—yet, pushing and "going to smash" or appearing "hard pushed" exposed his weaknesses to all.[8]

To a nation on the verge of anointing individualism as its creed, the loser was simultaneously intolerable and indispensable. Failure was the worst thing that could happen to a striving American, yet it was the best proof that the republican founders had replaced destiny with merit. Rising from laborer to entrepreneur was the path to manhood. "Every man thinks himself qualified to be a merchant, as if by intuition," a U.S. Circuit Court judge remarked in 1839. "A man but says, 'I will be a merchant,' and he is a merchant. The creation of light was scarcely more instantaneous."[9]

Nineteenth-century Americans understood that solvency and selfhood were speculative ventures. Buying and selling, borrowing and lending, acquiring and forfeiting were not simply economic behaviors; they were liberal virtues that remade daily life, individual selfhood, and national culture in the antebellum era. The talents of good businessmen—investment, management, innovation—became hallmarks of personal autonomy and growth. The entrepreneurial self, the speculative soul, thrived on perpetual advance. As Joseph Ropes sensed in Petrograd in 1839, "the *go ahead* principle" extended far beyond Wall Street and the merchant class. Ropes's cousin Waldo agreed in 1843, when he wrote that "there is no maxim of the merchant which does not admit of an extended sense. The counting-room maxims liberally expounded are laws of the universe. The merchant's economy is a coarse symbol of the soul's economy." The fact that cousin Waldo happened to be Ralph Waldo Emerson bolstered the notion that liberal virtues were the means to self-reliance and individualism. But "the *go ahead* principle" said bluntly what a man must do to save his "soul's economy."[10]

The Panic of 1819

Joseph Hornor was a Philadelphia hardware dealer who prospered in the decade before 1819. The United States' defeat of

Britain in the War of 1812 reconfirmed the young nation's independence and lifted a trade embargo. Victory also established American control of the Mississippi and its eastern tributaries, securing inland waters as commercial highways to link disparate regions into a national market. So Joseph Hornor bought a boat. Not just any boat—he invested in *The Maid of Orleans,* one of only sixty-nine steamboats churning western rivers. Embracing innovation, entrepreneurs like Hornor fueled a market revolution: concurrent developments in transportation, communications, manufacturing, banking, and individual endeavor. Between 1815 and the 1850s, the Erie Canal, the railroad, the telegraph, a national postal system, steam-powered mills, the expansions of wage and slave labor, political democratization, and above all human desire and duress converged into one rushing current of commodities and credit. Entrepreneurship and speculation had not been the way of life for most in the early republic; the choices made by men like Hornor helped raise entrepreneurial individualism to an American ideal.[11]

But in the summer of 1818, the Second Bank of the United States blinked. Money and banking systems had been in flux for a quarter-century, since the days of Jefferson and Hamilton. The postwar boom made the bank directors increasingly nervous about unchecked inflation. Fearing a bubble, they called in loans and hard money—leaving men like Joseph Hornor unable to pay bills or redeem limp banknotes for hard specie. Panic ensued. The initial crisis of 1819 settled into a depression that ebbed and swelled during much of the 1820s. "Go where you will," cried a New Jersey farmer, "your ears are continually saluted with the cry of *hard times! hard times!*" After five years of this chorus, a Virginia gentleman sent his nephew a letter. "We have nothing new here," he wrote, recalling "the old song Hard times":

> *Well since you request it, I'll sing you a song,*
> *And tell you how people do jumble along;*
> *But the times are so bad that we scarcely can live,*

So I nothing shall ask, if you've nothing to give,
In these hard times.[12]

The crises of 1819 and thereafter were different from the hard times of "the old song." Earlier economic dips had obvious, tangible causes like drought, revolution, or wartime embargoes. But *these* hard times, in the words of one historian, "appeared to come mysteriously from within the economic system itself." The panic of 1819 gave most Americans their first jolt in the boom-and-bust cycles of capitalism. The handiest villains were those tabloid monsters the "speculating madmen and visionary schemers," in Washington editor John Jacob Niles's words. One epithet rang out from the counting house to the meeting house. *Speculator!* The word lumped cheats and "stock gamblers" with legitimate traders who capsized in unknown waters: prudent men who should have known better.[13]

Like many a man since, Joseph Hornor learned too late that a boat is a money pit. "I hope the boat is sold before this and money on the way," Hornor anxiously wrote his partners in April 1819. Hornor knew hardware—he had done a brisk trade in that line for years—but what did he know about the freight business? Why had he gotten involved in something he knew nothing about, with men he knew hardly at all? "What is to become of us on the 3d and 4th of May I know not," he wrote, as the deadline for his spring-season bills drew nearer. He knew that he would not be able to pay on the day of reckoning. "I have struggled very hard to get along and have sacrificed all my comforts in the trial," he wrote. "If I fall it will not be my fault."[14]

Was it Joseph Hornor's fault when he failed? This was the question of the day—here writ small, in a letterbook hardly different from any other in which merchants copied outgoing dispatches. Were men always at fault for their failures? Was the answer best reached by invoking legal or moral standards? Did a man's moral responsibility to pay his contracted debts persist even if the law let him off the hook? Hornor offered the commonest excuse for his broken fortunes. Despite his speculation, he claimed that he could settle his debts if only others had paid what they owed him. Hornor cursed his associates ("John R. C. hangs like a dead weight on me") just as his creditors damned him. Such were the hazards of a credit economy, delicately laced with the ritual fraternities of borrowing and lending. The essence of a merchant's life, a Federalist congressman insisted, was "to involve himself in the fate of others." Independence in commercial society risked perilous interdependence. In the panic, it seemed as if everybody owed everybody and nobody could pay anybody. "It is impossible to imagine a greater stagnation to every kind of business. . . . The streets wear the appearance of gloom and silent despair," wrote a debtor in Richmond, Virginia. "The failure of Ellis & Allan . . . is tho't a serious one, and likely to injure many others, particularly old Mr. Glat to a considerable amount." Debtors everywhere blamed circumstances beyond their control; men fell in succession like a house of cards.[15]

Beyond the panic, the politics of bankruptcy law left Hornor in particularly narrow straits. Debt laws had not kept pace with expanding credit and interstate commerce. Pennsylvanian Joseph Hornor owed money in Louisiana, Alabama, and even in England. Which jurisdiction could discharge him? Congress had given the U.S. Bankruptcy Act of 1800 a five-year term but repealed the unpopular law in 1803. Despite perennial debates, no federal bill passed until the Act of 1841 (repealed in 1843). Men like Hornor maneuvered in a byzantine environment of contradictory state laws. Definitions of bankruptcy varied, as did distinctions between bankruptcy and insolvency. Common law traditions treated bankruptcy as a crime (fraudulent nonpayment), whereas insolvency signaled "mere inability" to pay. Bankruptcy warranted involuntary prosecution, while insolvency permitted voluntary surrender of assets. These lines blurred in antebellum legal theory and daily practice. Colloquially, farmers, artisans, and laborers became insolvent, but only commercial "traders" and merchants went bankrupt—and cheats and innocents populated both groups.[16]

Honest debtors like Joseph Hornor often "compromised" with their creditors, an informal settlement allowed in some states, often by the assent of two-thirds of the creditors. Debtors surrendered their assets to one or more "assignees," who meted them among creditors at so many cents per dollar owed. Abuse by one party or another was common. Vindictive creditors could obstruct the compromise and have the debtor arrested or put through a long grilling, known as "squeezing a dry sponge." Assignees colluded with debtors to pay more (or all) to a few "preferred" creditors at the others' expense. Rascals shielded property by transferring it into a confederate's name—at last finding use for a shiftless cousin or brother-in-law. By 1850, when new laws permitted married women to own property, the insult "protects himself under petticoats" tarred men who shifted assets into their wives' names. Scoundrels fled; so many that a Philadelphia wag suggested a direct railroad line to Texas, to carry mobs of absconders to their favorite refuge. The rogue's stratagem tainted all who failed and made recovery more difficult. Many compared "mercantile character" (meaning commercial reputation) to "a woman's chastity, which a breath of dishonor may smirch and sully forever."[17]

Feminized and defiled, the failed man embodied primal fears inherited from the revolutionary generation. Merging classical ideas and colonial experience, the ideology of republicanism bred fears of ambition, corruption, entangling debt, dependency, and extravagance—the last two being especially imputed to women. But if nineteenth-century men doubted republican virtues as a formula for success, defying them often became a formula for failure. Frederick Westbrook cursed "Broken down Speculators and Stock Gamblers" for "living in princely dwellings furnished in proportion and adopting that style of living generally which is known in our Republican land as being the First in point of extravagance." But after erecting a fine house with "Mahogany

Doors," Westbrook himself failed in 1842—which prompted a confession in his diary: "My living in a style comformodable [*sic*] to the manner in which my Wife was brought up . . . , together with my building [the house] and consequent neglect of what little business I could get are principally the cause of the misfortune that I now so deeply deplore." In hindsight, Westbrook saw that ambition and surrender to womanly luxury had undone him. Under the canons of "our Republican land," he stripped himself of the foremost virtue of manhood: "publick usefulness."[18]

Such usefulness was a cultural and practical resource in the early republic, part of a manly ideal that esteemed the pursuit of material independence as a service to the community. When Joseph Ropes wanted to remain in Russia in 1839, he wrote to his grandfather that he feared not being "useful in America." Joseph knew very well that his grandfather, Samuel Ropes, born in 1778, was a fortunate son of the Revolution. So was Henry Van Der Lyn, born in 1784, whose father had been a Continental Army surgeon. The son practiced law in the western New York town of Oxford from 1805 to 1865. When a former "trinket peddler" died rich in 1843, Van Der Lyn, in his diary, called the man "a miserly misanthropic hateful being . . . nearly useless as a Citizen & *poor in good* deeds." He wrote of another miser, "His neighbours rejoiced at his death, as at the removal of a Nuisance." Such men were independent, but they were not useful. Republican usefulness was the precursor of self-made manhood, which began not as a synonym for aspiration and business success but as a "heroic ideal, . . . an expression of the meaning of life." When an old friend sank into misery after the panic of 1837, Van Der Lyn wrote, "On the whole, it is a cure for Ambition to read Clark's letter."[19]

Absent a cure for ambition, failure had many ways of making life meaningless by making men useless. Unpaid debts could keep a man from starting again—or keep him in debtor's prison, an institution that endured until almost 1850. *The Debtors' Journal* (doomed to a brief run, since its readership could not afford sub-

Supposed feminine extravagance was often lampooned, as in this cartoon, where a plainly dressed "lady sans crinoline" confides that because of "this horrid panic," her husband can no longer "afford me thirty-seven yards for a Skirt." ("Dreadful Effects of the Financial Crisis," *Harper's Weekly*, 24 October 1857.)

scriptions) pointed out the obvious in 1821: an honest debtor could not raise the cash needed to pay his debts in jail—"where he catch no skins." In some states, prisoners could gain release by taking the "Poor Debtor's Oath," swearing that no fraud had been committed. But first, the debtor had to pass cross-examination. In the early 1830s, John Carter of Worcester, Massachusetts, was asked: "Have you not stated since your arrest . . . that you had enough to pay all your honest debts?" He answered, "I have not. I have stated that I wished I had." Presumably, Carter was not being droll; jilted lenders had broad rights to crush defaulters. The law clerk in another case wrote in his diary, "The Insolvent is an honest man in the strictest sense of the word." All but one creditor agreed to his release: "a perfect *Shylock* by the way, [who] would not on any terms come into the arrangement." A contemporary political cartoon, "Shylock's Year, or 1840 with No Bankrupt Law," mixed anti-Semitic imagery with dialogue from the Gospel of Matthew. "Pay me that thou owest," says the top-hatted creditor while throttling a fresh-faced debtor, who pleads, "Have patience with me."[20]

Melodrama sometimes carried the day, as in a case tried by attorney Henry Van Der Lyn. In 1831, a mulish creditor demanded the last pennies of one Pliny Nichols. "I waxed warm & pathetic, dwelling on the hopelessness of a distressed debtor," the lawyer wrote in his diary, and bade the jury "to grant him a reasonable indulgence to recover himself & preserve his station in society." Having lost "himself," the debtor had to recoup selfhood as well as property to keep his manhood. Nichols was not on trial; two clement creditors and a deputy sheriff were being sued by the unyielding creditor for plotting to stall the seizure of Nichols's assets. Van Der Lyn extolled the trio as uncommon heroes. "I told the jury that humanity was a rare plant, requiring encouragement and sunshine, & should not be rooted up in the jury box." When the compassionate cabal were acquitted, he crowed, "It was a fine case for displays of feeling & sympathy in support of justice & honesty." Who knew better than a lawyer that feeling was a display and justice a performance? "I have great reason to be thankful to god for my success at this court," he concluded, "& for having blessed me with powers of oratory, for the protection of honesty & the punishment of fraud, &c." Evidently, Van Der Lyn's ambition needed no cure, given his exemplary republican usefulness.[21]

Joseph Hornor was less eloquent but more revealing. His letterbook voiced his efforts to "recover himself" and documented the legal and cultural impasse that made this so difficult. "I am comparatively but a young man in business," he wrote at age forty, "with . . . means that recent misfortunes have reduced to a very small compass." The image conjured lost horizons, equating business capital with tools of navigators and surveyors. Hornor saw his radius of achievement and identity narrowing. His intrepid investment in the vessels of western commerce had scuttled his expansive, liberal vision of his own future. The liberal's founding virtue was the republican's cardinal sin. The root of his success— ambition—was also the root of his failure.[22]

On Hornor's Dilemma

The paradox of ambition hindered efforts to pass reform and re- lief bills through Congress. Then as now, hardhearted lawmakers declined "to feed a train of lazy dependents" based on sob stories from "the pencil of fiction." The republic would survive without the likes of Joseph Hornor, whose problems were of their own making. "Part have failed, from causes beyond the control of hu- man power," conceded an opponent in 1822, but "this latter class must be comparatively small." How would society benefit by re- lieving "those who failed from an ignorance of their business, and the want of prudence and economy"? Ruin justly punished republican vices, which the *New-York Commercial Advertiser* lam- pooned in 1820:

> *There is a cause, we needs must own,*
> *Why much distress and want are known:*
> *Extravagance—our country's bane,*
> *Is spread o'er city, town, and plain: . . .*
> *To dress, to visit, and to play,*
> *To get in debt, and run away,*
> *Are common vices of the day.*[23]

Men in Joseph Hornor's predicament were suspected of run- ning away not only from debt but also from moral responsibility, and this belief proved to be the most enduring obstacle to le- gal reform. The antebellum press lionized "the man who labors to pay his debts, instead of creeping out of his responsibilities through any small hole in the crevices of the law." Canceling fairly contracted debts through the enactment of federal bankruptcy or insolvency laws would threaten sacred principles. One congressman insisted that to abrogate the rule of a gentleman's word was "a price almost too great to be paid for the preservation of one generation of the human race." Men who failed in the early republic faced not only volatile markets, but a moral vocabulary that could not make sense of new experience, guide conduct, or direct public policy.[24]

Even ardent reformers conceded that bankruptcy laws voided only a debtor's legal obligations, not his moral ones. "Not that the legislative authority can release a man from the moral or conscientious obligation to fulfill his contract—that transcends all human power," Congressman John Sergeant assured other lawmakers in 1822. Congressional debates throughout the antebellum era reiterated the national regard for this ethic. "Let the *moral* obligation remain, as it will, as strong as ever," conceded the sponsor of a short-lived federal bankruptcy act in 1841. "It is the legal liability only which is touched." If he prospered later, a legally bankrupt man bore the onus to "cancel the *moral* obligation" by paying his old debts "to the uttermost farthing."[25]

The fable of the conscientious debtor papered over a schism between the spirit of go-ahead and the cult of moral obligation. An entrepreneur who failed in the early nineteenth century faced inadequate state and federal laws, vengeful creditors, and forced idleness in debtor's prison—and if he successfully ran this gantlet, there was still the matter of moral obligation. These conventions ignored or denied the impact of larger economic and cultural trends and reinforced a dogma that blamed failure on individual imprudence, iniquity, or inadequacy. On New Year's Day 1820, a newspaper bard composed a bit of doggerel for a nation immobilized by bewilderment and indecision:

> Old "Uncle Sam," in chasing bubbles,
> Has jump'd into a peck of troubles'

Troubles, 'tis said, which sorely vex him,
And which 'tis feared will much perplex him.[26]

In such a maelstrom, Joseph Hornor tried to save himself in the panic of 1819. His letterbook showed how perplexing it was for even an honest man to see the right course. Having always relied "on the honour of Gentlemen," on moral rather than legal obligation, Hornor had never sued another man for payment. "It is neither my habit nor my disposition to press those indebted to me," he explained to a customer, "but when the Salvation of my Mercantile Character is at Stake there is no alternative." Like someone who is traumatized and awakens suddenly gray-headed, Joseph Hornor turned modern overnight. He wrote bluntly to one debtor, "My friend, the days of sentiment have gone by with me and I would rather read your draft on a good house here for the amount of your account than any romance either in prose or poetry that this age has produced. . . . [T]he *sinequa non is money*—that is the one thing needful in my present situation and that I can not do without." Only cash would redeem Hornor's commercial manhood.[27]

This was Hornor's dilemma: aspire the new way, but atone the old way. To borrow his description of an associate, Hornor was "a man wrestling with fortune in behalf of justice." Straining to do the right thing, he saw that he could not save both his property and his reputation. The initial panic settled into the hushed terror of being lost. Should he struggle on or admit defeat? Should he satisfy his creditors or support his family? His letters betrayed a sense of ethical disorientation as he toggled between frameworks for making economic decisions. He esteemed promises more than lawsuits, cherished "honour" but needed "money," and at last forsook "sentiment" for a "draft on a good house"—a check that could be cashed. Hornor's letterbook recorded the economies of a man and of a nation evolving from standards of honor and promises to those of money and contracts.[28]

Joseph Hornor lost everything in the summer of 1821, when there remained no "reasonable hope that my embarrassments would be but temporary, that by struggling and privations I could get on without relinquishing my standing as a merchant." Going on with a countersigner would have compounded his republican vices by entangling others. "To bring my immediate friends and connections into responsibility and danger . . . I never could for a moment consent to," he wrote; "nothing will be withheld for myself or family." The formerly good provider suffered his wife and ten children to be turned out of their home at 63 Spruce Street in Philadelphia. Weeks later he vacated another symbol of manly autonomy: his letterbook. Surrendering it to the assignees who conducted the final disbursal, Hornor's "wrestling with fortune" had come to defeat. He became a third party in the annals of his own wrecked ambitions, talked about and acted upon by others.[29]

Hornor's creditors permitted him to keep another volume because it had no worth, and into it he inked the twist in his tale. For a quarter century, this sensitive soul had copied beautiful verses into a "commonplace book," perhaps as a sanctuary from business worries. In these pages he composed an original ode to failure on 2 August 1821, two weeks after doing the right thing:

> *But me, placed on Life's middle stage*
>   *Doom'd to review a downward path*
> *No pleasing visions now engage*
> *The victim of Misfortune's wrath. . . .*
> *Shall I to gloomy fears resign*
>   *My life, because its hues are faded?*
> *No—this exulting thought be mine*
>   *Although* depress'd *I'm not* degraded.

Who could say whether the name Hornor tried so hard to save would ever again grace the pages of the Philadelphia city directory? But as the decade passed, with help from his father, Joseph

Hornor settled old scores and regained his name. By 1829, he was back selling hardware at his old High Street stand.[30]

Though Joseph Hornor's story may have ended happily, it is for that no less revealing a tale of ethical disorientation in the age of go-ahead. In the 1830s, a freshly painted sign announced "Joseph P. Hornor & Son" soon after Henry Clay coined a sonorous phrase that caught on rapidly: the self-made man. Not long after Hornor's death in the 1840s, the *Daguerreotype* magazine endorsed the myth that all successful businessmen were self-made and had been tested by risk and adversity: "You must throw a man upon his own resources to bring him out," it declared. Republican public usefulness evolved into the liberal virtue of self-made manhood—the basis for the American gospel of success, the doctrine of achieved identity. But if the self-made man was the go-ahead spirit made flesh, where did this leave the unfortunate debtor?[31]

The Market Reformation

The panic of 1819 revealed a new article of American faith: thereafter, the second coming of the goat-god would be ever at hand. Panic rose again, too soon and too often, in antebellum America. Red ink seemed to inspire prophets and pundits, who were never in short supply. Three weeks after Hornor sank in Philadelphia, New York merchant John Pintard preached in a letter, "Americans are an active restless people impatient of slow profits." A former imprisoned debtor and bankrupt himself (and all the more self-righteous for that), Pintard wrote that American habits "must undergo, not a reformation, but a complete revolution. A new race must arise on the broken fortunes of the present, who different[ly] educated may be content to plod & earn an honest living, to ac[c]umulate by slow degrees." Two decades later, *Hunt's Merchants' Magazine* made the same point: "Not to be content with slow and certain gains is characteristic of the American people." Was discontent the old vice or the new leaf? Either way, doomsaying did not make Pan's next visit any easier to bear, nor any less inevitable.[32]

The panic of 1837 ended a decade of national prosperity that rested largely on credit and land speculation in the continued absence of sound banking and currency systems. Andrew Jackson in 1829 became the first Democrat to become president, but to his public the old war hero was always "General Jackson." During his two terms, this scrappy Tennessean waged a blood feud against banks, corporations, and money men whose privileges and schemes (he claimed) made life harder for common people. Old Hickory's 1832 veto of recharter for the Second Bank of the United States and his 1833 transfer of federal accounts into regional depositories mortally wounded the "monster bank." So began a "full and fair experiment" to decentralize the already disjointed money system. In the summer of 1836, the U.S. Treasury issued the infamous "Specie Circular," an attempt to curb frontier speculation by requiring buyers of public lands to pay in gold or silver. Inflation and overdependence on foreign capital spiraled as a result. A Jacksonian congressman coined the motto "Perish credit, perish commerce," sending a message that financial casualties had no one else to blame for going too far, too fast. Jackson's hand-picked heir won the 1836 election. Taking the oath in March 1837, Martin Van Buren vowed to stay the course of "my illustrious predecessor." The next month, panic erupted. Drygoods merchant James Morris Whiton witnessed the chaos in Boston and wrote in his diary, "Every day a crowd gathered at the news room to see a list of New York failures the day before. The list would often contain 20 names. The regular questions of the day were 'Is the mail arrived? Who failed yesterday?'"[33]

Hard money grew so scarce that citizens began minting their own, many with comic vignettes and slogans. Copper "hard times tokens" circulated widely in lieu of pocket change and in favor of policy change. A penny tribute to Jackson was stamped "Perish Credit Perish Commerce" on heads and "My Experiment, My Currency, My Glory" on tails. A closer look at a coin bearing a shipwreck revealed the vessel's name: *Experiment.* Another rendered the "Executive Experiment" as a slow tortoise hauling a strongbox; on the reverse, a Democratic donkey galloped "In the Footsteps of My Illustrious Predecessor." Likewise, satirical currency changed hands as retail or wage scrip, despite public mistrust of paper notes as an intangible and oft-counterfeited medium. Most whimsical bills or "shin plasters," however, pulled nothing more than a wink from an empty purse. "Hickory Dollars" and sundry other denominations drew upon the "Rag Bank," the "Rogo Vilo Dishonesto Associato," the "Printer's Bank," the "Sucker Institution," or the famous "Humbug Glory Bank." Hard-times tokens and scrip made assets out of irony, giving real value to funny money while the genuine article remained scarce or worthless. But petty cash, as it were, could neither buy national recovery nor discount public fears of fraud and mendacity in commerce. Bankruptcy and unemployment plagued the country until the mid-1840s, with individual and international consequences. "It was indeed said across the water," a U.S. Circuit Court judge wrote, "that 'the Yankee nation, from General Jackson to a shoe black, was a fraudulent bankrupt.'"[34]

Voices of doom echoed in lyceums, churches, and political halls of the republic, wherein reckless ambition was garbling ancient moral conviction. Scattered heretics insisted that "a complete revolution" had already occurred and that another sort of reformation loomed: a new ethics of capitalism. In 1841 in *Hunt's,* legal writer Joshua Marsden Van Cott advocated federal passage of a "General Bankrupt Law." The "political duty" to enforce contracts, he wrote, also entailed a utilitarian duty to annul contracts: "the good of the few must yield to the good of the many." To enforce "mere *moral obligations* to pay money" served neither duty nor any utilitarian purpose, he insisted. In an 1842 essay for *Hunt's,* another writer endeavored to debunk two harmful myths. First, wrote John N. Bellows, too many people believed that the creditor did a sort of favor for the debtor by selling now and allowing him to pay later. Bellows asserted that the creditor "is as much interested to sell as [debtors] are to buy" and thus "must bear his share of the risk" inherent to a credit economy. The second myth was that failure resulted from individual "laxity of principle, or, at least, some culpable carelessness." Such myths gave rise to "Quixotic" standards of moral obligation, he wrote. For example, the fable of the conscientious debtor (who repays every cent) "substitutes a wild heroism" in place of fairness and good sense. This was a classical liberal answer to Hornor's dilemma: archaic idealism impeded progress and justice. Moral duty pushed to absurdity, Bellows argued, becomes "a kind of infatuation with honesty. It looks too much like praying in the market-place."[35]

Louder and more numerous voices roared back that the marketplace needed more praying and less policy. The redoubtable Reverend Henry Ward Beecher's Thanksgiving sermon of 1850 (published the following year) dripped with sarcasm. "It is well that men have a *half-dozen separate characters*," America's best-known parson sneered. Beecher mocked the idea that one man could have "a social character, a political character, a religious character, and a professional character, and he may conduct himself very differently in each." He went on to ridicule the idea that "a man may be honorable in private, and yet dishonest in public affairs; a man may be a good neighbor and kind householder, yet a very trickster in traffic." In this context, maxims of the Ben Franklin variety came under harsh scrutiny, especially "Honesty is the best policy." An 1852 business manual clucked, "*Honesty* ought never to be named in the same category with *policy*." Boston reformer Thomas Wentworth Higginson worried in 1853 that merchants knew no morality except this eminently bendable rule: "it is not always *the best* honesty which is the best policy." Taken literally, "the cunning maxim" debased honesty as a mere business ploy. Eminent commentators like Higginson (and Beecher) decried this "separation between the man and his profession, between personal character and business character."[36]

The market revolution begged the question of a market *reformation:* a dual realignment of economic relations and the moral and legal codes that gave them meaning. Even those who worked toward this goal tripped over it—as Daniel Webster did one evening in 1837. Because of the panic, the Senate had stayed in session that Sunday. Webster was a man of legendary eloquence, but after a long day his guard came down with the gavel that banged adjournment. That night, he told a group of citizens, "There are no Sabbaths in revolutionary times." This bit of impiety sparked a brief furor, albeit nothing the gentleman from Massachusetts could not smooth over. As a Whig, the party of progress and enterprise, Webster advocated bankruptcy relief and banking reform, which were repeatedly defeated by Jacksonian Democrats. The nonpartisan truth of his "sabbath" quip was its précis of a cultural stalemate: new morals had not accompanied new markets. By 1841, a hard-times token had lionized Webster and his mission with the legend "Credit—Current." That year, he pushed an unpopular bankruptcy bill through Congress, only to see the law repealed two years later amid moral outcry against discharging contracted debts. Even the *American Whig Review* beheld the mess with ambivalence, admitting "Our virtues are the virtues of merchants, and not of men." America aspired to the liberal virtues of the entrepreneur at the cost of republican manhood. Hornor's dilemma had become his nation's, and not even the great Daniel Webster could talk his way out of it.[37]

2 A Reason in the Man

In the winter of 1846, a young attorney subscribed to a seven-lecture series at the Lyceum in Worcester, Massachusetts. "I did not understand it," wrote J. Henry Hill in his diary, after the third lecture. The opening address, "Montaigne the Sceptic," fascinated him, and the second night, on Napoleon, was passable, but the discourse on Plato lost him. "I expected it would be full of the mystical and of course was not very much disappointed. I never very much relished the doctrines of abstractions, of entity, oneness, duality, &c." Such "quiddities" had no relevance to Hill's career as a bankruptcy lawyer—which was precisely why he attended all seven lectures. His diary alternated reviews of the lectures and complaints about his caseload. "Insolvent proceedings and insolvent records are completely the order of the day now," he wrote between orations on Swedenborg and Shakespeare. Then came Goethe, who stirred up storm and stress. "It is after all the most difficult thing in the world for a young man to do, to fix upon the kind of business he will pursue through life," Hill despaired. "No one can know what it is till they have passed through the ordeal for themselves." At twenty-seven, he hated lawyering and hated seeing "ruined fortunes & blighted hopes" across his desk every day. From where he sat, failure looked like an inner deficit as much as a monetary one, and his clients' inadequacies aroused his own fears. Certain he had achieved "nothing at all," he wrote, "I am more and more ashamed of myself every time I think of it."[1]

The diarist learned more than he imagined from attending "Mr. Emerson's Lectures" in 1846, later published as *Representative Men* (1849). Ralph Waldo Emerson and Henry Hill were uncommon men, born in 1803 and 1818, respectively, though they had little in common with each other (much less with their fellow Americans). At the same time, they *were* representative—unelected aldermen working for constituencies of ambitious and unfortunate men. The attorney and the philosopher spent their days drafting arguments about the perils of contemporary identity—a matter of growing concern to men of every station. "A person needs to live one life in this world to know how to live," Hill mused in his diary. "We want to learn [to] know ourselves & when learned it is too late to be of any avail to us." Yet Emerson's way to self-knowledge held no allure for him. "A man of books is to be pitied truly. I mean a man of nothing but books," Hill wrote. "He finds in his library beautiful theories of life and codes of morality & goodness, and as he goes out into the world he is sadly disappointed to find nothing of them there. He has learned the theory, but cannot find the practice & application." Henry Hill lacked the philosophical apparatus of transcendentalism, but he did not need Emerson to teach him self-reliance.[2]

While Hill practiced in his cluttered office and Emerson pondered in his airy library, both worked to reconcile the law of the marketplace and the moral basis of achievement. Each beheld failure and success as incarnations of self-reliance: the wages and taxes of individual effort and vision. Both upheld the law of achieved identity, yet vacillated about its ostensible corollary. In his own journal of 1842, Emerson scribbled a business maxim.

"The merchant evidently believes the State street proverb that nobody fails who ought not to fail. There is always a reason, *in the man*, for his good or bad fortune, and so in making money."[3]

The panic of 1837 popularized such cries of economic and political discord, and against this background, Emerson and Hill reassessed Joseph Hornor's dilemma. What did self-reliance mean without personal responsibility, without the presumption of "a reason, *in the man*"? In 1846, a Boston merchant assured a lecture audience, "Failures that arise from inevitable misfortune alone, are not so numerous as they are generally supposed to be. In most cases insolvency is caused by mistakes that originate in personal character." Like the Puritan sermons of old, commercial jeremiads beheld the panic as retribution upon a nation that had strayed from the path of righteousness. The evangelists and money-changers agreed for once. The rhetoric of moralists and business leaders quarantined failure like a plague. The whole community had sinned and must atone, but ruined men were the *causes* of pestilence, not its casualties. Theirs was a solitary affliction, contracted through individual error and excess; and it must be contained to avert further outbreaks.[4]

Emerson's "State street proverb" combined market logic and moral creed, both of which always presumed "a reason, *in the man*." This alliance amounted to a powerful ideology, a canon of cultural beliefs and practices that shaped the ordeal and aftermath of economic loss: "nobody fails who ought not to fail." Conventional wisdom is not official rhetoric, like presidential proclamations or church doctrine. Yet "a reason, *in the man*" expressed potent cultural assumptions about failure. Resonances among personal meditation and public speech—Emerson's lectures, Hill's diary, commercial jeremiads—show how ideologies mature in a process of continuous flow. The ideology of failure was not just the bombast of preachers and senators, nor the gossip of neighbors and associates, nor the imagery of tabloids and balladeers, nor the pain in diaries and family letters. The circulation of ideas among such diverse communities and types of communication defined failure within a matrix of achieved identity. "A reason, *in the man*" could make the difference between a temporary setback and a lifelong identity, in some cases. But which cases?

Confessors and Storytellers

Self-reliance and self-criticism went hand in hand. Hill and others in similar good repute tormented themselves, dissecting "mistakes that originate in personal character" before such flaws led them to ruin. Virginia planter Charles Dabney used the genteel "we" to rebuke himself on New Year's Day 1838. "We want very much, a habit of energy and application—a habit without which there can be no success," Dabney wrote in his diary. "We still procrastinate, still neglect things, and still idle our time." These were "the causes of all my failures. . . . I have been more inconsiderate and selfwilled than ignorant—rather careless indolent and selfindulgent than unlucky." Henry Hill's deadly sin was sloth. In 1841 he contemplated suicide and berated himself for "indecision and misspent time." He wrote, "Misfortune & Poverty stare me in the face at every turn and keep alive these feelings & . . . without a remedy I am condemned to suffer the consequences."[5]

Such confessions echoed the abasement rituals and testimonies of early American Protestantism. Like evangelicals bearing witness to their own depravity, some men overstated their vocational sins in the hope of salvation. Henry Hill's shame hardly compared to the humiliations seen in his office; eternal damnation was no literary metaphor to a prostrate merchant whose past lay in ruins and whose future remained in doubt. "Henry this is a Situation I never meant to be placed in," Timothy Whittemore wrote from New York in 1832 to his brother in West Cambridge, Massachusetts. "Now have got patiently to wait till deliverance comes, and am sure shall look out for the future." Conventionally, men reassured failed brethren that "a new beginning in life" was nigh, as attorney Henry Van Der Lyn wrote to a bankrupt friend in 1839. But there was good reason to fear that commercial and social redemption would never come. Van Der Lyn observed many cases of irretrievable ruin in sleepy Oxford, New York. Part scribe and part pharisee, he kept smug accounts in his diary of neighbors who fell from grace. He wrote of a lifelong friend in 1835, "It is now understood that this busy, meddling, unprincipled & immoral Man has failed." In 1837 he wrote, "These two extinguished stars are now wandering about our streets shorn of their influence and false consciousness." In yet another entry, he noted, "Dodge's case is hopeless. The mad fellow, built a large new House on his farm, of 2 stories & painted it last summer & was a Bankrupt at the time. . . . He is gone in toto."[6]

Henry Hill's diary revealed even more clearly how public imagery colored private attitudes about failure. Six months after the Emerson lectures, an old associate turned up at Hill's door, bankrupt. "When he stepped in to the office this morning with his bloated face, staring eyes & careless appearance," the diarist remarked, "I could scarcely believe that it was the same elegant ladies man that we had among us only two or three short years ago. How sad the change!" Did the man really look so bad? Even if he did, was Hill inspired by sketches from contemporary fiction? "Who has ever seen a man when his affairs are becoming desperate, and has forgotten the picture?" asked the writer of an 1841 short story; "his form shrinks, and his coat hangs loose upon him; his cheeks grow lank, and his eyes stick out." In the 1830s and 1840s, stock fictional characters rose and fell; certain sins meant certain failure. Conventional plots and characters helped to contain failure and reinforce the idea of achieved identity. Didactic narratives understood by all fixed blame and made every dilemma seem crystal clear.[7]

Henry Hill used these cultural conventions in his diary. Given to brooding over his own vague sense of failure, Hill portrayed his friend's breakdown as an open and shut case. The two had "read law" together as students in a senior attorney's office, but the other man went into business. "'Tis the case of a young Merchant of this Town," Hill began. "What this reverse in his fortunes arises from I know not save what every body in the community conjectures as they ever assume the right to do in every case." Hill had always disliked him. "He was of a prepossessing appearance, well educated & accomplished withall, who was handsome, well-educated, [and] married to a young lady of princely estate." Formerly a wild bachelor known for fast horses, the fellow was undone by his marriage to a rich girl. Hill explained, "His was a temperament which easily gives way at the presence of prosperity. He could not endure it. . . . Dissipation stepped in—liabilities were incurred thoughtlessly—& his step has been downward till the present." Hill admitted he was guessing; "perhaps the key of the present transaction, perhaps not. One thing is certain, that the failure has come," he added; "another is probable, that 'tis a bad one."[8]

Hill's diary told a fable of extravagance by fitting actual events into a familiar plotline: the spoiled rich boy finally gets his come-uppance. Hill tossed in some literary flourishes ("'Tis the case of a young Merchant," "accomplished withall," "a young lady of princely estate"), enhancing the semblance of a morality tale. Hill's story resembled *Strive and Thrive*, a British novel by Mary Howitt (1799–1888). Hill read the American edition in 1841 and reviewed it in his diary. "Mr. Walingham is a young man," he wrote, with "a classical education & refine[d] and elevated taste, but gay and reckless withal perfectly disgusted with any thing like business." But the protagonist is duly punished. "He finally (Mr. W.) marries," "plunges into every extravagance," and becomes bedridden. His wife must find employment, and when he finally dies he leaves nothing to support their children. "The story is pleasantly told and illustrates with much force and beauty the values of perseverance," Hill concluded. "Indeed I have seen nothing of the kind for a long time which has so much pleased me in its perusal."[9]

The affinities between Howitt's novel and Hill's diary reflected the continuous flow of ideas among public and private idioms. Extravagance was only one "reason, *in the man*," one variant of achieved identity, that was circulating in the antebellum public domain. *Hunt's Merchants' Magazine* noted similarly in 1848 that "most men fail in business not through overwhelming . . . misfortune, but generally through disregard of the simplest principles of morals." A typical litany followed. "In most cases . . . the ruined man has brought his affairs into hopeless condition by his grasping spirit involving him in ruinous extensions and speculations; or by his overreaching disposition, which, becoming notorious, has driven off his customers; or by his meanness, which has disgusted them; or by some other ingredient in his moral mixture."[10] Despite its brevity, this indictment not only specified three reasons, it glanced at three *stories* about achievement and identity. Character and plot, such as an "overreaching disposition" or driving off one's customers, told how men became hopeless, notorious, or disgusting. In private communications, people borrowed from popular culture and rewrote formulaic plots to narrate failure in real life. These "master plots" lent a generic shape or outline to organize bewildering experience into an intelligible story.

"The past Season has unfolded a pretty general bankruptcy on the West side of this Village," Henry Van Der Lyn wrote in his diary in 1827. Among the wounded were three blacksmiths who had opened a mercantile shop in partnership: "industrious & thriving Mechanics but not content it seems with their station & business." The diarist concluded, "The idea of being elevated to the superior rank & profits of Merchants led them astray & in an unguarded moment, They entered into this untried & perilous undertaking." Ten years later, in 1837, Charles Russell of Boston penned a consoling letter to his niece Sarah Gilbert, whose husband had been ruined in the panic. "I am sorry to learn that the severity of the times should have reach'd in any manner your peaceful dwelling," he wrote. "Scarcely any one however has escaped—The calamity which has prevailed thro the Country for the last ten months seems to have fallen upon all in a greater or less degree. Yours I hope will soon be succeeded by the bright sunshine of future prosperity & may past events teach us all a moral lesson which will be suitably improved." During the panic of 1857, Caroline Barrett White of Roxbury, Massachusetts, relayed to her diary worries expressed by her husband. "Frank came home with a sad story of 'Hard Times'—new failures every day— He that trusteth in riches, trusteth vanity, nowadays."[11]

Master plots shaped even firsthand accounts, but abstract lessons fell short in real life—where failure was anything but abstract. The trouble with blaming "a reason, *in the man*" was that "the man" was always a unique human being and usually somebody's loved one or neighbor. These three observers upheld "a reason" generally, yet all bent the rule to some degree. The uncle's blessing ("Yours I hope") and Frank's reports to Caroline about men in their circle empathized more with family and friends than the mass of ruined men. Van Der Lyn showed the least pity, but even he hedged, holding veteran merchants and upstart mechanics to different rules. In the abstract, he wrote, "This spirit of speculation will undermine the Religion & Morals of the people of the U.S. [and] upset the Government or totally change its character." But in the aftermath of the 1837 panic, he remarked, "My friend Sidell has been somewhat damaged by his speculations, which have disordered his finances & given a cast of care to his lively & gay countenance." In addition to writing such formulaic, literary flourishes in his diary, Van Der Lyn immediately sent John A. Sidell a letter of condolence. "I cannot omit the performance of a sacred duty which one friend owes to another in misfortune, to send you my heartfelt grief & sympathy," he wrote, asserting "that the best of men (of whom I consider you one) are exposed to such misfortunes," adding, "To look misfortune in the face, is the way to rise above its depressing and blighting influences." Wives, uncles, and even lawyers wavered between universal censure and particular sympathy, between generic plots and extenuating circumstances. "To look misfortune in the face" was much easier if the face were anonymous.[12]

Losers, Monsters, and Squatters

All eyes were on the man who failed. By the 1850s, a visual culture of failure illustrated the master plots that circulated in private and public writings. Beginning with the panic of 1819, caricaturists taxed their cleverness to depict this new American, the broken man. Thomas Kensett's engraving "Brother Jonathans Soliloquy on the Times" featured a character resembling a young Benjamin Franklin, with a sheaf of unpaid bills fluttering from his hand and a bankruptcy notice jutting from his pocket. The country cousin of Dame Columbia and Uncle Sam, Brother Jonathan was the early republic incarnate. A homespun Yankee, he wandered a village square lined by broken banks and sheriff's sales, while shady brokers (according to Jonathan's verse) "laugh in their sleeves at the loosers forlorn." The "looser" got the short end of a bargain and ended up the scapegoat of those who robbed him. The common man had always been poor, but the "looser forlorn" had known better days. He was a ghost who had lost his spirit, a fallen republican angel in a land of rising liberal entrepreneurs. Unlike eighteenth-century caricatures of frenzied gentleman speculators, this was the face of everyman.[13]

Swept along in the course of events, the "looser forlorn" embodied a crisis at once civic and intimate. Satirists, more than other commentators, disputed the belief that achievement defined identity, that "nobody fails who ought not to fail." The panics marked "the first time many Americans thought of politics as having an intimate relation to their welfare." These forces operated and proliferated every day, but the imagery in both the public press and private writings restored flesh and bone to the disembodied powers of the market and the state. "He is prone to the ground," one congressman said of the "looser" after the panic of 1819, "and he is only viewed as a silent monument of grief when he surveys from a corner her desolate streets."[14]

The loser as "silent monument"—a national emblem wandering like Brother Jonathan in Kensett's engraving—evoked well-

Fretting over his unpaid bills, circa 1819, one of the earliest personifications of the nation was also an early portrait of "the looser," in this detail from Thomas Kensett's engraving "Brother Jonathans Soliloquy on the Times." (Courtesy of the American Antiquarian Society.)

known master plots. The *Debtor's Journal* printed this 1820 version of the familiar story:

> *Do you see the poor bankrupt, who totters along,*
> *His countenance fallen, his spirits oppress'd?*
> *No pity he gains from the cold-hearted throng,*
> *While his deep-bursting sighs tell the throbs of his breast.*

Artistic imagination fleshed out the bankrupt, but people saw him in the flesh every day. Van Der Lyn opened the seventh volume of his diary with a mise-en-scène: "The appearance of Washington Square in 14th April 1853, 9 P.M. Commerce has departed from it &. . . . [t]he withdrawal of all business from this once busy mart of trade, has left several melancholy wrecks behind." In his own soliloquy on the times, Van Der Lyn surveyed decaying buildings and derelict men, street by street.[15]

Men who failed lost money and gained an identity: the broken man. "He seemed like a bow which had been kept bent too long & thereby lost its vigour & Elasticity," Van Der Lyn wrote about a friend in 1855; "I fear he has been overtaken with business." Artists rendered such men in tattered finery, with beaver hat respectfully doffed, and they appeared in political cartoons and dime novels, on posters and song sheets, and in sentimental prints for the home. The rise of the penny press and chromolithography after 1840 heightened demand for fresh pictures of vivid places and characters. Old anecdotes inspired new engravings and woodcuts, like "The New Orleans Sock-Seller," a much-published rendering of a real case, in which speculation reduced a merchant to street-peddling. "The merchant, broken in fortune," read the caption, "mutters to himself, and smiles, half insanely, as he praises his wares to his real or pretended customers!" The commonest motif showed the ritual meeting of a lean debtor and a stout creditor. Drawn and redrawn for decades, this power play could be seen in the flesh on many a village green. In a student essay about 1835, Virginian James Holladay depicted a debtor facing his creditor on the day of reckoning: "The man that once appeared so gay in the eye's [*sic*] of the world is, now thin pale and his spirit's sunk to the lowest pit's of despondency, and wretchedness." The stigmata of failure were so familiar that even a schoolboy knew them.[16]

Such tableaux made it easier to see how failure connected the public square, the family hearth, and the political scene. In 1841, a self-described "broken merchant" ventured to tell his own story. Born in western New York in 1800, at twenty Milton Buckingham Cushing ran away to become a merchant on the Ohio frontier. He prospered and acquired land, but overconfidence and overextended credit broke him by 1833. He freely admitted these "reasons, *in the man*," but he also blamed "Genl. Jackson's 'experiment,' upon the Currency & business of the country." As Cushing described the bank war's impact on him, "the compass was unshipped from the binnacle, the vessel ceased to mind its helm,

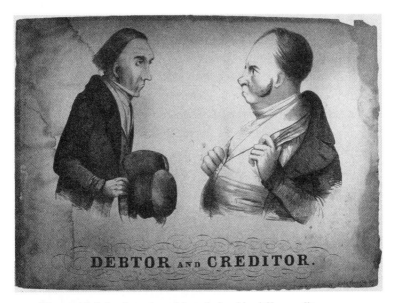

The motif of the obsequious debtor facing his pitiless creditor, one gaunt and the other corpulent, conveyed the power relationship behind failure and success. (Lithograph by W. W. Chenery, Boston, circa 1841–1853. Courtesy of the American Antiquarian Society.)

and darkness that could be felt came over the face of the deep." Holding on, "at last I was driven upon the huge and jagged reef of *Broken Banks,* and my vessel became a complete wreck." Shipwreck was a common metaphor of financial distress in popular fiction. Cushing's writing exemplified rhetorical exchanges between the public and the private spheres.[17]

Cushing had nearly recovered from the bank war when the panic of 1837 flattened him again. "Late in the fall of 1837," he recalled, "I gathered up my *little all,* a *lovely wife & four children,* and paddled up the great lakes." Their new start in the remote "Wiskonsan" territory ended when hard times trailed west after them. "[A] stranger in a strange land, there seemed no alternative for me but to 'dig, or starve,'" he recalled. "I followed the example of others in like circumstances, and became a *'Squatter,'* on the public lands." Squatting was widely denounced as akin to speculation, the pursuit of something for nothing. Eventually, he got title to the parcel and settled his family "in a 'Log Cabin' built with my own hands." Their life was hard. Cushing's wife proudly descended from "the Adams & Hancock families of Revolutionary memory. In the veins of my children," Cushing boasted, "flows the blood of Patriots, heroes & Statesmen, whose memory is dear to every true American." He hated to see his "buds of promise" grow up unschooled, "like wild flowers of the country we inhabit." Out of money but not out of ideas, he sat down to rewrite the master plots that held him down.[18]

The squatter's tale filled four pages of a dense round hand in an 1841 letter to congressman Caleb Cushing (no kinsman, but a fellow Whig). Invoking the Gospel of Luke, Milton Buckingham Cushing prayed for commercial resurrection. "I am as unfortunate as the Poor Widow in the gospel," he wrote, "and with your aid . . . I hope to be alike successful." Brazenly asking to be made head squatter, he begged a lucrative patronage job: Register of the Land Office.[19] Cushing's epistle to Cushing was the sort of yarn critics ascribed to "the pencil of fiction," but the writer foiled the master plots by inserting his personal story into the nation's. He confessed his sins but refused to be the scapegoat for economic or political crises. Instead, he framed a panorama of manifest destiny with himself as trailblazer, surrounded by vivid characters and plots, including Old Hickory, the Monster Bank, Bible stories, shipwrecks, the blood of patriots—even a log cabin, the political symbol that won the 1840 election for old Tippecanoe. Cushing posed as a monument, but not a "silent monument." Escorted by the stalwart icons of history and current affairs, "a broken merchant" was as valuable an American character as any other familiar face.

Articulate losers like Cushing hardly fit the part of the ragged, stooped beggar of contemporary writers and illustrators. A cartoon parody of Andrew Jackson's bank war showed the "Poor fellow!" extending his hat toward two matrons in black veils, financial widows without a penny to spare: "Alas, We were ruined with the Bank!" Behind them, Jackson rides roughshod over the Constitution, in a cart hauling money from the "monster" bank—poking his oxen with a giant veto pen. A suicide hangs from a dead tree on the horizon. The era's best-known engraving, Edward Clay's "The Times," likewise had no role for respectable families like the Cushings. "The Times" depicted the Fourth of July 1837, on the same square (based on Manhattan's Five Points) Brother Jonathan had roamed in 1819. With the stars and stripes snapping overhead, idle mechanics mingled with rum-soaked men and women, begging mothers, a fat capitalist, and the hydra of panic: a bank run. In the gutter, a handbill quoted Jackson's war cry against the evils of credit: "All those who trade on borrowed Capital, should break." Individual and collective sins remapped America as a financial Sodom and Gomorrah. But hallucinations of a market society run amok did not look like the "dig or starve" efforts of a family man to save his *"little all,* a *lovely wife & four children."*[20]

Local and intimate disasters like Cushing's made it easier to imagine the broader transformations going on in the commercializing society, easier to discern how buying and selling on cash and credit tightened the connections among family hearth, public square, and the highest echelons of national politics. But Cushing's vivid imagination failed to conjure up the appointment he sought. In 1844, the "Wiskonsan" squatter moved his family to Chicago—where he resumed practicing medicine. Oddly, he failed to mention that calling in his long letter, although his claims about business losses and bloodlines were true. This is known because his youngest son grew up to be a Civil War naval hero: Commander William Barker Cushing. "Lincoln's Commando" was not yet four when his father died suddenly at forty-six, while on a travel cure for his chronically weak health. His widow, Mary, took her husband's body and their brood home to Fredonia, New York, where she made her way by living yet an-

*Displayed above shop counters, this color lithograph discounted the
reality that cash was often scarce, obliging merchants to sell on
credit or not at all.* (Warshaw Collection of Business Americana, Archives
Center, National Museum of American History, Smithsonian Institution.)

other master plot: the broken man's wife who survives as a schoolteacher. At home, Mary taught her five children to revere their father and his admirable, if futile, quest to succeed.[21]

We notice the clock most when it stops running, and so with
broken banks and broken men. Here and there, a lone voice challenged the master plots. "When a long life has been passed in a
meritorious pursuit, and the result to the individual is not competence, but poverty," *Hunt's* conceded in 1849, "there must be some
great and fundamental error at the basis of the system." Blame
mongering impeded reform: "accusations of extravagance, imprudence, speculation, &c., are always adduced in individual cases;
but the effect, being general, not individual, the cause must also
be general." These causes, however, were harder to see than a broken man. As much as the canals and railroads that plowed up the

landscape, or the telegraph and mail system that consolidated it, or the new products that cluttered it, the "looser forlorn" was the market revolution's impact made visible. To depict him was to examine the face, hands, and works of the republic itself.[22]

People like Milton and Mary Cushing understood all too well that sentimental master plots shaped their experience of failure, proving the rule that "nobody fails who ought not to fail." In the public imagination, pictures and plots confirmed assumptions about achievement and identity faster than individual cases could challenge them. Back in 1819, Joseph Hornor needed hard money more than "any romance either in prose or poetry that this age has produced." Recounting the miseries of failed men in 1822, a U.S. congressman added, "Sir, these are not pictures of the imagination; they are scenes of real life. They are not singular, but are examples of thousands." Master plots wrote contingency out of the story, substituting fables and effigies of reasons "*in the man.*" Tycoon Stephen Girard's 1845 guidebook to New York City warned visiting merchants, "The freaks of fortune are at all times strange enough, but the last few years have witnessed some instances that would astonish even those who have dealt mainly in fiction. Wall Street has been the theatre on which have acted scenes that have surpass[e]d in interest the fabled days of Aladdin." Always ready with corroborating testimony, diarist Henry Van Der Lyn pasted in an 1845 clipping from *Cist's Advertiser* of Cincinnati. "What are the fluctuations of romance writers," it began, "compared to some of the realities of human life?" Failure was ushering in an age of realism.[23]

Imaginary Characters and Real Ones

Reality was the last quality Henry Hill associated with his legal work. He was the junior partner of a firm that handled insolvencies under Massachusetts law and bankruptcies under the federal act of 1841–1843, a short-term law that generated a long-term caseload. Hill's cases provoked him to vow never to declare bankruptcy, come what may. Besides its ritual humiliations, he wrote in his diary in 1845, "should the poor wight be successful enough to get his discharge[,] his moral obligations are not in the least affect[ed]." Hill alluded to the moral of a story then going around, about a man who declared bankruptcy. Although the court decree cancelled his legal obligations, he stepped forward years later to "cancel the *moral* obligation" and paid his arrears with interest. Like today's urban legends, variations of this story arose in many cities; often, the folk hero became "my neighbor" or someone else known by the storyteller personally. The most common version was known as "the debtor's banquet," wherein the host (often a Quaker) gave a feast for his creditors and put a bank draft under every plate! Henry Hill perceived his job in the same light; he gained for his clients "a *Legal* discharge to prevent any effect which a legal process might have upon their persons or property. But a man's moral feelings must be blunt," he added, "not to consider himself in a moral point of view just as much holden to the payment of his just debts as before." However tempting legal remedies might seem to ruined men, he maintained, "the inducements held out are more of an imaginary character than real."[24]

The lawyer who conceded the "imaginary character" of his paperwork was a marvel indeed, but was Hill's confession another restatement of Hornor's dilemma? Was "the poor wight" at fault when he failed? Why were "moral obligations" required above the "*Legal* discharge"? Hill's work ethic, pursuit of education, and habit of introspection aided his quest for self-reliance, but he saw achieved identity and the path to it as practical matters. "I never very much relished the doctrines of abstractions," he wrote after hearing Emerson's lecture on Plato. How odd, then, that moral concepts seemed more concrete to Hill than legal procedures. Six months later, he found himself in a position to reconsider. "Had opened to me to day another source of business in the way of clerkships in Insolvent cases," he wrote, "before a Master in Chancery." These administrative judges handled such matters as debt and divorce, and in July 1846 Hill jumped at a chance to boost his income by clerking in veteran attorney Henry Chapin's chancery court. On the paper trail of failure, the law clerk was the pack horse: copying records, taking minutes at settlement meetings of debtor and creditors, and transcribing the master's grilling of the debtor. Hill did this galling work from 1846 until at least 1849. "One of those interminably long insolvent meetings today which are always annoying," he complained after a year of it, "where there seems but little to do for any one save the Debtor and the Inquisitor."[25]

In the clerk's diary, the master became "the Inquisitor" as Hill daydreamed his way through "dull tedious affairs." He lived for the occasional oddity, an excuse to spin legal hearings into comic yarns. "The day opened with a pretty dark affair . . . of a character a little novel. I refer to the insolvency of a black man—a very Falstaff of a person in size," Hill wrote in 1848. "However the thing went off well and it seems rather to bad to make *light* of the subject." To Hill, the failure of an African-American man was a tautology; neither law nor culture presumed he could succeed, so how could he fail? It struck him as "a little novel" when the race, class, or gender of the parties contradicted his expectations for the type of case. Rustic debtors vexed the learned "Inquisitor," who grilled one yokel for two days and got nothing incriminating. "The Debtor was too unaccountably stupid," Hill smirked, having witnessed evasion "from trickery, & obstinancy, but very seldom from stupidity." Hill's favorite was the fellow convicted of "breach of promise of marriage," who was driven into insolvency by court-ordered damages—with the jilted woman as his major creditor! "She pursues him with the vengeance of a tiger," Hill wrote. "'Tis decidedly the best joke of the season & might prove available capital for writers of 'Romances founded on fact.'" Even in jest, he ascribed a durable value ("capital for writers") to strange but true tales like these.[26]

While few and far between, such episodes broke the crushing tedium of "Insolvency, insolvency & nothing else," as Hill juggled two clerkships besides his own practice. "If I could live without clerkships I would gladly sweep every thing of the kind from the board," Hill wrote in December 1846. "But I cannot. I must bear it though it swallows up every atom of my time: & it really does." This solitary hell conjured more than boredom. "The mind left to itself naturally falls upon the work of self-extermination," he mused two years later. "I am sorry to admit so much of a feeling of melancholly. . . . But sometimes the demon will come [in] spite of my endeavors." He did not try suicide, but "depression of spirits," "listless inactivity," and "blue days" plagued Hill. It was no solace that others also scribbled until their fingers were inky black. "I am now in one of [those] terrible flurries that I so frequently find myself in by means of the accumulation of labor—as a young professional brother of my acquaintance would say—mere mechanical labor," he wrote in 1848, adding the next day, "I am tied down to my desk from morning till night—pursuing the same dull, wearisome avocations." Still, it had to be done, both procedurally and economically; the law required the documentation, and Hill needed the income—lest he "be left behind for want of friends." He hated genteel society, but felt obliged to mingle as a wife-hunting young bachelor. "I prefer," he wrote, "any time to be tied to a whipping post to going to a fashionable party." He preferred not to, but Hill copied by day and cavorted by night, sulking his way through both shifts.[27]

The diary of Henry Hill's clerkships could have been the first draft of the 1853 short story "Bartleby, the Scrivener: A Story of Wall-Street," had Herman Melville written it from the standpoint of the title character. A literary "looser forlorn," Bartleby was hired as a "law-copyist" by a master in chancery. At first, he was an exemplary (if gloomy) clerk, who "wrote on, silently, palely, mechanically." Bartleby copied legal contracts for a few days, then inexplicably stopped working. He shirked all further tasks with the benign mantra "I would prefer not to." Henry Hill dreamed of mutiny, too. "I wish I could feel more like work—toil hard and unremitting," he complained in his diary, "but I do not and I may as well own up." But he wrote on—to curry favor with his mentors. Hill's senior partner, Judge Benjamin Franklin Thomas, and Master in Chancery Henry Chapin were valuable patrons for an ambitious novice. Both were old friends of Massachusetts Chief Justice Lemuel Shaw, who dedicated the new Worcester Courthouse in 1845. Hill attended the ceremony, in awe of Mr. Justice Shaw—whose daughter Lizzie was soon to marry her suitor, Herman Melville.[28]

Henry Hill need not have been the inspiration for Bartleby. Thousands like him made up the shock troops of American capitalism: the army of clerks drafted during the market revolution to point steel at parchment and make the curves, swirls, strokes, and capitals that ornamented the endless drafts, fair copies, duplicates, triplicates, and quadruplicates of the memoranda, prospecti, pleas, proxies, promissories, inventories, briefs, deeds, duns, liens, wills, codicils, registers, charters, tenders, transfers, foreclosures, seizures, dossiers, debentures, demurrers, petitions, depositions, extensions, evictions, conveyances, references, cross-references, discharges, mortgages, indices, appendices, sureties, licenses, summonses, certificates, dockets, affidavits, accounts, consents, warrants, judgments, testaments, assignments, attachments, endorsements, abstracts, and binding contracts that transformed ink and paper into both the nourishment and the excrement of commerce. By these weapons combatants lived or died, won or lost, succeeded or failed.

Lurking in or around most of these documents was the basis of modern American law, economy, and society: contract theory. Contract was the framework of achieved identity; by his own toil and acumen, any free man could make deals to advance himself. Hence, "nobody fails who ought not to fail." The law's proper role was to preserve liberty of contract unfettered and to refrain from hindering its exercise. Massachusetts Chief Justice Lemuel Shaw, as one historian put it, was the central force in raising "the paradigm of contract to its supreme place in nineteenth century legal thought." Shaw died in 1861, but after the Civil War, contract brought forth a new ideal of freedom: every citizen an entrepreneur. In theory, every man—white or black—enjoyed unfettered choices to sell his labor for wages or not, to accept the boss's terms or not, to incur debts or not. Those injured on the job or tricked into debt peonage had no recourse, because the law presumed that individuals freely chose their situations. Like presumptions applied to economic failure. Legal release from debts seemed to violate two rules of capitalism: keeping your promises and taking responsibility when your actions harm others. Failure was at once anathema and endemic to maturing capitalism, because a contract was a promise to succeed—to uphold your end of a bargain or else to "plague and curse" your associates, their associates, and their associates' associates.[29]

In "Bartleby," Herman Melville parodied his father-in-law's doctrines. To claim that men freely accepted or rejected contracts ignored facts of poverty and power. Men worked for peanuts and risked life and limb, not as truly free agents but as hirelings who lacked realistic alternatives. Pushing the scrivener's rebellion unto absurdity, Melville showed that the theoretical free agent was not meant to make real choices. "I would prefer not to" fell short of outright refusal, yet the master in chancery was so flummoxed that he never thought to restate his "request" as a command. Bartleby's preference was gibberish in Lemuel Shaw's contractual world. A hireling does not prefer, he complies—willingly, to spare the boss an embarrassing show of naked power. The scrivener's mantra is so perplexing that it overshadows something more significant: when Bartleby stopped working, he stopped copying *contracts*. His "passive resistance" (Melville's term) dammed the flood of paper that carried men to success or failure. Bartleby, however, was a naïf, not a revolutionary. Credulity, rather than audacity, made him such an oddball. Exercising the free agent's hypothetical choice would have been cheeky; believing that choice could be exercised at all was downright loony.[30]

Legal Fictions and Practical Truths

Henry Hill was the son-in-law Lemuel Shaw never had: an awe-struck legal disciple. A member of the bar from 1844 until he died in 1890, Hill's practice spanned the period when the "free agent" of contract theory recast American citizenship, labor, and enterprise. Indeed, he learned the law not only from books but also by watching the great man preside, whenever the circuit brought the Chief Justice to Worcester. He saw Shaw decide the fate of a fugitive slave, a child, and pronounce a death sentence on a rapist, a retarded boy of seventeen. Compared to the logjam of insolvency hearings, Shaw's jurisprudence and decorum revealed another side of Hill's profession. Told that in Boston they set aside a whole day for each case (an archaic rule honored in the breach), Hill marveled, "rather a 'Legal fiction' as some would call it; but then there are so many fictions in the Law itself it would be a pity really if there could not be occasionally one in the practice of it."[31]

A "legal fiction" referred to something not literally true but deemed true "in the eyes of the law." It was "a metaphor that had certain legal results," as when courts decreed that husband and wife were one individual, corporations were real people, and workers were free agents. Hill noted the "Legal fiction" in his diary, and the next day he penned the blunt distinction between the "imaginary character" of insolvent law and the "real" force of "moral obligations." Such was Hill's version of contract theory. To relieve debtors, courts had to annul contracts. Could they, under the Constitution? Should they? Would moral obligation endure? If so, was legal discharge spurious? If not, was legal discharge unrighteous? "The sacredness of private contracts" was a notion that repeatedly foiled proposals for debt reform from 1819 through the Civil War. To Henry Hill, voiding contracted debts was a useful pretense: a legal fiction.[32]

Leave it to a bankruptcy lawyer moonlighting as a scrivener to solve Joseph Hornor's dilemma. Doing double duty, Hill wrote and voided contracts daily. A contract signified obligation but was not the promise itself; promises were sacred, but contracts were breakable by definition. Filing the paperwork to terminate an illusion did no harm whatever to the real thing. So what if "nobody fails who ought not to fail"; why should moral responsibility thwart legal release? Hill practiced the fiction of legal discharge but preached the reality of moral obligation. After the panic of 1819, Joseph Hornor wrote, "If I fall it will not be my fault." Thirty years later, Henry Hill filed his rebuttal: the man who failed *was* at fault, but the law would forgive him anyway. This distinction made an acute difference. Rampant failure moved Americans to bolster moral obligation, to construe it as being at odds with legal and economic change, and to pronounce it worth preserving. However, to enshrine moral obligation was also to sequester it—literally to order it from the court. Ironically, a magnified sense of moral obligation as a thing apart, a truth immune to the legal fictions of contract, laid the foundation for U.S. bankruptcy reform after the Civil War. The reason stayed "*in the man*," but the remedy did not. Breaking contracts was not equivalent to breaking promises if society recognized an immutable (if unenforceable) moral obligation to pay. Like the one-case-a-day policy, a rule honored in the breach was still a rule.[33]

By the 1840s, Alexis de Tocqueville had given a name to this unprecedented democracy of contracting free agents: "individualism." Discontent and ambition drove the striver, he explained, whose desire to rise was exceeded only by "the most imperious of all necessities, that of not sinking in the world." This was not hyperbole; antebellum diaries and business records showed such precepts in action. A credit-rating agency evaluated a Virginia merchant in 1858 and 1859, calling him "sober & industr[ious] & honest, but rather green about bus[iness]" and concluding, "he has been on the sinking list all his life." Honest toilers could make shipwrecks of their lives, drowning perpetually without ever going under. They joined the town drunk and the neighborhood gossip as familiar characters in the American community. The man "on the sinking list" proved the negative case of achieved identity, reminding his fellow citizens of something they forgot or denied. The self-made man who fulfilled his contracts embodied the free agent—individualism made flesh—but so did the broken man who could not fulfill them. Twins were born in antebellum America; success and failure grew up as the Romulus and Remus of capitalism. Failure was intrinsic, not antithetical, to the culture of individualism. "Not sinking" took both self-reliance and self-criticism, lest a dream become a nightmare.[34]

Sinking Lists and Dead Letters

Hill's vow never to declare bankruptcy did not shield him from another kind of failure. "I really accomplish nothing," he wrote in January 1848; "I am the more ashamed of this when I see so many around me accomplishing so much more at a much earlier age—I want to hide my head for very shame." Anxiety over "not sinking" was even harder to remedy than being sunk. In the panic of 1819, Hornor's dilemma moved him to pen an ode to failure in his commonplace book. Thirty years later, Hill's solution all but eradicated his diary. In May 1848, he wrote in the final volume of his journal, "When there is nothing but insolvency in the orders of the day there is nothing to speak of in such a place as this. There is too much monotony in the administration of the insolvent law to get much of poetry or incident from it." Beyond the boredom, "nothing to speak of" marked a cultural absence—the frustrating lack of words and grammar pertinent to the new models of selfhood. Individualism had no poetics of its own. Henry Hill was a lawyer, not a literary man; but, like Melville, he felt a spiritual bankruptcy that defied easy description. "Whatever name you apply to it, it is an uncomfortable feeling to say the least," Hill wrote. This kind of failure could not be written off as a legal fiction.[35]

Henry Hill drudged for his fees; insolvency and bankruptcy cases racked his fingers whether he held the pen of attorney or scrivener. Often, he felt like a snake-oil peddler; he mused on the "singular state of things that one class of men should live in a measure upon the poverty of another." His clients praised his exertions, yet he felt no pride of achievement. "Today is the thirtieth anniversary of my birth," he wrote in August 1848. "A day that of all others in the year I most dislike to see—a pretty sure indication that my life is not what it should be." Two years after taking on clerkships, the achieved identity of success eluded him; "a tolerable indication that all is not right—that there should be some change." Instead of a poem he composed a prayer: "God grant that these saddened feelings with which I enter upon this fourth decade of my life may be profitable to me—that they may result in revolutions which may be carried out & produce a change in my whole manner of life—& that then that life may be better and more satisfactory to myself—and more useful and pleasant to all around me." Six months later, he was still clerking for the extra income that kept him from sinking in the world. "If it was not for my insolvent business I should be dry enough," Hill sighed on 9 January 1849. The next day, he scrawled, "Nothing of any particular moment to day—the most is or that can be said of it is an Insolvent Court without a Commissioner to preside—wherefore the Clerk himself has been obliged to do it." This sentence made up the final entry in the diary.[36]

Hill's deliverance came in 1850, when he rose from lawyer-scrivener to "the good old office . . . of a Master in Chancery." Himself becoming an employer of clerks and "Inquisitor" of debtors, Hill gained the power to condemn or spare many a "poor wight" from Bartleby's fate. Melville's scrivener died in jail at the end of the fable, "a man by nature and misfortune prone to a pallid hopelessness." The master's subsequent inquiries about Bartleby turned up only a record of former employment at the dead letter office in Washington, D.C. "Dead letters!" the master grieved, "does it not sound like dead men?" Bartleby had mistaken legal fiction for reality; figuratively and literally, exercising his theoretical choice was suicidal. Henry Hill met a happier end after practicing bankruptcy and probate law for nearly forty years. Three of his sons graduated from Harvard Law School and another became a physician. Newspapers printed his obituary when he died at seventy-one in 1890, and local antiquarians profiled him in Worcester history volumes. He mastered contract law and its fictional solution to failure, but no surviving record tells whether he ever subdued his chronic "feeling of melancholly." A man might go through life "not sinking," yet feel "prone to a pallid hopelessness," eluding failure, yet wondering why success eluded him.[37]

3 We Are All Speculators

A dead letter miscarried without being missed, finding neither its destination nor safe passage home. In nineteenth-century folk tales and romantic fiction, undelivered messages killed love or luck or magic. Such images tormented ambitious young men, for whom lack of direction or destination felt like social death. "I have gushed into tears many a time," New Hampshire's John Flagg wrote in 1825, when "I was afraid I should never be able to get into business." On his birthday in 1833, Philadelphia Quaker Samuel C. Morton remarked, "What a note for reflection! that I should have lived *one fourth of a Century*, and yet have done so little good for any—self or others—nothing by which I am to be distinguished from the common herd of mankind." Henry Hill felt this way in 1841: "Thus far my life has quite too much the appearance of *blankness*. What can I show as the fruits of twenty three years of my existence? Nothing!" Although Hill's luck improved in time, his mood did not. "The thought that I am living so little to my own profit or the service of any body else," he wrote in 1846, forced him to admit "a lack sometimes but too severely." A man might remedy bad habits and blunders caused by inner faults, but what if he simply lacked the elements of success? The bogeyman-speculator of commercial fables erred by "his overreaching disposition," but in actual letters and diaries, men feared underreaching. Instead of an inner flaw, dead letters and blank ledgers signified an inner void—a reason *not* in the man.[1]

"A new race must arise on the broken fortunes of the present," New Yorker John Pintard had warned after the panic of 1819, "who different[ly] educated may be content to plod." To the next generation, however, contentment looked too much like stagnation. What fresh hell was it, to "never be able to get into business," to languish "with no fixed plans," to achieve nothing but *"blankness"* among "the common herd"? The dead letter was no mere metaphor. In May 1849, "having no business of any profit to pursue here," Charles Hunt hanged himself, alone in a barn not far from Henry Van Der Lyn's law office. Three months later, *Hunt's Merchants' Magazine* noted that "to have no business is to be cut off from the rest of the world, and to exist in a state of listless isolation and exclusion . . . a looker-on where all are busy; a drone in the hive of industry; a moper in the field of enterprise and labor." When looking on did not claim the body, it deadened the spirit. In Providence, Rhode Island, in 1852, Hiram Hill wrote in his diary, "I need employment most of the time to keep off the blues," but that cure was not always available. "Business is dull and my spirits low," he noted in 1855; "I have made many mistakes in my life which has been a Blank nearly." Men thought that bankruptcy might be the least of their worries.[2]

Feelings of terminal *"blankness"* bespoke a way of life, not a mere setback: failure as identity, not calamity. To the first generation reared on steamboat levies, canal embankments, stage platforms, and railroad beds, boyhood fascination with perpetual motion grew into an ideal of manhood. "The true business man," editor Horace Greeley enthused, "knows how to set new wheels running" and "make himself a sort of driving-wheel." The name "business man" (usually two words) came into common usage in the 1830s. When British traveler Thomas Brothers grew curious about the phrase "real, enterprising American citizens," which he seemed to be hearing everywhere, he pressed users for its definition. The consensus, he wrote, was that "real" Americans were "'business-men;' 'go-ahead men;' such as adorn the country in every quarter, and such as are, for ever, held up above the rest." A rising "business man" embodied true selfhood and citizenship: the man in motion, the driving-wheel, never idle, never content. "Few American merchants seem to think they are doing business enough," a Boston editor claimed amid the panic of 1857, "so long as there is any chance of doing more."[3]

Perhaps nobody knew this better than the wife of a striver. Roxana Turner and Thomas Wall married in 1829 in Leicester, Massachusetts. Barely twenty-one, Thomas had a notion to get rich manufacturing scythes—soon to be standard gear for those going West. The couple spent five unavailing years in upstate New York before trailing Thomas's customers to the frontier. Roxana wrote to the home folk in 1834, "it seems to me to be a great undertaking to go to Ohio, and live so far from my friends. However if it is for our interest I must be content in so doing." Manly discontent demanded wifely contentment, but she also defended the move: "I suppose you may think we might be contented where we are and perhaps may think we are doing well enough," she wrote, portraying ambition as a joint venture between man and wife. Five years later she reported, "all I have to say is that we are in Ohio and get a comfortable living." They were still not doing "well enough" for Thomas; but, Roxana confided wearily, "Ohio . . . is not what it is cracked up to be." She closed a July 1839 letter saying, "I have to work hard this summer and have considerable care on my mind, it makes me look rather old. I am loseing my red cheeks fast and so good bye." This dispatch included a note from Thomas. "It has been very bad times since I have been in this state," he wrote, nodding to the panic of 1837; "business very dull a great many failures among businessmen which has made it rather bad for me as well as for all others that were dependent on that class of men for support." Still hoping to succeed as a manufacturer, he did not yet rank himself "among businessmen," but clearly Thomas and Roxana Wall were working and scrimping and scheming to win that title for him. Whether he ever made it is unknown, but she did not: Roxana died a "lunatic-pauper" in the New York state asylum in 1850.[4]

With commercial and civic identity at stake, husbands and wives risked everything for the rank of "business man," which was no mere synonym for "merchant." It came into the American language as an honorific for the ideal citizen, "held up above the rest." Daily speech differentiated among merchants, traders, brokers, agents, factors, jobbers, importers, speculators, manufacturers, and peddlers. "Business man" encompassed them all, not so much negating the differences among men as assuming that all white men were entrepreneurs. Edgar Allen Poe satirized this idea in an 1840 short story, "The Business Man," about a failed merchant turned mugger. Conducted methodically, banditry became "The Assault and Battery Business." Poe mocked the managerial jargon of success manuals, which extolled a systematic approach to life that blurred occupational and class inequalities. Before the panic of 1857, the author of *How to Do Business* assured readers, "We are all to a greater, or less extent, men of business." Such blather had a nice populist ring; by 1896, William Jennings Bryan was milking applause with "The man who is employed for wages is as much a business man as his employer." Lumping together manufacturers and mechanics erased inequality much as contract theory did; "business man" pinned a street name on the abstract "free agent." If astute trade unionists did not buy it, many a poor boy on the make did. Lawyer Henry Hill did not make a living buying or selling, yet he called himself "a business man."[5]

Dead letters, blank pages, and broken wheels stood as grave reminders of an entrepreneurial culture that looked upon failure as a capital crime: assets and identity perished, even if the body survived. Ralph Waldo Emerson reconsidered the "State street proverb" from his journals of 1842 and elaborated his ideas in "Wealth," an 1860 essay. "Commerce is a game of skill, which every man cannot play, which few men can play well," he wrote, emphasizing that reality before considering popular assumptions. "There is always a reason, *in the man,* for his good or bad fortune, and so in making money. Men talk as if there were some magic about this, and believe in magic, in all parts of life." How was it that proverbs and superstition held sway in this epoch of the skilled "business man"? Why did people rush to judgment when one man fell, yet stand in awe when another rose? Children could recite the mundane causes of failure, yet the greatest sage could not impart the secret of "making money." Why did the failed man provoke a witch hunt, if the successful man was the alleged sorcerer? The striver's ethic drew upon this medieval logic: if success be a magic touch, failure was the conspicuous absence of magic.[6]

A Flunky Born Every Minute

Few Americans had P. T. Barnum's magic touch. In 1841, he bought the seedy American Museum in lower Manhattan and carted in curios, relics, and hoaxes of all species. At the corner of Broadway and Ann Street, he suckered his patrons, made them like it, and made a fortune. When he lost everything in 1856, associates consoled him while the press and public erupted in howling, foot-stomping delight. A falling star was a crowd pleaser, a carnival of *schadenfreude*, where the humdrum "reason, *in the man*" became a grand spectacle. The self-crowned "Prince of Humbugs" owed half a million dollars, but his lapses were a disappointment: land speculation and investments in clockmaking. "Those who have been fleeced by his ingenuity," teased the *Boston Chronicle*, "had a sort of moral claim on him to the effect that he would not be ruined, except in a novel, original, and striking manner." Common men took heart "that our own poverty cannot be attributed to our folly [except] by a process of reasoning that would make men who have money as great fools as ourselves."

The impresario put on a fine show of contrition but intended to laugh last. Little bothered by dilemmas of failure or "a sort of moral claim," he hoped to exploit the state debtor laws of his native Connecticut to outfox his creditors. "I shall soon be relieved of all liabilities . . . under the 2/3 Bankruptcy Act," he boasted privately, "leaving it to me to give them what I please. It will not take me long to make another fortune." Nor did it, despite vigilant creditors having Barnum arrested on the steamer *Arabia,* as he prepared to sail for England in September 1857.[7]

A bankrupt Barnum reflected the times like a clever hall of mirrors: humbugs tricking humbugs, tricksters humbugging tricksters. You needed double vision to see him clearly. The *New-York Times* regarded his career as exemplary and illusory all at once. "Barnum is the embodiment and impersonation of success," read the paper's 1854 review of *The Life of P. T. Barnum, Written by Himself.* A hoax-by-hoax retelling of its author's rise, the book parlayed controversy into best-sellerdom. "He calls it *humbug,*" huffed the *Times,* but behind this carney barking, "his wealth has been acquired by a complicated system of falsehood and fraud." Everyone yearned to know how he did it, especially young men eager to replicate his success. The newspaper groused that by long example, and now by close instruction, the showman aided and abetted the petty humbuggery that already had given merchants a bad name. "Other men do the same thing on a small scale," noted the *Times.* "They sell sand for sugar,—chicory for coffee,—counterfeit bills for good ones; they seldom get rich and more frequently get into the State Prison." These midget humbugs lacked Barnum's magic touch. "They are mere prosaic, common-place, and therefore unsuccessful, swindlers." Mendacity was as old as humanity, but nineteenth-century capitalism paid a golden premium for novelty: all things quick or clever, curio or jumbo. Humbug set a fresh standard for the scrupulous and unscrupulous alike: to avoid the shame of a "mere prosaic, common-place, and therefore unsuccessful" life.[8]

"Barnumization" was a newly coined word synonymous with

running out on deals and debts. Shape-changers and money-changers pulled so many "tricks of trade" that upright men in financial distress faced new scrutiny even as they inspired new anxiety. Could honest men succeed anymore? An 1850 handbook, *How to Get Money: Or, Eleven Ways of Making a Fortune,* gave uncommonly blunt answers in chapters like "Making Fortunes by Suspension of Payments." Mocking "that fool," Poor Richard (and hence Benjamin Franklin, the patron saint of success), this pocket-sized primer taught readers to run up vast debts, hide assets, duck and default on payment, and abscond into the night. The book scrapped "honesty is the best policy" for a new motto: "Smile at honest men for lack of brains." The real joke was on aspiring cheats who shelled out for *How to Get Money,* because its author had already published a manual on detecting fraud and collecting from rascals who might follow the advice in his new book. In a credit market, every buyer was a potential defaulter and every defaulter a potential sham. Hence, everyone from writers and illustrators to phrenologists and credit-rating agents tried to detect dishonesty and predict failure. *Caveat venditor!* A credit agency warned sellers to beware of an Ohio tailor who shirked payment and shielded assets. "Made a fraudulent sale to his bro[ther] & pretends to have fail/d," read an 1849 report. Such cases confirmed public fears of commercial and personal deception. The broken man had become the bogeyman.[9]

Pretending to fail: what could be more cunning than to feign disgrace? In Barnum's written statement for a court hearing, he testified that many creditors refused to believe he was broke. Who could lose half a million in half a year? "Oh, it is all humbug," they snorted; "BARNUM has got plenty of means!" Humbug mixed puffery and perfidy into profitable amusements, yet it also provided a school for skeptics. Friends swore "unshaken confidence in his integrity," but most people knew Barnum as a *shaker* of public confidence, with hoaxes like the "Feejee Mermaid." Playful deceit played a dangerous game in an era when "confidence" measured the level of trust needed for the economic health of individuals and the nation. With a monetary system of "a mixed character made up of confidence and . . . precious metals," explained an advocate of bankruptcy reform in 1840, mutual trust was a keystone of credit. Panic ensued when "unlimited confidence gave place to universal distrust," one of the fathers of modern bookkeeping warned. Barnum's case redoubled public distrust of failed men. Not even self-destruction was sincere anymore. "The Last Confidence Game—The Suicide Dodge," read an 1859 headline in the *Cincinnati Gazette*. The subject had faked a suicide attempt in a hotel, citing business losses in a note "fully up to the standard of suicide literature"—then bilked $25 from those who "saved his life."[10]

Everyone knew "tricky men" who "made money by failing" or had heard about compassion shown to a broken man who turned out to be a confidence man. Local gossip, tabloids, and merchant manuals told cautionary tales about drifters "of prepossessing appearance, and that suavity of manner," who lived on hard-luck stories. "A Confidence Man at Cincinnati," that city's *Inquirer* reported in 1859, put his wife and five moppets in a boardinghouse, cadged $50 from tycoon Nicholas Longworth, "and left for parts unknown—bequeathing his wife and five children to the landlord. The question is, where will he turn up next?" Everywhere, it seemed; charlatans no sooner appeared than they absconded, or "funked out," again. The folklore of capitalism nicknamed such men Peter Funk—master of "all kinds of petty humbug, deceit, and sham, especially in business." In an 1834 novel, Peter told an honest bankrupt to feel no shame. "What! man, do you go moping about the streets, with your head down," he says. "A failure is nothing—it is the only way to get rich, man." Peter stood for "moral gum-elasticity" in an 1848 newspaper column by Walt Whitman. No mere legend, Peter was seen in the flesh hawking bogus watches or shill-bidding at mock auctions. Credit-rating firms dubbed a Cleveland auctioneer "a veritable Peter Funk." In 1854, agents warned that a Cincinnati watchmaker "*is a Peter Funk* . . . a man that takes advantage of the ignorant & unsuspecting."

Credit evaluations from Connecticut profiled "a tricky slippering unreliable fellow" and urged, "It would be well to have bargains clearly defined as he is apt to wiggle out if he can." This wiggler was P. T. Barnum himself—who drew catcalls from the credit-rating agent: "he is a consumate humbug!"[11]

So there they were, practically a three-ring menagerie of failure: "consumate humbugs," "great fools," and "honest men." One failed by trickery, another by stupidity, and the third by some blend of adversity, delinquency, and mediocrity—but none should be trusted. "The green stranger is as liable as ever to the seductions of Peter Funkism," the *New-York Times* warned in 1852. A thief and a naïf were equally dangerous (if not equally heinous) to their trading partners. New modes of travel and communication eroded trust by multiplying encounters with "strangers." Codes of middle-class etiquette arose to regulate interactions and engender trust, based on how "respectable" people dressed and behaved. A "cult of sincerity" or emotional transparency guided social occasions, and canons of "moral obligation" ordered business relations. Crowded markets meant more buying and selling but also more bilking and stealing. Veterans had a name for novices "who, unacquainted with the manner in which stocks are bought and sold, and deceived by appearance, come into Wall street without any knowledge of the market." Some blundered and others got hoodwinked, but they were all *flunkies.*[12]

Trading with strangers risked falling victim—but *not* trading with strangers risked falling behind. The dread of flunkydom and the appeal of humbuggery tempted "honest men" to practice deceits short of outright fraud. If the character ethic was not obsolete, it looked rather dull. "A merchant ought to acquire and maintain an easiness of manner, a suavity of address, and a gentlemanly deportment," advised the book *Hints to Tradesmen* in 1841, "without which the finest talents and the most valuable mental acquirements are often incapable" of success. Ambition required a mastery of social and commercial masks, but what separated them from the mask of a confidence man—known for his "suavity of manner"? The weekly *Philadelphia Merchant* frankly admitted in 1855, "There is a kind of magnetism in trade that goes a great ways towards explaining the greater success of one man over another who seems to have equal opportunities." Others conceded the point, yet warned that "personal magnetism" operated "entirely independent of character." These admissions and admonitions did not reveal (or refute) an insurgent humbug manifesto, but neither did they disentangle self-presentation from self-manipulation. The secret of success, divulged by the *Dry Goods Reporter*, was to cultivate "a ready tact in adapting one's self to the different humors of the various classes of buyers."[13]

"Adapting one's self" and "personal magnetism" were attempts to demystify the "magic" of the successful entrepreneur, and some men pronounced themselves lacking. "I have none of that sort of cunning which constitutes a talent for making money," Peyton Harrison of Virginia concluded in 1824. He begged his father to accept this and not force him "to spend my life in ceaseless endeavors to climb the ladder to wealth & reputation, when as often as I begin to advance, I feel a *clog* about my neck which drags me to the bottom!" Out in Ohio, another young man established a general store in 1837—bad timing, but Comfort Avery Adams held on for a decade. In 1848, he folded and played his only ace: groveling to Uncle Elisha. Lucky was the man with a moneyed uncle, and Adams's just happened to be Elisha Whittlesey, Comptroller of the U.S. Treasury and a czar of patronage jobs. Adams addressed him in a proper tone of rambling contrition. "I am poor, and I have been weak enough, to allow my misfortunes, (although I must blame myself principally for them), and my long continued ill health," he wrote, "so to sour my temper, that I do not believe I shall ever be fit for a merchant again." Adams felt unfit, being unable to adapt. "I find that often, when I am really anxious to please," he explained, "by my unpleasant manners I offend." Certain this flaw would not matter in government service, Adams solicited and got a postmastership in 1849; he later became a tax assessor. Men without connections appointed themselves to assess their own liabilities, as did Hiram Hill of Providence in 1852. "Business rather dull," Hill wrote in his diary. "I don't know how to take advantage of circumstances. I should have been a wealthy man if I had." Taking advantage meant good business to some and bad conscience to others. Either way, downtrodden men looked like frauds or flunkies, too shrewd or too naïve. Hiram Hill eventually wised up; by 1865, he stood "rich & undoubted" in the eyes of credit-rating agents.[14]

Hiram Hill's penchant for self-doubt reflected popular beliefs that some men were too honest for their own good. Hill made his diary entry in June 1852; in the same month a rejoinder appeared in *Hunt's Merchants' Magazine*. "We frequently hear the expression made in reference to some good-natured, inactive, old-womanish man, '*O, he's too honest to get along*,'" reported *Hunt's*, but "in nine cases out of ten the honest man's failure does not arise from the practice of an honest course, but from his unfitness for the business in which he is engaged." The "too honest" theory of failure incited the punditry against conventional wisdom to deny the effects of changing markets and morals. Yet both sides drew an emasculated portrait of failure: a "good-natured, inactive, old-womanish man" unable to *"to get along."* The men themselves used this phrase to contrary effect. "I have struggled very hard to get along," Joseph Hornor wrote in 1819. Frederick Westbrook mused in his diary in 1842, "I have been struggling to get allong [*sic*] and have found my expectations blasted." Uttered in self-defense, "getting along" sounded a note of ambivalence that echoed more loudly in consolations by kith and kin. When a Massachusetts farmer died in 1854, his son wrote, "He was always too honest to get along in the world and get to be very rich. But he managed somehow to just about hold his own, but I suppose it has been tight work for the past few years." Was this a eulogy or an apology? Why did an honest man who "just about held his own" need vindication?[15]

By midcentury, "getting along" often meant "getting ahead," the magic words some men could not say. The standard given by the dead farmer's son in 1854, "to get along in the world and get to be very rich," showed up almost verbatim in *Hunt's* two years later: "By *getting along* you mean that you are advancing in your worldly interests, that you are increasing in prosperity, gaining riches." This advice ran under the headline "Getting Along Slowly," recommended as the safest way to climb "up the ladder of fortune." That very month, P. T. Barnum asked for mercy from the court and his creditors, "to be permitted to go ahead in some kind of enterprise." His words distinguished between plain "getting along" and a more dynamic mode: "to go ahead." One might have read this between the lines of *Hunt's;* "advancing," "increasing," and "gaining" voiced higher expectations than "getting along." Life on a horizontal footpath could not beat a vertical ascent on "the ladder of fortune."[16]

Onward and upward sloganeering drowned out the older ideal of yeoman competency, which valued the maintenance of current status and plenitude more than the cultivation of risky ambitions. The man with "a competency" (in the language of the eighteenth and early nineteenth centuries) sustained his independence by land ownership and contentment, providing for his family today and squirreling away necessary resources against tomorrow's troubles. William Cooper Howells took this approach to life on the Ohio frontier between 1813 and 1840, recalling, "on the whole I got along tolerably well." His son, novelist William Dean Howells, sounded no more eloquent than that Connecticut farmer's son in trying to defend such a life. "The real hurt which adverse fortune did him was to make him contented with makeshifts," wrote the younger Howells. "Consequently, he was not a very good draughtsman, not a very good poet, not a very good farmer, not a very good printer, not a very good editor, according to the several standards of our more settled times; but he was the very best *man* I have ever known." However poignant, the tribute nevertheless heeded "the several standards"—as if only "the very best *man*" deserved pardon for a makeshift life. "I got along tolerably well" was a failure's epitaph.[17]

Humbugs and flunkies stood at the ends of the spectrum, but Barnum's America gawked at the men in the middle: could any breed of failure be more bizarre than "the very best *man*"—the "good-natured" fellow who "managed somehow to just about hold his own" or "got along tolerably well" or was "*too honest to get along*"? In 1858, *Harper's New Monthly Magazine* sorted all species of failure under the heading "Freaks of Fortune." *Harper's* had grown since its 1850 debut into the colossus of reads: circulation 200,000 in a country of 40 million. The nation's most popular magazine granted that the panic of 1857 humbled every man before the powers of chance. Yet, failure mostly downed "mad caps or cowards"—hotheaded or fainthearted aberrants—while "the practical man masters Fortune in spite of her changing chances. He will succeed, and can not be put down." Talk about a sucker's choice: the new way of hustle and humbug might be the road to perdition, yet the old way of contentment and competency might be the road to oblivion. By 1858, Barnum was in England remastering fortune by lecturing on "The Art of Money-Getting, or Success in Life." Some 2,000 Londoners jammed St. James Hall to hear the once and future Prince of Humbugs: "A man may appear to be honest and intelligent, yet if he tries this or that thing and always fails, it is on account of some fault or infirmity that you may not be able to discover, but nevertheless which must exist."[18]

Americans who deemed themselves "honest and intelligent" did not need Barnum to send them looking for hidden faults and inner voids to explain their disappointments. A busted storekeeper and out-of-office Whig named Abraham Lincoln considered his restless ambition an "infirmity" even as he hated the "unambitious, unsuccessful way of life" of his male kinfolk. Lincoln skipped his father's funeral in 1850, then scolded his stepbrother, "Your thousand pretences for not getting along better, are all nonsense—they deceive no body but yourself. *Go to work* is the only cure for your case." Sound brotherly advice; yet Lincoln's own approach to "getting along better" favored wit over grit. Showmanship in court and on the stump gave him an edge; he acted the artless yokel as shrewdly as Barnum played the artful dodger. Lincoln understood humbug (a word he used often) but had prior claim on another Barnumism. Before it ensnared dupes and losers generally (around 1840) the word *sucker* sneered specifically at clodhoppers from Illinois, called derisively "the sucker state." The rail-splitter felt little in common with his woodenheaded kinsmen, yet this one amazingly elastic word caricatured the lot of them. In 1858, with Stephen A. Douglas standing perpetually between him and high office, Lincoln amused a supporter with a bitter pun: "Just think of such a sucker as me as President!" Like Barnum's crazy mirrors, *sucker* made little men mistake themselves for giants and big men doubt their own stature. Words and images of failure distorted how men saw themselves and others. For all his hard-won distinction and prosperity, sometimes Honest Abe glimpsed his own reflection and thought he saw a born loser.[19]

"Zip Coon" Was Not a Dashing Fellow

Humbugs, suckers, flunkies, freaks of fortune, great fools, mad caps, mopers, meteors, loafers, lookers-on, driving-wheels, magic men, self-made men, old-womanish men, too-honest men, good-natured men, broken men, makeshift men, business men, confidence men, and go-ahead men—the expanding lexicon of capitalism redefined white masculinity in the era of Lincoln and Barnum. In 1850, a twenty-one-year-old clerk cringed when a veteran Manhattan dealer cornered him, "telling me 'that I could never make a Merchant.'" Ned Tailer fumed in his diary, "He also imagined that I lacked energy, and wanted that bustling, and go ahead spirit, which characterizes the active and persevering Salesman." Tailer's indignation recalled misgivings voiced a decade earlier by the American in Petrograd, twenty-four-year-old

Joseph Ropes. Summoned home by his Boston family, Ropes pleaded unfitness for "the American *go-aheadism* . . . to be continually letting off steam and puffing away as you do in America." Call it steam or spirit, bustling or puffing—the driving-wheel momentum of the "active, persevering Salesman" shaped the culture of modern capitalism. Supposedly open to any white male who did not "lack energy," this fraternity hooted and hollered about "our go-aheadative spirit" and "American *go-aheadism*." Even the staid *Scientific American,* founded in 1846, warned of "the fearful blot of a wasted life" and beat the drum for "Yankee go-ahead-ativeness."[20]

Young men starting out in the 1850s were dubbed "the 'go ahead' boys of 1835." Having been in the crib or at school in that tumultuous decade, they were too young to remember severe hard times. Now grown and impatient, they scorned their elders as "slow coaches" or "old fogies" when advised to be cautious. As the partisan *Democratic Review* put it in 1851, to them "the experience of 1830–1840 is a dead letter. They know nothing of the disasters of those years, their causes or consequences, and care less. The future to them is bright, and the times are propitious." Certainly, electoral bitterness over Jacksonian losses to Whig boosterism skewed the opinions of the *Democratic Review,* but the "'go ahead' boys" were hardly alone in measuring their manhood by "the absurd vanity of 'doing a large business.'" In competitive markets, to lack the "go ahead spirit" (in reality or allegedly) counted as a fatal flaw. In 1851, a credit-rating agency blacklisted a New Yorker, noting, "R. is not a 1st rate business man, has not enough energy to go a head." Another agency recommended a Philadelphia dry-goods dealer as "a driving, pushing fellow" and lauded a tailor as "a pushing go ahead young man." In 1852, another magazine depicted the nation in just these terms: "[Brother] Jonathan is a pushing, enterprising, surprising fellow" full of "go-ahead mobility." The following year, George Washington Light, Boston editor of *The Young Mechanic* and *The Young Men's Magazine,* composed this chant for a new generation:

Better days are drawing nigh;
  Go ahead:
Making Duty all your pride,
  You must prosper, live or die,
For all Heaven's on your side.
  Go ahead.[21]

What exactly was this masculine "go ahead spirit" that "a 1st rate business man" dared not lack? Bartlett's *Dictionary of Americanisms* defined it in 1848: "To proceed; to go forward. A seaman's phrase which has got into very common use." In the literal sense, the *London Spectator* in 1851 reviewed *Moby-Dick* as a fatalistic parable about "the go-ahead method." Colloquially, the term hailed "Yankees who are the most 'go ahead' in energy, ambition, and success." Popular songs like "Go Ahead Polka," "Go-Ahead Quick Step," and "Go Ahead Galop" set a new tempo for the nation. Bartlett's 1859 edition accelerated the meaning: "GO AHEAD. Rapidly advancing, progressive." Bartlett cited the *Philadelphia Press* on cockiness as national style: "In our opinion, which we express, of course, with our wonted and characteristic diffidence, America is a dashing, *go-ahead,* and highly progressive country." A dashing fellow was not only manly but speedy and still accelerating, and not all could enter this race. When a minstrel song sheet showcased "Zip Coon on the Go-Ahead Principle" or *Harper's* printed an antifeminist cartoon of bloomer girls declaring "*we* go ahead"—both wrung laughs from the absurdity of an ambitious woman or Negro. Among blackface characters, "Zip" was the dandy, but he could no more be a "dashing fellow" than could a woman in bloomers. Velocity and stamina defined white manhood—being "the most 'go-ahead' in energy, ambition, and success." Doing tolerably well was no shield from reproach, much less from reversal; men worried that other men suspected "that I lacked energy" or had "not enough energy to go a head."[22]

Young men who measured themselves by this standard often berated themselves for feeling languid and slack. "Every jot of en-

ZIP COON

ON THE GO-AHEAD PRINCIPLE.

I went down to Sandy hollar t'other arternoon,
I went down to Sandy hollar t'other arternoon,
I went down to Sandy hollar t'other arternoon,
An de first man I chanc'd to meet war ole Zip Coon,
   Ole Zip Coon he is a larn'd scholar,
   Ole Zip Coon he is a larn'd scholar,
   Ole Zip Coon he is a larn'd scholar,
For he plays upon de banjo, "Cooney in de hollar."
   Tudle tadle, tudle tadle, tuadellel dump,
   O tuadellel, tuadellel dump,
   Ri tum tuadellel, tuadelleldee.

Cooney in de hollar an racoon up a stump,
   Cooney in de hollar, &c.
And all dose 'tickler tunes Zip used to jump.
   Oh de Buffo Dixon he beat Tom Rice,—*(repeat.)*
And he walked into Jim Crow a little too nice.

Ole Sukey Blueskin she is in love with me,
   Ole Sukey Blueskin, &c.
An I went to Suke's house all for to drink tea,
   An what do you think Suke and I had for supper,
   An what do you think, &c.
Why possum fat hominy, without any butter.

My old missus she's mad wid me,
   My ole missus, &c.
Kase I wouldn't go wid her into Tennesse.
   Masa build him a barn to put in fodder,
   Massa build him, &c.
'Twas dis ting an dat ting, one ting or odder.

Did you eber see he wild goose sailing on a ocean,
   Did you eber, &c.
De wild goose motion is a mighty pretty notion,
   De wild goose wink and he beacon to de swallow,
   De wild goose wink, &c.
De wild goose hollar google, gogle gollar.

I spose you heard ob de battle New Orleans,
   I spose you heard, &c.
Whar ole gineral Jackson gib de British beans;
   Dare the Yankee boys do de job so slick,
   Dare de Yankee, &c.
For dey cotch Pakenham, an row'd him up de creek.

Away down south dare close to the moon,
   Away down, &c.
Dare lives a nullifier what they call Calhoun,
   When gineral Jackson kills Calhoun,
   When gineral, &c.
Why de berry next President be ole Zip Coon.

He try to run ole Hickory down,
   He try to run, &c.
But he strike a snag an run aground,
   Dis snag by gum war a wapper,
   Dis snag by, &c.
And sent him into dock to get new copper.

In Phil a del fie is old Biddle's Bank,
   In Phil a del fie, &c.
Ole Hickory zamin'd him an found him rather crank
   He tell Nick to go and not make a muss,
   He tell Nick to go, &c.
So hurrah for Jackson he's de boy for us.

Possum on a log play wid im toes,
   Possum on a log, &c.
Up comes a guinea hog and off he goes,
   Buffalo in canebreak, ole owl in a bush,
   Buffalo in a canebreak, &c.
Laffin at de blacksnake trying to eat mush.

Nice corn's a growing, Sukey loves gin,
   Nice corn's a growing, &c.
Rooster's done crowing at ole niggars shin,
   Oh Coone's in de hollar and a Possum in de stubble
   Oh Coone's in de hollar, &c.
And its walk chalk ginger blue, jump double trouble.

Oh a bullfrog sot an watch an alligator,
   Oh a bullfrog sot, &c.
An jump upon a stump an offer him a tater;
   De alligator grined an tried for to blush,
   De alligator grined, &c.
An de bullfrog laughed an cried oh hush.

Oh if I was president ob dese Nited States,
   Oh if I was, &c.
I'd lick lasses candy and swing upon de gates,
   An does I dina like why I strike em off de docket,
   An does I dina like, &c.
De way I us'd em up was a sin to Davy Crocket.

Sold, wholesale and retail, by LEONARD DEMING, at the Sign of the Barber's Pole, No. 61, Hanover Street, Boston, and at MIDDLEBURY, Vt.

A minstrel show stereotype speaks about Jacksonian politics and culture, in "Zip Coon on the Go-Ahead Principle." (Boston, circa 1834.
Rare Book and Special Collections Division, Library of Congress.)

ergy if it can be said that I ever had any seems to have departed," lawyer-scrivener Henry Hill wrote in 1847, hoping to "blunder upon something that will serve to arouse me." To waste manly vitality, in the so-called "spermatic economy" of the time, ensured failure despite hard work. Men whimpered about bad luck, "but the fact is, they miscarry because they have mistaken mere activity for energy," *Hunt's* retorted in 1856. "The person who would succeed in life is like a marksman firing at a target; if his shots miss the mark, they are a waste of powder. . . . Everybody knows some one in his circle of acquaintance, who, though always active, has this want of energy." Not indolence, but impotence, caused failure. From its origins as a sailor's cry to its adoption as a capitalist cheer, the "go ahead spirit" named a kind of masculinity wherein some delivered while others "miscarried." Men failed because they lacked spunk.[23]

Private discussions corroborated public images of failure as deficiency rather than catastrophe, absence not mischance. Abolitionist editor Lydia Maria Child observed these defects in her husband, David, a serial bungler dependent on her throughout their marriage. On a sleigh ride in 1847, David and a family friend got lost in unfamiliar woods. "It was *so* characteristic of him," Lydia wrote. "At last they met two surveyors, and Mr. Child asked, 'Can you tell us where we are?' 'Where do you wish to go?' inquired one of the men. 'Nowhere in particular,' replied Mr. Child. 'Very well,' rejoined the man, 'you are on the straight road there.'" His wife's conclusion expressed the mixture of empathy and disgust that welled in her during "fourteen years of uninterrupted adverse fortune." She wrote to a friend that she could not stop thinking about that sleigh ride. "Poor David! He drives on at much the same result in *all* the affairs of life. He constantly reminds me of Emerson's remark that 'Some men expend infinite effort to arrive nowhere.'"[24]

Failure was the lost horizon of American manhood. The sponsor of an 1822 bankruptcy bill argued that if Congress voted it down, the failed man would have "no ray of hope—no power to be useful; he would have in truth nothing in prospect before him." Another reformer pleaded, "Let the unfortunate debtor have a FUTURE." A prospect was a ticket to strive, a chance to grab hold of one's future. The crime of the drunkard was that he "destroyed his own prospects." Nothing seemed more precious to those on the make, nor more indicative of manly identity. New Hampshire's John Flagg bragged and hedged in a typical 1825 letter. "My prospects are very flattering," he assured his brother Charles, "and if nothing happens to interrupt me I think I shall make money." On the Ohio frontier in 1839, Thomas Wall tried to recoup from the panic and wrote home, "Things now look better the prospect before me has a better appearance and I look forward in hopes of seeing better times hereafter." As a mirror of speculative identity, a phrase like "the prospect before me" made future gains look even handsomer than current assets. Such talk was less a sign of individual narcissism than of cultural fetish. Capitalism made a fetish of the future, seeing nothing better than profit except the prospect of more. By midcentury, Americans were mad about prospects, from the gold prospectors of California to the paper prospectuses of corporations and speculators. A man with "nothing in prospect" blew the chance to speculate on the future, to bet on himself.[25]

The "go-ahead system" meant living the life of a futures trader, to chase the masculinity of another day, another deal. The speculating self thrived on continuous risk and obligatory advance. "The American is always bargaining," traveler Michel Chevalier reported in the summer of 1835; "he always has one bargain afoot, another just finished, and several more in meditation." Stopping in Johnstown, Pennsylvania, he noted, "Every body is speculating, and every thing has become an object of speculation. The most daring enterprises find encouragement." Wherever he went— New York, Lowell, Pittsburgh, Erie, Cincinnati, Richmond, and Charleston—Chevalier heard the cheer, "*Go Ahead!*" He depicted a culture of incessant striving: "all is here circulation, motion, and

boiling agitation. Experiment follows experiment; enterprise succeeds to enterprise."[26]

This was literally true in Buffalo, where omnibuses named
"Experiment," "Enterprise," and "Encouragement" clattered up
and down Main Street. Englishman Thomas Brothers sketched
the owner of the streetcars as "a real enterprising American citizen, a regular 'go-ahead' man." Benjamin Rathbun's holdings in
transportation, communications, and real estate were so vast that
in 1836 he actually owned Niagara Falls. But his dominion over
the mists was as fleeting as Lear's. Massive debt and a forgery
conviction struck flat Rathbun's empire, and his thunderous fall
exacerbated the panic of 1837. Rathbun was called a "meteor," a
speculator who soared and plummeted with spectacular velocity
and destruction. Fellow citizens denounced him and other "wild
and reckless speculators, [for] destroying the enterprise and para-
lyzing the efforts of the prudent, honest, and industrious man."
Yet sharp distinctions and extreme examples deflected awareness
that even the simplest Americans were becoming part of this
world—whether they knew it or not. "We may believe it, but
never do we live a quite free life, such as Adam's, but are enveloped in an invisible network of speculations," Henry Thoreau remarked in his journal in 1838. "Our progress is only from one such
speculation to another, and only at rare intervals do we perceive
that it is no progress."[27]

In theory, the "go ahead (i.e. go-headlong) speculator," as one
critic put it, was an enemy of the people. In practice, he *was* the
people. "There are speculators of many kinds," Federalist representative John Sergeant told Congress in 1819; "the variety is
infinite, and in no country on earth greater than this. Every thing
about us invites to speculation." Scotsman James Flint visited
Cincinnati and found that speculators came from nearly every
walk of life; he commented on "the designing amongst lawyers,
doctors, tavern-keepers, farmers, grocers, shoemakers, tailors,
&c." Little had changed when the next great crisis came along.

"The spirit of speculation and adventure pervaded the entire community," read an autopsy of the panic of 1837; "and crowds of individuals of every description,—the credulous and the suspicious—the crafty and the bold—the raw and the inexperienced—the intelligent and the ignorant—politicians, lawyers, physicians, and divines, hastened to venture some portion of their property in schemes of which scarcely any thing was known except the name." Workers, who were conspicuously absent from such lists, knew the booms as times when wages did not keep pace with rising prices and rents.[28]

Definitions of speculation were as broad as the continent the land grabbers coveted. "*Speculators*, That is those who live on buying & selling Lands, stocks," Van Der Lyn wrote in 1838, "have become a profession & have in many instances accumulated vast fortunes by luck & chance." The next year, Horace Greeley printed a more benign definition in *The New-Yorker:* "the buying of an article, not for personal or immediate business use, but with the hope of selling it again at a profit." This sounded like what merchants did, and much ink got spilled to draw a line between legitimate trade and speculation. "The trader depends upon small but regular gains; the speculator looks to sudden and eccentric enrichment," Edwin T. Freedley wrote in his best-selling *Practical Treatise on Business*. But his chapter "How to Get Rich by Speculation" concerned "daring, dashing, hazardous, break-neck adventures" suited to a man "large of faith—a believer in things not seen." To demystify speculation, he set ground rules and explicated popular commodities. He concluded with a wink: "Never speculate; but *when* you do, be sure to mind our rules."[29]

Breaking the rules by speculating, oddly, made failure seem as much a matter of chance as defect. "Industry appears as a vast lottery," Alexis de Tocqueville wrote in *Democracy in America*, in a famous passage about bankruptcy. "The Americans, who have turned rash speculation into a sort of virtue, can in no case stigmatize those who are thus rash." Either Tocqueville exaggerated, or he misconstrued the American lack of a national bankruptcy law. The stigma depended entirely upon the outcome, as Whig journalist Richard Hildreth explained. "When speculation proves successful," he wrote in 1840, "however wild it may have appeared in the beginning, it is looked upon as an excellent thing, and is commended as *enterprise;* it is only when unsuccessful that it furnishes occasion for ridicule and complaint, and is stigmatized as a *bubble* or a *humbug.*" Hildreth added that "a certain spirit of speculation must at all times exist, otherwise there could be no improvement." Likewise, in 1851 the magazine *Littel's Living Age* remarked upon "the go-ahead habits of the people, and . . . the success which attends such rash or resolute determination, till it fails." Whether rashness turned out to be enterprise or humbug, the old deadlock endured. To risk and fail had consequences, but so did not risking at all. Alabama and Mississippi land fever inspired the 1853 quip "He who does not go ahead is run over and trodden down."[30]

What would it mean to fail in a new world that deemed every man a speculator? Old knavery became a new testament, an American gospel. "This principle enters into all the ramifications of life," claimed the *Wall Street Journal* in 1851, "that those seeking the gain of money are not the only speculators: but that men, women, and children, are all endeavoring to acquire something of which they are not now possessed—in fact, that we are *all speculators.*" Betting on himself meant something to Samuel C. Morton, the Quaker whose twenty-fifth birthday in 1833 left him ashamed to "have done so little good for . . . self or others." A month later, commodity investments in Liverpool flour went bad, and Morton took "a considerable loss on the adventure." *Adventure* was a telling euphemism for speculation. Morton's escapade sank "nearly all I have made & saved for several years past," he grieved; "it has never been my case, to float on that 'tide which taken at the flood leads on to fortune,' as I have ever encountered the ebb." Failure audited the person as well as the purse; it meant more than an outcome, like a bad debt or a great panic. It revealed a man's inability to achieve or sustain a venturous mode of living. "Nothing venture, nothing have" was the rule of the day.[31]

Going bust in the age of go-ahead begged questions about capitalism's impact on morality and identity. As a model of white manhood, the "business man" had many critics. Grammarians quibbled when "man of business" devolved to "business man," and moralists warned that the new title reduced men to mere creatures of ambition. As the insignia of a "dashing" temperament, "business man" touted mettle, not morals. "He is an active, resolute, go ahead fellow," wrote a Michigan credit reporter in the 1840s, "with no regard for obstructions, principles, or consequences." The market revolution ran along faster than its counterpart moral reformation. During the second half of the century the heirs of the panics enacted structural changes—laws, procedures, and institutions to reform banking, bankruptcy, and credit. Still, master plots and stock imagery of individual moral blame infused the culture of American capitalism. In this way, failure proved the doctrine of achieved identity. "Men succeed or fail . . . not from accident or external surroundings," a Massachusetts newspaper reiterated in 1856, but from "possessing or wanting the elements in themselves." Deficient or degenerate, the specter of the Broken Man gave proof through the night of many a nationwide panic that the flag of "Yankee go-ahead-ativeness" yet waved.[32]

Words over America

The panic of 1857 hit in late summer. European demand for Yankee grain plunged when the Crimean War ended. The Ohio Life Insurance and Trust Company went broke, sending ripples through the financial world. And with a touch of melodrama, the steamer *Central America* sank in a storm with $2 million in California gold (and, incidentally, six hundred souls). Philadelphian Sidney George Fisher studied causes nearer home. "A bank is a machine to facilitate trade, just as a railroad is," Fisher wrote in his diary. "Our people require a machine to make money fast although now & then it produces bankruptcy & confusion, and they require a machine by which they can travel fast & cheaply, altho now & then a collision occurs, by which fifty or a hundred people are maimed at a blow." What the bankrupts called "going to smash," Fisher concluded, was not so different from a train wreck. Both were calculated risks of life at full throttle.[33]

A Greek chorus in the age of go-ahead, Fisher defined America in 1857 as a set of familiar actors performing an epic of contemporary hubris. Olympian banks lured investors and borrowers with "fictitious capital," he explained, no better than the crookedest confidence men. The credit economy depended entirely on confidence. "So long as confidence is maintained all is well, but a failure must at length occur, & then the fiction becomes apparent. . . . [M]any families, lately rich, are plunged into actual poverty." In an October 1857 letter, New Yorker C. H. Luddington gave the panic narrative shape: "Things are rapidly approaching a climax. Three more Banks failed to day. . . . This will be a blue week." New York's *Evening Post* gave rhythm to the blues:

Merchants very short,
Running neck and neck
Want to keep agoing—
Praying for a check;
Dabblers in stocks,
Blue as blue can be
Evidently wishing
They were "fancy free."[34]

Running, praying, dabbling, wishing, and agoing articulated how the market revolution transformed identity. Americans became a people of the gerund—"rising and falling, going and coming, making it or not making it," as Nelson Aldrich put it recently. This ideal reshaped masculinity. An 1853 success manual emphasized, *"a right measure and manner in getting, saving, spending, giving, taking, lending, borrowing, and bequeathing, would almost argue a perfect man."* A business lecturer remarked in 1857, "Striving, struggling, inventing, contriving, executing are the inseparable characteristics of the present condition of man." In 1864, a physician reviewed the past forty years: "Every one is tugging, trying, scheming to advance—to get ahead. It is a great scramble, in which all are troubled and none are satisfied." Identity was as fit for speculation as any other commodity. Solvency and selfhood both demanded prudent but bold management of ambition and risk. The speculating self spoke in the gerund; to the first Americans born and raised in the "great scramble," success meant risking and failure meant stagnating. The two differed as much as the Overland Express differed from a dead letter.[35]

Perennial restlessness raised the stakes of American life. "The word is, 'Go ahead; be something; make a pile, and make your mark,'" observed *Putnam's Monthly* in 1856. Three years later, *Harper's* concurred: "'Fast,' is the word: and it irks us terribly. Society is tumbling 'ahead' neck and heels." Both magazines took exception to "the word," but who could deny that "go ahead" had become the national anthem—or, more specifically, the measure of white manhood? In an 1860 article for *Atlantic Monthly*, Ralph Waldo Emerson lauded "the word of ambition" as the basis of American culture. He explained that the rewards and penalties for personal endeavor revealed worth and restored balance, in society as well as in men. On the eve of the Civil War, some said "the word" for America was "fast," others said "go ahead," and still others said "ambition" or "individuality." In more formal speech, the word was *individualism*—a grandiloquent name for the go-ahead creed. The self-made man was individualism's favorite son; the broken man, his black-sheep brother. In national pictorials and local sightings, the failed white man proved the rule of achieved identity: individual merit determined payoff or punishment in the market. Even more than an achiever, a ruined man was individualism incarnate; success always drew a crowd, but failure often stood alone. "The loosers forlorn" of 1819, as the famous Brother Jonathan cartoon dubbed the fraternity, dispersed as the lonesome losers of 1857. That year, a sensational new tabloid called *Harper's Illustrated Weekly* ran this bit of tomfoolery:

> *For fate is fickle, and Fortune fails,*
> *And life is a game of heads and tails,*
> *And mixed-up losers and winners,*
> *And the same retributions now and then*
> *Happen to fall on nations of men*
> *As on individual sinners.*[36]

By proving the rules that undid him, the loser in this game personified both individualism and its discontents. *Harper's Monthly Magazine* pondered such riddles in December 1857: "Discontent, indeed, is a prominent characteristic of our age and nation, visible in our virtues as well as our vices." Only two months into the crisis, a spirit of universal contrition still prevailed; everyone had been "'going ahead too fast,'" hell-bent on becoming an Astor or "oh! help us, genius of anti-climax!—a Barnum!" But in April 1858, after six months of hard times, collective guilt had given way to the usual finger-pointing. "In situations of financial responsibility, incompetency is a moral offence," *Harper's Monthly* wrote, putting the bungler on par with the swindler; "the wrong man in the right place is the plague and curse of modern society." So there it was: whether felled by sin or circumstance, a failed individual was literally and figuratively "the wrong man."[37]

Any fool would have wondered if he were that man and looked for contrary indicators. Men commonly rated themselves at year's end, as a Maine diarist did in 1858. "At the commencement of the year I considered the hard times and scarcity of employment, and thought if I earned my living for the year it would be all I should do. But the Summary . . . shows that I have done a little more," wrote Albion W. Clark. "The Summary" balanced his assets and earnings of $406.59 against debts and interest of $32.58, leaving a bottom line of $374.01—not bad for a lean year, even to a twenty-three-year-old keen to do "a little more." Indeed, Clark did a little of everything—farming, fishing, teaching, carpentering, hatmaking, peddling, and storekeeping.[38]

Clark was one of "the 'go ahead' boys of 1835," born thereabouts in Piscataquis County, central Maine. He married in 1856 and spent the next half-decade living the word: "Go ahead; be something; make a pile, and make your mark." At loose ends in 1861, he rode south as a private in the First Maine Cavalry (once inspected by President Lincoln himself, whose smiling face took Clark by surprise). Private Clark survived Gettysburg and a prisoner exchange before riding home. After Appomattox came Aroostook—the frontier, Maine's northernmost county—where he tried homesteading for two hardscrabble years. By then past thirty, he spent New Year's Day 1867 with "a little book called *The American Chesterfield*," the perennially popular success manual young George Washington had read. Clark quit his farm that summer for Newburyport, Massachusetts, where employment in a hat factory only depressed him. He worried that he would never make his pile, never make his mark. "It seems to me that I cannot bear prosperity," he moped. "If I ever prosper I must brace up to it and try to be content and not be in too much hurry to get more money. Discontent was all that ailed me this year." His wages did not buy contentment, however; clothing, room, and board "takes all I can earn," he wrote. "I want to do more than make a living." After a decade of striving, New Year's Eve 1867 found the diarist again writing up "the Summary," showing him still $513.50 in the black. "I have made some hasty recapitulations and estimates of my own affairs," he explained, "so that I may look back and see my situation in life, from a standpoint away ahead in the future when I am rich." Half-serious, he added, "I expect that time will keep far enough in the future to be out of my reach but I can do as others do, be always agoing to be rich." Summarizing, estimating, expecting, and reaching were his calling; Clark was a man of the gerund if ever there was one.[39]

"Always agoing" was the down-easter's pronunciation of the "go ahead principle." Clark embraced ambition as a way of life, a kind of success in itself. Perpetual striving tipped the balance between identity and oblivion for his generation of men on the make—including another son of 1835, Samuel L. Clemens. "We were always going to be rich next year," he recalled in *Mark Twain's Autobiography*. "It is good to begin life poor; it is good to begin life rich . . . ; but to begin it poor and *prospectively* rich! The man who has not experienced it cannot imagine the curse of it." Twain and Clark shared a knack for irony, each grasping that "go ahead" logic made every man prospectively rich. This was at once the dream and the delusion, the chance and the curse. "Every man a speculator" took identity itself for the dearest and riskiest commodity of all. To be "always agoing" was a duty of manhood, though any payoff be "away ahead in the future." That day never came for Albion W. Clark; dead within a decade of writing those words, barely forty years old, he left a widow and two small children to try their own luck.[40]

What is the American Dream but an astrologer's chart, a collective reading that fits some lives but not others? The frontier ideal of Manifest Destiny claimed not only the far continent but also the big sky above it. Riding up to Aroostook or rafting down the Mississippi, "'go ahead' boys" scanned the heavens for their own star and any sign that the sky might fall. We became a land of fortune tellers; the winning bid and the bragging rights went to the man who read his own future (and his competitor's). The entrepreneur lived by prophets as much as by profits, using foresight not only to best his neighbor but to decide whom to trust and not trust in business dealings. Commerce now traveled farther and faster—but so did panic, bad news, and the ripple when one man failed and took others down with him. Striving on credit made prophesy a valuable commodity. If only a financial douser could point out who would succeed and who would fail, sort those "mixed-up losers and winners," and tell "the wrong man" from the one who was "always agoing to be rich."

4 Central Intelligence Agency, since 1841

anging around Wall Street in the summer of 1843, Henry Thoreau witnessed the birth of the information industry. To explore literary Manhattan, he took a job tutoring Emerson's nephew on Staten Island. Emerson had asked two protégées to welcome him. "Waldo and Tappan carried me to their English Alehouse the first Saturday," Thoreau wrote Emerson. Giles Waldo seemed shallow to Thoreau, but not William Tappan: "I like his looks and the sound of his silence." The pair clerked near the stock exchange, where Thoreau visited and "spent some pleasant hours with Waldo and Tappan at their counting-room, or rather intelligence office." Tappan's father, Lewis, owned the enterprise, a city marvel that Thoreau noted to impress the folks back home. "Tell Father that Mr. Tappan, whose son I know . . . has invented and established a new and very important business," he wrote his sister. "It is a kind of intelligence office for the whole country, with branches in the principal cities, giving information with regard to the credit and affairs of every man of business in the country." Thoreau quit New York by summer's end, having discovered little else besides the first modern credit bureau, Lewis Tappan's Mercantile Agency. A direct ancestor of Dun & Bradstreet, the Mercantile Agency sold "information with regard to the credit and affairs of every man of business" and rapidly established itself as a national bureau of standards for judging winners and losers.[1]

The Mercantile Agency managed risk by managing identity: a matrix of past achievement, present assets, and future promise. Neither rating consumers nor granting credit, it graded commercial buyers for wary sellers. Lewis Tappan—an ardent social reformer—did in the marketplace what others did in asylums and prisons. He imposed discipline via surveillance: techniques and systems to monitor and classify people. Local informants quietly watched their neighbors and reported to the central office. "It is an extensive business and will employ a great many clerks," wrote Thoreau, whose grotesque penmanship disqualified him for such employment. "Mr. Tappan" kept a stock as legible as it was categorical. "We have no confidence in his success or bus[iness] ability," a typically blunt report said of "an honorable man" who later "Bursted up." Another case noted approvingly, "Bus[iness] on the increase & parties here who sell [to] him largely have confidence that he will finally succeed & become well off." That good word —"confidence"—meant access to major markets for rural buyers. "No confidence" warned urban sellers of fools. Then there were the swindlers: "He is a perfect confidence man" with "a happy faculty of deluding the people around him, many of whom believe him an honest & respect[able] man." Annual subscriptions to Tappan's service began at only $50—the cost of a good horse.[2]

People often said that credit rested on "confidence between man and man," a cliché as early as 1803. Adopting this motto, the agency cited an 1834 speech by Daniel Webster, who had actually said "intercourse between man and man." A harmless revision perhaps, but it mimicked the problem at hand: neither men nor money nor even words were trustworthy anymore. Telegraphy, improved postal service, and fast freight by rail and steamboat encouraged citizens to strike bargains over vast distances. Transportation and communication linked regions into a national market, yet technology outpaced economic, legal, and social infrastructures. Trading beyond the horizon precluded looking another man in the eye. Confidence men now moved faster than their reputations, and even if the man was good his money might not be. Financial systems went from bad to worse in Andrew Jackson's "bank war" of the 1830s. States, cities, and private banks still printed local currency. Buying in Boston with Ohio banknotes meant fussing over exchange rates and checking *Bicknell's Counterfeit Detector and Bank Note List* or another guide to genuine bills and known fakes. Falsity of any kind—from outright confidence games to just idle gossip—might cause panic in the marketplace. The agency system revolutionized a vital business tool, facilitating stability and growth in an era with few other national economic institutions.[3]

When Tappan began in 1841, no comparable system of surveillance had ever existed. Within five years, he enlisted 679 local informants; after ten, his network reached 2,000. Their first decade of dispatches filled "more than 100 books, of the size of the largest ledger, extending to 600 and 700 pages each." One 11-by-17-inch page held up to 1,500 words of tiny calligraphy, the handiwork of "a great many clerks." By 1851, the inflow kept thirty scriveners busy. Indexing within and among volumes sped retrieval of any given entry among thousands and later millions. Cross-referencing aided continuous tracking, even when subjects changed pursuits or locales. In 1871 alone, clerks added 70,000 *new* names and closed 40,000 files because of failure, death, or retirement. On an average day, the firm received 600 new or updated field reports and answered 400 inquiries. It all flowed in and out of "the largest ledger"—the master volumes in their impressive red sheepskin bindings. The agency upgraded the most adaptable and dependable technology in human history—the book—by building networks and systems around it.[4]

The marketplace now had a memory, an archive for permanent

Thousands of words about dozens of men covered the 11-by-17 inch folio pages of a Mercantile Agency ledger. (R. G. Dun & Co. Collection, Baker Library, Harvard Business School.)

records of entire careers. Each page looked more like a series of stories than a column of statistics. Individual cases spanned decades, while accumulating updates chronicled a subject's beginning, middle, and end. When did he start, and where? What has he achieved? What happens next? Whatever became of him? The life and times of a Charleston shoe dealer accrued for more than thirty years. "Makes rather a swell here," said his first entry, "can't be much; is smart enough to carry on his bus[iness]." The ink traced John Cummins from upstart in 1850 to absconder in 1859: "Has been closed up by the Sheriff. Left for parts unknown." The agency tracked him to Texas and home again in six months. "John is a curious fellow, he has got back, but is doing [nothing]. Let him alone." Southern reports ceased with the Civil War, but Cummins's story picked up in 1866, taking him from privation ("Always hard up & slow pay") to stagnation in 1880: "In bus[iness] many years but has never been successful, owing to want of capacity; though is an honest man." The June 1881 up-date—"Old man in bus[iness] here many y[ea]rs but never made anything"—ended his serialized tale of comings and goings, tenacity and futility. John Cummins lived an unremarkable life, which a remarkable company monitored for thirty-one years.[5]

More than a bank balance or a character reference, a credit report folded morals, talents, finances, past performance, and future potential into one summary judgment. As a credential of such broad scope, it resembled the modern concept of identity. First outlined by psychologists and sociologists in the mid-twentieth century, identity reflects two ongoing processes: evaluation of self and verification of credentials. Early credit reports addressed both. In 1857, a subscriber asked about "Henry J. Hull" of Utica, New York. The agency had nothing on him but queried its informant there, who replied, "Is not w[orth] a Dollar. a *miserable Vagabond!*" The client demanded more details. In three days came a clarification, equally brief and blunt, plus a spelling correction: "His name is 'Henry J. Hall.'" The central office tried again: what was Hall's exact occupation? Clearly irked by the third inquiry within a week, the informant retorted, "Loafer. Bad." The agency could find and appraise nearly anyone in a crowd of 29 million (the U.S. population in 1857)—even *loafers*—in seven days. The system managed identity not as a legal or psychological abstraction, but case by individual case, while doing a volume business.[6]

Managing identity meant more than guarding one's name as a priceless asset. Benjamin Franklin supposedly drew that lesson in America's first motivational poster, "The Art of Making Money Plenty"—the "art" consisting of a rebus (or picture puzzle) with maxims from *Poor Richard's Almanack.* An eyeball stood in for the middle vowel in "creditors," a reminder that someone was always watching. Dating from 1811, it became a popular Currier & Ives lithograph. The eye of Providence had watched over America, atop the pyramid in the Great Seal that Franklin helped design. "Making Money Plenty" substituted the eye of commerce; besides the creator, "thy creditors" and competitors also observed and

A popular poster since about 1810, this rebus attributed to Benjamin Frank-lin challenged viewers to decipher its word pictures—which admonished that watchful eyes followed one's every move. ("The Art of Making Money Plenty in Every Man's Pocket; by Doctor Franklin," New York, 1817; Printed Ephemera Collection, Rare Book and Special Collections Division, Library of Congress.)

judged you. As a young printer, Franklin showed how to use so-cial surveillance to advantage. Instead of having paper delivered, he fetched it "thro' the Streets on a Wheelbarrow," a street perfor-mance to show himself not above such exertion—and thus to be "esteem'd an industrious, thriving young man."[7]

This scene enlivened *The Autobiography of Benjamin Franklin*, fulfilling Poor Richard's maxim "He that can compose himself, is wiser than he that composes books." A life set in movable type, Franklin's memoir showed how to rise by making a good story of yourself. Failures were like typographical errors, it winked: forget small ones and revise "great Errata" in "a second Edition." Frank-lin's gospel made him the patron saint of American ambition—but only after 1840, as public schools raised literacy and the first cheap editions of *The Autobiography* appeared from publishers like Lewis Tappan's brother Charles. Indeed, the Tappan brothers were great-grandnephews of Franklin; "I have the honor to be collaterally descended from this eminent & industrious country-man," Lewis Tappan wrote proudly. While Charles publicized their role model, the Mercantile Agency would catch the errata, set the type, and publish the definitive edition of a striver's life.[8]

From Almanacks to Spy-Books

In Benjamin Franklin's day, transatlantic traders wrote highly rit-ualized letters to create a grammar of long-distance trust. Euro-pean firms solicited intelligence from colonial agents and clients. English tobacco importers Farrell and Jones relied on a Virginia planter named John Wayles. Thomas Jefferson wed his daugh-ter, Martha (whose dowry included her enslaved half-sister, Sally Hemings, fathered by Wayles). Wayles was a colonial insider whom Farrell and Jones could rely on to know other gentle-men's affairs, and in 1766 he sent them written credit appraisals of his fellow Virginians. Such informal reporting was common, but early confidence men easily ducked such scrutiny, and none of Lewis Tappan's antecedents achieved the scope and influence of the Mercantile Agency. Four decades into the nineteenth century, with banking and currency in disarray, the only permanent economic institutions were proverbs. "Trusting too much is the ruin of many," saith Poor Richard. But quaint sayings from old almanacs were no guide to trusting the businessman at the other end of a telegraph wire.[9]

Trust was the trickiest pun in the capitalist idiom. In the vernacular, it meant not only interpersonal confidence but also financial credit. "I am ruined by . . . trusting others," Thomas Emerson wrote from a Vermont debtor's prison in 1838, blaming deceivers and defaulters and warning his sons, "trust no man with your name as long as you live—as soon as they are poor they become villains." Like much fatherly advice, this was easier said than done. Emerson had debts in Boston, Manhattan, Buffalo, Indiana, and even Chicago. Dealers both great and petty used credit (as did aspirants without capital), not only in local and remote transactions but also because hard cash was often scarce. "Trusting" and "getting trusted" were offers not easily refused, as a young baker learned in Andover, Massachusetts. "It is my intention to sell what I sell for cash after the first of *January*," Jonas Prentiss promised his mentor-uncle in December 1839. "I do not expect to sell so much for *cash* as I should by trusting, but I think it will be beter [*sic*] for me in the end." Still, Prentiss needed credit to get supplies. When the flour miller went unpaid in February 1840, Prentiss's uncle feared for his reputation: "You very well know that *Credit* is a very important thing to you, and you ought to make every possible exertion to acquire confidence in those from whom you obtain it." Like much avuncular advice, this simple rule was beside the point. By year's end, the baker sat insolvent before a Master in Chancery. "Keep up a stiff upper lip," wrote his uncle (himself a failed merchant turned postmaster). Prentiss replied in his own defense, "a cash business . . . is out of the question alltogeather [*sic*], I cannot sell for cash and if I do not trust I cannot sell."[10]

To "acquire confidence," as the baker's uncle enjoined, or to prevent "no confidence," as the credit report warned, became a kind of commercial holy grail. Old maxims and rules for face-to-face dealings offered scant help for trusting invisible men who lived upright, corrupt, adroit, or inept lives hundreds of miles away. Before the invention of credit reporting, city merchants sent clerks on expensive western crusades to collect bills from frontier debtors, hired "commercial travelers" to dun and snoop, or consulted the few single-industry credit reporters who preceded Lewis Tappan. Far cheaper was asking the man most likely to know others' business: the local postmaster, who might answer queries or collect debts for a fee. In Warren, Ohio, a busted storekeeper and political string puller named Comfort Avery Adams held the office. Adams informed a Peoria lawyer hunting for a local debtor, "He is a wild fellow and has no property and consequently nothing can be collected of him by process of law." For $2, Adams pestered the wild one's father-in-law to cosign the debt. Unofficial services, a postmaster's bread and butter, demonstrated the commercial value of a network of agents but lacked central coordination and record-keeping.[11]

Blacklists and "spy-books" met these needs but operated informally. The former were printed rosters of absconders and bankrupts. The latter began with urban sellers keeping notes on shifty buyers. When his old student chum failed, lawyer and sometime scrivener Henry Hill noted in his diary, "Jobbers in Boston have a long time had certain memoranda against his name something like this: 'Drives fast horses, sprees it often, handsome wife, rather extravagant.'" An 1841 exposé, *A Week in Wall Street,* told readers that "Mr. Solomon Single-Eye" was watching. Like the Franklin poster with its eyeball, "Solomon Single-Eye" personified informal but "rigid . . . *surveillance.*" Lumping market watchdogs with usurers and swindlers, the anti-Semitic name turned old prejudices to new suspicions that the eye of commerce favored urban titans over petty or rural dealers.[12]

Similar resentment coined the epithet "spy-books" when informal note-taking spawned printed registries. On 10 April 1837,

New York's *Commercial Advertiser* depicted Chicago in an uproar about "one of the New York mercantile spy-books." Such books described out-of-towners who traded in New York—"country merchants," as New Yorkers derisively called them; Chicago was then a frontier town of 4,400. Trouble ensued after someone doing (or feigning) business at a Manhattan emporium purloined a copy of the book (literally from "under the counter") and slunk back to Chicago. Western blood boiled over a book illicitly printed and passed around like mercantile pornography! Page after vile page sullied the "the fair character" of Chicago merchants and saw them "most villanously traduced, by a pack of knaves hired for that purpose by the merchants of New York." Chicago editors were howling for a grand jury probe of the "spy system" when a bigger story unfolded at the end of April: the panic of 1837.[13]

Lewis Tappan stood in the eye of that storm. A decade before, in 1827, he went broke milling textiles and took a job as credit manager for his elder brother Arthur, a Manhattan silk importer. That same year, with their friend Samuel F. B. Morse, famed artist and inventor, the brothers established the *Journal of Commerce* (it was Wall Street's oldest business daily when it ceased print for online publication in June 2000).[14]

Entrepreneurship and evangelism coexisted for the Tappans, who were sons of a devout Calvinist family in Northampton, Massachusetts, and active in moral reform movements. Arthur and Lewis became prominent advocates of prohibition and sabbath laws. In 1833, they cofounded the American Anti-Slavery Society, which elected Arthur its first president. A year later, they advanced interracial education by organizing Oberlin College. Arthur Tappan & Co. prospered despite its link to unpopular causes. But in 1834, "anti-Tappanist" mobs ignited a week of violence against abolitionism. Several thousand strong, the raiders sacked the brothers' storefront and burned Lewis's home on Rose Street. Southern newspapers offered $50,000 for Arthur's head.

Vigilantism and terror did not stop the Tappans, but vicissitudes of trade did. The familiar concatenation began in spring 1837; the Tappans defaulted because their own credit buyers reneged. Nicholas Biddle, the brothers' friend and director of the Second Bank of the United States, guaranteed their debts up to $150,000. Even so, the million-dollar failure of Arthur Tappan & Co. shocked New York and helped spark the panic of 1837. While the elder brother rebuilt his enterprise, the younger (who was nearly fifty) went in search of another calling.[15]

Lewis Tappan's experiences in business and reform led him to exalt "the Christian self-made man," according to one historian, "the person who partook in vigorous profit-making ventures along lines that fortified basic Christian morality." In the next four years, Tappan proceeded to merge the duties of moral reformers, postmasters, bill collectors, and spy-bookers into a unified system of commercial surveillance. In 1839, he championed the mutineers of the slave ship *Amistad* until the Supreme Court upheld the Africans' freedom in January 1841. The case benefited from his talents for moral righteousness and organizational efficiency. That same year, Tappan saw his chance to fight the evils of fraud and ineptitude in the credit economy. Systematic verification would revitalize moral responsibility in commerce. By linking national surveillance to central record-keeping, Tappan meant to archive market memory. An intelligence agency would reward men of integrity and punish rash lenders and crooked borrowers. Thus, after being ruined by defaulters and doing the same unto others, a famous abolitionist set out to break the chain of broken promises.[16]

The Mercantile Agency opened in the summer of 1841, and the founder immediately faced the problem of recruiting agents. Like the "spy-books," Tappan intended to monitor "country merchants" who ordered from urban wholesalers—a goal unlikely to win friends in the hinterlands. Tapping into the wide, communicative circles of antislavery men, he solicited comrades like Ohio's

Salmon P. Chase (future Treasury Secretary and Chief Justice). Using an existing network was canny but also risky. Their cause was no business asset, and in conspiracy-minded times, any mobilization of abolitionist agents could be misread. Even before he opened, New York's *Courier and Enquirer* faulted "the business of a secret inquiry into the private affairs and personal standing of every body buying goods in New York." The *Courier* also reprinted an item from Virginia. The *Norfolk Beacon* lauded a local attorney for spurning Tappan's invitation "to act as a spy"—and added that even a slave would balk at the low-down offices of a snitch.[17]

Tappan regarded his "correspondents" more as sentinels than snitches, but he often had to defend himself. Taking a half-page in *Doggett's New-York City Directory* for 1843, he wrote, "It is not a system of espionage, but the same as merchants usually apply— only on an extended plan—to ascertain whether persons applying for credit are worthy of the same and to what extent." The firm's "resident and special agents" made similar inquiries, but on a larger, more systematic scale—"an extended plan." Reports circulated in strictest confidence, "so as not [to] injure any one. . . . It is not known that injustice has been done to country traders by this plan." This notice likely met less skepticism than the one at the bottom of the same page, for P. T. Barnum's American Museum. But careful readers may have inferred that harm befell some traders—except not unjustly, since the agency adjudged them scoundrels or incompetents. The founder himself set the sanctimonious tone that later subjected his firm to numerous lawsuits for libel and slander.[18]

The advertisement showed that by his second year of operations, Tappan's antislavery friends were off the hook. Correspondents included "attorneys, cashiers of banks, old merchants and other competent persons." Lawyers seemed most inured to the heavy paperwork; besides, people were used to them nosing around town, asking impudent questions. Obtaining candid reports from covert sources required anonymity at both ends.

The agency shielded informants behind code numbers, rarely copying their names into its volumes. Correspondents were expected to send updates every six months, answer urgent queries, and warn of imminent collapses. In lieu of payment, they earned a cut of any debt collected from local defaulters. Entrusting evaluations and collections to the same agent, however, invited conflicts of interest. In 1850, for example, an Ohio druggist asked for extensions on his New York bills, a common request. Instead, the correspondent urged creditors to send him their claims and promised, "I can make the money." The druggist soon failed.[19]

As commerce moved faster and farther, credit agents trumped individual self-control with institutional surveillance. Forebears drew identity and selfhood from community, church, kin, and guild. Ranking individual achievement bolstered the idea that you are what you do. In the 1840s and 1850s, issues of work and identity stirred abolitionists and trade unionists, inspired inventors and medical quacks, and sparked creative departures as singular as Walt Whitman's poetry and Lewis Tappan's ledgers. The Mercantile Agency imposed standards that no ambitious man could ignore. "Failed & now in Boston," warned an 1848 entry for J. B. N. Gould, a tailor who absconded from Worcester; "be sure & never trust him, will always be worthless." Debtor laws could punish or forgive failure, but credit agencies predicted it. In Jackson County, Alabama, the name T. R. Mattox prompted this 1860 report: "The general opinion here is, that he is in a v[er]y critical & embarr[asse]d condition, and that there is a strong probability of his *failure*." Reporters noted more than financial omens; grocer Alexander W. Bateman appeared "close & steady to bus[iness], but dont think he will succeed, he is unpopular. He is rather of an unhappy disposition." Such reports institutionalized Ralph Waldo Emerson's axiom "There is always a reason, *in the man*, for his good or bad fortune," by fixing moral blame with greater authority. Confirmed systematically and preemptively, the "reason, *in the man*" became the identity of the man.[20]

Lewis Tappan. (Engraving
by G. R. Hall, Prints and
Photographs Division,
Library of Congress.)

Mr. Tappan Takes a Walk

In the early 1840s, a new kind of market appeared in lower Manhattan. It ran from the Mercantile Exchange on Wall Street to City Hall Park, stretching ten blocks up and down Nassau Street and Broadway. Lewis Tappan canvassed these streets for charter subscribers in the summer of 1841. He took offices on Hanover Square, behind the domed Greek-revival temple at 55 Wall Street: the Merchants' Exchange, rebuilt in blue granite after the Great Fire of 1835. Brokers and jobbers made all sorts of deals in its environs, but the newest commodity was identity. To procure it, they applied science to character—not codes of general morals but traits of particular individuals—delineated precisely, by the latest methods. Tappan sold profiles of out-of-towners, which vetted "their character as business men," according to the handbill he carried on his rounds. His "intelligence office" was novel, but the neighborhood was buzzing with competitors touting other ways to fix and sell identity. They transformed lower Manhattan into a hub of technical and aesthetic innovation.[21]

The walk up Nassau Street took one past newspaper offices and optical and chemical suppliers. Mercury, iodine, lenses, and copper plates were in demand by the makers of perfect "indices of human character": daguerreotypes. New York's first photography studio opened in March 1840. At Nassau and Beekman, Tappan surely called on a family friend who had set up shop in the spring of 1841. The panic having disrupted government funding of his telegraph, Samuel F. B. Morse was experimenting and giving lessons in daguerreotypy. Up the block, scientific publishers Fowlers & Wells operated the Phrenological Cabinet. In this salon, Lorenzo Fowler mapped clients' skulls, filling in "charts of character" derived from his brother Orson's best-selling books. No mere fad, phrenology influenced medical and social science for decades, and the publishing imprint lasted until 1912. Antebellum crowds visited the Cabinet's displays of plaster: a thousand life masks and busts of statesmen, businessmen, and madmen. Lewis Tappan had reason to stop in, to inspect a cast that featured a strong nose, high forehead, and pursed lips: his brother and former partner, Arthur Tappan.[22]

Nassau Street ended just past Fowlers & Wells, where Park Row angled sharply into Broadway and pointed the way back to Wall Street. P. T. Barnum's American Museum commanded this crossroads, and the walk downtown passed the fanciest daguerreotype parlors, soon to include Mathew Brady's at 205 Broadway, Gabriel Harrison's at 203, and Jeremiah Gurney's at 189. In the 1850s, the Mercantile Agency stationed an uptown branch at 111 Broadway. A later move to 314 met familiar neighbors: the enlarged Phrenological Depot at 308 Broadway and Mathew Brady's gallery at 359. With offices on Broadway and at 83 Wall Street, the agency stood sentinel at the top and bottom of the ward, in decades when those two avenues became the main concourses of American culture and enterprise.[23]

Never before and nowhere on earth (let alone within a short walk) had a cluster of businesses shared the goal of observing, recording, and selling the distinctive traits of individuals. Myriad sciences of the self, including "the science of credits," hit the American market about 1840. Technology and systematic inquiry underlay their rhetoric, but most of the innovators were less interested in science for its own sake than for its marketability. More than adjacency and acquaintance, they shared a business plan: making a commodity of identity captured by new methods in new formats, and selling the accuracy and objectivity of the whole process. People "anxious to obtain a true analysis of their characters" could send $4 and a tintype to a mail-order phrenologist. Editors praised the "unerring truthfulness" by which "the daguerreotype, like the faithful historian, takes us—just as we are." *Hunt's Merchants' Magazine* endorsed the quality of Mercantile Agency intelligence: "the plan pursued insures accuracy; for they deal in *facts,* and not in opinions."[24]

The cranial index, the exposure index, the credit index: all bolstered the idea that failure entailed identity and personal responsibility, recordable by objective, not subjective, means. Emerson's précis of the daguerreotype captured the promises made for all sciences of the self. "The artist stands aside and lets you paint yourself," he wrote. "If you have an ill head, not he but yourself are responsible." The innovations of the day shared two methods of expert surveillance: inventing keener ways to see and evaluate people, and creating a tangible record of what the expert saw. "Men's past successes and misfortunes, their triumphs and failures—in a word, the daguerreotype of man's material condition," noted one merchant, "is only imperfectly preserved in history." Phrenologists claimed to practice "the first means of deciding, with anything like certainty, the talents or character of a stranger." Mathew Brady's early commissions included criminal portraits for a phrenological textbook about deviant character. Reformers advocated hidden cameras to catch crooks, and by 1859 the New York Police Department began a photographic archive dubbed the "Rogues Gallery." Photography offered a new way to tag and classify people. "Men shall ultimately be known for what they are," one theorist enthused; "the inward unworthiness, despite all effort, will glare through the fleshly mask." In 1856, *The Independent* magazine extolled credit agencies precisely for their power to expose unworthiness and to "act as a detective police." The Mercantile Agency itself touted its power to expose and fix reality: *"It has made men take their real character along with them,* the character they bear at home," in local markets—in fact, "wherever they go to do business."[25]

Phrases like "real character" denoted rapid social change. Amplifying old words for new situations showed the inadequacy of existing vocabularies and taxonomies. Character was no less inscrutable for being "real," but no word in common usage captured the modern facility for individual assessment. In 1848, Webster's *American Dictionary* recommended a distinction between *"real character"* (inner endowments) and *"estimated character"* (public reputation), but it did not catch on. Surveillance experts promised to record both, by fixing one's moral essence in observable form. Developments in transportation, communication, and commerce had blurred identity, but novel techniques for seeing and registering the whole person could refocus it. Technicians distilled "real character" into a fuller concept of identity, as both a credential and a sense of self, in an era when occupations took on new import. At midcentury, wage labor looked increasingly like a life sentence. From 1800 to 1860, the number of whites employed by others grew from 12 to 40 percent; the 1870 census found that hirelings comprised 60 to 85 percent of the northern labor force. Poor boys who made good, like Vanderbilt and Carnegie, fueled the myth of self-made manhood, even though social mobility occurred incrementally, with individuals making small gains, if any, within the class into which they were born. Meanwhile, a new middle class did the office and managerial work created by industrialization, and medicine and law began to professionalize. Such trends drew attention to the links between achievement and character but also raised the stakes. He who misread his own character might pursue the wrong career to certain failure. Reading the character of strangers was necessary to avert fraud. Who are you? Who am I? True and correct answers could be had for a nominal fee, from an expert equipped to survey one's whole person.[26]

Americans lined up to plunk down their money for practitioners and inventors of tools to validate identity. About 1840, a client named A. V. Champney saw a phrenologist and took away a form rating his "acquisitiveness," "constructiveness," "approbativeness" (self-doubt), and other qualities suggesting his vocational aptitude. Even people with few career options affirmed their trades through modern means. A photographic genre arose, "the occupational," showing sitters in work clothes instead of their Sunday best. Men and women posed clutching tools—hammers, brooms, account books, sewing baskets, and odd gadgets. Daguerreotypes of wiggling babies and sleeping corpses etched birth and death into an unbreakable mirror; "occupationals" registered the prime of life. Sitters made their work ethic visible, demonstrating what antebellum political rhetoric only averred: that freedom and free labor were inseparable in a nation of strivers. Individual achievement, not hereditary status, would define identity. Men would be free to succeed and free to fail.[27]

This nexus of achievement and identity presaged the Civil War. Tappan and his ilk reengineered the cultural infrastructures of freedom. A regular client of phrenology and daguerreotype parlors put it best: "Neither a servant nor a master am I." Walt Whitman coined this motto in *Leaves of Grass,* its revolutionary style owing much to the sciences of identity. The poet came to Manhattan from Long Island in May 1841, just as Tappan was organizing his agency. Whitman found work at 162 Nassau Street— in the *Aurora* newspaper's print shop—rising to editor within a year despite his daily two-hour walks. People watching and news gathering, he ambled down "that part of Nassau Street which runs into the great mart of New York brokers and stock-jobbers." Whitman preferred the Battery and Broadway, "that noted ave-

Taken around 1850, this "occupational" daguerreotype conveyed a young peddler's pride in the life of a salesman, unbowed by the leather harness and brace he wore to carry his heavy sample cases.
(Prints and Photographs Division, Library of Congress.)

nue of New York's crowded and mixed humanity," where he first sat for a photographer. He got his head examined at "the 'Phrenological Cabinet' of Fowler & Wells" and went often to see "all the busts, examples, [and] curios." The eugenic implications inflamed his democratic passions, but how could the aspiring poet resist a thousand faces from all walks of life? Faces could be acquired by the gross in this neighborhood, and here Whitman started a collection to rival any gallery of browlines or tintypes.[28]

In the summer of 1841, Whitman loafed where Tappan bustled—that being the least of their differences in their approaches to life. And yet, Whitman styled himself a surveillance agent, a voluminous cataloger of intelligence. Self-published in 1855, *Leaves of Grass* displayed specimens without placards, presenting untitled poems and declassified faces. "Neither a servant nor a master" declared emancipation from such categories, and this antitaxonomy began the poem later entitled "Song for Occupations." It rattled off countless trades and tools and mulled their impact on "the curious sense of body and identity":

> *Manufactures . . . commerce . . . engineering . . . the building of*
>   *cities, and every trade carried on there . . . and the implements*
>   *of every trade,*
> *The anvil and tongs and hammer* [. . . .]
> *The directory, the detector, the ledger* [. . . .]
> *The implements for daguerreotyping* [. . . .]
> *In them the heft of the heaviest. . . . in them far more than you*
>   *estimated, and far less also,*
> *In them, not yourself. . . .*[29]

Whitman revised this poem through three decades of political and economic change, adding new industries and enterprises to its roster while asking, "What have you reckon'd them for, camerado?" Tallying your life's work or wages won't compute your true value. Trying to "rate" self and others resulted only in this paradox: "Objects gross and the unseen soul are one." In other words, in a commercial democracy, commodity and identity melded. Although Whitman hailed the liberty to be neither servant nor master, he called it a "paradox" because new freedoms spawned new ironies. Computing identity from achievement might demean human worth, not affirm it. To readers expecting validation by some "agent or medium," Whitman sang, "you and your soul enclose all things, regardless of estimation." How could *he* know their enclosed souls? "I see and hear you, and what you give and take." Even as he tried to lure readers to another country, the poet's distinctively omniscient tone recalled the enterprises of Broadway and Nassau Street.[30]

Walt Whitman and Lewis Tappan worked at cross-purposes, but each devised new techniques for observing and cataloging identity. Tappan's ledgers, like Whitman's leaves, kept both individual and society in focus. Whitman did not compute his "divine average" (the elaborate proof of equality that *Leaves of Grass* became) by multiplying flowery couplets. He enumerated workaday identities, adding them in ever longer columns. *Leaves* offered only twelve poems in 1855, but the 1892 "deathbed edition" bulged with nearly four hundred. Whitman emended and appended ceaselessly, like a clerk updating a ledger with the last word on "an active enterprising trustworthy man on the light road to success." That 1856 credit report might have been drafted by Whitman: "Afoot and light-hearted, I take to the open road,/ Healthy, free, the world before me." Yet if the poet and the agent stood the same watch, they saw with different eyes. An 1844 Mercantile Agency entry concluded, "Honest & likely man but not attentive to his bus[iness]—is a 'Singer' which takes up too much of his time . . . sh[oul]d be watched a little." An entry from 1860 harumphed, "Has failed—turns his att[entio]n now to fiddling & dancing." Whitman might have recognized a *camerado* in such men and given them credit for being neither servant nor master. Still, the poet's licentiousness did not rule out his officiousness. In Whitman no less than in his times, contrary philosophies of identity did not preclude convergent methods of managing it.[31]

Nobody said so better than Whitman, who chanted democracy in the voice of a detective. "It is useless to protest, I know all and expose it," he wrote in "Song of the Open Road." The poet admired his own acuity, but no more than Lewis Tappan or other peddlers of observed and cataloged identity. Conceit was their occupational hazard. Using surveillance as a creative method, Whitman made poetry from exhaustive catalogues of people and things observed—then basked in his own prescience. "I project the history of the future," he proclaimed while throwing down a gauntlet entitled, "To a Historian." He whistled with the confidence of a sage who had already peeked—and why not, having borrowed techniques from the sciences of the self? No historian could have guessed that the first commercial printing of *Leaves of Grass*, in 1856, would be published by the phrenologists Fowler & Wells— with a frontis engraving of the author from a daguerreotype by Gabriel Harrison of Brooklyn (formerly of 203 Broadway). The chance meetings and crisscrossing ambitions of that place and time signified nothing—except the dawning of modern identity management. "Now I will do nothing but listen," the poet demurred in "Song of Myself." Credit-raters, skull-readers, and picture-takers made similar disclaimers, to publicize their objective and accurate methods for listening, watching, measuring, indexing, focusing, projecting, and selling identity. After all, they heard America singing, too.[32]

Only one called the tune, however. Tappan's central intelligence agency realized Whitman's audacious boast "I am large, I contain multitudes." Among the old neighborhood gang, only the Mercantile Agency used surveillance to make catalogs with direct power over subjects' lives. "The science of credits" withstood future challenges to objectivity, while phrenology turned out to be bad science and photography lost its aura as a perfect record of reality. As for Whitman, when have Americans ever taken a poet seriously? Only fiddlers and dancers flouted credit agents, who imposed involuntary surveillance 150 years before security cameras and facial recognition scanners could tell one noggin from another. Credit reporters kept a lower profile while more than keeping pace with their nearest rivals. In 1849, a famous writer claimed in *Godey's Lady's Book* that some daguerreotypist was "busy at work catching 'the shadow'" in almost every county in all states. The U.S. Census listed 938 photographers in 1850—when 2,000 credit correspondents supplied Tappan's agency and six branches as far west as St. Louis—not counting imitators like Woodward & Dusenberry's Commercial Agency (founded 1842), W. A. Cleveland's Mercantile Agency (1844), J. M. Bradstreet & Son's Improved Commercial Agency (1849), and Potter & Gray's City Trade Agency (before 1851). A decade after his first walk around the block, the whole country had become Mr. Tappan's neighborhood.[33]

Confidence Men of a Different Kind

The first generation raised in that milieu, the so-called "'go ahead' boys" of the 1830s, came of age in the boom that burst in 1857. Ned Tailer, a twenty-seven-year-old New Yorker, had been a merchant only sixteen months, after seven years on a clerk's stool watching old men go broke. On 25 April 1857 he heard "'by a set of croakers,' that a large Barclay St. jobbing house, were going to cave." Croakers were nay-saying rumormongers, and Tailer mused in his diary, "If people would cease croaking, a want [of] confidence in certain doubtful concerns, would not be created, and they would not be compelled to fail & cheat their creditors." If the jobber "caved," the creditors would include Winzer, Tailer & Osbrey: Importers & Wholesalers of Fine Woolens. Deciding not to file a preemptive legal protest, the diarist explained, "the day has wore away, and as yet the 'agentcy' has not been informed of any protests." He ignored rumors and heeded reports—from Dun *or* Bradstreet, heir and rival (respectively) of Lewis Tappan. In 1857, Robert Graham Dun was managing the Mercantile Agency; he bought the company the following year. John M. Bradstreet's Improved Commercial Agency had opened in 1849. Bradstreet &

Son competed with R. G. Dun & Co. for seventy-five years before the two household names became one in 1933. Whichever agency got Tailer's business, his diary gave a subscriber's view of the system amid a context of social and economic change.[34]

On the same day Tailer blamed "a want of confidence" on the croakers, the New York publishers Dix & Edwards failed—three weeks after issuing a book that blamed "the want of confidence, in these days" on "public Bibles" (counterfeit detectors) and "Intelligence Offices . . . wreaking their cynic malice upon mankind." Released on April Fool's Day 1857, *The Confidence-Man* folded with its publishers, and Herman Melville never published another novel. The failed book's riddles were perennial, however—as when the swindler disarmed his mark with the credit agent's motto, "did you never observe how little, very little, confidence there is? I mean between man and man—more particularly between stranger and stranger?" Observers like Ned Tailer had little use for any satire of this most uneasy fact of life. "Our city is now at the flood tide of the business season," the diarist had written four years earlier. "The numerous trains of cars on the various lines of railroads which centre here, all come crowded with passengers, & the city is rapidly filling up with strangers." Who were they? Could they be trusted? Discerning readers skimmed a true 1857 best-seller, the first edition of *Bradstreet's Commercial Reports,* a biannual ratings directory of 17,000 firms in nine cities. By 1862, it covered 200,000 establishments in 6,400 northern locales. Not to be outdone, the Mercantile Agency published its own *Reference Book,* so full of secret intelligence that its fine leather binding came equipped with a sturdy brass lock. Literary satire paled beside the newest counterfeit detectors—for people.[35]

The credit agent was a confidence man gone legit—a promoter of market confidence, with the best of intentions—preaching from a new good book. Ned Tailer subscribed to both the principles and the products of the "agentcy." In 1854, he reported, "There is a general panic among the dry goods merchants, and it is extremely difficult to decide who is good or who is bad." Tailer was still a clerk then, but already he was making decisions much as the agency did—by logging and judging ruined men around him. "F. E. Radcliffe has failed after having been in business eight months, or just as his first notes fall due," one such entry began. "How he could have used up a cash capital of $75,000 no one can tell." Tailer and the Mercantile Agency considered many cases in common and often agreed. The credit ledger showed that Radcliffe's dry goods career ran only from February to November 1854. As the agency reported on 3 October, "Nothing in particular has taken place to injure [his] cr[edit]," but he was "unpopular with the trade. There is a lack of confidence . . . in regard to his success in bus[iness]." On 30 October, the agency put him down as broke. Was "lack of confidence" in this "unpopular" man a self-fulfilling prophecy? Tailer claimed, "no one can tell," and the agency blamed "nothing in particular." To all but poor Radcliffe, the report seemed to matter far more than the reason.[36]

The diaries lacked the influence of the ledgers, but both sets of books rendered the judgments of maturing capitalism, as each bolstered confidence and determined value through categories and catalogs. Tailer kept a journal from age sixteen until his death at eighty-seven, from the Mexican War to World War I—1846 to 1917. Beyond parsing merchants' failures and successes, he described lost dogs and fallen women, gossiped about suicides and embezzlers, copied business maxims and Bible verses, reviewed *The Poor of New York* at Wallack's Theatre and Barnum's Baby Show at the American Museum, correlated literacy rates and capital punishment, judged servants ("Colored Gentlemen with white aprons") on Fifth Avenue and promenaders "decked in the gayest of colors," tallied shipwrecks and warehouse fires, witnessed drunkards and wife beaters on trial at night court, tested the steamboat and the daguerreotype, mourned a Bowery tramp ("Alex[ander] McFarland, alias the Lime Kiln Man") and a bankrupt restaurateur ("George Downing, colored—oysters in every style"), glued in clippings from the *Tribune, Herald,* and *Journal of*

Commerce (founded by the Tappan brothers), and surveyed Niagara Falls and the Mississippi—all before 1861. When that year ended, he had completed another black leather diary, letter-sized, two inches thick: book 13 of an eventual 57 volumes.[37]

Compulsive note-taking was no quirk; it was the mode and impetus of capitalism. Inking in volume after volume, Tailer and Tappan joined a fraternity driven to assess, authenticate, index, abstract, and archive people, places, and things. Such methods managed identity and enterprise, helping discern "who is good or who is bad" and encouraging self-assessment. Tailer jotted away as if any event and every detail might be the ticket to achieving his desired identity. At twenty, he complained that an elder told him "that I lacked energy, and wanted that bustling, and go ahead spirit." At twenty-three, he recorded the death of a merchant: "he was a self made man, and stood amongst those of the foremost rank." At twenty-six, he recorded his birthday wish: "I hope the future may be fraught with happiness and success, and that I may eventually be numbered amongst the hard-working merchants of this Metropolis." He worked hard at self-improvement, drilling at a gymnasium, trying phrenology, and discussing books at the Knickerbocker Literary Association. When his debating society put the question "Which is the greatest incentive to action, Ambition or necessity," he reported they "decided it in the favor of Ambition." Tailer benefited from Franklinesque exertions toward being "esteem'd an industrious, thriving young man"; yet these old maxims fell short of his modern ambitions. A "self made man" had to be more than "esteem'd"—he had to "be numbered" and "rank[ed]."[38]

Mercantile Agency ledger 199, page 276, vouched that "ᴇɴ Tailer Jr" joined the firm "Winzer & Osbrey" in January 1856. "'T' has fine acquaint[an]ce a g[oo]d knowledge of bus[iness] and will be a val[uable] acquisition," the initial entry read; "the new p[artne]r has been in the employ of 'Sturges Shaw & Co' and is well spoken of as to char[acter] & bus[iness] talent, the ho[use] is tho[ugh]t to be strengthened by his accession." Lots of men were "well spoken of," but here was a genuine asset. "EN Tailer Jr" sounded as bankable as prime Manhattan real estate.[39]

"'T' has fine acquaint[an]ce" understated the case for Edward Neufville Tailer, Jr., son of a Wall Streeter descended from Puritan merchants who governed colonial Massachusetts. The Dutch forebears of his mother, Ann Amelia Bogert, had settled Brooklyn and Harlem in 1663, acquiring large tracts in upper Manhattan. Ned grew up in a downtown enclave named for its old Nederlander farms; a Bowery boyhood in a Broadway mansion. A class of 1846 graduate of "Penquest's famous French school in Bank street," he became a clerk in order to learn business. He courted Miss Agnes Suffern, of Suffern, New York, and 11 Washington Square North: one of the Greek revival edifices in "The Row" near Fifth Avenue. After a parlor wedding in December 1855, the groom's father and father-in-law gave him the partnership stakes to join Winzer & Osbrey on New Year's Day 1856. "His fa[ther] is well off, & his fa[ther]-in-law, 'Thos. Suffern' is rich," sufficed for background in the credit report, "and he will [have] th[ei]r friendship & aid."[40]

With friends like that, this merchant prince needed no bootstraps, but American success mythology often favored outlook over origins. With the right attitude, even a rich boy could become "a self made man." Tailer made his confession of faith in "that bustling, and go ahead spirit." Upon confirmation, the credit agency baptized and entered him into its registry. Born with a valuable name, he now had a valuable identity. The "agentcy" abetted Tailer's energetic management of his own identity. A sense of independence and a source of information kept him cool when croakers reported "a want of confidence" in a certain jobber Tailer was doing business with in April 1857. Tailer's course of action during that year's panic showed how useful innovation and technology could be in managing identity; yet, when tested, he would not pray to the "go ahead spirit." The story of his brief ordeal and easy salvation confirmed that self-made success still owed much to family fortunes.[41]

The End of an Old Story

The first Monday in May disappointed New York's croakers. "The 4th of May was a heavy day in N.Y.," Tailer wrote, "but the jobbers here met their payments punctually." This proved to be the calm before the storm that blew in the next day. "It was nearly 6 P.M., when the agentcy informed us of the failures in Boston," he wrote—"too late" to catch a northbound train "to see if I could not recover some goods purchased lately." He took the train to Boston on Wednesday, and a steamboat sped him down the Ohio River a week later, to collect debts in Nashville; by early June he was back home again. Shocking news came over the western wire in August: Ohio Bank & Trust, the largest firm in the country, had failed. Panic! "A sad list of names to contemplate" in the diary grew day by day, as failure and suicide winnowed Tailer's circle of friends and business associates. In September, "my Father came forward & loaned us $vcww." (Tailer had devised this financial code after marrying, in case Agnes or a servant peeked.) In December he wrote, "We at present owe Mr. S[uffern] $DV,www." Thanks to fatherly interventions, he suffered only a brief hour of panic, when a deposit error left him overdrawn. Fortunately, he heard before the croakers did. Once the problem was fixed, he had time to note with a shudder, "The least thing might give rise to the rumor of 'failure.'"[42]

Tailer wrote "failure" in quotation marks—just as he set apart "agentcy"—as if to flag new concepts or meanings. The word "failure" gave pause, even to one who embraced innovative enterprise, communication, and transportation. Old money, not new methods, had saved him; but his diary of the panic exposed larger ironies than a "go ahead boy" who was being carried by his father. After racing to Boston on newfangled rails, he was hearing old-fashioned wails. "Upon calling upon the different defunct concerns, I could get no better consolation, than the old story," he wrote. The Bostonians claimed they could not pay because *their* debtors had not paid. "The truth is that they were all second rate

*Smaller rivals and one-industry credit agencies often borrowed the
authority of the "Red Book," as shown in this trade card for a
"Clearing House of Trade Reports" and "Invaluable Information."*
(Warshaw Collection of Business Americana, Archives Center, National Museum of American History, Smithsonian Institution.)

houses," Tailer grumbled. His words were actually a credit rating,
not a metaphor; ordinals like "second rate" cued subscribers to ask
higher interest from weaker buyers (second- or third-raters). The
best deals went to "first-raters" like Tailer, who here regretted
trusting men below his grade. Having paid for expert advice and
ignored it to boost his sales, he now stood behind old fools in the
long story line of "failure" after "failure" after "failure." Tailer's diary flagged keywords of identity management, reaffirmed by the
panic's hard lessons. "The truth is," he should have listened to
"the 'agentcy.'"[43]

What is a capitalist, after all, but a bookkeeper? In the archives
of the market, lesser men could not hide behind "the old story."
The few hundred master ledgers of 1857 had become thousands
by New Year's Day 1892, when Tailer retired to spend his last
twenty-five years hobnobbing with the Astors and Cooper-
Hewitts. His career had spanned forty-five years—and twenty-

nine diaries, "MADE FROM THE BEST LINEN PAPER AND BOUND IN THE MOST DURABLE MANNER," according to his stationer's label. In that half-century, clerks at the Mercantile Agency had used 2,580 ledgers likewise made to last. Tailer's file was among the first that were transferred to a new technology. Handwritten notes on Tailer ceased in 1879, after R. G. Dun became the first major firm to adopt Remington's typewriter—another way the "agentcy" rewrote the story of American business. Published ratings stood guard behind teller windows, shop counters, and rolltops. "The mammoth red-edged quarto volume known as Bradstreet's Reports," that firm boasted in 1883, "is as familiar a sight as the Bible is, or should be, in the homes of those who have a household at one end of the line and a counting-room at the other." Long before Dun and Bradstreet merged, their products melded in the vernacular. Genuflecting to the morocco bindings, people just asked for *the red book*. Upstarts like "International Mercantile Agency," "The Furniture Commercial Agency," and "the Red Book Company" embossed the icon on cards and letterhead. The big red book helped install business methods as the American way to judge self and others. Strivers vied for honorable mention in these catalogs of identity, and subscribers weary of "the old story" got what they paid for: the new story.[44]

5 The Big Red Book of Third-Rate Men

oser is a title with no story. Calling someone "a success story" evokes familiar outlines of achievement and identity, but failure disrupts our stories. Life's journey stalls, maybe for now, maybe forever. Antebellum citizens found fault by recycling old stories—quaint fables and master plots wherein haste made waste or borrowing went a-sorrowing. They told hard-luck stories when bad things happened to good people. Ten such characters sat in a lawyer's anteroom telling *Bankrupt Stories:* the title of an 1843 novel, framed as a pecuniary *Canterbury Tales* that the group had published to raise money. Several actual memoirs tried to "make book" on deficit identity as a literary commodity, but misadventure never cohered as well as the "strive and thrive" genre did. Success ostensibly followed a single story line, but failure told a thousand and one tales with as many loose ends—seldom gathered until credit agents took the rating out of narrating. "Failed & Worthless" labeled more than bad bargains. Commercial idioms became colloquialisms: "Are said to be loosers by the failure of Thos. W. Griffin." Market jargon computed manhood: "K. is industrious attentive and a good buyer, but not quite the man to give them a first-rate credit." Even losers had long shelf lives in the big red book; making a durable commodity of failure made it a more indelible identity.[1]

Rating required narrating because Americans had not learned to think of one another as mere numbers. We had faces then, and getting a feel for a stranger took more than an abstract ranking. Red books used plenty of scales and classifications in assessing "the three C's" of capital, character, and capacity—but they also supplied character sketches, flashbacks, foreshadowings, and trick endings. A steamboatman's case rambled like a dockside yarn about "one of those unfortunate men who have to spend a lifetime mending the evils of a few years in early manhood." Notes from Ohio romanticized "a clever goodhearted, illiterate man who gives way to impulses & by education & early associations, rather than by lack of principle, associates with men of unenviable character & notoriety." The tragedy of a Philadelphia collegian began with a prophecy ("Rather too magnificent in his plans & projects") and ended with his fall from owner to clerk ("Failed Badly & out of bus[iness]"). Greenhorns turned blackleg. "Has just comm[ence]d—is a worthy young man" served to introduce a country storekeeper in New York who eventually "absconded to Iowa . . . a Villain." Fates reversed; plots twisted. "Matters seem to have turned out well, there was a report of [his] doing badly," admitted a Worcester shoemaker's entry, but a sobering correction came quick on its heels: "hung himself—cause unknown—many think Embarr[asse]d circumst[ance]s." Closing the book on a man generally came after less poignant final exits. "Broke & run away," read an Alabama entry; "not w[orth] the powder to kill him." Such fragments recorded American lives otherwise deemed a waste of paper, tales untold until they could be sold.[2]

Ordinary Americans had never before inspired big books of their comings, goings, hits, and misses. Credit ledgers reflected new vocabularies of success and failure. *Loser* was once a neutral word for anybody who lost property, often by theft or natural disaster. After the Boston fire of 1820, one newspaper wrote, "the keeper of the hotel, is a great loser, particularly in furniture and liquors." In credit reports, losers were men who had taken the brunt (and often the blame) in a deal gone bad. "Old dealers . . . and in their legitimate business always prosperous," wrote a Baltimore credit agent, "but have been pretty heavy losers by outside undertakings." Credit reports popularized monikers like "small fry," belittling the petty dealer operating a "sm[all] twopenny conc[ern]." They wrote "dead beat" beside a name when suing for payment seemed as pointless as lashing the fabled dead horse. Sluggards were set down as "not a 'fast horse' in bus[iness]" or "naturally a slow man in his temperament." The race went to "an active, driving man," in a phrase from an 1860 entry, or to "a man always on the go" in 1867. The winner was "active & stirring & aims to do more than ordinary bus[iness]" or was deemed "remarkable for his energy of char[acter]." Clerks copied incoming reports wherever they would fit in the master ledgers; winners and losers mingled as they perhaps never did in life. Open to page 31 in Georgia volume 28, cases from Savannah, and there is George W. Hardcastle. "Indus[trious], attent[ive] & consid[ere]d hon-[est]" in 1854, he was broke by January 1857, months before the panic: "No Means, No Capital, No honesty, no Cr[edit]." Farther down on the same page, W. H. May & Company could do no wrong. "They are all self-made men," read a June 1854 entry. May and Hardcastle cut unequal figures on the red-dirt avenues and in the red-leather archives, but the Mercantile Agency made money on both of them. By remembering and retelling their stories to subscribers who might wish to solicit or to boycott them, the service earned its fees.[3]

Bad Egg, Bad Risk, Bad Investment

Fabled biographers like James Boswell or Parson Weems had been outdone: the value of a man or his exploits no longer decided the value of his story. Whatever befell the hero, the saga itself was a valuable commodity. Subscribers paid for this 1857 tip about a man who seemed to be "wading into the pockets of the people, no probability of any cr[editor] suffering." And they paid for an 1860 warning in the same case: "The general opinion here is, that he is in a v[er]y critical & embarr[asse]d condition, and that there is a strong probability of his *failure*." In this context, "probability" was a rhetorical, not a statistical, science. Reporters figured "the average opinion" (as one Philadelphian put it) around town to distinguish "a v[er]y likely man" from someone "not calculated to succeed." Often they placed subjects along an informal continuum, from "Is hardup. a hard risk" to "is consid[ered] a good risk" to "Is w[orth] $15[,000] no risk with this man." An 1854 remark about a Cincinnatian captured the vagueness of such nomenclature: "he's ab[ou]t a fair risk, he is honest, but men that have no money must live off of somebody." Although reports had to be plainspoken to be useful, the times and the task at hand demanded finer gradations. Few cases were as clear-cut as an 1862 report: "The whole lot of the 'W[eatherby]s' are Bad Eggs."[4]

"Bad egg" was newly minted American slang in 1862, typical of the commodity talk that made credit reports both understandable and concise. In the 1850s, speculators caught "hen fever" and railroads brought rural staples to urban markets. Preserving eggs or telling fresh from stale was not easy; *Scientific American* endorsed Burt's Patented Oonoscope as a gadget "no household should be without." A "bad egg" was a market commodity that turned out to be worthless, an apt metaphor for gauging a trader's current and future value. An 1853 line from Virginia, "he is as tight as the bark on a black gum," invoked a tree notoriously hard to cut, the very trait that had recently made it valuable—for railroad ties. Commodity comparisons took the measure of a man in terms subscribers knew well. Was he a bad investment or a good one? How good? Ledger entries for a Charleston cotton king read "as good as gold." A Manhattan clothier was *"making money; good as wheat."* In 1863, "Good as wheat" comprised the full update on a lumber baron worth $30,000 to $50,000. At the low end, informants wrote, "Think he is worth oo [nothing] & that he never was & never will be." Another man's update read in full, "Good for oo whatever."[5]

"Good for nothing" was more credit lingo, a label so useful that its economic origin disappeared into an all-purpose epithet. Idioms like "a man of no account" and "good for oo" (or "good for nix") literally described the loser without a cent in the bank, untrustworthy for any credit—as opposed to men "considered good for $100." Such taxonomies sounded informal but practical, like home recipes calling for a smidgen of this or three fingers of that. Agencies measured men by loose increments. "Not in bus[iness]. g[oo]d for nothing" meant damnation, and next came faint praise: "put him down 'all right'. . . . he might be probably g[oo]d for his wants." A little headway garnered "g[oo]d for a Small am[oun]t," "a limited am[oun]t," "a mod[erate] am[oun]t," or, with petty assets, "prob[abl]y w[orth] a little, g[oo]d for reas[onable] am[oun]ts." Up another rung, subjects were "careful & prompt, g[oo]d for $1[ooo]" or better yet, "a driving, pushing fellow . . . thot g[oo]d for $1[ooo] at least." And so on, from the "money m[a]k[in]g fellow cr[edit] undoubted" to the titans "called rich, no 1" or "No. 1 g[oo]d for all eng[agemen]ts."[6]

Number one. What flagged success more clearly than that? Every report addressed the same sweeping question: what is this man good for? "Rated A no. 1" meant unlimited credit. Derived from naval and insurance classifications, in this context great wealth ("A") and superior ability and reliability ("1") stamped "*A no. 1* & no mistake" beside a man's name. Such ratings allowed more precise financial assessments, yet in practical usage they often imparted a sense of identity: "Is a Capital good man and is A No. 1 in all respects." The barb in Ned Tailer's diary about Boston's "second rate houses" likewise seemed aimed at more than weak businesses. Such tags turned unsureness into consensus. In 1857, a Charlestonian reported "some diversity of opinion as to his respons[ibility] but it is pretty generally conceded that he is not strong . . . does not rate higher than No. 3 if as high." Besides judging a third-rate enterprise, these lines added to the continuing story of a third-rate man.[7]

First-rate or third-rate, good as wheat or good for nothing, credit reports calibrated identity in the language of commodity. Distinctions like second-rate or "fair risk" evaluated by means of ordinal scales—a common way of expressing a hierarchy when exact increments are unclear. Americans picked up credit slang so readily that colloquial senses of the terms even crept into field reports. Although an 1854 entry about a partnership worth $150,000 called them "1st rate men," by 1857, "a 1st rate clever fellow" turned out to be a rural druggist with $500 to his name. Whether or not its statistical logic was consistent, every credit report relied on simple addition: line by line, entry by entry, page by page, the stories accumulated. "Small Man, Small Means, d[oin]g Small Business" summed up the life of a New Jersey carriagemaker who failed after the Civil War. Behind market prognostications about eggs, wheat, gum, and gold, the only durable item on sale was a narrative. And that was a commodity to haggle over.[8]

The Emancipator and the Aviator

In May 1844, the Mercantile Agency took note of Dr. William Henry Brisbane, who was running an apothecary shop in Cincinnati, Ohio. His own statement of assets listed two houses (mortgaged), two government bonds, and lands in Ohio and Kentucky—all tallied, over $22,000 free and clear, plus 100 acres in Pennsylvania. The local agent verified these facts, seemingly the portfolio of a go-ahead man; but numbers did not tell the whole story. An 1846 note from Ohio described Brisbane as "an honorable high mind[e]d man & generous South Car[olinia]n, who inher[ite]d $100[,000] & has run thro with all of it but $20[,000] in R[eal] E[state]." Like other "changeable" men who switched jobs or moved often, Brisbane appeared fickle. "Has been a planter, preacher, publisher, physician, & farmer but has never succeed[e]d at any[thin]g & probably never will," the informant predicted. He added that Brisbane "w[oul]d pay his last cent to Cr[editor]s & trust to Provid[ence] to keep hims[el]f & fam[ily] f[ro]m starvation." This entry from April 1846 was a model report: a detailed account of a good soul and a bad businessman, a log of migrations from south to north to east, and a forecast. In February 1847, this reporter's next and final note on Brisbane read simply, "Out of bus[iness]—Moved to Phil[adelphia]."[9]

Brisbane's case took the linear shape of classical narrative— Aristotle's beginning, middle, and end. *The stranger came, failed here, and moved on.* Times and places beyond the agent's purview lent context and trajectory, weaving in Brisbane's past and foreshadowing his future. Such details bolstered the credit report's authority to adjudicate; however objective in tone, all narratives pass judgment by choosing what to include or exclude. *This man squandered his birthright, came here as a jack-of-all-trades but master of none, and seems unlikely to succeed.* Narratives are not only linear but cumulative; besides creating a sequence of events, they select patterns and give them meaning. As updates about Brisbane accrued, hints of stories left untold and glimpses of his integrity, idealism, and charity deepened the portrait and complicated the plot. *A gentleman came here after trying many things to save his inheritance, and although indecision and ineptitude cast doubt on his success, as a man of honor he would sooner deprive his family than rob his creditors.* As a story, Brisbane's report invited many readings but only one conclusion: *no confidence.* The prudent subscribers got what they paid for, and the prodigal southerner got to see Philadelphia.[10]

Another version of this story survived, not in big red books but in pocket diaries kept by the man himself. Brisbane recorded that he had "run thro" a fortune because it had come to him in human currency. An only son, on turning twenty-five in 1832, he inherited a plantation near Beaufort, South Carolina, "Milton Lodge on Ashley River . . . & 22 negroes." The heir's aversion to credit enhanced his success, but his aversion to the whip ensured his failure. He farmed profitably but hated slavery. "I am no abolitionist," he told himself in 1835; but three years later he divested. His lands and slaves sold cheap, hardly a year after the great panic. "He became, to the white population, the most hated man in the Beaufort District," local historians wrote. Nor did his pro-slavery family understand, not even his wife (and first cousin), Anna Lawton Brisbane. Nonetheless, with their three boys and a few house slaves, she followed him north in February 1838, crossing the ice into the free state of Ohio. Brisbane "suffered great distress of mind" over the "22 negroes" left behind; he had sold out those families to deliver his own. Now an abolitionist lecturer and preacher, he vowed to buy them back and free them. He made good his promise over three years, but buying two dozen northbound passages left him "greatly embarrassed financially." Anna took in boarders for $50 a month, Mr. Brisbane being called to preaching and doctoring, whether he got paid or not. To ease her homesickness, in 1844 they sent for her brother and set him up in Ohio. Willy Lawton ran the drugstore and Brisbane ran for Congress—almost. Nominated by the Liberty Party, he declined, saying that religion and politics should not mix. Instead, he founded an antislavery journal, *The Crisis*. November saw his cause outpolled and his business undersold. "It seems to me that nothing prospers that I engage in. What is the design of Providence in all this," the diarist wondered. Like old Job, his only balm was to "trust in him & be prepared to die though I know not how to make a living."[11]

Two tales about William Henry Brisbane—one a confessional and the other a commodity—rendered his story differently yet reached the same conclusion. A closer match could not have been achieved if the informant had copped a peek at Brisbane's diary. The reverend sighed, "nothing prospers that I engage in," and the reporter assayed, "never succeed[e]d at any[thin]g & probably never will." Where the diary offered "the design of Providence" and "trust in him" as the last best hope, the ledger supposed he "would trust to Provid[ence]" as his only refuge from privation.

*Dr. William Henry Brisbane, slaveholding physician turned aboli-
tionist.* (Detail from an 1853 daguerreotype, WHi-2248, Wisconsin Historical
Society.)

The diary explained motives, but the ledger evaluated outcomes.
Beyond helping subscribers avoid him, however, the firm traced
Brisbane's career and personality with startling accuracy.

Perhaps this owed something to the ties between the subject
of the report and the founder of the agency. Traveling in 1841,
the Rev. Dr. Brisbane called at the Brooklyn home where Lewis
Tappan's family moved after mobs burned them out of Manhattan in 1834. The two men shared not only ideals but recent ordeals, each having been driven from his home and changed

careers in midlife. Likewise, each won a victory over slavery in 1841. Tappan helped to win the Supreme Court's January decision to release the mutineers of the slave ship *Amistad,* while Brisbane freed the people he had once enslaved. "In N. York took tea at Lewis Tappan's," his diary noted on 24 April. Did his host mention the credit office he would open in July? Surely the visitor brought regards from Salmon P. Chase, of whom both wanted a favor. Tappan asked Chase to furnish reports, but Brisbane wanted only a signature. In August, when the former slaveowner signed manumission papers, Chase cosigned as his witness and friend. Probably neither Chase nor Tappan wrote Brisbane's report; whatever the case, friendship certainly did not boost his ratings.[12]

Brisbane's vitae ("Has been a planter, preacher, publisher, physician, & farmer") changed many times after he quit Ohio for Philadelphia. Nothing took hold there, and in 1846 the family moved again. Leaving the competitive sphere of business, they visited the utopian community at Brook Farm, Massachusetts. There Brisbane wrote a novel of slavery and a biblical exegesis of abolitionism. Next, he secured a pulpit in Camden, New Jersey, but resigned in 1849. Back in Cincinnati, he resumed printing what proved to be his short-lived paper, *The Crisis.* Off to Wisconsin in 1853, he acquired the ferrying rights on the Wisconsin River and made "a dead loss." Doctoring did not pay (not in cash, anyway), and the Rev. Dr. Brisbane even failed as a tavern keeper. Who wanted to take his daily nip from a Baptist preacher? Appointments as local tax assessor and state senate clerk gave him a modest income, which he spent on federal land patents, eventually piecing together a 600-acre farm.[13]

When the war over slavery came, the Second Wisconsin Cavalry rode off with a son of South Carolina as its chaplain. Brisbane enlisted with two of his own sons; careworn and white-bearded, he looked much older than his fifty-four years. In 1862, the war took him home after twenty-five years—as the Union tax commissioner of occupied Beaufort, South Carolina. Appointed by his old friend, Treasury secretary Salmon P. Chase, Brisbane oversaw sales of confiscated plantations. New Year's Day 1863 thus found Brisbane proclaiming the Jubilee on his native soil, as a federal officer reading the Emancipation Proclamation aloud to thousands of freedmen. He served in the post until 1870 and died in 1878 at Arena, Wisconsin, where his Stone House Farm survives as a landmark. A great emancipator if not a good provider, his only steady living came from patronage jobs (the last refuge of a man without pluck, people said). Vocationally, the credit agency had been right: he "never succeed[e]d at any[thin]g."[14]

Solomon Andrews succeeded at practically everything. If the Brisbane case magnified contemporary tensions between prosperity and integrity, more surprising qualms about innovation shaped the Mercantile Agency version of Andrews's career. Watched from 1844 to 1872, he often looked like "a v[er]y unsafe man to trust." An 1851 entry hedged with a "man of intellect & genius . . . v[er]y clever, hon[est] man, but eccentric, cant say as to him." Asked to clarify, the source listed debts and risks: "He is an inventor and a man of great ingenuity, been engaged in building a flying Machine." If nothing else, Andrews owned land whose value rose sky high in 1855, a fact duly noted: "not so eccentric as before." An 1856 update found him "connecting the Telegraph Line from Sandy Hook passing thro' Amboy." Summed up in 1859, "He is a man who has been all his life stirring up some new invention; such as padlocks, Sewing Machines &c. he once invented a padlock approved by the General Government and contracted with them for its use at some $10[,000]. he is a Physician by Profession but never practiced, only the poor when called upon Gratuitous." Doctoring, tinkering, and office-holding occupied him: "he was at one time Collector of the Port of Entry at this place and also Mayor . . . he is a very eccentric man, no estimate can be had of his means." Year upon year, informants shrugged their shoulders when asked to rate Dr. Andrews: "up-

*Dr. Solomon Andrews,
physician and aviation
pioneer.* (National Air and
Space Museum, Smithsonian
Institution, SI 2003-35052.)

right Char[acter] but extreme notions and odd peculiarities." His credit appeared to rise in 1861 and 1862, only to plummet in 1864: "His p[ro]p[ert]y is all adv[ertise]d to be sold at Sheriff's sale."[15]

Agency correspondents wove together a good story, full of vivid and accurate details. Other records verify that Solomon Andrews took his medical degree in 1827 from Queens College (now Rutgers). His practice included tending the indigent in yellow fever and cholera outbreaks, which moved him to design and build a sewer system in Perth Amboy. Thrice elected that city's mayor, he also served as Collector of the Port. In 1840, he patented a "clam shell lock" that earned him $30,000 as sole manufacturer and supplier of padlocks for U.S. mailbags. Andrews spent his fortune building the "Inventors' Institute," a fully equipped research laboratory. Buying the decrepit but spacious British army barracks abandoned after the American Revolution, he established a membership cooperative, a fraternity where access to the best facilities would stimulate American innovation. It languished; Andrews was the type whom agents derided as "visionary"—delusional or mercurial, in that day's usage. "Has been at many things," from Andrews's 1858 report, understated his output and versatility. His inventions included a sewing machine, a kitchen range, a gas lamp, a barrel-making machine, a tobacco filter to remove "harmful substances," a velocipede, and U.S. Patent 43,449—a mysterious craft that proved the agency's worst fears of his "various experiments with Balloons and flying machines."[16]

Aereon, he called it: "the age of the air," a conceit made good when it became the first airship to fly against the wind. Tall and handsome, with golden hair, Andrews made a dashing pilot and publicist, and his credit rose and fell with his daring invention during the Civil War. Not "a flying Machine" but rather a tri-celled balloon filled with 26,000 cubic feet of hydrogen, *Aereon* navigated by a method akin to the tacking of a sailboat. Designed to carry passengers and freight, by 1862 its motorless and sound-less operation suggested military potential. A $10,000 prototype tested in September 1863 landed on the cover of *Scientific American* and led to an audience with Abraham Lincoln. Thereafter, red tape kept *Aereon* tethered during 1864, when Andrews lost vital equipment to the "Sheriff's sale" noted in his credit report. Major General Robert C. Schenck, an Ohio congressman and Lincoln partisan who chaired the House Military Affairs Committee, appointed "a scientific commission" (including the Secretary of the Smithsonian Institution) to study Andrews's design. He got his patent in July 1864, and that month the commission report advised Congress to fund the airship. But in the summer of 1864, the Lincoln administration hit its political and military nadir—and the report went astray. Andrews heard nothing until March 1865, when, with victory assured, Schenck's committee denied the contract. The inventor tried to save his "Aerial Navigation Company" by attracting investors. In 1866, "Aeronaut" Andrews made two flyovers and brought Manhattan to a standstill with *Aereon II* as crowds gawked up at "a Brobdignagian lemon." But the postwar recession, coming on top of the lost contract, grounded Solomon Andrews. This "very eccentric man" died in 1872, a footnote in aviation history.[17]

The story of Solomon Andrews revealed tensions between innovation and financial safety in the credit-reporting industry and paralleled antebellum beliefs about failure. Founded on the ruins of speculation after the panic of 1837, the Mercantile Agency's mission was to "render safe and profitable to all concerned, the great credit system." Low assets and high ideas made Andrews "unsafe to trust"; he might have fared better being content with postal locks instead of being "always at Something new." A man labeled eccentric or "visionary" appeared deluded, not foresighted. An Ohio civil engineer who invented and manufactured rolling mills for steel production earned this report: "We learn that he is reg[arded] a man of good char[acter] & hab[it]s but visionary in his ideas, a poor bus[iness] man & that all his undertakings so far have been failures." Risk and ambition remained hazardous but estimable commodities. Entry upon entry gave empirical proof to the precept that failure came from overreaching: running too much debt, giving too much credit, keeping too much stock. "Are inclined to extend & do too much," warned an 1856 entry from Georgia. "In good cr[edit] now but hard times might blow them over." Some cases related fables of failure, morality tales like that of a New Jersey grocer. "Would do better if he would not try to do too much," the first report said, followed a year later by the second: "Failed. Went too far, too many irons." The paramount objective was to minimize risk, not to encourage it as a source of growth or innovation.[18]

If red books did not tell the whole story about Brisbane or Andrews, they told stories that would sell: accounts worth buying if you wanted to grant credit on an informed basis. Both cases ignored key episodes; like all narratives, choosing what to omit or include spawned the power to judge. Neither stolid nor formulaic, both provided more than dates, places, and dollar amounts. Subscribers met a man of God and a man of science, neither of whom was a man of business. No mere audit of achievement or nonachievement, the reports sketched multidimensional characters to give subscribers a sense of the identity of a stranger. "The man who gives his neighbor credit does so because he believes he knows him, and has confidence in his integrity and ability to pay," *Hunt's Merchants' Magazine* wrote after the Mercantile Agency's first decade. By its methods, "a continuous history of the customer is thus preserved, by which the creditor's knowledge of him is made to approximate, as nearly as possible, to a personal acquaintance." The agent drafted a biography ("a continuous history") sufficient to convert identity ("personal acquaintance") into a commodity. Both men of "upright Char[acter] but extreme notions," Brisbane and Andrews were trustworthy yet not to be trusted. Foresighted and uniquely successful in their own ways, these good men were not "good for" much if any financial credit. In the agency's ledgers, the moral of these failure stories became clear: redeeming characters sometimes had no book value.[19]

How to Save a Rateable Soul

A commodity is something made or procured to be sold. Build a chair for your own use, and it's a chair. Build it to sell for profit, and the chair becomes a commodity. It exists because it can be swapped for money—theoretically, at any time. But a commodity that is not useful is a hard sell. "Use value" attracts the buyer, but "exchange value" prompts the manufacturer. Credit agents got no direct use from recording other people's business; they wrote for the market, and clients bought the product for its usefulness. In another sense, the report became a commodity by assigning dollar values (the subject's credit and the agency's fee) to assets and traits the subject had cultivated for his own use. The conscience of William Henry Brisbane, in his life and ratings, attained high use value but low exchange value. Ditto the ingenuity of Solomon Andrews. Yet the agency traded on their names just as it stamped others "good as gold," making money in all cases. Systematic reporting inspected and graded men like commodities. "The man who seeks to purchase goods on credit, or otherwise to contract a debt, virtually challenges investigation," *Hunt's* declared in January 1851. The true measure of a man's worth loomed as the great puzzle of that generation, for enterprisers and freethinkers alike. Henry Thoreau wondered in October 1851, "Now is not your manhood taxed by the great Assessor? Taxed for having a soul—a rateable soul." Was this the coming standard of success: identity as commodity? The good doctors Brisbane and Andrews evidently had souls but not "rateable souls," the common denominator among successful men.[20]

Questions about human commodities inflamed conflicts over slavery and industrialized labor in the mid-nineteenth century, even as new models of freedom like self-made manhood confirmed the power of market principles as arbiters of identity. Credit reporting engaged with these trends, commodifying identity by describing, sorting, and labeling people. In early America, the word *character* meant reputation as well as honor; colloquially, a letter of recommendation was often called "a character." As suppliers of written appraisals, credit agents literally sold characters, but in a more modern sense they sold identity. A commodity "made to approximate, as nearly as possible, to a personal acquaintance" represented both major senses of identity, verification of credentials and evaluation of character. The old value of "a good name" hardly matched the new value of a good credit report, which meant more than good marks for capital, character, and capacity. "The three C's" had to be discernible, verifiable, and recordable within the purview and language of the agency. Be the sort whose activity and personality could be branded in a certain way, and your identity (like other commodities) could be converted into money—into credit, a supplement and often a substitute for capital and cash on hand. An 1858 report about James Wirick of Earlville, Illinois, likened him to yet another American staple commodity. "Is No. 1 p[er]f[ect]ly respons[ible] for all cr[edit] he may need," the entry stated; "no man here is *'neater cattle.'*" Such a man exceeded his own sum; the use value of his composite identity underwrote extra exchange value to help him succeed.[21]

A good credit report would tell a recognizable success story. "Com[men]c[e]d life poor, by indus[try] & strict atten[tion] to bus[iness] & the aid & counsel of 'S & S Halsted' he has been v[ery] successful," described a merchant whose annual sales in 1852 neared $100,000. Such entries corroborated the archetypal American success story—itself one of the best-selling commodities in American literature. Rags to riches tales were scarcer in life than in national mythology, yet credit agents beheld ample instances of rags to respectability. "Commenced 10 [or] 12 y[ea]rs ago in a v[ery] Sm[all] way, came from the Country poor, got a loan of $15 & bought his first bill at auction," read the first entry for a New Yorker counted "among the most indus[trious] enterprising, and persevering men in the trade." Still others witnessed money begetting money. "Sons of 'James Fassitt'—the whole fam[il]y rich," gushed a Philadelphia informant in 1852; "they are all constitutionally wise & prud[ent] as to worldly affairs—none have even made much of a dash, but all they touch turns to Gold." By contrast, failure stories sounded uneven and unmanageable; misfit careers traced ignoble or unstable outlines. "Capital enough Cr[edit] very good, but a great rascal," a Georgia agent wrote in 1847; "will never fail, unless by so doing, he will be able to make money." The owner of the Black Bear Tavern in Cincinnati, according to 1854 reports, "Has prop[erty], ought to make money, but is dissipated, vacillating, wasteful at times. . . . Clever man, but this world concedes him but little." Some men were too fickle to be bankable commodities. Any tale might take a bad turn; indeed, every case in this paragraph ended in failure.[22]

Surprise upsets made narratives of identity as erratic as other market commodities. An entry headed "Robert L. Brown" concerned a merchant and planter in Tye River, Virginia. "In a word, he is one of nature's best sons, that takes things as they are," a Mercantile Agency correspondent wrote in 1855. Perhaps this sounded too little like a rateable soul, because the agent quickly added, "we do not mean that he is a lazy or slovenly man, no! he is a nice g[oo]d gent[le]m[an]; a little liable to be imposed on by sorry men that profess to be gentlemen." Albeit gullible, being a "Large Land & Negro holder" Robert L. Brown stood "v[er]y good for debts, indeed he is considered rich high minded and honorable but spends more than he makes." The reporter played dueling adjectives: "Rich in prop[erty]: much in debt, a g[oo]d fellow, poor manager, fast liver, slow pay." Presumed to be worth $20,000 to $40,000, Brown kept on until December 1857, two months into the panic. "To my surprise he has failed," came an urgent dispatch. "I knew he was in debt but had no idea he owed one fourth as much as he does." In fact, Brown owed $50,000 and took several creditors down with him, proving that one "fast liver" hurt the wider community. Brown relocated and settled into another stereotype, that of the dependent husband: "has moved to Lynchburg, where his wife on the bounty of some of her friends is teaching a female school." Margaret Brown (née Cabell, an illustrious Virginia clan) went to work to feed eight children and one husband. Her kinfolk gave them scant help after paying his debts in 1858, yet strangers shared one of Margaret's main chores (probably unbeknownst to her), "looking after Robert" until he died in 1880 at age sixty. He had done little for decades, but the agency kept watching him for a quarter of a century.[23]

Robert Lawrence Brown came up short in Virginia, but "Robert L. Brown" had a long run in New York. The report certified the man as risky business. His talents and choices shaped his ratings, yet the logbook also laid out the life. If the community forgot or forgave his sins (especially after he fought for the Confederacy in middle age), his postwar ambitions would have involved distant lenders with total recall, courtesy of a credit agency. Cumulative reporting carried forward Brown's old deficits; "Caution advised" ended each new entry two decades after his "surprise" ruin in 1857. Even in those hard times, the agency blamed moral imperfection, not market fluctuation. "One of nature's best sons" and "a nice g[oo]d gent[le]m[an]" before the fall, Brown in subsequent reports became a stock character of failure: "I understand he has no energy & will never make a dollar, I reckon." Had the ordeal changed Brown or only the reporter's opinion of him? Either way, the market memory of credit ledgers often reinforced the moral master plots of popular culture. Even more efficiently than the jeremiads of editors, preachers, and legislators, the judgments of credit agents tended to sequester "a reason, *in the man.*" In the man Robert L. Brown, a financial ordeal changed his story and (possibly) his character. In the report "Robert L. Brown," failure altered not only his history but also his identity. One of the agency's final entries about him could have been an epitaph: "has always been unsuccessful."[24]

In part, credit ledgers echoed master plots because the professionals and community leaders who wrote the reports evidently shared the presumptions of contemporary preachers, statesmen, didactic novelists, and writers of prescriptive advice manuals. Taking it upon themselves to judge the whole community or subsets of it, public moralists were merely self-righteous, but credit agents were disciplinarians. The system institutionalized moral judgment—making such judgment a vital business tool and recruiting agents to supply it. Rather than nagging anonymous congregations of sinners, credit reporters performed individual audits. "That Kind of cr[edit] that can get our recommendation," explained the reporter in an 1854 Ohio case, "must consist much more in a man's virtues & g[e]n[era]l char[acter] than a few [thousand] $ in prop[erty] that may be easilly transferred." Implementing structural solutions to the era's debates over the morality of failure and success, agencies not only prescribed virtue, they tried to enforce it.[25]

Indeed, "moral regulation" was among the industry's founding objectives. The Mercantile Agency grew not only from Lewis Tappan's business failures but also from his success in reform movements. Building associations and communications networks, antebellum do-gooders papered the land with temperance pledges and codes of conduct to keep drunkards dry and factory girls pure. They installed "Overseers of the Poor" and built panopticons, octagonal prisons and asylums that facilitated central observation of oddballs and miscreants. Similar disciplinary aims moved Tappan to deploy surveillance and to devise performance standards. In a private letter about his firm in 1843, he bragged, "It checks knavery, & purifies the mercantile air." His agents checked and purified with zeal, as samples of their work showed. "Failed some two years or so ago, & subsequently became insane, was abt. a year in the Asylum." "Stone is too lazy to be honest." "'Wood' has no cap[ital] or char[acter] that I ever heard of." "He is v[er]y steady & plausible, but no one that I know of has any confidence in his honesty." Two Alabama farmers became "liquor sellers" in 1856, earning this final note: "Busted & returned to their legitimate bus[iness], tilling the soil." Such remarks backed moral and commercial prescription with institutional surveillance. Branding weak men, bad men, and madmen, a credit agency was a panopticon without walls.[26]

Moral fables and credit reports not only sold well, they also shared the question of what men were "good for." Is he "a money m[a]k[in]g fellow cr[edit] undoubted" or "an idle loafer, wor[th] oo, no cr[edit] & never will have"? The latter characterized a blacksmith in New Jersey, whose file spanned the years 1845 to 1859. Excepting a solitary notice of his "steady, industr[ious]" character, most entries reiterated one from March 1858, which read in full: "Not worth naming on paper." Who would recall his name—William J. Manning—or notice that he had ever lived the if the credit agency had not spent ink and paper on "a continuous history" of "an idle loafer"? Evidently, Manning could not keep a steady home for his wife and four sons (two of them blacksmiths), because the U.S. Census found them only once. The Mercantile Agency, however, managed to keep him under watch for fifteen years. On top of life's disappointments, a permanent narrative of those disappointments now existed as a separate commodity, keeping track of broken men like damaged or unclaimed freight. Manning's worthless name faded from an 1859 entry ("not in bus[iness] in his own name now"), he disappeared, and the story ended. Nonetheless, agency ledgers preserved that story and could sell it ever after. All souls now were rateable souls; whether high or low, all got saved.[27]

When in Doubt, Speculate

A credit report was a tip sheet, which advised clients to risk their money on this fellow but not the other guy. "If your *sub*[scriber] asks the advise of this office," wrote one agent, "the best you can give is to let him severely alone." If those who maintained credit ledgers and published ratings directories were not quite bookies, surely they were identity brokers. Was a given individual "worth naming on paper" or not? Trivial queries might bring curt replies from the field, such as this 1848 note from Chenango County, New York: "A sm[all] 3 cent concern, not w[orth] reporting." Combining money talk and moral codes sorted people into useful, if offhand, categories of worth and worthiness: "plausible men" and "doubtful char[acters]," "fast livers" and "steady fellows," "small fry" and "Large Dealers." Such labels communicated present and projected value, both being indispensable "unless those giving Cr[edit] want to be fleeced."[28]

Credit narratives commodified identity so adroitly that informants grew querulous if they encountered an enigma who defied estimation. Theodore B. Guy of Charleston, South Carolina, owned an ice house and sold other goods on commission from the mid-1830s until the Civil War. A reporter picked up his trail in 1847. "Is of v[er]y little ac[count]," an 1850 entry guessed. "Cannot be w[orth] anything tho has the strange faculty of being always in bus[iness] & yet doing nothing." An update in 1852 repeated, "it is a Mystery how he gets along from year to year Owns no p[ro]p[ert]y & paid no tax last year." Reporters seemed to try various master plots about Guy—"Appears to have no energy," "He is a clever, lazy fellow"—but none fit because he kept going. "Have hunted all over Charleston & can find no Man who can tell me abt. Mr. Guy," the agent carped in 1856. "He has been here 20 yrs with a store, doing nothing apparently & always has a roll of money in his pocket. My rule would be to sell for cash, & *every body* will say the same." Apparently, *"every body"* knew that a sphinx could not succeed. "I have known him 16 yrs & nobody can get head or tail of him," the entries for 1857 began. "As much a wonder as ever. No Body k[no]w[s] how he lives. V[er]y quiet Steady man. Never Seems to do anyth[in]g or be intimate with any body. Smokes his Cigar as usual & Keeps a sign up over his store, in wh[ich] you will find a pile of B[il]ls & Boxes, but whether they contain anyth[in]g is problematical as [nothing] is seen to go in or come out of his Store." Always in the money and yet a bad risk, the man simply was not a known commodity.[29]

In a similar way, profitable reprobates vexed reporters by defying their predictions and moral assumptions. "Indus[trious] & money making, but somewhat inclined to dissipation tho not so much as formerly," read an 1849 entry about Isaac Thorne, a baker in Rahway, New Jersey. Six months later, agents warned of trouble brewing. "Has been in good circums[tances] but is intemp[era]te as yet he is able to pay his debts but don't know how long he will be so." A year later, the baker's hearth stayed hot while informants kept saying it would cool. "A poor drunken fellow," an 1850 update began, "has been a drunkard for 10 yrs & has made money all the time." The subject hardly fit the mold of "a poor drunken fellow," but the entry frontloaded the stereotype before conceding, "wor[th] prob[abl]y $5 or $6 [thousand], a wonderful fellow always has money, very shrewd chap but he must run out." And he did, finally, eighteen months later. "Used up with Rum, cr[edit] & reput[atio]n gone," the reporter gloated, as if all were again right in his moral universe.[30]

Moral imperatives helped to gauge integrity and predict achievement. "Pays now, but must fail . . . drinks . . . think will fail sometime." Such formulas closed inscrutable or incorrigible cases. In 1855, word came that Virginia planter J. N. Phelps "promises to break off gambling and drinking." A year later the agent huffed, "Drinks pretty generally. Cr[edit] getting v[ery] low, he still boasts of hav[in]g ab[ou]t 20 Negroes. I suppose he is good for what he owes and perhaps a g[oo]d deal more; but any man that gambles and drinks, you know how far he ought to be trusted." Informants applied everyday morals, not high ideals; the evil in this case was not slavery but debauchery. The update for 1857 recommended discipline. "Generally drunk & gambles . . . better make him pay, lest he fail without doing so." Same story in 1858: "good for his debts now, without a reformation he cannot reasonably be expected to hold out." The last prewar entry read, "drinks liquor yet I understand. he has astonished me that he has not failed yet, if indeed he has not. I understand he has yet a few negroes." The notes resumed after the war and Phelps was broke by 1868, ruined by postwar recession, not personal dissipation.[31]

Credit reports imposed conventional moral imperatives to keep the "reason, *in the man*," even when the master plot did not really fit. The system was not made for cheery drunkards like Phelps (or dreamy abolitionists like William Henry Brisbane); it preferred men "called g[oo]d pay & said to be punct[ua]l & . . . consid[ered] respon[sib]l[e]." Datelined St. Louis, July 1860, those words described "Corbin Thompson. Slave Dealer, 6th Street near Market." Tappan's successors had by then shelved his goal of "purifying the mercantile air." If not entirely ineffectual, such an aim seemed immaterial to the service's growth and profit margin. Nonetheless, credit ledgers never became mere balance sheets; the reform era had set the genre's moralizing tone and standpoint. The tenor of an 1876 entry for hotelier Lewis W. Spencer of Old Bridge, New Jersey, differed little from that of earlier cases. "In bus[iness] here 25 yrs, m[a]r[rie]d, but too fond of a spree." Unable to reconcile a "h[ar]d drinker" and "a man who will make money anywhere," agents cautioned, "you can't tell where 'Rum' will take a man." The facts were on Spencer's side; he was worth $5,000 outside his profitable business and owned $3,000 in real estate besides. But subscribers needed more than material facts. They paid for estimation and prediction, even intuition—but not for intervention. The system need not reform drinkers, gamblers, or even dreamers to label them commercially unredeemable.

Long after agents gave up on moral objectives, moral imperatives ("if it be true that he drinks he will fail") remained the quickest way to commodify identity—to figure a man's present and future value.[32]

On the eve of the Civil War, after two decades at it, many agents sounded like soothsayers as much as storytellers. "He is steady and honest," one wrote in 1858, "but unless I am mistaken he will make many bad debts." He did. An 1860 case signaled, "The indications are favorable to their future prosperity." They prospered. Another from 1860 read in full: "W[orth] but little: of bad habits & cant succeed we think." He didn't. "Parties here," a Philadelphian reported in 1860, "have confidence that he will finally succeed & become well off." He did, until he began "giving [too] much attention to spiritualism, being rather fanatic on the Subject." Speculation of the more worldly variety was unavoidable; credit reporting required an educated guess and a calculated gamble. Agents weighed available evidence and projected future performance, and subscribers took a chance by heeding the advice or not. Sellers and buyers of credit reports thus traded in the commodity of identity. And for once, the speculators had morality on their side; moral codes and master plots figured value and prefigured results. "Worthless, & always will be," an agent reported in 1847, selling wholesale generalizations by the case. "Worthless pecuniarily & otherwise." "Worthless & contemptible," "worthless but still here," "a worthless cuss never was wor[th] anything."[33]

On the page as on the street, these were one-liners. Heard the one about the Cincinnati dry goods merchant? "[I]f he succeeds 'twill be contrary to the expectations of all I have heard speak of him," an informant cracked in 1852. How about the blacksmith from Chenango County? "Don't think w[orth] anyth[in]g never heard of any one that ever had any suspicion that he was," came the 1876 reply. Unfair or inaccurate in some cases, such quips aided a high-volume and high-risk service. Every man, even a "worthless cuss," had a story with commercial value, if not to himself, then to an enterprising narrator who knew how to tell it. What was a speculator anyway, if not a storyteller, who wrote the ending before the beginning? Popular scenarios and moral platitudes helped creditors hedge their bets.[34]

The One about the Rat Hole

Failure becomes fact when it becomes a story—when somebody makes a rumor stick. "Can't say that he has failed & presume it is not so," an Ohioan hedged in 1854, "but we repeat such was the current rumor as utter[e]d by a thousand tongues." A week later came an update: "*Confidential.* I think he will fail before long if he has not already." He had not—but did within the year. If a town had "a thousand tongues," how many did an agency have? As a narrator, it liked to give away the end of a story. Six months before a Virginia druggist's last report in 1869, the informant wrote, "it is concluded that he is going down hill and it is best to stand from under." Another shut the book on an Illinois case in 1873. "Am satisfied that they will go under soon & think it is only a matter of time," he wrote. Years passed. "It is a mystery to the bus[iness] community here how this conc[ern] gets along & Keeps going," he wrote in 1875; "no one seems to know how they stand, but it is believed they are not wor[th] a cent." Systematic investigation and communication could stop—or spread—rumors efficiently. A Cincinnati agent wrote in 1862, "the impression here is that they are bound to go under, for the present would say 'hands off.'" Among the market's invisible hands, how much power did this one wield?[35]

Etched into the master ledgers, could a rumor become a revelation, a prophesy that fulfilled itself? On 31 October 1848, a final entry from upstate New York confided, "It looks dark." Sometimes correspondents protested inaccuracies filed by others. "The rep[or]t is a false one without any foundation," a Philadelphian wrote in 1850; "he has been a victim to a number of reports & by g[oo]d managem[e]nt has entirely outlived them. . . . *he is entirely safe* but such rep[or]ts must injure him." A telegram came ten days later. "The rumor here is that he has suspended." The correction was evidently too late. Correspondents were in a bind, neither able to ignore gossip nor always to verify it. "People have taken the liberty of talking ab[ou]t them for some time past," a New Yorker wrote, sending news that proved untrue. Fortunately, the victim blamed others: "'Mr. Edwards' says that he never thought the report of the failure of his house came from this office." Wherever the story started, "Mr. Edwards" broke a week later. Another case had a happier ending—that is, no ending—when the all clear sounded. "Have emerged from the cloud in which they were represented by us as being enveloped a fortnight Since & now [stand] out bright." Wary businessmen learned to be more guarded, and critics raised questions about the system.[36]

"The man who *objects* to such investigation," warned *Hunt's Merchants' Magazine* in 1851, "gives, in doing so, *prima facie* evidence that the result would be unfavorable to himself." But not only tricksters and losers feared the system; prominent critics suspected bias and error. "What man whose credit is his bread, does not feel anxious to know whether he has been misrepresented or not?" asked Edwin T. Freedley in *A Practical Treatise on Business* (which went through twenty-eight printings from 1852 to 1854). "It is a system that is fraught with danger," he warned; "the credit of the mercantile community, which is its life and soul, would be in the hands of a few men, self-constituted umpires, and their unknown and irresponsible agents." New York's *Independent* disagreed. "They should know everything that *can be known* about everybody in trade. They should point out wrong-doing in every quarter. They should act as a detective police." *The Independent* was an abolitionist weekly with ties to Lewis Tappan, but *Hunt's* seconded its view in reprinting this piece.[37]

Part umpire, part detective, and part soothsayer, credit agencies and their informants did police the market. Sometimes acting as enforcers but usually as lookouts, correspondents sent all news, great and small. "I think there is some shuffling here," advised an

1855 report; "such may win for a while but cant succeed. such men will bear watching." Shufflers aroused extra vigilance, but the system's premise was that *everybody* in the new economy bore watching. A Massachusetts jeweler looked "Good for a reas[onable] am[oun]t. still sh[oul]d be watched a little." A source in Cleveland wrote, "he is p[roba]bly g[oo]d for sm[all] am[oun]ts well looked after." A St. Louis saloonkeeper's 1860 entry read, "Dunning & watching dont hurt him." Everybody kept an eye out for rascals, but credit agents watched even upright and prosperous traders. Filing an update about a grocer who seemed *too* successful, an Illinois informant vowed, "Will be watching, as there is something mysterious about this house."[38]

The Mercantile Agency booked nearly three decades of reports before formally instructing informants about "what to look for." Tappan's antislavery comrades submitted the company's first reports, but the agency soon lined up lawyers, bankers, aldermen, and veteran merchants. Until 1869, the firm presumed that the sagacity of its correspondents would suffice. "They dont look like men who could carry so big a load as they have to shoulder," began an 1855 report from Cincinnati, about the manufacturers of "a New Patent Steam Engine on the Chronometer Principle." The writer conceded, "they are strangers here & therefore I k[no]w [nothing] of their means," but added, "I predict the concern will fizzle out tho no one has expressed that opinion to me." They fizzled. To defenders, the agencies' profitability proved the accuracy of their reports and the perspicacity of their reporters.[39]

Yet neither experience nor a knack for minding other folks' business ensured fair or uniform standards. Often local snooping turned up little. "Nobody can tell any thing ab[ou]t him. he is an energetic stave ahead fellow & may have p[ropert]y," read a note from 1858. "The most that can be said in reference to such men, is they want close looking to." Close looking uncovered all kinds of transactions. In Ohio, a druggist "became too well acquainted with a 'Calif[orni]a Widow'" left behind during the gold rush; "her husband returning, made a fuss." A few sources mocked their own vigilance. "The way 'S' spells his name looks suspicious," an agent in Cairo, Illinois, wrote of one Thomas Smyth; "afraid to acknowledge himself a 'Smith'?" Maybe field correspondents made jokes as a fleeting gift, to relieve the inky tedium they shared with copy clerks who toiled in faraway New York City. "First of all, he has a wife and baby," one allegedly wrote; "together they ought to be worth fifty thousand dollars to any man. Secondly, he has an office in which there is a table worth one dollar and fifty cents, and three chairs worth, say one dollar. Last of all, there is in one corner a large rat-hole which will bear looking into. Respectfully yours, A. Lincoln."[40]

Prairie lawyer Abraham Lincoln really did furnish reports to the Mercantile Agency from Illinois in the 1840s and 1850s. But the rat tale looked mighty tall when it first saw print about 1885, and in the next fifty years Carl Sandburg and Dun & Bradstreet publicists gave it a good stretching through many retellings. As a purported scrap of Lincoln's wit, it had the added charm of improbable history: Honest Abe meets Dun & Bradstreet. Like any good yarn, it hinted at larger truths and winked at the new system's ironies. In a nation beginning to doubt the rightness of slavery, the antislavery Tappan devised a new way to calculate human value. In a culture that exalted the separate spheres of men and women, agents ciphered a man's wife and family into his economic worth. In an era that invented scientific and social surveillance (think of the asylum and urban reform movements), informants peeped into bedchambers and rat holes because nobody quite knew what to look for. And in an industry that boasted of its facts, this, its most famous report, was probably a legend. Lincoln used the "rat hole" metaphor often in his known writings, but if such a letter ever really existed, the original has never surfaced, either at auction or in an archive.[41]

A true relic of Lincoln's services to the Mercantile Agency survives in an Illinois master ledger: "This Office has had the honor of having Old Abe as a correspondent," a clerk wrote after Lincoln won the White House, near-contemporary proof of the fu-

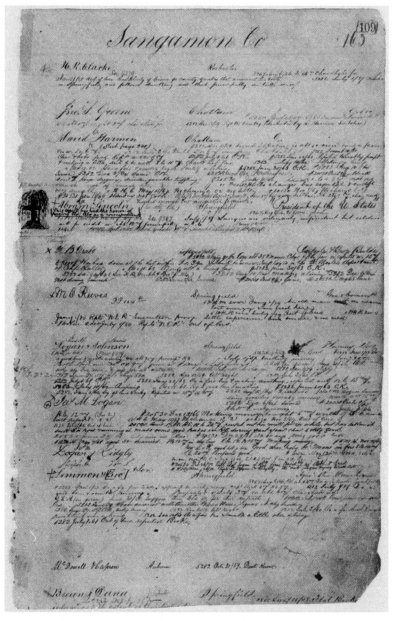

Abraham Lincoln's credit report from the 1850s (with a postmortem cross and weeping willow in the left margin) shows white space where several lines of ink were "systematically abraded," as determined in April 2000 by the Paper Laboratory of Straus Center for Conservation at Harvard University's Fogg Art Museum. (Courtesy R. G. Dun & Co. Collection, Baker Library, Harvard Business School.)

ture President's work as a field informant. The clerk jotted this above an entry *about* Lincoln, created because agency watchmen were themselves watched by others. Lincoln's affairs would "bear looking into," and the agency induced one of his neighbors in Springfield, Illinois, to do so. "Lawyers are ordinarily impudent but seldom ask for credit," the informant wrote, adding that the subject was "w[orth] ab[ou]t. 12m/$ [$12,000] principally in R[eal] E[state]." Between January and July 1858, however, as Lincoln prepared to debate Stephen A. Douglas, the shadow reported something else—which has been lost to history. Someone purged Lincoln's credit report after his assassination, leaving only the passage just quoted and a black cross doodled in the margin. Maybe the entry mentioned his extravagant wife or echoed Wendell Phillips's unkind remark that Lincoln was "a first-rate second-rate man." Whatever it once said, even a martyr's blood was not thicker than waterproof ink. This job took a knife. Someone pared the writing off the page, scraping the surface so clean that even ultraviolet and infrared scanning cannot raise the dead words. And yet the crime left more telling evidence behind.[42]

History's trickster holds up a nonexistent letter and a blank ledger, saying, Pick a story: the one about the rat hole, saved but maybe untrue; or the nosy neighbor's report, shredded but perhaps all too true. What surfaces is not a revelation about Lincoln; like any other life, his was a mess of stories true and false, lost and found, told and untold. Whoever butchered the 1858 reports evidently erred on the side of "untold." Yet that act itself acknowledged the power of narrative—not only Lincoln's, but the whole system of reporting. Rateable souls accrued neatly on crisp pages. Nothing got buried in unkempt files or fell down any rat hole. No more the confidence game of pick a story, any story. Sturdy red books preserved an official story, rated and narrated, recounted and resold. A striver's tale was no longer his own.

6 Misinformation and Its Discontents

A patch of woods still grows between two brooks that meet behind Main Street in Bridgton, in Maine's lake region. Before the Civil War, some joker dubbed the spot "Little Canaan," since it looked like a promised land but stank to high heaven. Caustic breezes of sulfur, dung, and death stung the eyes. Rural people knew how money smells up close, and here it smelled like Horace Billings's tannery. He started in 1842 and made a name by sweat, temperance work, and marrying the local tycoon's granddaughter. Fifty men tended vats in his tanyard, which was crisscrossed with drying hides and stacks of hemlock. Bark mills turned by draft horses ground a thousand cords a year to brew a tanning liquor for the dark, red leather prized by shoemakers and bookbinders. In time, Billings bought out rivals locally and in Portland (forty miles southeast), built a corn cannery, and dammed Stevens Brook for power. Go Ahead! By 1880, the tanner reeked of a quarter million greenbacks and built his family a brownstone in Boston's newly filled Back Bay. The home folks crowned him "Bridgton's Business King."[1]

But even kings cannot count future blessings. Success still lay ahead of Billings in the autumn of 1854 when rumors began to swirl around him like the dry leaves of Little Canaan. *Billings from Maine is in trouble.* But the tanner knew his accounts to the penny, and by trade he knew an ill wind when he smelled it. *Billings is "getting ready to fail."* The word on the street led back to the Boston Mercantile Agency, Lewis Tappan's first branch, opened in 1843. *Horace Billings "is worse than nothing."* A friend of the tanner confronted the manager of the Boston agency, who allegedly replied in "High horse" tones that he would not be "dragooned" into altering his books, adding that he "w[oul]d go to his death before disclos[ing]" the name of his informant.[2]

So the tanner got a lawyer: Richard Henry Dana, Jr., fresh from defending fugitive slave Anthony Burns. Dana was more famous for his 1840 memoir *Two Years before the Mast,* part of which time Dana had spent tanning hides in California. Bringing suit for $10,000 damages, Billings appeared before the bar in an attempt to clear his name. Subpoenaed to prove the libel, the red-leather book hemmed and hawed. "I am not intimate enough with his bus[iness] affairs to go into any particulars, as to what he is w[orth]," Billings's entry read in part; "I have no doubt, he is a man of handsome prop[erty] but it is impossible for me to name any Sum. I have no means, of knowing any thing about him." Where was the alleged libel? On closer examination, according to the published decision, "it appeared that the unfavorable report had been erased, and a favorable report substituted in its place." Defendant's counsel conceded the point. After hearing from Billings's friend, the agency manager deleted the original entry and solicited another—albeit without notifying Billings or subscribers. By agency policy, no duplicate books were kept; the erasure had destroyed the only copy of the disputed words. No proof of libel existed but what this or that trader said he heard at the agency or on the street. Hearsay was fair in credit reports but foul in court; the jury acquitted. Billings got neither apology nor recompense, and after clearing his name he kept his own counsel. "Is

very silent about his own affairs," the agency noted in 1856, "&
very little is known by the Public about his worth."[3]

Anyone ever beset by a computer error can pity the tanner's
tale, but his frustrations were novel in 1854. Bureaucracy, surveillance, and information management had just begun to affect everyday life. Agencies did not warn those whose commercial and
private lives they watched. Sources enjoyed anonymity, and subscribers pledged not to leak reports. Richard Henry Dana sneered
at unnamed agents and deleted files—"Never tell any one! Secret
corrections!"—to no avail. Billings the "Business King" could neither avoid becoming a subject again nor be sure they got his story
right. Many other businessmen sued credit reporters to fight being called a *failure*—showing how that label impinged on new
concepts of privacy, ties between home and market, the value of
life stories, and ultimately the value of the people who lived them.
Such cases posed the first challenges to bureaucratic conceit and
lack of accountability in the information industry.[4]

The Mercantile Agency was an early information system, even
if its moving parts were human and its only electric component
was the occasional urgent telegram. Tappan, John M. Bradstreet,
Robert Graham Dun, and others established networks to amass
and transmit data, languages to value and encode it, and protocols
to store and retrieve it. Central coordination of local informants
was crucial, as were indexes to access, track, and update data.
Each function enhanced case management—but as an integrated
system they all supported an expandable database with millions of
interlinked files. More than making old lines of business more
efficient, the pioneers opened a new field of enterprise—and a
new way of life.[5]

Information Please

"Please call at my office and receive *important* information. LEWIS
TAPPAN." A printed form with handwritten names, an "Agency
Ticket of Invitation" summoned those who previously had

checked on a man or firm now in trouble. A client explained, "there were two forms, one for ordinary information and the other extraordinary." The more routine form said "call at my office at your leisure, if interested." Either ticket admitted the bearer to a marvelous exhibition. The reporting room resembled a post office or train ticket depot. A dozen or more clerks manned a battery of tall desks, like teller windows, ledgers visible in the stacks behind. Inking in a call slip, a visitor "handed up a ticket of inquiry" to the clerk's "raised desk." A page boy fetched the correct volume, which thumped on the desk impressively, like a family Bible. The subscriber could judge this book only by its cover, as it was "laid at an angle of about 40 or 45 degrees, so that a person outside the desk, cannot see the inside of the book without difficulty." The clerk made no copies of the report; he read the entry aloud and permitted the hearer to take notes. House rules were strict, but the intelligence seemed to be worth the inconvenience. In 1851, a satisfied client wrote in the *New-York Times,* "for every dollar I pay for information, I save one hundred."[6]

"Information" was a fresh word back then, in the sense of authoritative knowledge that could be stockpiled and sold like any other commodity. Often associated with the computer industry after World War II, an information system was already emerging a century earlier, when Lewis Tappan set about "procuring, by resident and special agents, information . . . for the benefit of such merchants in this city as approve the object and become subscribers." So said an 1843 advertisement, but Tappan revealed his vision more fully in a private letter that same year. "In prosperous times," he boasted, clients "will feel able to pay for the information, and in bad times they feel they must have it." If Tappan reveled in his own advantage, he also foresaw the growth potential of this new industry. Subscribers and subjects might rise and fall, but the information broker could not lose.[7]

Tappan's early rivals tried to best him (rhetorically if not operationally) with offers emphasizing "*full* information." A rival's agent recruited in 1845 agreed to send "the required information" and promised, "I shall endeavor to give correct information." Such modifiers conveyed the value added to narratives made and disseminated systematically. J. M. Bradstreet's Improved Commercial Agency earned its name by enhanced delivery. He printed rating books for his clients to use anywhere, when his forerunner still required office visits for "obtaining the necessary information." Like a yardstick or an interest table, knowledge formatted for useful reference became a vital business tool. *Hunt's Merchants' Magazine* hailed a new "Basis of Prosperity" in 1860, "the vast modern increase of the facilities for diffusing and obtaining full and correct information on everything pertaining to trade." Bankers and insurers collected and analyzed data, but only credit agents sold nothing else. Something new unfolded from local news compiled, evaluated, indexed, updated, and retailed nationwide. Tappan's quaint motto, "Man's Confidence in Man," evolved into a modern mania for "full and correct information."[8]

Information systems and bureaucratic surveillance seemed to exemplify the process of economic rationalization. Theorists from Adam Smith to Joseph Schumpeter explained how capitalism matured as policies and methods superseded personal relations and community mores in doing business. Max Weber studied rationalization as bureaucracy—"written documents ('the files') . . . preserved in their original or draft form" by "a staff of subaltern officials and scribes of all sorts." Weber saw bureaucracy as "a power instrument of the first order," and his droll aside "('the files')" bespoke the authority vested in carefully controlled information. At the Mercantile Agency, "the files" expanded to 2,580 volumes in fifty years. However rational they were, credit reports were never impersonal. Tappan meant to enforce moral discipline ("it checks knavery"), using new systems to fortify old values. "It tends to promote a high standard of mercantile honor," applauded *Banker's Magazine;* critics said the agency imposed "moral quarantine." Either way, moral regulation and economic rationalization coalesced. Far from trading morality for policy, credit reports projected the rules of face-to-face bargains onto richer, long-distance markets. Moral prescription and commercial description fraternized on every page.[9]

Failure and success were the information industry's first products; it arose to clarify such categories by converting achievement and identity into "necessary information." Credit reports began as local knowledge—rumors, meetings, sightings—bits of oral culture to be transformed into systematic writing. Stories gained authority and value as "the files." The "three C's" of character, capital, and capacity merged into taxonomies like "A number 1" and "second-rate," judgment calls that sounded commonsensical. Unheard-of capacity and efficiency bred resistance to challenge, as a generation of scriveners came of age, mad for record-keeping and truth telling. Demanding a correction, Billings and dozens like him chased a new type of wild goose into the courtroom. The first suit against the Mercantile Agency, brought by a "country merchant" named John Beardsley, was a public spectacle complete with salacious testimony, surprise witnesses, conspiracy theories —even a prisoner of conscience. A question loomed: what if efficient corps of clerks and agents had the power to make their predictions come true?[10]

Old Evils and New Goods

John Beardsley just missed the trial of the century, back in September 1807. Born six days after the verdict, he grew up ambitious and left rural Goshen for Gotham, sixty miles east. The country boy in New York City soon fell under evil influences—becoming a law clerk for Aaron Burr, slayer of Hamilton and accused plotter of treason. Acquitted the week of John's birth yet guilty in public opinion, the former Vice President had fled to Europe in 1808, only to return later to practice law in Manhattan. Ostracized, Burr minded his own affairs and hired the usual crew of student clerks. By the 1820s, the name Aaron Burr may have meant nothing but opportunity to a young man like John, whose surname probably opened the old man's door. Burrs and Beardsleys had founded Fairfield County, Connecticut, intermarrying and going to war together. Aaron Burr had been an aide-de-camp at the battle of Long Island in 1776, where John's grandfather had been a regimental surgeon; and the surgeon's brother wintered with Burr at Valley Forge in 1777. But if old family ties launched John's career in the 1820s, a reviled mentor opened few doors. Success eluded Beardsley in New York, but not love; he wed Mary Rutherford in 1828. Indirectly, she would entangle him in their own trial of the century twenty years later, when ambition and scandal tainted his good name.[11]

The case of *Beardsley v. Tappan* ran from 1848 to 1871. Set off by a rumor in a frontier village, it was settled by a ruling in the U.S. Supreme Court. At issue were entries about John and his brother, storekeepers in Norwalk, Ohio. "July [18]48, Has been sued. [R]eport says that 'J[ohn] B.'s wife is about to file a bill for divorce & Alimony & that he has put his p[ro]p[er]ty out of his hands," the informant warned; "if so their store will probably be closed at once." The agency was an early warning system; word soon got back to Norwalk. Scrambling for cash, the Beardsleys advertised a clearance sale, "in consequence of certain wicked, false, and slanderous reports which have been industriously circulated in New York against them." John protested to the agency and filed suit when Tappan stood by his information. Neither side blinked for two decades, as the case weighed "a valuable aid to our merchants" against "the evils incidental to it." For John Beardsley, both his business and his manhood were in doubt. For the Mercantile Agency, "the most serious crisis in its brief history" tested its accuracy and also its legality. For Mary Beardsley, the proceedings questioned her autonomy and even her sanity. For the local informant, his integrity and anonymity were at risk. And for the public, new ventures like "industriously circulated" information collided with new values like the right to privacy. *Beardsley v. Tappan* argued about surveillance as a business method and a daily presence: the new arbiter of individual success or failure.[12]

John Beardsley chased success down any road that would go

*Several African-American men are among those gathered on
Norwalk's Main Street, beneath the awning of "Beardsley & Bro.
Dry Goods Head-Quarters." The man in the white smock may be
John Beardsley, who became sole proprietor when Horace retired in
1865.* (Courtesy of Henry R. Timman, Firelands Historical Society.)

ahead. After New York, he took Mary to Lanesborough, Massachusetts. In the spring of 1832 they joined Connecticut settlers in
Norwalk, Ohio, sixty miles west of Cleveland. They opened a
millinery, but in November it went up in a "DREADFUL CON-
FLAGRATION" that consumed half the town. John boldly put more
irons in the fire; in 1835 alone, he formed partnerships with a lawyer and a saddler while managing a livery stable and seeking public office. A Whig, he stood for Huron County recorder and in
1844 he ran for county prosecutor, losing twice yet building a
name. He also dealt in real estate, lost some to back taxes, and
speculated in silkworms. In 1845, his brother, Horace, came west
and they opened H. Beardsley & Co. on Main Street. "New
Goods–New Goods!!" they advertised in the weekly *Reflector;*
"Staple and Fancy Dry Goods, Groceries, Hardware, Crockery,
Hats, Caps, Boots and Shoes." Fashions "direct from New York"

included "Leghorn Bonnets" and "Calicoes, of every description and style." John's legal, political, and commercial ventures established himself and an extended family, including his father and Mary's siblings and in-laws. On Main Street near the store, their homes were known for gardens tended by Horace's wife, Elizabeth, whose green thumb and lavender ribbons lingered long in local memory. Befitting their station, the brothers rented pews at St. Paul's Episcopal, where Lizzie chaired the Church Aid Society. By any standard, this family had succeeded.[13]

The Mercantile Agency picked up their trail with the store opening and watched until John retired thirty-three years later, in 1878. The initial entry, dated September 1845, flashed back a dozen years to his arrival in Norwalk "poor." In his first ten years there, lawyering and "fortunate speculations" had earned him a farm, a lot and house in town, and now a store. The first biannual update came in February 1846. "Com[men]c[e]d last fall. 'H[orace]' is recently from N.Y. city, he appears well, ag[e]d ab[ou]t 28," it stated. "'J[ohn]' ag[e]d abt. 38, marr[ie]d, is a lawyer, his reputation for honesty & integrity is not first rate. [H]e is ambitious & attends strictly to the bus[iness] of the store, is w[orth] [$5,000]." Although John had not paid debts promptly in the past, "the firm appears to be d[oin]g a g[oo]d bus[iness]. safe for the present." Further updates found the brothers prosperous and audacious, stocking goods worth up to $23,000. "It is hardly possible to sell that amount here," the correspondent scoffed in 1848. Despite hard times, a year later the writer had to admit that "they appear to have sold off their goods rapidly considering the scarcity of money." Up against more doubtful reports later, the brothers "put forth very strenuous efforts and are apparently doing well." Complementary temperaments made them an effective team—Horace the cajoling salesman, John the calculating businessman.[14]

In the summer of 1848, however, doubts arose that could not be quelled. The Norwalk informant wrote in July that divorce would likely ruin the store. Tickets of Invitation went out in Manhattan, but some recipients doubted the warning of failure and fraud.

"I think you are doing this man or this firm an injustice," one jobber told agency manager Benjamin Douglass, adding that he got $500 that very day from Beardsley & Co., who had also remitted $2,000 to other houses. A Norwalker in New York on business, Charles L. Boalt, was escorted to the agency by a subscriber. "The report must have come from some malicious source," Boalt said. Douglass refused to pull the report, but promised to inform Tappan and solicit confirmation. Meanwhile, Boalt reassured the brothers' creditors, but some took legal action anyway. In August, an emphatic reply came from Norwalk: "(Confirms prev[ious] rept. & says in addition) Two suits in com[mon] pleas Court, besides those commenced by 'Judge Baker.' 'Mrs. B.' petition for a divorce will soon be filed & I am informed 'J[ohn] B.' is putting his R[eal] E[state] out of his hands. I do not doubt but the firm has the ability to do a prosperous bus[iness] so long as they are honest which I think will be just as long as it suits their intentions." More tickets went out, heeded this time, and the system worked as it was meant to. "I declined selling [to] Mr. Beardsley after I got this report from Mr. Tappan," a New York merchant said later.[15]

Damned and double-damned, John Beardsley journeyed home to New York to redeem himself. On 18 November 1848, he visited the agency behind Wall Street, bringing a tea trader who had refused his orders because of the reports. They found Tappan himself in the reporting hall, a hive of clerks and clients at tall desks, abuzz with questions and answers on a busy Saturday. According to the trader, "Mr. Beardsley told him that he called for the purpose of asking him to correct his report of him, that [it] was doing him great injury in his business and wronging him—that it was a slander; Mr. Tappan said he 'would show him before he got through that it was no slander.'" With twenty clerks in earshot, he told the tea trader to leave and took Beardsley into his private office. Tappan refused to kill the report or to name the reporter. Beardsley had come of age playing the games of New York lawyers, but if he hoped his adversary would flinch at litigious talk of "slander," he was wrong. If Tappan thought Beardsley was bluffing, he was wrong. They had nothing left to say but *See you in court.* Tappan's office door had been closed barely five minutes.[16]

The Truth about John Beardsley

Opening the trial proceedings took three years. Lewis Tappan sold out to his brother Arthur and Benjamin Douglass in 1849, but his diary of 1851 found him "daily in the Circuit Court of the U.S., attending the trial of H. Beardslee & Co's suit against me for Libel, growing out of words recorded July & Aug. 1848 on the Books of my Mercantile Agency." Retired but still "defendant in law," he drew a caret next to "& Co" and inserted "(John Beardsley)"—plaintiff in fact. The store was in Horace's name, but it was John who literally made a federal case of it all. Tappan noted big names: "B. F. Butler & Ch. O'Connor are counsel for defendant, & Mess. Cutting & Hoffman for the plaintiff." F. B. Cutting was a noted lawyer-politico and Ogden Hoffman a former U.S. District Attorney and future New York Attorney General. They faced former U.S. Attorney General Benjamin F. Butler and Charles O'Conor (his spelling). Widely regarded as America's finest lawyer, O'Conor broke Boss Tweed, defended Jefferson Davis, and became the first Catholic to run for president. His Honor Samuel R. Betts presided, a federal judge so intimidating that he sat for twenty years before any higher court overruled him. The Tappan case would go to a jury and be second-guessed by the newspapers.[17]

Betts called for opening arguments on 22 November 1851, in the U.S. Circuit Court chamber at New York City Hall. Butler and O'Conor claimed the agency's reports were not public defamation but rather "privileged communications" (as between lawyer and client), immune from prosecution even if derisive or false. This doctrine was not upheld until 1882, but the gambit revealed that "doubt [of] the general legality or usefulness of the business" was seen as more of a threat than John Beardsley. Regarding Beardsley, Tappan's lawyers entered "a plea of justification," or truth defense. He had no case if "the said libellous [*sic*] words . . . were, at the time of the composing and publishing thereof, in all respects true." The defense ordered depositions from Ohio to prove a failed marriage and a failing business. This testimony showed that folks gossiped about the family, but was otherwise useless. Indeed, the plaintiff introduced several of the defense's own depositions to show that reported lawsuits against Beardsley were retaliatory actions for liens he placed. Vague testimony about the timing of local gossip fit Beardsley's claim that the stories began when townsmen "hear[d] that reports had been circulated in New York." Had a correspondent's insinuation come back home as *information?* Cutting and Hoffman forced the defense to object to its own witnesses. Eventually, it emerged that the reports were not true—not exactly; but the truth hardly mattered in the larger battle over making and selling truth.[18]

Plaintiff's Exhibit A, by subpoena, was "a certain folio manuscript book, marked on the back, 'Record,' and on the side, 'Ohio,' 'A to H.'" Behold, the big red book! Laid open, it was the size of the *New-York Daily Times* (founded two months earlier) and nearly as gray with fine print, albeit handwritten. The dramatic bulk of the thing (600 pages in crimson covers) fit diverse scenarios. Cutting and Hoffman waved it like a bloody club, evidence of character assassination. Butler and O'Conor made a fuss about clipping envelopes on the disputed page—to frame the Beardsley reports but maintain confidentiality of the adjacent ones. On the witness stand, subscribers got their first peek at the disputed entries, noses having almost to graze the page to focus on the tiny script. "I should think that was about the substance of the report read to me," several nodded, but some detected omissions. "I don't see the words 'Mr. Beardsley was not a man of good character,' here in this book," defense witness Samuel Frink swore under cross-examination; "I recollect distinctly that those were the words used to me and not my own inference; 'not an honest man' were the precise words used."[19]

Besides individual inference or bias, the trial revealed that routine factors could skew "the words used." Clerks might color readings in word or tone. Clients might ask questions that prompted clerks to editorialize. Urgent news might not wait for transcribing. New Yorker Thomas Lawrence, Jr., conceded on defense cross that "the information may not have been read from the book; it may have been read from a letter." By policy, the correspondent's missive would have been destroyed once copied; but copying could change wording. Tucked here and there in many volumes, original letters survive for comparison to page entries, showing that clerks did not always copy verbatim. Such variables might explain why Charles Boalt (the Norwalker who confronted Douglass) heard different words when he visited Tappan three days later. "I also recollect the language, 'They will probably fail,' as a part of the report read the second time," Boalt said. Conflicting testimony showed how everyday contingencies revised even "*important* information."[20]

Otherwise, how could words vanish from a page? According to Boalt, Tappan said that regular correspondents were not his only sources, and that news from others was copied in pencil, not ink. For whatever reason, many penciled remarks can in fact be seen on the books, as in P. T. Barnum's entry and that of an absconder from Bangor. "I got the impression . . . that [Tappan] wished me to understand," Boalt added, "that some parts of the report that bore the hardest on Messrs. Beardsleys' credit was in pencil." Strange, given the red ink and blue notes illustrating another innovative agency practice: color-coding. So, why pencil? The firm did erase reports about Horace Billings and Abraham Lincoln. Penciled notes in the Beardsley entry include one from Benjamin Douglass: "Let *no person* attempt to read this rep[or]t off [without] consulting B. D. (under penalty)." Beside this command, "(how much?)" was added by a cheeky clerk, perhaps the same fellow who pulled extra duty because of the lawsuit.[21]

His chore was to recopy a full page of the disputed entries, and he left traces of his work. A single hand and pen wrote all the entries from 1845 to 1850, which would have been unlikely had reports been entered as they came in. The copyist misdated entries, writing 1858 instead of 1848. Updates on later pages carried a headnote, "For prev[ious] rep[or]ts See p. 359," but page 359 is missing. Extant records begin at 316, on different paper from adjacent pages. Such clues narrow the recopying time frame between May 1850 and July 1852, contemporary to the 1851 trial. Recopying did not prove tampering; deceivers, one assumes, would take more care, and a few omitted phrases would hardly have won the case. Perhaps the original page was simply damaged by overhandling during the trial or retained by defense lawyers afterward. Besides, the suit went on for twenty years, and nobody seemed even to notice the recopying, much less to cry foul.[22]

Yet *Beardsley v. Tappan* disputed not only "words . . . on the books," but the power of words when investigators became storytellers, the authority of words when agencies rated identities. Boalt and Frink testified that key phrases stuck in their heads, markers of identity and adversity: "not a man of good character"; "will probably fail." Defense lawyers moved for dismissal on a technicality: "a fatal variance between the words of said alleged libels" in the lawsuit and "in said Record-book." Judge Betts refused to dismiss over quibbles such as "Wife is about to apply for divorce" versus "Wife is abt to file a Bill for divorce." Even defense briefs quoted the Beardsley reports inaccurately or inconsistently. No keener record-keeping system had ever existed than "this business of collecting and collating information." Yet neither side produced a consistent or authoritative text. Words on the books might never fade—but they always changed.[23]

This truth undercut the agency's truths. "We presume the proprietors do not pretend to infallibility," *Hunt's* wrote in 1851, "but we are satisfied that the records of the office are rarely inaccurate, and never seriously so . . . for they deal in *facts*, and not in opinions." But they actually dealt in a commodity made of more than ink and facts. Whether or not "fixed facts" stayed that way, information *moved*—from rumors heard on town squares, to reports etched in big books, to recitations and reinterpretations at tall desks, back to rumors on city sidewalks and town squares again. Each entry synthesized oral and scriptural, communal and institutional texts. An accountability system that found uses for pencils and unnamed sources sounded *un*accountable. Formal and informal communications enlarged the net of information—and perhaps the margin of error. *Hunt's* presumed wrong: agents *did* "pretend to infallibility." The manager in the Billings case "was not in the habit of altering his reports." To a client who challenged the Beardsley entry, Benjamin Douglass allegedly snapped, "What the report states is undoubtedly true, and I don't think it necessary to enquire of any one." Despite lofty claims about the integrity of information, the agency *did* alter its books, inadvertently and willfully. Written error and erasure were occasional; oral exaggeration and elision, constant.[24]

Star witness Benjamin Douglass upheld his information under oath but refused to name the source—or even to confirm that he had one in Norwalk. Stating that "his answer . . . would tend to accuse or incriminate him," Douglass took the Fifth Amendment, yet asserted that conscience, not crime, silenced him. Ordered to answer, he told Judge Betts, "I gave, a solemn pledge, under no circumstances, to disclose the names of the agents . . . but to keep them an inviolable secret within my own breast." He would never tell, even if the court threatened "to deprive me of my life." Judge Betts gave him twenty days in the Eldridge Street Jail for contempt. "The Imprisoned Witness" ran the agency from his cell via messenger boys, rather than give up the name to reclaim his liberty. Editor Horace Greeley led well-wishers at his release, urging the martyr to run for mayor! Tappan announced that Douglass stood mute as a point of honor, not to carry out a gag order. Twenty-seven clerks signed a testimonial to their boss's "manly stand" against "a violation of the rights of man." In ornate script, they defined the principle at stake: "We cannot suppose that the law recognizes a right to coerce an individual into a public exposure of his private business."[25]

The Truth about Mary Beardsley

In the two decades since the Beardsleys had married in 1828, "private business" had taken on new meanings. In the Beardsleys' day, *public* and *private* became labels for male and female spheres of life, symbolic divisions that braced underlying connections. Middle-class norms wedded manly ambition to wifely domesticity ("true womanhood") through fashions, spaces, and manners. "Loquacity," warned an 1842 *Ladies Repository* article, "leads families to discuss their private business in the presence of strangers, which is improper." The Beardsleys did exactly this to refute a libel. For the sake of a business, they discussed "private business."[26]

Telling trade secrets and family secrets had long irked the agency's critics. "It is not a system of espionage," Tappan asserted in an 1843 advertisement; yet even his supporters voiced abiding fears. *Hunt's* assured readers in 1851, "We think ourselves incapable of saying one word in defense of a system of espionage." Two years later, underworld journalist George F. Foster's *New York Naked* exposed "an organized system of espionage" at "the office of the central inquisition." He described truly lurid "secret ledgers" detailing "the business, the family, and the personal habits of every man engaged in trade." Worst of all, "no possible means of escaping it exist." Polemics were met by puff like the *New York Independent's* 1856 avowal "They should know everything that *can be known* about everybody in trade. . . . They should act as a detective police." No wonder folks worried that "information" was simply gossip at so much per word.[27]

The Mercantile Agency sold information, but early alerts required prediction: facts not yet true that would become true.

"'J[ohn] B.'s wife is about to file a bill for divorce," clients heard in July 1848; and in August: "a divorce will soon be filed." Despite hints of fraud, both the dossier and the discord focused on salacious details. "Mr. Tappan inquired very particularly about the circumstances and character of . . . John Beardsley," Boalt testified of their late July interview, "and about the report as to his infidelity to his wife." But the entries said nothing about adultery; was this alleged remark in pencil? "I had heard reports against Mr. John Beardsley to the effect that he was unchaste," Boalt conceded, adding, "I did not know of any fact to justify the charge." He could say only one thing for sure: "I knew he did not live pleasantly with his wife." Actually, he did not live with his wife at all. She left him (and their seventeen-year-old daughter) while he was away on a New York buying trip in June 1848—clearly the event that prompted the July credit report. Mary Beardsley moved in with her sister's family around the corner, yet six months later she still had not filed for divorce. The agency's prediction remained unfulfilled when her husband confronted Tappan in New York in November 1848. The only complaint filed that month was John's—against Tappan, for libel.[28]

Soon after, the stale prediction became "undoubtedly true." *Mary Beardsley v. John Beardsley* was filed in Huron County Court on 5 December 1848. She accused him of affairs with seven women, including a mother-daughter pair; Elizabeth Beardsley (Horace's wife); and Mrs. Ezra M. Stone, the wife of John's divorce lawyer. John denied "each and every charge of adultry [*sic*]." Ultimately, this was not a case of "he said, she said"—but rather "he said, it said." The husband and the agency both gathered depositions about the wife and her intentions. Divorce testimony dominated the libel trial—as if the truth about John Beardsley and the truth about Lewis Tappan's reports depended on the truth about Mary.[29]

All agreed: it was a bad match. An agency witness said, "I knew his wife and daughter well; there was a difficulty between him and his wife for some years"—twenty years, according to Mary's siblings, who testified on behalf of John. Mary's brother, Charles Rutherford, said that the couple left Massachusetts because she "had fits of phrensy (for I can call them nothing else)" whenever other women spoke to John, "and would call them whores and strumpets." New to Norwalk in 1833, they boarded with Cornelia Mason, who told how John ran an errand on horseback and met "a company of young ladies riding in the same direction." They were "respectable" maids, but Mary cursed John ("You smooth-faced devil") and "commenced beating her head violently against the wall." When he intervened, "she struck him about his head repeatedly." He pointed out a scar on his forearm where Mary had stabbed him; she announced, "I wish it had been in your heart." The landlady told John to leave his wife, saying they would never be happy together.[30]

Scenes from a marriage revealed a trying but lasting union that had neither impelled divorce nor injured John's local credit. Neighbors often heard Mary drive him from the house: "Now you can go out and see Mrs. Stone and Mrs. Beardsley" (the lawyer's wife and Horace's). On such nights, John would "sleep at the store, on a pile of sheeting on the counter" rather than ask for shelter. But the testimony revealed injuries deeper than social embarrassments. Clerk Sam Skinner met his boss "coming to the store one morning with a black eye." Another time, he saw Mrs. Beardsley strike her husband, "to provoke [him] to defend himself." He "always put up with it," to his clerk's dismay. "I thought at that time a good whipping would do her good." No idle metaphor, wife-beating was all but legal in 1848; states began to criminalize it during the next decade. But Skinner's boss never lifted a finger when "she would lose all control of herself . . . in a perfect phrensy." He only "requested me after I had witnessed these scenes, not to mention them." Rutherford agreed. "I have seen his face marked . . . his eyes black in two or three instances," he testified, although his brother-in-law tried "to conceal these things, and not make them public."[31]

So why did Beardsley reveal these stories at the Tappan trial?

Why tell degrading secrets to refute a libel? Federal court would bring far more exposure than divorce court. To fight a "private memorandum book" that linked his standing as an economic partner to his standing as a domestic one, he opened the books on his troubled marriage. In line with contemporary beliefs that market and home were separate but closely linked spheres, this man and wife became a study in contrasts: she hysterical, he unflappable. "He has treated his family with kindness, and provided for them well," said Mary's sister, Catherine Lapham. Her husband, Stephen, agreed, saying, "I believe it would be impossible for any man to live with her any great length of time in peace." John kept trying to do just that for twenty years. Testimonials to his integrity as a husband exhibited traits the agency said he lacked as a businessman. Who would not extend credit to one who honored his contacts so faithfully—even a marriage contract that was evidently a losing bargain? Predictions of a final break invited the obvious rebuttal: *Reports of my divorce have been greatly exaggerated.*[32]

Nothing backed this claim more than what happened in divorce court. Sebastian F. Taylor, a longtime judge and legislator from nearby Milan, represented Mary. Oddly reluctant to prosecute, it came out that he had never met his client. Deposed by John's lawyer, Taylor admitted, "I saw a lady that was called Mrs. Beardsley some time ago"—*two years* ago. Did she hire him by mail? No, "I was spoken to." By whom? "It was a man"—someone in Norwalk. His occupation? "I can answer no question tending to show his identity." Was it "the Reporter of Lewis Tappan's Commercial Agency"? Taylor knew nothing of that firm. How did he know for certain that the envoy really spoke for Mrs. Beardsley? Her lawyer replied, "I have no positive knowledge that she did authorize him." When the divorce was heard in June 1849, Taylor withdrew straightaway, explaining that his client "refuses further to prosecute."[33]

Such irregularities fueled John's theory that Mary had been used as a pawn to change libel into truth. Why had Mary waited six months, then promptly sued for divorce after John's libel complaint? Why had she never appeared in court at any time? Not one word of her own went "on the books" to tell her side of it all. Yet a suit she had no part in—her husband's against Lewis Tappan—exposed her private business more intimately than any ledger. "Mrs. John Beardsley" in the documents was neither a "true woman" nor a real one. She was *represented* in both legal and literary senses—by an anonymous informant, by a lawyer she never met, by an agency that disclosed a wife's business to discredit a husband's, and even by a spouse who confessed insanity (hers) to deny insolvency (his). Betrayed wife or hysterical pawn? When debate focused on who really initiated the divorce, no one—neither her husband, nor her family, nor the agency—ever suggested that it was Mary Beardsley herself.[34]

The Privilege of Privacy

The libel trial uncovered a genuine conundrum: the emerging conflict between the businessman's need to buy and sell confidential information and the individual's desire to control access to his private business. Charging the jury after nearly a month of argument, Judge Betts began, "The time occupied by this trial may seem disproportionate," yet it posed "a question of importance to the commercial community." How to balance the benefits and drawbacks of modern ingenuity? "This agency saves expense, and tends to promote the business of the country," but did it show "sufficient regard for the rights of others?" Legal privilege forgave good faith but not malicious error, he explained. Was it malice to keep circulating reports after receiving notice of mistakes? The defense conceded that the agency was unable to prove its facts. Yet having failed to deliver the truth, it withheld the source of a lie. Tappan exposed Beardsley's secrets but expected to keep his own. Betts pointed out that "secret establishments are invidious in their nature. These agencies are increasing. They may soon be conducted by men of no responsibility, and unable to respond to damages. The feature of secrecy must be guarded as not to infringe on the rights of others." Thus charged, the jury awarded the Beardsleys $10,000 damages on 17 December 1851.[35]

"HEAVY DAMAGES," proclaimed the *New-York Times*. A trade paper declared "the perfect justice of the verdict," adding that John Beardsley "appear[ed] 'more sinned against than sinning'" in both his commercial and private life. The *Norwalk Experiment* reported the local man's moral and legal victory over "the New York Secret Agency Association" under the headline "A Righteous Verdict—$10,000 damages!"[36]

"It is a most unrighteous verdict," Lewis Tappan wrote in his diary. The agency, not he, would have to pay the fine if it ever came to that; but, ever the moralist, he objected that "a most unprincipled man, as I believe, has succeeded thus far in obtaining a verdict to wh[ich] he is not justly entitled." Tappan was among the few who actually knew whom to blame. "The Correspondent, whose name we would not disclose, has behaved either corruptly or foolishly." Firing off a letter to him, Tappan complained that the truth defense hinged upon "what you asserted over & over again could be proved," adding that "the whole matter is involved in such mystery that you must satisfy me that you acted correctly." Tappan expected fast communication. After a week, having received no response, he sent a warning: "If you do not reply to this promptly & satisfactorily, I shall consider that you consent to my disclosing your name."[37]

John Beardsley had already disclosed the name on this letter: Jairus Kennan, Esq. John's divorce rebuttal spent two paragraphs on Mary and two *pages* on a conspiracy theory. "Jairus Kennan, of Norwalk," he wrote, "is the secret informer and correspondent of the said Tappan in Huron County." Beardsley charged that Kennan and Tappan "employed counsel and caused a petition for divorce to be filed . . . getting up a foul record to be used by them on the trial of the . . . suits for libel." Kennan was an obvious choice for a local correspondent. A lawyer, he was also mayor in 1848—and a sometime Commissioner of Insolvents, school board clerk, Whig committeeman, and master in chancery (in which office he sometimes foreclosed on Beardsley's land speculations). Kennan's brother, John, had gone broke in a silkworm scheme endorsed by Beardsley. Jairus himself (like Tappan) had failed in dry goods, going bust while Beardsley went ahead. Kennan married better, to a sister of the town banker, by whose grace theirs was Norwalk's *second*-best Greek revival house. She had the money, he had the blood. Senior deacon at First Presbyterian, he came from a line of New England Scots longer than his patriarch's whiskers or the pew their eight children filled at three services on Sunday. Tappan could not have found a better surrogate or keener watchman. Not for nothing did Kennan's many hats include the secretariat of the "Huron County Horse-Thief Detecting Society."[38]

Tappan's threat drew two apologies from Kennan; although Kennan's letters have not survived, Tappan's response suggested their contents. "The suits, as it appears, should not have affected the credit of H. B. & Co. at all," Tappan wrote. "John Beardslee's putting his property into his brother's hands was not an act to impair the credit of the firm." Tappan mentioned "Mrs. B's communication to you," noting that only Kennan and an associate had known of her plans. If so, divorce rumors had *not* swept Norwalk before New York reports filtered back. "The circumstances attending its commencement—the date—the non appearance of Mrs. B. &c: appeared to the Jury here," he added, "as if my Cor[respondent] had invented what he reported & after wards tried to fulfill his predictions at Norwalk. The information you produced was, in my judgment, wholly insufficient to justify the report you made." Refuting Kennan point by point left only one question: "If J. B., is, as you represented him how can it be that so many persons in various & respectable positions, testified so strongly in his favor?" The letter makes clear that Tappan and Kennan were not in cahoots.[39]

And yet Lewis Tappan *did* conspire against Beardsley. If "the information" that Tappan got from Kennan was not true of Beardsley, neither was the notation in Tappan's diary: "a most unprincipled man . . . not justly entitled." Falsely reported, denied a correction and his accuser's name, rumored from New York to Norwalk, defamed for three more years, and put to the cost and shame of a suit, "J. B." had been wronged. Soon after the verdict, Edwin T. Freedley condoned "the generally just prejudices against these agencies." His popular 1852 business manual warned of errors in the system: "all who believe in the golden rule should watch it with the most jealous scrutiny." Untrue equaled un-Christian, in Freedley's view (perhaps a dig at Tappan's famous piety), judging others by means "subject to the errors of ignorance and mistakes of carelessness, with no guaranteed exemption from the influence of private malice, favoritism, bribery, or corruption." Instead of owning up, Tappan and his heirs covered up. They buried the truth, shielded Kennan to his grave, and appealed "a righteous verdict" for twenty years.[40]

In 1867, a federal judge rejected a retrial motion from R. G. Dun & Co. (née the Mercantile Agency), writing that to broaden legal privilege abetted "an organized system of espionage and inquisition"—and echoing old polemics word for word. The Beardsley case upheld, the *New-York Times* editorialized, doomed the "immense establishments, with numerous corps of clerks and with long rows of desks on which lay numbers of immense volumes in which could be learned a story, true or false, of every merchant in any part of the country whatever." Abiding fears of evil twins—bureaucracy and secrecy—made Beardsley's conspiracy theory plausible to a judge and jury shown no hard evidence. Possibility outweighed probability. After a quarter-century, a profitable and powerful firm was still fighting for life. Without privilege for its "numerous corps of clerks" and "immense volumes," the information system would shut down. In 1870, the U.S. Supreme Court reviewed *Beardsley v. Tappan*—now called *Tappan v. Beardsley*. The erstwhile defendant—at age eighty-three, a "testy, vigorous, obstinate, intrepid old man," according to his obituary eighteen months later—became "plaintiff in error" when R. G. Dun & Co. challenged flaws in the 1851 trial. When

Hundreds of patrons, messenger boys, and an "army of clerks" confer at the Mercantile Agency's high desks in 1875. (Special Collections Research Center, University of Chicago Library.)

the Supreme Court heard oral arguments in 1870, the *Brooklyn Eagle* scoffed, "We seem to want the dead Dickens brought to life again, and another such novel as 'Bleak House,' . . . founded on the real case of Tappan vs. Beardsley." Running down the particulars, and calling the Mercantile Agency "a sort of volunteer espionage of other people's business," the *Eagle* could not resist evoking Dickensian nightmares of immense files and armies of clerks.[41]

"An army of clerks! Yes, there is an army of clerks," boomed Charles O'Conor in the great chamber; "but like all other armies, they are disciplined and regulated." It was 16 December 1870, nineteen years (minus a day) since the verdict—and decades before William Morris and Max Weber immortalized the phrase "armies of clerks" as shorthand for bureaucratic capitalism. O'Conor hailed Dun's army as the vanguard of modernity, "acting in great haste, and with mighty machinery and vast 'bureaus,' as my learned friends on the other side suggest." Beardsley's team battled "this monster—this Mercantile Agency," as if central archives and surveillance networks equated to "an instrument of mischief." In that light, the divorce depositions cast "Mr. Tappan as a thorough fiend," directing a regime of truth. O'Conor presented this as the main issue. Nobody liked a tattler, "particularly the tattler for pay," he granted. "It is easy to excite disgust against this business on the ground of 'espionage,'" yet "so far as it may be conducted discreetly and properly, without any undue violation of private rights, [it] is not in itself criminal or mischievous; nay, it is necessary." Modern enterprise required choices between "private rights" and commercial privilege. Information was an essential commodity, and *Beardsley* was "a stumbling block in the path of a useful pursuit, a barrier against progress."[42]

The high court vacated *Beardsley* in January 1871, on narrow grounds. Associate Justice Samuel F. Miller's opinion held that the divorce testimony tainted the libel trial; "the record of a suit is not evidence in another suit against one who is not a party to it." The court was silent on privilege versus privacy, but two members were already on record against the firm. Justice Samuel Nelson had denied the 1867 retrial bid, and Chief Justice Salmon P. Chase's qualms were as old as the agency. Recruited by Tappan in 1842, Chase declined: "I entertain as you know doubts respecting the propriety of furnishing such information. We may mislead—and on the other hand we may be instrumental in doing unintentionally, great injustice." Neither Chase nor Nelson recused; possibly they swayed their brethren to rule on procedure rather than principle. Two days before the decision, the agency was indicted for libel in Philadelphia, where a judge wrote: "its operations are secret; everything is sent out under the garb of confidence, and thus the poisoned arrows which are launched in darkness, may strike down the purest and most solvent in the land; no business man is safe, if this can be recognized and protected by the law as a privileged communication." The high court granted only a new trial, which Beardsley never pursued.[43]

Who is a failure? The question weighed public shame against

private pain. The answers weighed privacy against information. An 1876 book castigated the agency system as "an enterprise which possesses *the coercive power of rating every man in the community as its managers or clerks may see fit.*" Federal courts ruled in 1882 that credit reports were privileged communications (with a caveat against the agencies' *"meddlesomeness")* and gave them copyright protection in 1896. The law defined information as the property of the seller, not the buyer or the subject of a report. The strange case of John and Mary Beardsley raised early alarms about modern problems: the ordeal of arguing with an information system, the arrogance of bureaucratic error, the scope of commercial surveillance in public and private life, and the obstacles to limiting (or even learning) who knows what about you. Worries over what's in "your permanent record" (compiled by others) began over 150 years ago. "The lines of communication are now so perfected, that the movements of every trader within the bounds of the United States are chronicled with astonishing expedition," an agency critic noted in *Hunt's* in 1853, two years after the Beardsley verdict. "Your character, from such a source, is circulated by post and telegraph, east, west, north, south; while you are pursuing the equal tenor of your life, you have become notorious for something. A thousand folios include a page or more about you and your affairs, without your knowledge or consent."[44]

The Tanner's Revenge

Beardsleys' emporium yet stands in a landmarked row at Main and South Linwood in Norwalk, Ohio. Nearby at 115 West Main, a local history plaque marks an 1845 cottage. More survivor than showplace, it gave no ground when Victorian behemoths took over the street. John bought it when he remarried in 1865—nine years after divorcing Mary. Consumption ended Mary's trials in 1881, the summer after the second Mrs. Beardsley's fatal fall on the ice. Whiskey got Horace; hurt on a spree, he died a one-legged pauper in the county asylum in 1886. Almost eighty by then, John "became something of a recluse and a miser," at least in the eyes of a girl who still remembered him (and his link to Aaron Burr) in 1938. He died of "mouth cancer" on April Fool's Day 1887. Horace and John lie in unmarked graves in the old burying ground at St. Paul's Episcopal, maybe near their father's tall slab. Mary is lost in Woodlawn, across town. The registry puts her in perpetual indignity beside John's second wife on Lot 253— but Mary's tombstone dominates Lot 287. The obelisk is scarred by a century of acid rain, but a rubbing still resurrects the word "Mother." Nothing else remains of this family in local lore; memory corrodes even faster than marble.[45]

Another family monument rots in the catacombs of a Harvard library. Ohio credit volume 101, once elegant in sheepskin, now rusts irrevocably. The same airborne pollutants found in acid rain react with the sulfuric acid in its bindings. After 1850, new chemicals tanned faster and cheaper, but produced inferior leather. "Red rot" eats most of R. G. Dun's ledgers; call it the tanner's revenge, for Billings of Maine, whom the agency routed in 1854.[46]

Touch volume 101 and you draw blood: crimson platelets stain your hands. But open it, and the ragstock is bright and supple. Scattered leaves follow a family for thirty-three years. Horace Beardsley retired in 1865. His brother took a new partner to brew beer and sold dry goods alone. John got rich on lager and lace, then lost 60 to 90 percent of his assets. In 1869, the informant protested that R. G. Dun & Co. lowered his appraisals of Beardsley: "Has not been rated high Enough as to pecuniary strength. He is wor[th] more than 25 [thousand]." Dun raised him a notch, but not to its reporter's 1871 estimate of $75,000 net worth. John lost nothing in the panic of 1873 but had only $8,000 in autumn 1878, when a clerk wrote the last word about him, on page 372. Volume 101 omitted a fact advertised elsewhere. The Supreme Court made the loser pay the winner's lawyers—"probably $20,000 in costs." John Beardsley died broke. Company brochures made an example of him, to "any person contemplating proceedings against the agency."[47]

And Jairus Kennan? Dead in 1872, at age fifty-nine, his misinformation shaped our world, setting off legal wars that upheld a new order of business. During the Beardsley ruckus, Jairus's nephew studied law with him, 1847 to 1851. Thomas Kennan never forgot his mentor's "strict honesty and integrity," and at age ninety, Thomas taught family values and stories to a bright grandson. By this short mentoring chain, part of old Uncle Jairus left for Princeton in 1921 with George F. Kennan, whose Cold War diplomacy remapped the world. The July 1947 issue of *Foreign Affairs* featured his plan for the American strategy of Soviet "containment"—a memorandum signed only "X." A century before, in July 1848, a secret correspondent's report appeared in "the private memorandum book" of a central intelligence agency. The anonymous missives of Jairus Kennan and his great-grandnephew were not causally linked, of course—few men (and fewer uncles) cast that long a shadow. Yet each helped build a subterranean America of covert agents, classified files, and blacklists—a culture of "trust but verify" in which failure was unthinkable.[48]

More than a family tree, this genealogy traced a new branch of American freedom. What Thoreau called "an Intelligence Office for the whole country" arose amid battles over individual rights, from Jacksonian Democracy to the Civil War and Reconstruction. Self-determination was the heart of antebellum hostilities and the soul of postwar hopes. Fair access to credit meant freedom or unfreedom for African-American and poor white sharecroppers. Credit was literally seed money in that context, as it was figuratively in commerce. Pass the agent's tests and your name went into a registry of commercial citizenship that granted access to a vital tool of self-determination. Advancing this nineteenth-century ideal, the agency's red book undercut a freedom of the twentieth: the right to privacy. Samuel Warren and Louis Brandeis outlined it in the *Harvard Law Review* in 1890—the same year a credit agent's manual, *Whom to Trust,* detailed his own "inquisitorial functions" and remarked, "it is paradoxical, the free citizen of the United States is the only one on the face of the globe

"*A Chain of Offices Embracing a Continent,*" in the logo of the
North American Mercantile Agency, asserted the power of commercial surveillance in post–Civil War society. With its patriotic post-
mark and map of the nation, this 1898 envelope seemed to herald a
new order of American enterprise. (Author's collection.)

who tolerates it." Paradox is the taproot of American freedom: we
have often sold the souls of others to buy our own.[49]

Rumors of Men, Rumors of War

How could one know the soul of a stranger when it was so hard to
know oneself or bosom relations? If John Beardsley was the intelligence agency's constant legal antagonist, its cultural antithesis
was embodied by its strange visitor of 1843: Henry Thoreau. "We
falsely attribute to men a determined character—putting together
all their yesterdays—and averaging them—we presume to know
them," he wrote in 1841. Yet the narrator of *Walden* called himself
a "reporter," and he logged two million words in forty-seven journals. He painstakingly indexed and cross-referenced his notebooks, believing that such methods aided unconventional thinking—about wild apples, wild hogs, wild men, or his wild idea that
individualism meant more than conventional choices between

success and failure. "It is hard to know men by rumor only," he complained. He hated how commerce sorted people by price and grade, yet his own creativity owed much to information management. Thoreau had become a credit reporter, after all.[50]

If Lewis Tappan and Henry Thoreau never again crossed paths, they had a mutual acquaintance who declared bankruptcy in 1842. A failed surveyor, farmer, speculator, schoolteacher, tanner, and cattleman, he showed up as a wool dealer in an 1848 credit report: "his condition is questionable." Winter 1849: "may or may not be good." Summer 1850: "his means are equally obscure." Still in his forties, he looked sixty to credit reporters. The agency lost him when he switched lines of work yet again, only to fail yet again. Like many another misfit who pushed a doomed venture too far, he quit when he had no other choice. Having grown whiskers for the first time, his craggy face looked still more ancient. Everyone had an opinion of this broken man. "Served him right." Overhearing such comments, Thoreau said he felt proud even to know him and questioned why people "talk as if a man's death were a failure, and his continued life, be it of whatever character, were a success." The bankrupt court had restored this loser's freedom in 1842. Now it was 1859, and no earthly court could save John Brown after his failure at Harper's Ferry.[51]

7   The War for Ambition

One summer afternoon in 1864, U.S. representative Thomas A. Jenckes urged "emancipation" for all Union soldiers who wore a mantle of oppression under their blue tunic. "What to them are the guarantees of the Constitution?" he asked the House. Their loyalty had been repaid with grim choices: "to lay their bones upon the battle-fields, or to return to a life-long servitude." Had they not earned legal freedom? If given "the opportunity of liberating themselves from their bondage," these men could "walk free in the exercise of those rights which the immortal Declaration declares inalienable." Jenckes, a Lincoln Republican from Rhode Island, left no doubt that Congress could take such a bold step. "The power to make this declaration of freedom stands written upon the face of the Constitution," he asserted. By 1864, freeing the slaves and saving the union had become a single objective for Abraham Lincoln, whose "new birth of freedom" meant the universal chance to better oneself. How would "the right to rise" redefine the risk of failure? This question is what drove Jenckes's attack on "life-long servitude"—since he spoke not for "Colored troops" but for white men held in "the bondage of debt."[1]

Jenckes's plan to free men in debt became the first comprehensive bankruptcy law in American history, the Act of 1867, which surmounted the politics of failure by invoking the Civil War legacies of abolition and ambition. Debtors neither bled like chattel slaves nor belied the terms of the Constitution, which charged Congress to make "uniform Laws on the subject of Bankruptcies." And yet, between 1787 and 1865, the stopgap laws of 1800 and 1841 lasted a total of barely four years. Bankruptcy and slavery met similar obstacles on the dead-end roads of antebellum politics. People in slavery were presumed incapable of moral responsibility; such was a white man's burden, a set of obligations that supposedly made unpaid debts inescapable. Freeing slaves divested masters of legal property, and discharging debtors stripped creditors of the fruits of legal contracts. Bankruptcy and abolition posed taboo questions: could the federal government narrow property rights to expand civil rights; and if so, should it? The two controversies intersected in theory and chronology. The panic of 1819 introduced a new order of economic crisis; the Missouri Compromise of 1820, a new era of political crisis. Secession in April 1861 induced cessation in May—debtors on both sides quit paying enemy creditors, ruining thousands. The Emancipation Proclamation of 1863 gave impetus to the bankruptcy bill of 1864. "Men ruined by the war" had begun to make noise about a debtors' uprising when Jenckes's "bondage of debt" speech hit the papers on June 1.[2]

A congressman made an unlikely Spartacus, even for rhetorical bondsmen, yet Jenckes's words rallied an army of debtors. "Allow me," one wrote on 6 June, "in behalf of the *thousands* . . . bound down with a bondage worse than slavery, to thank you for your efforts to release them through the medium of the bankrupt law." Overnight, the smallest state's freshman representative had a national constituency, whose letters brought individual voices of failure into federal politics. Metaphoric bondage couched their fears in racist jealousy, lest they be left behind when the war ended. In December 1864, a week after the completion of Sherman's march to the sea, an Ohioan looked toward Union victory "with grateful Emotions for your Efforts to Emancipate the *white slaves.*" If the politician spoke their language, he shared little else with his followers. Thomas A. Jenckes was property interests incarnate, a major industrial patent lawyer born into a century-old political and commercial dynasty. Friends joked that he had nary a wild hair in his long black beard. No rabble-rouser, neither was he a race-baiter. Ten days before the Emancipation Proclamation, he asked Lincoln to permit Rhode Island to recreate "her colored regiment in the war of independence." Arguing for Negro troops, Jenckes equated "the earnestness and efficiency of this race, as of the white race." Arguing for debtors, he intended the war to deliver both races from economic and social tyranny. Even so, how could anyone liken white debtors to black slaves?[3]

Emancipation inflamed such comparisons, but Civil War bankrupts sang an old song. Eighteenth-century whites complained of "the thralldom of debt," in spendthrift Thomas Jefferson's words. *Poor Richard's Almanack for 1758* quoth, "The Borrower is a Slave to the Lender, and the Debtor to the Creditor"—not to mention the thief, since Ben Franklin cribbed from Proverbs 22:7, "the borrower is servant to the lender." King James's servant became Poor Richard's slave—a glib revision, but a rude reminder of how far the colonies were from England, where slavery was only a concept. British lords lambasted the "thraldom of debt" in treatises about political economy, but in 1767 one in twelve Philadelphians was enslaved. Similar ratios held in Manhattan, Boston, and Rhode Island (a hub of the triangular slave trade). The familiar sight of the cat-o'-nine-tails made it easy to imagine being "strapped for cash." The founders also knew the republican precedents of Greece and Rome, which had condemned debtors to slavery. Feeling abused by king and Parliament, Virginians and Bostonians shared a metaphor: "Let Us not be enslaved." "We won't be their Negroes." These catcalls came not from the filthy maw of an overseer but from the Yankee pen of John Adams. At Valley Forge, General Washington ordered his army back to "the great work of rescuing our Country from Bondage" as spring approached on 1 March 1778.[4]

Four days earlier, sixteen-year-old Prince Jenks joined the First Rhode Island regiment (the state's "colored regiment," in the Civil War lawmaker's words). A *real* slave, his life denied white rhetoric yet hinted why slavery and debt became twin antebellum crises. Born in Guinea in 1761, he endured the "middle passage" aboard a slaver (perhaps Captain Silas Jencks's voyage of 1770) to a shore called Providence. By 1778, John Jenks Esq. owned the African, Prince. The master drew £36 state redress after the slave marched to war with little but a surname and a snare drum. In 1781 at Yorktown, N.Y., the drummer boy watched as loyalists "inhumanely butchered about fifteen" comrades and their white colonel in racist fury. Captured and exchanged, he survived Saratoga but lost a leg in 1783. He went home a free man, to the pauper's workhouse. Peg-legged and indebted by 1786, he took to sea until his army pension kicked in on 4 March 1789—the day the U.S. Constitution took effect—granting him bounty land and $60 a year. The first U.S. Census counted "Prince Jenks (Negro)" among the heads of families, and listed him with three dependents. He died at the age of forty in June 1801, shortly after Jefferson took office and outlined the American Dream: "our equal right to the use of our own faculties, to the acquisitions of our own industry, to honor and confidence from our fellow-citizens, resulting not from birth, but from our actions and their sense of them."[5]

A former bondsman and a future congressman, Prince Jenks and Thomas Jenckes belonged (in very different senses) to one family. Slaveholding and trading had contributed to the affluence and influence Thomas inherited. Born in 1818, he probably never heard the name "Prince Jenks (Negro)," but it stood for millions caught in freedom's paradoxes. Homeless and voteless, what made a crippled Negro free? Jenks consummated his liberty by doing as only free men could do: make contracts—hire himself out, run up debts, try to meet them. To repay £19, he gave a creditor power of attorney to garnish his pension. This surrender of autonomy hardly made Jenks "a Slave to the Lender," but it epitomized why his white kinsmen feared debt. More important, the career of this slave, freeman, soldier, pauper, sailor, pensioner, and householder showed why Americans could not conquer that fear. Whites fancied themselves slaves when unable to pay, forgetting that to incur liability in the first place was a privilege of freedom. To be sure, a privilege was not the same as a choice, and keeping out of debt was never easy. But what could be done to lessen a burden that was also a birthright?[6]

Social Death and Political Suicide

In ancient and modern times, debt servitude differed from lifelong or hereditary "true slavery." The contrast appeared in the masthead of the *Forlorn Hope,* published weekly in 1800 by debtors at New York Gaol. Above the motto "LIBERTY SUSPENDED BUT WILL BE RESTORED," a white man in rags stood beside a half-naked black man on his knees: an antislavery icon often accompanied by the slogan "Am I Not a Man and a Brother?" Chained together, a standing debtor and a kneeling slave were both pariahs; but only one was property. The common denominator of slavery in different societies, however, was not ownership of people but power over them. Legal systems varied, but many cultures saw slavery as social death. It buried self and will but spared the body. Failed white men imagined bondage in this sense: not as living chattel, but as social death. Debt meant dependency, a pox on republican manhood, which equated civic virtue with propertied autonomy. "I am enthrald in debt and I am far distant from any friend," a stranger wrote to Thomas Jefferson in 1807; "the galling yoke of bondage I may justly term it, for no one is at Liberty that is in my condition." Might the president lend him $300? (No.) The price of his freedom marked this debtor as no slave in 1807: that year Congress banned human importation from Africa and domestic prices soared. Liberty was cheap at $300; a prime Negro man cost at least twice as much.[7]

A "galling yoke" befit oxen and Africans but not citizens—a new status for many white men. Property criteria kept half from voting in 1787. All but three states had ended or eased such rules by 1821, but political rights hardly ensured economic justice. The Bankruptcy Act of 1800 seemed of, by, and for enterprising Federalists. Aristocratic speculators like Robert Morris (signer of the Declaration of Independence and the Constitution) got out of debtor's prison, but the law excluded traders who owed less than $1,000 as well as farmers and artisans. Once Jeffersonians repealed the law in 1803, its folly was never to be repeated, come war, plague, or panic. Handbills posted in 1812 pronounced bankrupts "politically dead," "no longer recognized as a citizen of the community . . . doomed to slavery, misery, and bondage for life." Not even the panic of 1819 persuaded Congress that "the debtor and his family have been condemned to slavery." From Jeffersonians and Federalists to Jacksonians and Whigs, bankruptcy reform fell between agrarian and commercial visions of a nation ruled by weak or strong government. In 1822, the sponsor of a doomed Federalist bill asked, "If such a power be given . . . by the Constitution is it immoral or unjust to exercise it? Hitherto we have only been looking at the rights and interests of creditors, forgetting that the unfortunate debtor is also a citizen; that *he* has rights, which we are bound to consider and respect." Epic feuds loomed over just whose rights Americans were "bound to . . . respect."[8]

White slaves, wage slaves, debt slaves: specters of dependent manhood proliferated after 1820. Trade unionists co-opted the slavery metaphor from their employers, the debtor classes of manufacturers and merchants. Whatever the context, in one historian's words, "a term like *white slavery* was not an act of solidarity with the slave but rather a call to arms to end the inappropriate oppression of whites." Philadelphia citizens said as much in an

1821 petition to Congress: "The poor African, . . . devoid of the intellectual torments which are produced by dependence and subjection, to a mind nurtured in the habits of liberty and intelligence, stands on ground far more enviable than that maintained by the insolvent debtor." This sort of talk moved creditors no more than the rhetoric of wage slavery kept union busters from saying that anyone could walk away from exploitation; supposedly, suffrage and freedom of contract were all the protection men needed. Stuff and nonsense, given the workingman's lot, and such fictions wore even thinner with debtors who believed their freedom of contract had lapsed. But getting Congress to act on bankruptcy meant defying constitutional orthodoxies. White debtors need not have felt "solidarity with the slave" to pray for reforms that might also undermine chattel slavery.[9]

As early as 1798, failed white men decried both "debt and personal slavery," standing with African Americans as orphans of the Constitution. Debtors were among the earliest Fourth of July protesters, seizing that day to declare their lost independence. An 1828 book, *The Patriot; or, People's Companion* (by "One of the People") urged abolition of debtors' prison: "this sort of *civil slavery*" must not "remain a foul blot upon the pages of our Code, no more tha[n] African slavery under the protection of the constitution." Federal and state reforms all but outlawed debtors' prison by 1839, but throughout the antebellum period, "our Code" remained a maze of state codes. Insolvency laws paroled honest debtors too broke to pay, unlocking the body without undoing the debt. Bankruptcy voided debts but usually covered only "traders" (merchants and others subject to commercial risk). Eligibility and household exemptions varied by state, as did the voluntary or compulsory nature of proceedings. Legal chaos perpetuated "Civil slavery," but so did order. In 1819, the Supreme Court upheld states' rights to legislate debt, but not *retrospectively*: no law could "impair the obligation of contracts" sealed before its passage. An 1827 case barred states from canceling debts in other states. To anyone with old debts or distant creditors, the Court was a rock and Congress a hard place. "As the States cannot, and the United States will not, relieve him," one senator explained, "even his personal liberty [is] at the will of his creditors."[10]

Some in Congress lacked political will; others doubted the meaning of "uniform Laws on the subject of Bankruptcies throughout the United States." Could discharge be for traders alone if "uniform Laws" meant the same for everyone? If it meant uniform "throughout the United States," then what of states' sovereignty? An 1822 petition to Congress from Charleston, South Carolina, blamed mismatched state laws for the debtor's "species of bondage," warning that inaction on bankruptcy would "destroy confidence between the citizens of the different states . . . foment sectional animosities, and . . . weaken their union." The South had always been "a debtor region" (where human chattel could be seized by a master's creditors), but now its leaders perceived a greater evil. In 1826, Senator John Randolph of Roanoke criticized "a centripetal force" in the bankruptcy power. A Georgian warned that states "would no longer have the right of controlling their own citizens, or the property within their limits." Southern debtor interests came second behind concerns about federal authority over property based on the notion of states' rights. Supreme Court Justice Joseph Story's seminal *Commentaries on the Constitution of the United States* (1833) held that federal power "to relieve the unfortunate and meritorious debtor from a slavery of mind and body" overrode the duty to defend property and enforce contracts. After 1837, Story's opinions inspired another bill for those who "find themselves bondsmen," Daniel Webster scolded the Senate, "because we will not execute the commands of the Constitution."[11]

Such rhetoric coming from antislavery New Englanders like Webster and Story antagonized Southerners, who tarred the bill with the odium of abolition. "We have no constitutional or moral right to pass . . . a law for the abolition of debts," roared Thomas Hart Benton in 1841, "calculated to free debtors from their creditors." Benton, slaveholder and master of the Senate, spat out "abolition of debts" like the Missouri tongue-lasher he was. A bushy-haired, barrel-chested, hard-money Democrat dubbed "Old Bullion," he had once shot Andrew Jackson in an 1813 duel but came to Old Hickory's defense in the 1830s. When the Senate censured the president, Bentonian bullying got the vote expunged from the record books. Comparatively, bankruptcy was a minor Jacksonian battlefront. The administration pitied honest insolvents but saw commercial bankruptcy as a special privilege for corporations and speculators: "the money power." Jackson left office weeks before the panic of 1837. Benton dug in until the Whigs took Congress and the presidency in 1840, ending Jacksonian rule. The Bankruptcy Act of 1841 narrowly passed the new Congress in its first session. In the second, Benton tried to stall implementation; in the final session, "the Great Expunger" persuaded two-thirds of his colleagues to vote for outright repeal. The nation's second bankruptcy law—the first in forty years—remained on the books only 562 days.[12]

Some later said—wrongly—that the 1841 act killed the Whig Party, yet the politics of bankruptcy did foreshadow the killing choices ahead: either some people would be deprived of physical and mental liberty or others must be deprived of property. By 1850, political economist Henry Carey discerned racial jealousy among failed entrepreneurs; "the time of Congress is so exclusively occupied by the *fugitive slave* bill . . . that there is no chance for considering the case of *fugitive freemen*," he wrote. "Everywhere men are seeing the day of their ruin approaching—they are hanging by the eyelids." Southerners pushed the point. George Fitzhugh's proslavery *Sociology for the South: Or, the Failure of Free Society* (1854) dared the North to see the "dark side" of its markets—not only the harm to free workers but also to entrepreneurs felled by cutthroat competition: "Those who rise, pull down a class as numerous, and often more worthy than themselves, to the abyss of misery and penury." Call them bondsmen or fugitive freemen, the social death of failure seemed incurable amid the

From the Globe.

WHITE SLAVERY!!

OR SELLING

WHITE MEN FOR DEBT!

—◦◦◦◦◦—

June 27, 1840.

We have received from Indianapolis a certified copy, under the 'broad seal' of the State of Indiana, of the 11th, 30th, and 31st sections of the act of 1807, approved by General Harrison, providing for the sale of white men and women in certain cases; and also the third section of an act regulating elections, approved in like manner, requiring a property qualification in voters for Representatives, &c. The copy is in the following words, viz:

AN ACT RESPECTING CRIMES AND PUNISHMENTS.

SEC. 11. If any person shall unlawfully assault or threaten another in any menacing manner, or shall strike or wound another, he shall, upon conviction thereof, be fined in a sum not exceeding one hundred dollars; and the court before whom such conviction shall be had, may, in their discretion, cause the offender to enter into recognizance with surety for the peace and good behaviour, for a term not exceeding one year.

SEC. 30. When any person or persons shall, on conviction of any crime or breach of any penal law, be sentenced to pay a fine or fines, with or without the costs of prosecution, it shall and may be lawful for the court, before whom such conviction shall be had, to order the sheriff to sell or hire the person or

---

This anti-Whig pamphlet from the 1840 presidential campaign portrayed small debtors at the mercy of commercial interests. ("White Slavery!! Or Selling White Men for Debt!" Lexington, Ky., 1840. Printed Ephemera Collection, Rare Book and Special Collections Division, Library of Congress.)

constitutional stalemate over *real* slavery. Bankruptcy awaited a consensus about federal power over property and states' rights that did not exist until the Age of Emancipation.[13]

A Beggars' Banquet at Delmonico's

Many traders had fresh scars from the bust of 1857 when the boom of 1861—at Fort Sumter—hit them again. Few bills got paid across enemy lines, and all but 16 of 256 New York dry goods firms went broke within a year. The "bankrupts of '61," according to R. G. Dun & Co., included almost 7,000 firms that owed more than $5,000 each. During the next four years, the patronizing line "no fault of their own" became patriotic, and people spoke of men being "ruined by the War." Many proprietors and breadwinners deserted firms and farms to join Union companies. In 1862, the *New-York Times* ran a plea for Congress to pass a stalled bankruptcy bill, "this great Emancipation measure for the liberation of white men." In January 1863, abolitionist Representative Owen Lovejoy declared, "As this is a year of jubilee to those literally enslaved, so let it be signalized by the disinthrallment of those who are entangled by pecuniary obligations." The antislavery *Independent* wrote the next year that "one hundred thousand good business men—mostly white men—are now in bondage, praying, at the doors of Congress, that their chains may be broken. They love freedom [as much as] black men." For decades, debtors and their political friends had urged the government to use the Constitution to make men free, only to see the Jubilee pass over them. "To President Lincoln," one citizen wrote in April 1864: "I am one of the victims who lost my property in the South and ask to be released from my shackles and try to recover myself." Lincoln no doubt recalled the mess created by the Bankruptcy Act of 1841, having handled many cases as a young lawyer. But as president, bankruptcy legislation hardly merited his attention. In 1864, unending war and unpopular emancipation threatened his reelection chances. Public opinion turned so sour that Lincoln tried to suppress a commentary written by the powerful editor Horace Greeley, which made reference to "our bleeding, bankrupt, almost dying country."[14]

Bankrupt citizens who had written to Lincoln and been ignored gladly turned their pens toward Thomas A. Jenckes when his legislation came up for debate in the winter and spring of 1864. For perhaps the first time, hundreds of losers got to tell their individual stories in the context of national politics. They wrote from Iowa, Illinois, Minnesota, Michigan, Ohio, Texas, Virginia, Maryland, Pennsylvania, New Jersey, New Hampshire, Maine. One of the first letters Jenckes received, in February, blathered on for three angry pages. "If the administration could *know* the *feelings* of the thousands who are tied in stronger chains than the Black man ever was, they would as a matter of policy (if not of justice) remove the shackles from off us," the writer argued. If Lincoln cared little about debtors, did he not require their entrepreneurship for the war effort? And with the election coming, did he not see them as a large voting bloc? Failed men lacked the coin to bribe the bill through, but "depend upon it . . . there will be an organization that will have power & one that will work with a will as we can use our *Brains* if we do not have *full purses.*" The letter was signed "George L. Cannon, Sect'y, National Bankrupt Association, Box 848," New York City.[15]

Could there really be a lobbyist for losers? Jenckes was a major patent lawyer, a member of one of the first groups to be vilified as "professional lobbyists" in the 1850s. But the letter at hand was hardly professional; its tone so bothered Jenckes that he sent it to McKillop's Commercial Agency in New York. "The organisation . . . is not 'secret,'" the agency reported back, but "the number and influence of the bankrupts of the U.S. ought not to be lost sight of. They are becoming exasperated and will be felt in some places by those who stand in the way of the passage of your bill." George L. Cannon turned out to be the ambitious son of a New Haven tinsmith. George had graduated from a private academy before coming to New York in 1852. Bankrolled by a Connecticut shipping magnate, he sold "Ranges & Furnaces," weathering the panic of 1857 and several warm winters, which were bad for business. A Democrat, he ran for city council in 1861 and drew 693 votes. Credit agents deemed him worth $10,000 before the war, but land speculation broke him in 1862. By 1864, Cannon was thirty-eight years old, with a wife, two small sons, a mother-in-law, a sister-in-law, and a niece to support—and he knew many like himself, men with little left but their votes. He wrote Jenckes, saying, "I cannot believe that any party are so foolish as to lose the lever which they have within their reach." And so he grabbed that lever himself.[16]

The National Bankrupt Association began recruiting in March 1864, luring would-be members to a well-advertised event at Delmonico's at Broadway and Chambers Street. The Manhattan eatery was famous for its 346 daily entrées and eye-popping prices (dinner for one cost $25!). But whoever brought his appetite to this beggar's banquet went hungry; all comers were pointed upstairs to a reserved meeting room. At least nobody would be able to tar them with the stereotype of the extravagant bankrupt. Cannon had a knack for such details, and for free publicity. He somehow got a letter stating the group's mission—"to exercise a controlling influence over the coming elections"—printed in the *New York Evening Post* with a favorable headline: "A Movement of the Bankrupts." Their anti-Lincoln agenda might have been quashed by the *Post*'s Republican editor, William Cullen Bryant, but for Cannon's acquaintance with him. Before going bankrupt, he had been the furnace man at 92 Hudson Street—Bryant's home. "The Press are speaking out plainly," Cannon notified Jenckes, "the Tribune to day & the Times & World are to follow—even the Bank Note reporters & the Banner of Light a spiritual paper have caught the fever." The lobbyist did all he could to turn up the heat during the next two years, promising that if the powers in Washington ignored his group, "there is a storm brewing that all their military power can not stop."[17]

Incendiary and flamboyant, George L. Cannon styled himself a rascal king: the ward boss of broken men. One of them wrote to Jenckes, "I can not sit waiting—silent & actionless while this movement is taking its initial steps." But it was Cannon himself who was the congressman's most faithful correspondent from 1864 to 1866, sending dozens of long missives. Becoming the man to see on his issue, Cannon fed squibs to the press, tallied likely votes in Congress, chased absent lawmakers back to Washington, led delegations to the Capitol, ran committees of correspondence "to reach every Bankrupt in the country," and helped set up new chapters of the National Bankrupt Association. His dogged efforts to collect funds for paying bribes ran afoul of Congressman (later President) James A. Garfield, who exposed "a money association having for its object the influencing of the passage of this bill." Cannon lay low for a week before resuming his "war upon those that keep us in chains." He seemed to know exactly which words carried the most political weight ("we are . . . *determined* to have our *rights*" was his constant cry) and to know exactly when to segue from rights talk to race-baiting. Lincoln's party would lose, he threatened, "if this administration refuse to grant us that which they do not refuse to the *meanest negro*."[18]

Whether Cannon incited or merely repeated such odium, many letters to Jenckes expressed the festering resentment Civil War bankrupts felt after emancipation. "I have passed Ten years in worse bondage than that of the black man at the South—more humiliating and degrading for I was no longer regarded as an equal amongst my old associates," a Philadelphian wrote, explaining that economic ruin had taken the equality and associations he expected as a white man. A New Yorker pleaded that "Congress emancipate from a slavery which to a high minded honest ambitious man is worse than that the poor African ever endured." Racist comparisons defined failure and rebuked the government for letting white men fall so low. Debt was the most abject form of bondage, as a letter from St. Louis explained this logic, because "the slavery of the colored man was upon one uneducated or refined." Hence, many letters articulated a fraternity of failure; ignominy and bigotry seemed to have bound together white men who imagined themselves "bound down." A Pittsburgh lawyer wrote that Jenckes's bill "would emancipate in this state at least many a man from the bondage of past debt, and put them in position to be of use to themselves, their families and society." Prevailing ideals of manhood prescribed not only that white men be free but also that they be useful to themselves and others. Another Philadelphian wrote, "Mine is not an *isolated case* but one among thousands, many of whom, had they the opportunity, might again become useful And enterprising Citizens that are now *cast down*, a burthen to their friends, and an incubus upon the Community."[19]

Such bromides sounded visceral, but they actually preserved careful distinctions between "the bondage of past debt" and "the slavery of the colored man." His servitude was perpetual, but "bondage" involved a contract and could, therefore, be revoked. When bankrupts complained about feeling useless, they meant that unpaid debts made them idle—kept them from starting again and making money to support their families or pay their creditors. By characterizing this as bondage or slavery, bankrupts used the language of enforced *labor* to describe a condition of enforced *idleness*. The image of an idle slave was, to say the least, an egregious oxymoron, one that drew upon insidious prejudices about the work habits of African Americans. Idle slavery made sense, however, to bankrupts worried about lost status, manhood, and economic freedom. "In common with thousands of others," a typical letter began, "I am living on the hope that Congress will break our chains and restore us to the activities and ambitions of life, ere it is—'too late'!" Melodramatically, the final words invoked the civic death long associated with slavery. Thomas Jenckes addressed this common fear in his speech of June 1864. "If hopeless insolvency be commercial death," he declared, "then the bankrupt laws open to the honest bankrupt freedom from his debts, and the road to a new commercial life."[20]

To the men who responded to Jenckes—and all but one of the

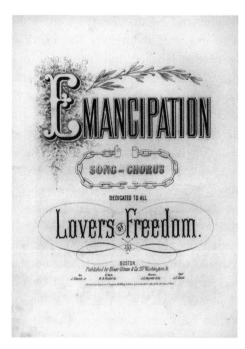

Meant to be sung "With Energy," this Civil War tune included the ecumenical lyric "A white slave or black, is a man for all that / Tho' the law may deny him his station / The birthright of all is to join in the call / For God and for E–man–ci–pa–tion." ("Emancipation: Song and Chorus," Boston, 1864. Alfred Whital Stern Collection of Lincolniana, Rare Book and Special Collections Division, Library of Congress.)

419 letters he received between 1864 and 1867 came from men— his legislation meant not only economic emancipation but a personal transformation as well. To an Albany leather merchant named Lott Frost, it promised that "we might be released from bondage and again Stand up and feel that we are men and be enable[d] to Engage in business and act like Men." Such rhetoric recalled the old abolitionist tableau of the kneeling African: "Am I not a man and a Brother?" Politically and artistically, that image depicted the actual moment of emancipation: when the slave would rise from his knees and stand free. A Washingtonian's letter sketched this moment by calling Jenckes's bill "the means of placing many a man upon his Feet again." Like the metaphor of bondage, this phrase was more than a cliché; it was a euphemism for the subordination felt by white men. Picturing themselves on their knees, they cursed the government—as one letter put it—for

"keeping the debtor in a position of the most abject Slave." To get back on one's feet was to be emancipated.[21]

The National Bankrupt Association came on the scene with perfect timing—in 1864, when the War Between the States finally became a war to end Southern slavery. Like true abolitionists, members of the association held that freedom was inalienable. "We do not ask the passage of a Bankrupt Bill as a *favor* to us," George L. Cannon wrote; "we demand it as our *right*." While manifestly jealous "of the liberty & freedom that [Republicans] are *apparently* so anxious to grant to the colored race," Cannon and his movement seemed to understand that inalienable rights made sense only as a universal standard, not as a privilege of race. Many of Jenckes's correspondents denied the equality of "the poor African," yet few voiced outright opposition to ending slavery. One debtor who fancied his own "bondage far more galling than slavery to the colored man" admitted that "the cruelties to him however were in many instances barbarous." Even a shameless race-baiter like Cannon, sniping at "the *meanest negro*," could go on to explain, "We think we are of some consequence & should have a little attention to our wants as well as the Negro." Political inclusion for themselves, not racial exclusion of the Negro, was their agenda. A few dared to hope that both white and black could thrive. In the fall of 1864, Lott Frost (the leather merchant who yearned to "stand up and feel that we are men") envisioned the nation reborn: "The time is not far . . . when She will Shine forth in greater briliancy [*sic*] glory and power than She has yet done, when She and All her children will be free." He prayed, "May God hasten the time when all this Shall be." Another wrote that although his fortune was gone, "with it would I give my Life could I today purchase by so doing a Righteous Just Peace attended with Liberty to the oppressed both White & Black."[22]

The legislation that might have answered their prayers went down by one vote in June 1864. In December, after it passed the House but died in the Senate, an enraged Chicagoan notified

Jenckes, "The opposers of this humane bill are *marked men*."
Ironically, many bankrupts felt like marked men—branded as
failures, even slaves. The screwy theology of antebellum Christianity led some people to believe that Africans were enslaved because they bore the Mark of Cain. Antiquarians reported that the
ancient Greeks had actually branded their slaves; so did some antebellum American masters—and so did the Union Army. Some
men who were court-martialed were branded (or tattooed) on the
face, hand, or hip. The letter "D" on the left side meant drunkard;
on the right side, "D" stood for deserter. If neither of those descriptions fit the crime, some courts used "R" for rogue—a nod to
"The Rogue's March," a tune often played on fife and drum while
the sentence was carried out. Private Daniel Callaghan lived out
his life marked "W"—as did privates John Shay, Barney Boyle,
Thomas Keller, Samuel Jenkins, and others: "W" for worthless.
Credit agents made such marks beside a man's name, if not on his
flesh. Compared to these harsh realities of Civil War America,
the wheedling bankrupt sounded mawkish, or worse. At least he
could still show his face at Delmonico's.[23]

Losers Must Be Punished

Whatever one thought of bankrupts, bankruptcy had become a
more urgent political and commercial question than it had been
before 1865, when the end of the war and the end of slavery began
to redefine freedom for both black men and white. In the Thirty-
Ninth Congress of 1866–67, the politics of bankruptcy got entan-
gled in debates over Reconstruction, and disentangling the issues
helped shape the postwar relationship between federal power and
individual rights. When Jenckes's bill again reached the House
floor in mid-February 1866, lawmakers were awaiting Andrew
Johnson's decision whether to sign or veto the Freedman's Bureau
bill and were pondering the rift between Congress and the president. On the afternoon of 14 February, as Jenckes fielded bankruptcy amendments the chair recognized Thaddeus Stevens of

Pennsylvania. Called "the Great Commoner," his craggy face and gaunt frame made him look far older than his mere seventy-four years. Having grown impatient with the endless haggling over Jenckes's bill, Stevens came out against it in *any* form. "I do not want anything stricken out or put in, or anything to pass," he snapped, recalling that the Bankruptcy Act of 1841 was "the most unpopular law the Congress of the United States ever passed." Stevens was chairman of the Ways and Means Committee (a powerful post akin to today's majority leader) and, with Senator Charles Sumner, was the architect of congressional Reconstruction. "This is not the time," he said, "when all rebeldom is in debt to us, to pass a law to free them from their debts." Stevens spoke the language of congressional emancipation better than any, and here he forcefully limited its application. Certainly, laws could be used to free people, but Stevens would not free the bankrupt traitors of the Confederacy. When Jenckes boldly asked the Speaker to instruct the senior member to address the specific amendment on the floor, Stevens yielded, saying, "the gentleman from Rhode Island thinks that would improve the bill, and I do not think the bill ought to be improved." Laughter filled the House, and Old Stevens left Jenckes standing alone.[24]

Consolation came to the Rhode Islander almost immediately, in a new wave of constituent mail. This batch was noticeably angrier than what Jenckes had received during the war. "I notice Representative *Stevens* Remarks in opposition to the Bankrupt bill," wrote a Philadelphian; "he seems to oppose any measure that will not benefit the *Nigger*. . . . [T]he Republicans has [*sic*] been Working for the Black man long enough—let them now help their Own Race—I am a Republican—and think like my Neighbors." J. DeWitt Sheldon (who in 1864 had written that bankruptcy was "a bondage worse than slavery") now wrote again: "It seems strange to me that so many members think only of the *black Man* & leave their poor White brothers to suffer under a load of old debts which they never can pay." He closed by urging Jenckes to "Make one more appeal for the *White Man*."[25]

The bankrupts' racial rhetoric was sharper than before, and their impatience with the priorities of the first Reconstruction Congress was palpable. A new irony entered the slavery metaphor that white debtors probably did not see. For a generation, they had aggressively vied for the mantle of slavery, hitting on the metaphor sooner and using it longer than their rhetorical competitors in the workers' movements. When the Thirteenth Amendment brought legal freedom to the real slaves, the bankrupts' self-definition must have chafed like a hair shirt. The government empowered itself to interfere with property, to redefine citizenship, and to protect individual rights—but not theirs.[26]

Five days after the Jenckes-Stevens exchange, President Andrew Johnson vetoed the Freedmen's Bureau bill and ignited the power struggle that would lead to his impeachment. Bankrupts kept writing letters throughout the political storm, and some picked up this new word, "freedman." A letter in behalf of "Thousands of poor slaves of the U.S." came from Ohio. "It seems strange that there should be so much sympathy in Congress for the Freed Man, Whilst there is so little for the White Slave," the man wrote. "The rebellion has made thousands of White slaves in the North." Adding that "too many of our Legislators seem determined to Keep us slaves," he concluded: "For the sake of Suffering Humanity do all you can for the poor White Slave. We admire the sympathy for the poor Freedman—But let us plead for sympathy and Mercy at the hands of those who Can give us aid to free us from the chains of despair." Once more, a white bankrupt ambivalently sanctioned black emancipation—if it were offset by expanded freedom for whites, who demanded first claim to the status of "Suffering Humanity." As it was, the government had allowed the bankrupt to become "the White Slave" while elevating the black bondsman as "the Freed Man." This new political vocabulary changed the status of "the poor African" from nightmare to aspiration. "For 12 long years I have wished for such a Bill that I might once more be a *Freedman*," wrote a Cincinnatian, "but it seems we are doomed." No antebellum debtor had ever "wished for" the status of a black man. In a feeble hand, this constituent asked Congressman Jenckes to "continue your noble efforts for the white mans liberty."[27]

Angry bankrupts even rebuked the Great Commoner directly. Several wrote to Stevens anonymously, but James Hume sent a polite and pensive letter from Arcola, Illinois. A farmer, not a merchant, he wrote that many "men have not become involved in debt by reckless speculation or extravagance in living or dressing, but by misfortune which was unavoidable to them." Rejecting the master plot that kept "the reason, *in the man*," Hume claimed another: emancipation. Bankrupts only wanted to be free. "Many of us sought the army in order to be freed for a short time," he explained; "many others seek death." He then turned to the politics of race. "While congress is legislating to aid the negroe to give him liberty (as he richly deserves) would it be be wrong for congress to aid the poore," he asked. "Give them a law that will make them free once more—make that law as stringent as you may[,] make it a capital offence to fraudulently take the benefit of it." They would accept any terms of surrender, he concluded; "we only ask once more to be free and we will work and support our families." These were common sentiments expressed with uncommon eloquence, but they were quite beside the point. Stevens opposed the bankruptcy bill neither to free blacks nor to fetter whites—but rather to punish "all rebeldom." Relatively few correspondents grasped this. "I do not see why hundreds of thousands of good business men should be Chained down on account of a few men who have tried to over throw the gov[ernment]," wrote one who did. Another complained, "Bankrupts will never 'return thanks' to Mr Stevens for being willing to chain them down yet longer lest a few hundred hopelessly bankrupt Rebels get free." Although not as numerous or visceral as complaints about freedmen, these letters engaged a political question that was more relevant to the bankruptcy bill.[28]

The question was this: Having seceded without paying their bills, should the former Confederates be readmitted to the Union without paying? Politically, giving individual Southerners access to a bankruptcy law seemed to reward traitors and punish patriots (the ruined Northern creditors who at war's end hoped for payment from the returning Southern debtors). But constitutionally, did Congress have the power to relieve the debts of some citizens but not others? Every version of the bankruptcy bill after 1863 included an exclusionary clause denying former Confederates access to the law, based on various criteria, which Jenckes tired of explaining. He had held his tongue when Thaddeus Stevens had mocked him, but he at last fired back when the bill came to a vote in March 1866. Paraphrasing Stevens's objection—"Why, sir, you may let some rebel debtor go if this bill becomes a law"—Jenckes announced that he would draw his rebuttal from the "piles of letters" he had received. "I will try to use their own language," he promised. First, he presented the creditors' position: "We know our debtors; we wish to meet them as commercial men, mercantile men, business men; we do not care to know whether they have been rebels or not; that is a political question. We want to meet them on the ground that business men meet each other upon." Jenckes thus dared to utter the sacrilege, aloud and on the record, that most Americans were ready to put Stevens's brand of vindictiveness behind them. The bill would exclude those who had actively aided the rebellion and "wasted their property in that direction," and that was sufficient.[29]

As for the debtors' perspective, Jenckes put to Stevens a demagogic question obviously taken from his constituent mail: "I ask the gentleman from Pennsylvania, who objected to this bill for political reasons, whether after so many years during which he has been known as the champion of the black man, he will now in his old age vote for the enslavement, the continued enslavement, of the white man." Jenckes, for one, would not cast such a vote. "I am in favor of emancipation," he asserted, "but I am for the emancipation of white and black alike." Jenckes poured forth the words his constituents had been writing for two years. "The slavery of debt is worse than the slavery of personal service," he con-

*Thomas Allen Jenckes,
congressional manager of
Civil War bankruptcy
legislation, is chiefly
remembered as the "father
of civil service reform."*
(Engraving by G. E. Perine,
Prints and Photographs
Division, Library of
Congress.)

tinued. "The latter can be performed and the obligations satisfied; the former never can be." The voices of failure had finally been heard; but they were not heeded. The bankruptcy bill went down again that day in March 1866; its constituents would have to wait another year for their dignity. "Why are bankrupts more to be pitied than idiots?" *Harper's Weekly* asked; "Because bankrupts are broken, while idiots are only cracked."[30]

Although his bill had again been defeated, Jenckes's repeated explanations of its rebel debtors' provisions had won him an important ally. "The day for amnesty, whether it be mercantile or political, has not yet come," said Senator Charles Sumner, and yet he perceived a utility in the bankruptcy bill that his House collaborator did not. Rather than blocking the bill, Sumner wanted to pass it *in order to deprive former rebels*. Outraged by Southern atrocities against freedmen and white unionists, he said, "Those people must be made to feel that they are no longer masters. The rebel spirit must be broken down. Now, I know no better way to break it down for the present, during this transition period, than by excluding them from these Chambers, by excluding them from office, by excluding them from the benefits of a great act of legislation" like Jenckes's bill. Naming bankruptcy as one of three vital interim policies of Reconstruction, Sumner acknowledged the social *and political* stigma of failure in nineteenth-century America. A week after this speech, on 12 February 1867, the House approved the Louisiana government bill, which disfranchised former Confederates for five years, and prepared to pass the Military Government bill. To Sumner, this was "the Beginning of a true reconstruction." That same day, the Senate passed a bankruptcy proposal for the first time in twenty-seven years. Minutes before the final vote, Sumner repeated his call to deny former rebels and current vigilantes their magic moment of emancipation. "We ought not to allow [them] to get on their feet," he said. Inescapable failure would deepen a culture of frustration and defeat that C. Vann Woodward a century later would term "the burden of Southern history."[31]

A New Birth of Freedom

The rebel debtors' question would fade into history, but the politics of Reconstruction and of bankruptcy intersected on a more momentous issue when Thomas Jenckes challenged Thaddeus Stevens over a provision in the draft Fourteenth Amendment to the Constitution. It was intended to define national citizenship for the first time and to guarantee due process and "equal protection" for all citizens. Stevens regarded it not only as the capstone of Reconstruction but as his life's crowning achievement; he had dreamed of it "in my youth, in my manhood, in my old age." Although the freedman needed its benefits most urgently, its broader rethinking of citizens' rights and the government's role in guarding them paralleled similar dilemmas in the bankruptcy bill.[32]

Jenckes and Stevens clashed over one of the Fourteenth Amendment's four sections—section two, which was the most overtly political clause of the historic measure. Section two provided that if a state restricted the franchise, its representation in Congress would decrease. The clause aimed both to encourage the enfranchisement of freedmen and, more urgently, to prevent the Southern states from dominating Congress. In tallying state population for congressional apportionment, freedmen were a potential windfall to the former Confederacy because they were now full persons rather than the three-fifths they had been designated in 1787, by the founders' infamous constitutional compromise. If freedmen were counted toward apportionment but denied the vote, defeat and emancipation would ironically have rewarded the white South with increased political power. Men like Stevens and Sumner could no more abide this than they could suffer rebel debtors to benefit from a bankruptcy bill. Stevens's solution was to reduce representation, in the words of the original version of section two, "whenever the elective franchise shall be denied or abridged in any State on account of race or color."[33]

This was the language to which Jenckes, a supporter of black suffrage and the amendment as a whole, objected on 23 January 1866, three weeks before he and Stevens quarrelled over the bankruptcy bill. On that January day, Stevens had moved for a final vote on section two, but before the clerk could call the yeas and nays, Jenckes interrupted. It was all well and good to punish disfranchisement on account of race, he pointed out, but the amendment "says nothing about the qualification of property." What if South Carolina, Jenckes continued by way of example, should reinstate the property restrictions in its 1790 state constitution? Freedmen could easily be prevented from voting if this were done, with no consequent loss of state seats in Washington. Stevens retorted, "All I can say is that if the law applies impartially to all, then no matter whether it cuts out white or black." Impatient for a vote, the old radical claimed not to care about potential disfranchisement of the poor, so long as the amendment treated white and black equally.[34]

Jenckes's question and Stevens's testy reply momentarily raised class politics in a debate largely dominated by concerns about race. Besides finding a loophole by which states could have disfranchised freedmen with impunity, Jenckes may have been thinking of bankrupts when he inquired about property qualifications. Whatever Jenckes's motive, Stevens quickly found himself ambushed on the House floor. A torrent of questions followed. Republican John Farnsworth of Illinois carried on where Jenckes left off, asking whether states could forbid freedmen from owning property. James Brooks, a New York Democrat, wanted to know whether the protections of race and color applied to the "one hundred thousand coolies" (Chinese laborers) in California and Oregon. Brooks continued, "Why exclude the Indian? Is he not a man and a brother? . . . Why not embrace them all, as we are making a liberal Constitution?" Remarkably, Stevens retreated. "I am so much astonished at the exhibition on this side of the House," he confessed, "that I withdraw the demand for the previous question and leave this matter with the House."[35]

Jenckes's query had exposed a flaw in the Fourteenth Amendment: it could not guarantee suffrage to freedmen or anyone else, because section two left unsolved the problem of states' rights versus federal power. This point became clear in the ensuing debate about the "basis of representation." Jehu Baker, a conservative Republican from Illinois who had planned to vote for the amendment, now saw that it failed, "in its very terms, to adequately effect its own object." He could not support a measure "which leaves any State in the Union perfectly free to narrow her suffrage to any extent she pleases." Others agreed. Rising again, Jenckes argued that states' power to set voter qualifications "has been used for mischief" and that it must be taken away for a truly national vision of citizenship to prevail. "When electors deposit their ballots," he averred, "they cease to be citizens of the small republics composing this great nation; they are citizens of the great Republic." Voting, like commerce, crossed state lines. Such anthems of economic nationalism echoed what Jenckes and his correspondents had argued on behalf of the bankruptcy bill; as one letter put it, "a sound bankruptcy system will do more in a few years to teach the people that we are a nation and not a confederacy than a million bushels of political pamphlets and speeches."[36]

The amendment at hand expressed a similar hope: that federal protection of individual rights might enable citizens to learn (or relearn) freedom, not as idealism but as everyday experience. Jenckes's challenge to Stevens spoke directly to this objective, but ultimately Jenckes won a pyrrhic victory. After much wrangling, lawmakers revised section two, and the Fourteenth Amendment passed on 13 June 1866. The final wording guaranteed suffrage "to any of the male inhabitants of such State," thus basing the right on gender instead of race. For the first time, the Constitution incorporated the word "male"—states would lose seats in Congress whenever *men* could not vote, regardless of whether race or property was the mechanism of restriction. Stevens had rejected Jenckes's broader assertion that the federal government must decide all voting qualifications, even in state or local elections. History would prove Jenckes right: the Fourteenth Amendment's capitulation to states' rights in section two would shorten its intended reach for a hundred years, until the passage of the Voting Rights Act of 1965.[37]

By contrast, the Bankruptcy Act of 1867 took only eighty years, after 1787, to overcome the ideological and constitutional obstacles to its passage. On the last day of the Thirty-Ninth Congress, on 2 March 1867, Congress approved both the Bankruptcy Act and the Reconstruction Act of 1867 (the first of four major provisions for readmitting former Confederate states). Both acts contributed to the "Yankee Leviathan," the rise of centralized government power in last quarter of the nineteenth century. Both laws asserted unprecedented authority over the political and economic nation that had been united by a divisive war. National bankruptcy promised a kind of national citizenship. Economic failure caused men to lose the capacity to transact, and in turn, to lose the chance to prove their ability and worth. The alienation and racial jealousy that bankrupts expressed during and after the war voiced a similar loss in the political realm. One's ability to command responsiveness, even protection, from the government had become another marker of freedom and value.[38]

Jenckes had often reminded his brethren of "a great unexecuted power" they could use, while struggling over Southern policy and constitutional amendments, to demonstrate their vision of the federal government as the guarantor of individual freedom. A national bankruptcy system would protect the civil and economic rights of individuals, even at the expense of property rights and traditional state jurisdictions over debtor-creditor relations. At the same time, Jenckes's legislation gained momentum from the Fourteenth Amendment and the politics of Reconstruction. A bankruptcy act could not survive as more than a temporary measure (as in 1800 and 1841) until Americans settled broader conflicts among property rights, individual rights, and federal power—conflicts about the meaning of freedom. The Bankruptcy Act of 1867 was hardly perfect; after much revision, it would be repealed in 1878. But unlike its stillborn predecessors, the 1867 law not only promised a new start in life, its political genesis helped to deliver a new birth of American freedom.[39]

Who better to prove it than George L. Cannon? The busted furnace man owed more than $30,000 when he declared federal bankruptcy in 1868. He kept personal effects worth $115, nearly all of it clothing except for "1 Dictionary"—perhaps a memento of his success at writing polemics. Soon he was writing prospectuses, under his middle name, "G. Lyman Cannon," for a Colorado investment scheme. In 1872, he settled Fannie and their boys in Denver and became a miner. Lighting out for a territory called "Spanish Bar," he joined the rush of 50,000 silver-crazed prospectors seeking "grub stakes and millions." Cannon filed six claims, including one mine he named the "Great Mogul." By 1890, he and George, Jr., were running the "Colorado Chemical Company" and living on Denver's fashionable Pennsylvania Street. Once America's leading bankrupt, George Lyman Cannon died at age seventy-three in June 1899 and was buried among the local gentry in Fairmount Cemetery. His rise from rags to respectability must have been quite a tale; perhaps, like an old Manhattan ward boss, he seen his (second) chances and he took 'em.[40]

If nothing else, Cannon's "second act" dramatized how the law he had worked for had in turn worked for him. It seems fitting that, having been a prime beneficiary of the Bankruptcy Act of 1867, Cannon long outlived its 1878 repeal—and perhaps equally fitting that the author of the law expired before it did. Thomas A. Jenckes died in Providence in 1875, having retired from politics after sponsoring the Civil Service Reform Act of 1871. He went home to practice law, and in 1872 and 1873 he helped prosecute the railroad profiteers and crooked congressmen of the Crédit Mobilier scandal. His obituary in the *New-York Times* described him as being neither "magnetic" nor "of the oily variety of politicians," but simply a "useful legislator" who won "the implicit confidence of the people."[41]

The people—Jenckes's far-flung constituency—had not forgotten to thank him for the Jubilee of 1867. "Your Bankrupt Bill," an Ohioan wrote in big blue crayon, "will make many a poor Devils heart glad and help him out of the mire. If you should ever be a Candidate for the Presidency Sir, you shall have my vote—It's all I have to give." An old gentleman from Baltimore wrote in a tiny, cramped hand, "Our beloved and lamented Lincoln, in his Emancipation Proclamation, gave Freedom to the Slaves of the South." He went on, "You Sir, by your persistent perseverance, indomitable energy, and ability as a Statesman, have literally forced Congress to grant the same boon to the *Slave-debtors* of the Nation." The struggle over bankruptcy had shown how markets, laws, and politics told disparate stories about failure. The narrative that proved to be most important was not the tall tale of how debtors resembled slaves but rather the political saga of how losers wrote themselves into the national story. Instead of a myth about rags to riches, this was a manifesto about the right to rise. Making up a new narrative for "a new nation" had consumed generations and spanned two revolutions: from the market revolution, which made men failures, to the second American Revolution, which made men free.[42]

A New Birth of Failure

Civil War bankrupts wrote their own version of history, yet they shared Abraham Lincoln's vision of a new nation. Even as the clash became a war for abolition, it continued to be a war for ambition—for the right to transcend one's origins. From Fort Sumter to Appomattox, Lincoln defined the war this way. "I almost always feel inclined, when I happen to say anything to soldiers, to impress upon them in a few brief remarks the importance of success in this contest," he said in August 1864, greeting the 166th Ohio Regiment as it made ready to muster out. "Hundred days men" like them were serving short hitches to ease troop shortages that summer. Lincoln often made time to thank such units—in words that not only defined the war but also presaged postwar capitalism. Lincoln addressed the Ohio troops on the White House lawn during the warmest August anyone recollected, in a city noted for torrid summers. At dawn and dusk, Lincoln commuted on horseback between the presidential mansion and a summer cottage on the edge of town. It was cooler there, and he could work undisturbed in an unceremonious white suit and Panama hat: small comforts in the war's bleakest month. With Sherman stalled in Georgia and Grant dug in outside Petersburg, opposition newspaper editors called Lincoln "an egregious failure." Even his own political advisors confided to each other, "I fear he is a failure." Friend and foe badgered him to withdraw from the 1864 presidential election.[43]

Three days before addressing the 166th Ohio, Lincoln consulted Frederick Douglass in the White House. Lincoln resolved to defy public demands that he repudiate emancipation and sue for peace. Making plans should he be forced to give in, he asked Douglass to organize a federally backed underground railroad, to help as many slaves escape to the North as possible. On 22

In stunning contrast to idealized portraits of the Great Emancipator, this life drawing by French émigré Pierre Morand (aka Joseph Hubert Diss Debar) was made at the presidential retreat on the grounds of the Washington Soldier's Home in the long, hot summer of 1864—when Lincoln declined to repudiate emancipation, even if it cost him reelection that fall. (Courtesy of the Missouri Historical Society, Acc. no. 1952.99.21.)

August—the same day the Buckeye regiment listened to the president's speech—the editor of the *New-York Times* sent Lincoln a private letter, warning that unless he would drop emancipation from his peace terms, he could not be reelected. Lincoln pondered what to do: when his cabinet met the next morning, he would ask them to sign a blind pledge to make peace on any terms if he lost. With such matters cluttering his desk, even working in shirtsleeves barely made the office less stifling. Maybe Lincoln welcomed the chance to step outside and greet the Ohio soldiers under the blistering sun.[44]

Who was more uncomfortable: almost a thousand soldiers in scratchy wool uniforms or the man in the long black coat? "The countenance of the President . . . was inexpressibly sad," wrote a member of another Ohio regiment Lincoln had greeted earlier in the summer. "He heard the music, saw the crowd, but his mind was evidently not there." The soldiers, at least, could daydream of going home. Hold out for victory, the president was telling them, "not merely for to-day, but for all time to come." In a great, muscular hand he held his stovepipe hat, because despite the heat he always uncovered to show respect for the troops. The front ranks could see him sweating with them. Rivulets moistened the face Walt Whitman had described exactly ten days earlier, upon glimpsing the president as Lincoln rode into the city that morning: "Abraham Lincoln's dark brown face, with the deep cut lines, the eyes . . . with a deep latent sadness in the expression."[45]

Lincoln's high tenor voice squeaked some, but it carried like a bugle call, each word a clear, distinct note that made him easy to hear and understand. "I happen temporarily to occupy this big White House," he was saying. "I am a living witness that any one of your children may look to come here as my father's child has." Perhaps wandering thoughts outnumbered his words—nearly a thousand visions of fathers and children back in Ohio, interrupted by scattered sighs in the ranks of men anxious to return to neglected farms and shops. Even if some barely listened, they knew that Father Abraham started out life as a poor boy with dreams like theirs. It did not take a Walt Whitman to recognize a tanned brow accustomed to manly sweat.[46]

"It is in order that each of you may have an open field," Lincoln was saying about why they fought, "and a fair chance for your industry, enterprise, and intelligence." A fair chance. He was speaking their language, telling them what the struggle meant and why it must go on, even two or three more years. The president talked fast—quicker than you might guess his Kentucky twang could go. He would spit out two or three mouthfuls of words before he paused to accentuate two or three phrases that he especially wanted you to remember. He was nearly finished now: ". . . that you may all have equal privileges in the race of life, with all its desirable human aspirations."[47]

The race of life. No one now knows which words Lincoln

stressed that day, but no phrase stuck longer in this intensely ambitious and competitive man's vocabulary. In 1852, he had exalted the race of life in a eulogy to Whig statesman Henry Clay, coiner of the phrase "self-made manhood," an ideal Lincoln deliberately embodied. In the presidential race of 1860, Lincoln promised "the humblest man an equal chance to get rich with everybody else. When one starts poor, as most do in the race of life, free society is such that he knows he can better his condition." He said, "I want every man to have the chance—and I believe a black man is entitled to it." The slogan graced his first message to Congress in 1861, only three months into a war "whose leading object is . . . to afford all, an unfettered start, and a fair chance, in the race of life." After 1863, "unfettered" took on a more liberal (and literal) meaning, yet emancipation enlarged Lincoln's creed without changing it. Individual success was devalued unless all could strive freely, and freedom was a meaningless abstraction without "a fair chance" to succeed.[48]

In those dog days of August 1864, when he risked his office rather than break the promise of emancipation, surely Lincoln tried all of his old stump-speaking tricks to make the soldiers hear "equal privileges in the race of life" and embrace it as their true cause. He spoke fewer words that day than in his brief elegy at Gettysburg nine months earlier, where on a pasture of death Lincoln heralded "a new birth of freedom." Now, on the White House lawn, addressing men lucky enough to have avoided the graveyard, he translated the poetry of Gettysburg into plain talk that the greenest private could grasp.[49]

"It is for this that the struggle should be maintained," he concluded, barely three minutes after he began. "The nation is worth fighting for, to secure such an inestimable jewel." The jewel of liberty, a new birth of freedom, the race of life: all three named Lincoln's vision of a nation of strivers, which gradually but irrevocably linked the war for ambition to the war for abolition. This duality encompassed what he meant by "a new birth of freedom": a fresh chance at self-made manhood, a right to rise for white men as well as for black men. This vision did not get Lincoln re-elected in 1864—military victories clinched that. But it did get him killed. John Wilkes Booth, after hearing Lincoln promote limited Negro suffrage, vowed that the tyrant had given his last speech. At first a reluctant emancipator, Lincoln's faith that individual effort alone should earn men success or failure in life ultimately cost him his own.[50]

After the war, the defender of this faith was the White House visitor of August 1864, Frederick Douglass. Virtually Lincoln's peer as a writer, Douglass was a peerless orator, gifted with a lordly, basso voice the emancipator lacked. Douglass's most popular lecture, which he gave more than fifty times between 1859 and 1893, was entitled "Self-Made Men." It asked why, "in the race of life, the sons of the poor often get even with, and surpass even, the sons of the rich?" An escaped slave who had taught himself to read, Douglass faced the public as living proof that indeed the race went to the swift, that people are "architects of their own good fortunes . . . indebted to themselves for themselves." Douglass's biography was so well known that he need not draw explicit parallels to the exemplar of his speech: "the King of American self-made men . . . ABRAHAM LINCOLN." No better model of work and self-improvement existed than "the fortitude and industry which could split rails by day, and learn grammar at night at the hearthstone of a log hut." Douglass baptized the freedmen in the entrepreneurial identity now vindicated by war. Our motto, he exclaimed, is "'Go ahead!'"[51]

Douglass was a politician, not a motivational speaker. His paean to the race of life exposed the fraud of Reconstruction to the "scorching irony" that had made him famous. Once the post-war twaddle about forty acres and a mule died down, the former slaves got nothing but freedom—no parcel of land made fertile by bondage, no coin to reimburse stolen generations. Night riders, sharecropping debts, crooked labor contracts, and segregation precluded anything like a fair chance. If self-made men "owe[d] little or nothing to birth, relationship, [or] friendly surroundings," asked Douglass, who fit that part better than the freedmen? "I have said, 'Give the negro fair play and let him alone,'" he explained. "It is not fair play to start the negro out in life, from nothing and with nothing, while others start with the advantage of a thousand years behind them." The race of life should not be rigged. "For his own welfare, give [the Negro] a chance to do whatever he can do well. If he fails then, let him fail! I can, however, assure you that he will not fail." Anyone who accepted the Lincoln myth and the race of life as articles of faith, Douglass implied, must concede that racial equality was unassailable. Politicizing the gospel of self-help, the great orator preached it in earnest.[52]

The war had changed the terms of political and economic identity in ways that expanded the constituency of failure. In Douglass's words, "Liberty and slavery" gave way to a new measure of human worth: "success and failure." Trying to live up to these normative ideals, postwar generations faced hazards that neither bankruptcy laws nor constitutional amendments could relieve. New chances meant new risks. Civil rights created a new basis of identity for all, but even if political equality were enforced, economic inequality was inescapable. One scholar explains, "even as Lincoln celebrates the freedom of opportunity . . . he also inscribes a new logic for assigning blame." The logic is this: in a fair race, losers have only themselves to blame. The problem in postwar America was that fortunate sons ran alongside former slaves, and bond brokers edged out ditch diggers; the contestants included black and white, rich and poor, male and female. If Lincoln overlooked the dark side of his ideal, Douglass did not. In "this eager, ever moving mass which we call American society," Douglass explained, "life is not only a race, but a battle, and everybody [is] trying to get just a little ahead of everybody else." Off the dais, Douglass beheld a painful example in his three hapless sons and a daughter who married a ne'er-do-well. Confessing his "many failures in life" in an 1876 letter to his implacable father, Charles Douglass admitted, "It seems that under any

A MESSAGE TO YOUNG AMERICANS · · PRESIDENT LOUBET
THE STORY OF THE GREAT MOGUL · · · ROBERT BARR

OCTOBER + 1900 + TEN CENTS

SUCCESS

A
MONTHLY
JOURNAL
OF
INSPIRATION
PROGRESS
&
SELF-HELP

IS
COTTON
ONCE
MORE
KING?

ALBERT
HENCKE

McGraw-Marden Company, Publishers
University Building, Washington Square, New York

THE CIRCULATION OF THIS ISSUE OF SUCCESS IS 175,000

*Celebrating the resurgence of the cotton industry in 1900, this
mass-circulation magazine blithely ignored the post–Civil War
irony that many Americans with little opportunity to succeed were
now free to be failures.* (Author's collection.)

circumstances I am to fail in my undertakings, and my life is to be one series of blunders." Identity seemed to be more a matter of new risks than new rights.[53]

This was a common story after the Civil War. The Douglasses were a rare family, black or white—except in their encounters with success and failure as the definitive categories of human worth in postemancipation America. Coming up from slavery only to go down in failure, they approximated a saying attributed to another self-made man, Andrew Carnegie: "Three generations from shirtsleeves to shirtsleeves." Entrepreneurial individualism ended with the war it won. The age of go-ahead became the Gilded Age when business innovators remade self-made manhood on an unimagined scale. Men like Carnegie and John D. Rockefeller embodied different myths from those of Douglass or Lincoln. In the same era when Reconstruction failed to establish political equality, corporate industrialization challenged the limits of "an open field and a fair chance . . . in the race of life." Black and white, workman and tycoon would be—in theory but not in reality—just so many equal competitors in the race of life. "Properly speaking, there are in the world no such men as self-made men," Frederick Douglass said. "The term implies an individual independence of the past and present which can never exist. . . . We have all either begged, borrowed, or stolen." Many families would resort to some of these strategies in the postwar decades, after learning the hard way that the celebrated "new birth of freedom" also brought forth a new birth of failure.[54]

8 Big Business and Little Men

One October night in 1888, a Mrs. Osborne of New Haven, Connecticut, dreamed that something horrid drove her from her home and chased her naked through the woods into the safe embrace of John D. Rockefeller. In her waking world, her husband, who had invented a product called "Osborne's Embossing Oil," had seen investors bilk him of the profits. His wife sold everything to save him—even her fine clothes—but they lost their home, ate by the grace of a grocer's credit, and now feared eviction from their meager flat. Bedridden and delirious with spinal meningitis, gray-headed at age thirty-two, Mrs. Osborne had her strange dream. She climbed a great hill, "weak and worn and with clothing torn off," and there stood Rockefeller. "I am the great Oil King," he said. He took her on a long train ride to his magnificent home, where he and his wife clothed and fed Mrs. Osborne and sent for her husband. Upon waking and recovering her mind, she told her husband about the dream and said it was a sign that Mr. Osborne must write for a job at Standard Oil. They had told neither family nor neighbors of their plight, but she became obsessed with the idea that he confide in a total stranger and tell "Mr Rockafeller" about her dream. Her failed husband was understandably reluctant to barter his naked wife (even in a dream) for employment by the richest man in the world.[1]

To indulge "a womans seeming foolishness," Mr. Osborne sat through the night by her bed and composed a long letter. It read like the sentimental stories in women's magazines—"Life's Ladder" or "The Bankrupt's Wife"—wherein a paragon of true womanhood suffered by the failures of her feckless husband. "I do not want to *beg* or *ask Charity,*" Osborne wrote, "only so far as a *position* is concerned, to earn an *honest support* for *wife* and *four children,* for I have one of the finest and best of loveing wifes and christian mothers." Both men and women routinely experienced sentiment both as a feeling and as a style of middle-class morality that valued qualities like sincerity and trustworthiness in everything from fashion to manners to mourning. Such virtues were as vital in business as in the parlor during times of boom and bust, when success seemed arbitrary and failure seemed to menace every entrepreneur. Sentimental culture, in the words of a literary historian, was "a value scheme for ordering all of life, in competition with the ethos of money and exploitation"—an ethos that seemed to rise with postwar corporate capitalism. Sentimental norms fostered order in a dangerous world of commodities and strangers, two value schemes that Osborne's letter presented as more complementary than conflicting. Osborne traded on the credibility of a Christian home to propose an honest deal in the marketplace.[2]

He tapped another genre to portray his own "struggles and triumphs"—surely an allusion to P. T. Barnum's popular 1869 memoir, a classic of its genre. If Osborne lacked the resources to walk the walk, at least he could talk the talk. "Here is a young man ambitious to try to get up the ladder," he wrote of himself, "and who if given a chance, might and with his Yankee courage and grit, would in a short time place him self right before the business world. . . . My *motto* is and shall be where there is a will there is a way." These were the earnest clichés of how-to-succeed manuals and fables of plucky newsboys—the masculine side of sentimental literature, still popular but growing quaint as little men tried "to get up the ladder" during what history remembers as the Gilded Age. That appellation had always been tongue in cheek, having been coined by Mark Twain in 1874. Shaken by the panic of 1873, contemporaries called the era by another name: the great depression. Andrew Carnegie's postmortem on business conditions "during the great depression" of 1873 to 1886 appeared in a national magazine a week or two after A. A. Osborne sent his letter to the "Oil King" in January 1889. Adversity was always just around the corner, especially in the years after the panic of 1893. The century petered out amid farmers' revolts, the advent of Jim Crow, currency wars over the gold and silver standards, antitrust debates, bloody labor strikes, and "Coxey's Army" of unemployed men marching on Washington. The 18.4 percent unemployment rate of 1894 would not be exceeded until 1932; until then, Americans were recalling earlier hardships when they spoke of "the great depression."[3]

Like a Gilded Age that was also a great depression, Osborne's epistle to Rockefeller combined two worldviews, making business and sentimental values work together. Osborne expended domestic sentiment to redeem worldly ambition, combined panhandling with a business proposition, and (perhaps) employed sincerity as a subterfuge—making a true confession into an artful dodge. Osborne's letter testified that ordinary people experienced the capitalist market and the sentimental home as intimately connected, not separate spheres. More remarkable is that his letter was one of thousands—*begging letters,* they were called—rambling requests by downtrodden men and women seeking jobs, money, or advice from icons of success. Like the Civil War–era bankrupts who wrote to politicians, thousands of citizens breached the domestic "haven in a heartless world" to reveal their "private business" to an outsider. Connecting the home to the market in this way, begging letters revealed strategies of self-representation. How did people understand the identity of failure and its context in the marketplace? Many of Rockefeller's uninvited correspondents challenged prevailing assumptions that failure and success were achieved identities, that people always deserved their struggles or triumphs. Most important, they articulated vernacular understandings of the market and the relationships formed in it—understandings based as much on sentimental obligations as on rational economics.

Begging letters gave voice to little men and women in the age of big business. In 1890, J. W. Bomgardner turned sixty and surveyed a life of unremitting failure. Above all, he regretted an opportunity he passed up thirty years earlier, when a novice grain dealer proposed that they become partners in Ohio. With higher hopes, Bomgardner instead bought an Indiana mill that folded in the panic of 1873. "I was forced to the wall," he recalled, "losing every dollar I had in the world." He then set off on the odyssey of the transient failed man. "I drifted Westward—Decatur—Springfield—Quincy Ill—2 years in Iowa." Ending up as a grain dealer in Kansas, he barely made a living in the same line he had once shunned. "The business has changed (for the worse) Very much in few last years," he noted. Small-timers were being squeezed out by "firms of large capital that . . . have advantages that I cant secure." Swallowing the dregs of his pride in 1890, he wrote to cadge a job from his long-lost "partner": John D. Rockefeller. Here, in a worried scrawl, was a meditation on manhood in a bygone "great depression," a prayer to the self-made man from a forgotten man.[4]

"It is so many years since you have probably seen my name, that you may have entirely forgotten me," Bomgardner began. "But I have watched your career with considerable interest, some times thinking how near I came to being a Millionaire." Bomgardner hoped that Rockefeller would remember him "kindly . . . from our business relations when we were young men." Rockefeller remembered, but in reply he rebuffed the job request and sent

Icons of failure and success met again—this time as a pair of petroleum wildcatters—on this sheet music cover, published in John D. Rockefeller's town the year he began his rise to become Oil King.

("Have You Struck Ile?" Cleveland, 1865. Courtesy of the American Antiquarian Society.)

only good wishes. Humiliated, Bomgardner wrote again. "Glad to know that you have not forgotten the friendship formed 30 years ago—though our paths have diverged so widely," he began. "In writing you, as a matter of course there was something of *Sentiment* in it. Or probably I should not have Ventured writing you at all. Yet in asking if you could do any thing for me, it was not in the light of charity." He emphasized that he could be an asset, in the right job. "I thought if the *proper* place could be found for me to *drop into*, I could fill it . . . with credit to myself, and serve your interests. What I am seeking is not a good salary for a *soft* and *easy* place. But I would like a little rest from this care and anxiety." To this businessman, sentiment was not out of place in the competitive market. A man who could neither support a family nor pay his debts violated the contracts of both rational economics and sentimental conduct. Bomgardner proposed a deal he hoped would serve the interests of both parties, a transaction whereby *"Sentiment"* might lead to "Venture."[5]

Theron S. Nettleton, a thirty-year-old harness dealer in Alma City, Minnesota, felt this duality when he wrote to Rockefeller in 1889. He and his wife, Mary Estelle, had seen much heartbreak. Sickness had "taken three little boys all the children we had," he wrote, adding that they adopted a baby son because "our home was too lonesome." Soon after, hard times and a crop failure depressed harness sales, and he compared the loss of his children to the loss of his livelihood: "I have suffered the same misfortune financially." Feeling keenly his duty both as a provider and as a debtor, he "desire[d] to make everything right man with man" (a conviction reminiscent of the credit agent's "confidence between man and man"). Nettleton proposed to borrow $2,000 to settle up and "get a good start." He provided a financial history and a list of references. "As to security, you may think me foolish and crazy and it insufficient," he concluded, "but I offer you my *honor* that is all to me, and if you try me you will find it so. . . . Oh it would make one family so happy and help us so much may God bless you whatever you may decide." Rockefeller decided not to help in this case. Mary Estelle and Theron S. Nettleton left Minnesota for Arkansas, where she died in 1905. Going to Texas, he made a last stab at independence, even getting rid of his foreign-sounding Christian name. "Samuel T. Nettleton" ended up an elderly bookkeeper in Arlington Heights, where he died in 1934. Bookkeepers could not reckon sentimental capital, but Nettleton had tried as a young man—not only because he had no money, but because keeping family and business strictly separate was a luxury many strivers could not afford.[6]

Bomgardner and Nettleton employed domestic pathos in an attempt to remedy economic failure. Yet middle-class entrepreneurialism had long since become the dominant template of American manhood. "Never before in the world's history was competition in every calling and pursuit so fierce as now . . . in this latter half of the nineteenth century," warned a best-selling business manual, *Getting On in the World;* "The slow, plodding, illiterate, chicken-hearted merchant has had his day." The race of life impelled forward men as much by fear of humiliation as by lust for profit. "Forced to the wall" and painfully aware that "our paths have diverged," Bomgardner begged his old friend to "take my *measure.*" Nettleton wanted to put things right "man with man" and asked the millionaire to "try me." Both asked to be recertified as men worthy of personal trust and economic responsibility. Could sentimental exchanges between sincere and honorable men provide a basis for commercial deals between ambitious and self-interested businessmen?[7]

Failure was hard for men to bear because economic impotence stripped them of the masculine prerogatives to buy and sell, to borrow and repay, to contract and exchange. These were the pursuits of "an active life," according to *Getting On in the World:* "true happiness consists in the *means,* and not in the *end;* in *acquisition,* and not in *possession.*" Deal-making for its own sake conferred manly self-worth now, even though breadwinning and social mobility were ever more difficult to achieve in a nation reshaped by "firms of large capital." The propertied individualism of early

America, which had idealized land ownership and a contented life, was giving way to the acquisitive individualism that propelled corporate capitalism. Stagnation, not only collapse, was failure. "Let a man stay year after year in a position and not be successful," the newspapers commented in 1884, "what does the world say? It says, 'He's a plodder.'" For middle-class men and all who aspired to be middle class, manhood was defined less by plodding autonomy than by unceasing increase. To be a man was to transact, to contract, to make deals perpetually. The art of the deal was that it made men as well as money.[8]

This ideal of achievement and identity took a toll on both husbands and wives. More than half of Rockefeller's correspondence came from women struggling to save men from mental as well as economic foreclosure. English-born Stephen Featherstone's Ohio bookbinding business failed in 1873 and ruined his health. He "can put on a poorer mouth when asked for a $ than any apology for a man we know of," reported R. G. Dun & Company, deeming him "Worthless & contemptible." Sarah Featherstone assessed her husband differently when she wrote to Rockefeller, without telling Stephen, in the 1880s. "I think a little success would be the best tonic there is," she wrote wistfully. Gone were the piano, all their lovely books, and other emblems of the sentimental home. After a decade of struggle, she ached to restore her husband as head of the house. "We are a very busy family," she wrote, "but when Stephen is out of employment, the whole machinery is disturbed." Rockefeller knew this family slightly and sent some money (perhaps thinking of their seven children); but, like J. W. Bomgardner, Sarah Featherstone wrote again to explain that charity would not solve her family's problems. Sarah pleaded that only a job for Stephen could make things right. "Did you ever realize," she asked, "what a terrible thing it is for a man of good mind, to feel that he is entirely left out of all the great and good work, that is occupying the busy men of the world. It is not only a matter of money, but it affects a man's entire nature."[9]

If fortune was a woman, *mis*fortune was surely a wife; many already knew what experts were beginning to tell them. In 1880, neurologist George Beard diagnosed "American Nervousness" as a form of "nervous bankruptcy." He listed among its causes the phenomenal increase in "business transactions" and "the stimulus given, to Americans to rise out of the position in which they were born." Male sufferers included Theodore Dreiser and John D. Rockefeller, Jr., although *neurasthenia* came to be known as a woman's problem. In 1892, Charlotte Perkins Gilman immortalized it in her tale of a young wife driven mad by "The Yellow Wall-Paper"—inspired by the author's 1887 treatment for "nerve bankruptcy" and her feelings of "utter failure" as a wife and mother. But Gilman had also seen anxiety and ambition destroy her father, Frederick Beecher Perkins (a nephew of Harriet Beecher Stowe and Henry Ward Beecher), who was never able to live up to his famous middle name. "What a sad dark life the poor man led," she wrote when he died in 1899. "So able a man—and so little to show for it. Poor father!" Ironically, chronic stress was becoming a mark of middle-class status, proof of one's relentless drive to succeed.[10]

But compulsive striving did not nullify sentiment. Indeed Bomgardner, Nettleton, and Featherstone, like thousands of other epistolary beggars, amassed sentiment as a form of capital. They expended sentimental capital not only to purchase relief but to underwrite their sense of manly dealings: to allow a failed man to "get a start," serve "with credit to myself," and rejoin "the busy men of the world." They hoped to strike a real bargain in the "interests" of both parties. If this was an artful dodge, it nonetheless revealed genuine subtleties in beggars' notions of the new economy. Sentiment was legal tender in this negotiation because it was understood as a contractual system of exchange (albeit usually social) among strangers, ordered by meaningful rules, promises, responsibilities, and transactions. Sentimental capital completed a circle from exchange to emotion and back again to exchange. In daily life, the market was always both rational and sentimental; "there was something of *Sentiment*" in every deal.[11]

Self-Made Manhood and Self-Made Surveillance

The curious practice of epistolary begging began in England about 1815. The American du Ponts received letters as early as 1822, and the "Swedish Nightingale" Jenny Lind and her manager, P. T. Barnum, received 120 daily during their 1850 tour. Barnum collected them for decades before figuring out how to milk them for publicity—which he finally managed to do in "My Museum of Letters," a syndicated article featuring "preposterously ridiculous" excerpts. Mark Twain saved his begging mail, too, finding "this sort of literature" so hilarious that he pestered Barnum and others to send him theirs. Thanks to the penny press, moneyed Americans became "the rich and famous" in the postwar culture of celebrity. Department store magnate Alexander T. Stewart, clergyman Henry Ward Beecher, and philanthropist Margaret Olivia Sage (Mrs. Russell Sage) got begging letters. So did William Jennings Bryan, Henry Ford, Thomas Edison, and Andrew Carnegie. Even the supplicants themselves used the term. "Now Mr. Rockefeller," one wrote, "I suppose you have come to the conclusion long before this that this is a begging letter, and I suppose it would be called so." The flow of the oil tycoon's mail increased with his fame and with the panics of 1873 and 1893; correspondence after 1894 was later destroyed by fire but apparently peaked at 15,000 per week. Many writers were barely literate, but their collective output constituted a vernacular genre, cobbled together from idioms of sentiment and business shared by isolated and scattered individuals. The intimacy of the letters was exceeded only by their lack of originality: beggars from Des Moines, Brooklyn, and New Orleans wrote the same things, in almost the same order, pouring what they must have felt as unique heartbreak into relentlessly formulaic letters. They apologized for intruding, recounted their troubles, and pitched a deal. Many pondered at length their own worthiness and culpability in the face of failure. "I clouded some years of my life by a foolish struggle for freedom from subordinating duties which galled

Actor John T. Raymond and Samuel L. Clemens posed in 1874 to promote the hit comedy Colonel Sellers, *adapted from the novel* The Gilded Age; *this handshake between the ne'er-do-well title character and the author-persona Mark Twain evoked conventional imagery of failure and success.* (Carte de visite by Jeremiah Gurney, courtesy of John Burke.)

me," one of Andrew Carnegie's correspondents wrote in 1886. "Of course I failed and suffered. But the discipline was useful though severe." More than clever panhandling, the begging letter was a confessional and a reflexive crucible of identity.[12]

Beggars forced a dialogue between fame and ill fortune. Men like Rockefeller and Carnegie received letters not only because of their wealth but because they embodied the anachronistic but resilient ideal of self-made manhood. It dated from 1832, long before "firms of large capital" remapped the road to success, yet it still had wide appeal in 1897, when President Grover Cleveland left office and began a lucrative tour promoting his new book, *The Self-Made Man in American Life.* The bootstrap myth defined contemporary masculinity even though few captains of industry had started life poor. A gendered ideal, self-made manhood implied not only that success was a male arena, but also that great men were born of themselves and triumphed without the aid of women. In contrast, men who failed were passive, weak, dependent, and broken. William Dean Howells pronounced a typical eulogy in his 1885 novel, *The Rise of Silas Lapham:* "He was more broken than he knew by his failure; it did not kill, as it often does, but it weakened the spring once so strong and elastic. He lapsed more and more into acquiescence with his changed condition."[13]

Even more than they had in antebellum America, the self-made man and the broken man represented the poles of an ideology of manhood based on achieved identity—the conviction that all men earned their fates and thus deserved whatever credit or disgrace they accrued. J. W. Cleland tried to address this in an 1888 dispatch to Rockefeller. A Kansas City lumber dealer, Cleland asked Rockefeller to rescue some property he owned and promised to share its eventual profits. Cleland began his letter, however, not with current failures but with past successes. "I am a native of Ohio. served in the army of the rebellion from that state," he wrote, "going into the army as a private I came home in the command of my company." Perhaps wanting to emphasize his continued vigor, Cleland did not mention what his military records showed: that the war had weakened his health. "Came to Missouri at the close of the War and started life for myself first by working for wages and afterwards in the lumber business for myself with only my credit as my capital at beginning." Martial valor, wage labor, and credit backed his conviction that he had achieved the status of a true man, not a "crank." Having earned $50,000 in business, he reported this "not . . . with any feeling of braggadoia [*sic*] but only to show that I have not been a '*dependent*'." This résumé represented Cleland as a man of achievement for two people: not merely for the letter's recipient but also for the letter's author. Nevertheless, the lumberman lost his business. After moving his family to Decatur, Illinois, in 1892, he invented a slot machine that paid out cigars and advertising cards—but it did not sell. When he filed for a $100 veteran's bonus, the government sent him a check for 48 cents. He ended up as a traveling sales-man and died at age sixty-nine, as he hurried to catch a train: "J. W. CLELAND FALLS DEAD ON STREET," a local newspaper re-ported.[14]

Men like John W. Cleland believed in working their way "up the ladder," but at the same time they understood that forces larger than individual aptitude spawned self-made and broken men. For some, a begging letter was their only venue for challeng-ing the judgments made about themselves and their loved ones. Fitch Raymond, a bankrupt grocer, knew what all around him must be thinking. R. G. Dun & Company deemed him "an hon-est, hon[ora]ble man" but had last reported on him in 1879: "evi-dence of weakness & cr[edit] not advised at present." In an 1887 begging letter, Raymond wrote about manhood in the voice of an aging striver (he was sixty-seven) who nonetheless bitterly resented the ideology that drove him without a respite. "I have been Struggling incessantly trying to re[g]ain a little foothold but without Success," he informed Rockefeller. "Not because I am an imbecile, shiftless, lazy, listlessly, loafing about, no, not a bit of it, but the reverse is true. I am worried to death trying to better my condition & keep my nose above water, but the trouble is, I have no capital with which to make a start, & it is utterly impossible to make something out of nothing."[15]

Making something out of nothing was a burden often left to the resourceful wives of failed men, for whom publishers issued practical guides to cheap living, such as *Six Hundred Dollars a Year* (1867). Who could afford the lofty ideals of "true womanhood"? Writing to a friend in 1866, the wife of a starving artist dismissed "Emerson's advice to 'suck the sweetness of those consuetudes that lie near you.' I find them saccharine. I think of Emerson as I do my washing." Women compensated for men's failures by penny-pinching, gardening for food, stalling landlords, finding "respectable" jobs like teaching, and starting or taking over busi-nesses—exceeding a contemporary expression, "The first-rate woman does not equal the first-rate man, but she stands far above the second-rate man." Begging letters offered glimpses of women's diverse enterprises. In 1880, one wrote to Rockefeller that she was taking in boarders, "hoping by my own exertions to keep us from real want, until my husband is successful in his efforts." A rural New Yorker wrote in 1891, "my husband lost his business two years ago," and keeping up the mortgage had fallen to her; "if I fail to make the necessary payment this week, all is lost. To lose everything means utter despair, all our hopes, ambitions and aspirations dashed to the ground." Many hastened to preempt stereotypes about the character flaws of failed men. "A truer better man never lived and in every community we have ever lived he has ever borne the most unblemished character," an Ohio wife wrote in 1887, "but he is too trusting for his own good blessing." Evicted in Syracuse without even being allowed to pull up her vegetable garden, a wife named Jane Johnson wrote, "I am *almost discouraged,* still when I see my husband doing his best to get a living and know that it is no *fault* of *his* that he does not succeed, . . . I hope against hope." Not succeeding collapsed the convenient fiction of separate spheres and rendered it all the more inconvenient. Women's letters depicted role reversals in marriages tested by economic failure. By writing, many wives asserted a measure of control, albeit reluctantly, over the problems created by the economic failures of men.[16]

Many wives defended their husbands, and a few boldly challenged the corporate system and its titan. In 1887, a woman from Toledo wrote to Rockefeller, "During the year 1865 I think it was my husband had a wheat transaction with you in which he not only lost every thing he had but was left with a heavy debt with which he struggled for years," adding, "when I used to ask him to explain he would simply answer let us not talk about it." When Rockefeller crushed an oil wildcatter in 1888, the man's sister-in-law confronted him by pointedly using sentimental imagery. "From my quiet corner, I look out on the world and see and read of many men to whom God has given great wealth," wrote Mary Tibbitts of San Diego. "The law exonerates the Standard Oil Co.

from the accusation of defrauding him, all the same . . . when I see a good man of sterling integrity, uprightness and good business ability crushed to the earth by misfortune, I cannot feel as though it is either just or right." In 1891, another wildcatter's wife wrote of her husband's lucky strike, which had fizzled because he could not arrange transport by pipeline and railroad companies—which were famously in cahoots with Rockefeller. "Consequently for many days the Oil run into the earth. . . . Ever since that time it has been borrowing money—paying—interest, mortgaging the home, and more interest—untill now our home must go. . . . I am not a Crank and dont think that I am crazy only a sympathetic wife." Such letters pitted sentimental capital against the more tangible kind.[17]

But if begging letters were part business proposition, part sentimental novel, and part ideological protest, they were also part police report. The begging letter evolved when people who failed were coming under more scrutiny by charity and reform associations, as well as the ever-present credit reporter. "Commercial agencies record every movement from the time one enters business . . . [and] wield a formidable power to benefit or injure," the Bradstreet Company warned young men in 1899. Agents belittled men who were supported by women, making notations such as "his wife is now the business man," "not very indus[trious] but his wife is," "His wife is the manager & much the better for bus[iness]," and "Her husband . . . is a sort of 'shop boy' for her." Just as credit ledgers exposed "worthless" men, "scientific charity" bureaus investigated families to weed out "home slackers" and other "delinquent husbands." The Charity Organization Society, founded in 1868, generated 170,000 case files for New York City alone. Rockefeller sometimes asked a charity or credit agency to verify the circumstances described in a begging letter. Under a thousand eyes—a bureaucratic gaze—prosperity flowed to men whose lives could bear moral and financial scrutiny.[18]

Both senders and recipients understood the begging letter's ties to an emerging culture of surveillance. Awash in letters, Rockefeller asked business acquaintances, charity administrators, and credit reporters to investigate his uninvited supplicants. In 1891, he finally hired a full-time administrator to make "the most careful inquiry as to the worthiness of the cause." Correspondents, for their part, literally begged for inquisition. "I want you to investigate the truth of the statements made in this letter," asked a typical missive of 1891, "and if after investigation you are willing to help me you will receive my lifelong gratitude." By inviting scrutiny, beggars accepted that surveillance and expert judgment had become crucial facilitators of exchange, identity, and obligation in the modern market. Uneasily, Americans conceded that seeking and submitting to investigation was necessary to authorize not only economic exchange, but also self-esteem.[19]

Reporting on their own homes and families, beggars radically extended the jurisdiction of surveillance into realms that even the prying bureaucrats could not tread. With few exceptions, letters from wives were written behind their husbands' backs. From Mrs. Coryell of Colorado came this 1889 letter: "My husband does not know I wrote this, as we have no secrets—I shall tell him, though he will censure me for he is so proud, but pride and poverty do not correspond." One of the wives who accused Rockefeller of ruining her husband nonetheless requested discretion: "I don't want my husband should know any thing about it especially if you must disregard as I know he would go to the stake before he would do what I have done in writing you."[20]

Both husbands and wives wrote out of a sense of family duty, but while men usually begged behind the mask of a business deal, women were more likely to trade in secrets. Sharing with a stranger intimacies they dared not discuss with family or neighbors, women wished to act discreetly to avoid compounding their men's shame. Rockefeller was asked to initiate contact with him out of the blue and say nothing of her letter—leaving the man his pride by keeping up the appearance of an ordinary transaction between two men. A woman aiding her brother noted, "I have said nothing to him upon the subject preferring that you write him." Sometimes female writers rationalized their indiscretion under the malleable rubric of true womanhood. "I feel I have done no wrong," concluded a wife who wrote on the sly, "and what will not a true, loving woman not do for her husband[?]"[21]

By informing on men who did not know they were being watched, wives inadvertently mimicked the controversial credit agencies. But the begging letters of both men and women made up an alternative mode of surveillance, one that differed markedly from official watching and reporting, ranking and rating. Rather than having an outsider's bureaucratic gaze imposed upon them, correspondents insisted on a sentimental gaze. They asked to be judged as complex characters rather than as superficial commodities. They sought redemption in both the spiritual and financial senses of that word. Seeking more than jobs or money, they believed that the Rockefellers, Twains, and Carnegies could turn their failures to success—just by looking at them sentimentally and seeing their authentic selves.[22]

Of course, John D. Rockefeller never saw most of his uninvited correspondents at all. Credit agents and charity investigators actually observed (and often met) their subjects, but the sentimental gaze operated on another plane. What kind of gaze does not actually see? What kind of eyes inspect without looking? This riddle unravels in market culture, where identity—which is to say, value—is always a distillation of hearsay, of rumors about the past and promises for the future. Fortunes are built on commodities traded but never seen, using money that does not exist. Market cultures thrive on the trading of representations: people buy and sell not goods but signs and promises. The answer to the riddle "What kind of eyes see without looking?" is: the eyes of the market, wherein long-distance transactions between unseen strangers are regulated by rationalization and surveillance. Many who labored under the resulting bureaucratic gaze felt that they were watched but not truly seen—by eyes that recorded everything but understood nothing. "The thought pursues me day and night," wrote a woman in her third appeal for her husband, "that if you understood it, you would come to my aid." A sentimental gaze would allow a person to be judged as they truly were, in red blood, not red ink.[23] Beggars sought not charity but conversion. Sentiment became sacrament as correspondents awaited monetary and masculine resurrection. "Man to man," asked a wistful beggar in 1889, "why am I so left to fight—fight without reinforcements?" His own abilities would bring him success, he believed, if only the millionaire demigod would intervene. "Before God, Mr. Rockefeller, I have been and am most sincere but weak in the presence of my possibilities," he concluded. "A kindly notice of my struggle or a word of encouragement, would give a little strength at least." Echoing Protestant conversion narratives (not to mention sentimental fiction), beggars hoped for secular transformation—ascension inside the sentimental market, rather than assistance outside the competitive one.[24]

Beggars' prayers to a tycoon as confessor and redeemer revealed more about the beggars than about the tycoon. Both the redemptive powers of sentimental surveillance and the exchange rate for sentimental capital were calculated in the act of writing itself. Like all autobiographical narratives, the begging letter was profoundly reflexive. Before they could ask for aid, beggars had first to admit to themselves that they had failed. "Believe me," a boyhood friend assured Rockefeller, "this has been one of the hardest tasks I ever undertook—Could you have but the faintest conception of the effort it has cost me, you would I feel convinced read it with a friendly interest." A bankrupt merchant admitted in 1889, "I humiliate myself by appealing for assistance." Writing one's life story, especially a confession of disgrace addressed to the lord of success, was indeed a hard and costly task. Addressing John D. Rockefeller obliged the writers to remake their own identities and to attempt to shape his as well. Although they begged the self-made man to look upon them, epistolary beggars were already gazing at themselves.[25]

The Kindness of Strangers

Beggars had to overcome a fundamental problem: Why should a millionaire help a stranger? "I have no claim upon you whatever and am a total stranger to you," wrote the wife of a failed businessman in 1891. Economic and social transformations in the nineteenth century increased contact and exchange among strangers, both in person and through long-distance transactions. The threat of deceit and distrust gave rise to diverse regulatory modes, such as legal contract and the rules of sentimental culture—and both were crucial preconditions of the begging letter as a mass phenomenon. Correspondents tried to establish trust in two ways: by adopting a sentimental voice of utter sincerity and, more subtly, by reimagining the relations among the people they encountered in the market. "I am no imposter [*sic*] I assure you," one woman wrote, "but come to you with a simple unvarnished story of my troubles." Correspondents emphasized that they were plain speakers. "I have given you a *full detail*," another wrote after seven pages. "I thought it to be the proper way to be candid, plain, & truthful." Begging letters passed between strangers with no basis of mutual trust other than the conventions of sentimental expression.[26]

Writing to a famous stranger was more than an act of faith; it was an act of imagination. Correspondents, many of whom were unschooled, collectively invented a genre that demanded sophisticated writing. To win the desired prize (be it a loan, a job, or just absolution) the writer had to construct two literary characters—a person worthy of being helped and a person capable of helping—and then proceed to imagine and inscribe an obligation between these two characters. The letter allowed these writers to narrate their own lives—to speak directly rather than letting their failures be told by credit reporters or bankruptcy lawyers or charity snoops. "Let us go back," a quarry owner began, "for such is the story-tellers privilege. . . ." A farmwoman in Ohio insisted upon Rockefeller's "hearing the end of the story . . . to show you that if we had missed success we had still done well and failed only by a cruelly small chance." Success and failure were arbitrary. "You have been fortunate, I have been unfortunate," one man wrote simply. Beggars offered up their past to acquire a future. They knew that the difference between success and failure lay in who got to tell the story.[27]

Most letters opened with some acknowledgement of the gulf between author and addressee. "You may consider this rather a strange letter comming [*sic*] from a stranger as it does, one whom you never met," wrote a self-described "broken down" veteran in 1885. Missives from admitted strangers signaled a new awareness of anonymity in an era that fostered exchange and communication between people who had no discernible connection, no common ground, except for the act of exchange. One recognized a stranger visually, by noticing an unfamiliar face. But a stranger "whom you never met" was further removed—this person appeared only in a realm of interaction that lacked both place and opportunities for face-to-face recognition. This placeless realm of blind exchange was one of the venues of the nineteenth-century market, wherein debtors and creditors incurred obligations by letter and telegraph over long distances without ever meeting. Such was the conceptual arena of the begging letter. Not just the hardship of failure but also, curiously, the logic of the market itself produced an epistolary genre that transformed strangers into intimates "whom you never met." Stripped of its pathos, the begging letter was simply a business letter, a facilitator of long-distance exchange among strangers. Its basis was not benevolence but rather market relations. If the epistle succeeded, money or resources changed hands between strangers.[28]

The genre almost certainly owed something to the older practice of political patronage letters, and some beggars imagined that a sort of cultural constituency existed between the famous and the obscure. "In reading your Successful career," a Brooklyn insurance agent wrote to Rockefeller in 1889, "I imagined you might aid me in my struggle to prosperity." A woman from Indiana began, "You will no doubt be surprised to receive this note from an entire stranger, yet I have seen your name so often in the Journal and Messinger [*sic*] that I feel like I might almost have the right of claiming kinship." Many correspondents solved the problem of natural versus unnatural claims in this way. Celebrity itself authorized something like "the right of claiming kinship." Market relations sanctioned sentimental obligations among strangers. The begging letter was a genre whose most basic grammar was that of the archetype; merely by writing to a famous stranger, obscure correspondents asserted on some level that the categories of success and failure ordered the market and connected the people in it.[29]

Even as they asserted sentimental ties, however, epistolary beggars employed the impersonal modes of human interaction that coincided with the integration of a national economy. Beggars traded sentimental capital, but they communicated by thoroughly modern and market-oriented means: by soliciting a geographically distant stranger in writing. After all, the world in which the industrialist had become rich and famous was the first to make intercourse among strangers common and conceivable. Market conventions minimized the mortification of seeking alms. As the wife of a failed rancher explained, "Oh it is so hard to ask aid, and I *could not* go to any one and ask them it is easier to write." Blaming the cold and cutthroat market for their humiliations, beggars retooled its conventions to purchase relief.[30]

But distance did not remove all distinctions between business and benevolence. "I certainly ask again your pardon for trespassing on your time," concluded a longtime office clerk who sought a small business loan in 1889, "& for laying before you my own personal matters." Importuning a stranger on "personal matters" was no routine transaction. H. B. Alvord of Jamaica Plain, Massachusetts, admitted as much in 1894. "What prompts me to do this very unbusinesslike thing, requesting a favor of a person who has never heard of me and consequently could have no interest in me I cannot say," he wrote. "I fully appreciate the ridiculous position in which I may place myself with you."[31]

Was the begging letter inherently "unbusinesslike"? By habit or calculation, the writers' language drew as much on the idioms of business as those of sentiment. The word "favor," which Alvord used, in his day could mean a business order or offer. Business letters typically began, "Your favor of Nov. 29, 1901, just received." A favor was the privilege of transacting business with someone. Still, although Alvord offered bonds as collateral for a loan, he admitted that "it is very hard indeed to ask a favor and hard to find it necessary to do so." He preferred to suggest a quid pro quo. "Much better than a loan would be a position which you might give me possibly. I would serve you to the best of my ability and . . . certainly with perfect honesty. Should you grant me the loan the details of the matter would be arranged as you would wish."[32] Once again, a beggar deployed the "perfect honesty" of sentimentalism to shore up a job or a loan that would be arranged by formal, rational procedures to benefit both parties. Saving face depended on deflecting charity by the pose of the transaction. Buying and selling was the ideal, but borrowing and repaying would do in a pinch. As J. W. Cleland of Kansas City explained, "Should you help me out of my present dilemma [it] will be the proudest effort of my life to honorably pay and discharge the debt." Being in a position to borrow and repay a debt would enable him to begin to redeem his failures and refinance his manhood. Men begged for credibility as much as for credit.[33]

The Political Economy of the Forgotten Man

Probably no beggars were warming themselves inside the Brooklyn Historical Society on 30 January 1883, when William Graham Sumner delivered his social Darwinist paean to the forgotten man, "the clean, quiet, virtuous, domestic citizen, who pays his debts and his taxes and is never heard of out of his little circle." They were forgotten by reformers too eager, in Sumner's view, to coddle "the shiftless, the imprudent, the negligent, the impractical, and the inefficient, or . . . the idle, the intemperate, the extravagant, and the vicious." Sumner railed against contemporary "glorifications of the good-for-nothing" because he viewed failure as the quintessence of natural selection. "A drunkard in the gutter is just where he ought to be," he thundered. "Nature is working away at him to get him out of the way, just as she sets up her processes of dissolution to remove whatever is a failure in its line."[34]

Sumner especially admired that the forgotten man never asked for help. "In a society based on free contract," he explained, "men come together as free and independent parties to an agreement which is of mutual advantage. The relation is rational, even rationalistic. It is not poetical. . . . There is no sentiment in it at all." Rather, Sumner claimed that sentiment had been rightly pushed back into private relations and was a cause of great mischief whenever it escaped into the public sphere. "A free man," he continued, "cannot take a favor. One who takes a favor or submits to patronage demeans himself. He falls under obligation. He cannot be free and he cannot assert a station of equality with the man who confers the favor on him. The only exception is where there are exceptional bonds of affection or friendship, that is, where the sentimental relation supersedes the free relation." This was a rigid interpretation of the contracting free agent, whose qualities of freedom and deal-making perpetuated each other. An Ohio wife understood these lofty principles intuitively when she appealed to Rockefeller for help in 1891. She sent her letter knowing that others "would say in the pride of their hearts dont do it, but I have seen the failure of human wisdom so mutch." She knew that charity and dignity, like liberty and indebtedness, did not mix. "We have tried so hard not to owe aney boddy aney thing," she wrote, but "the case grows more desperate all the time & I cry unto the Lord for deliverance from this bondage."[35]

In their begging letters, forgotten men and women built their own platform for expressing their vision of a free market and their place in it. If any had heard about Professor Sumner's brand of social Darwinism, they did not see fit to mention it. Nor did they seem familiar with Andrew Carnegie's "Gospel of Wealth" (1889), which explained why great corporations "must either go forward or fall behind; to stand still is impossible." Describing this new mode of freedom as "intense individualism," Carnegie insisted that unbridled competition was "best for the race, because it insures the survival of the fittest." The writers of begging letters hardly needed a Sumner or a Carnegie to tell them that their very survival was at stake. The holder of a $10,000 life insurance policy wrote to Rockefeller, "if I take my life now . . . my wife and babe though dishonored, God pity them, shall, at least, have bread." Seeking employment for her husband, an Ohio woman wrote, "Mr. Gordon has been in business has failed is depressed and almost discouraged. I fear for the result." She felt badly about writing a letter behind his back. "My only excuse is I do so long to save my husband."[36]

Although many beggars agreed that charity was worse than death—because it was incompatible with true freedom—unlike Sumner or Carnegie they understood that sentimental relations preceded, constituted, and outlasted all others—both at home and in the marketplace. They invited sentimental surveillance and conjured up tenuous transactions. "I've sat down time & time again to write you but my courage failed . . . ," a decorated Civil War veteran wrote to John D. Rockefeller in 1888, "but the burden of being indebted to so many *cramps* my freedom of feeling and robs me of my sleep at night." Having survived being a Confederate prisoner of war, he was now a traveling evangelist who could not earn a living. "My Andersonville privations and sufferings were nothing compared with what I now am passing through," he claimed. Proposing to sell his life insurance policy to Rockefeller, the writer concluded, "Now the question is will you stand by me and grant me freedom from that which is worse than my Prison life at Andersonville." Rockefeller had once met the man at church in Cleveland and sent him a small check. The veteran wrote in thanks, "The amount sent will at least grant me a breathing spell." Such men desired "a breathing spell," not to escape the market but to stay in it and to recover the freedom that went with active manhood. Letter after letter claimed that if the tycoon would help just this once, the writer would be made fit to seek success again. "I am in alarm lest my all should be swept away," a failed salesman wrote from New Orleans in 1891. "I will hold my grip however the best I can & feel I will come out all right yet[,] especially if some one would step up & give me a little boost & encouragement." Beggars asked neither for alms nor abundance; they asked for a chance to strive again.[37]

However artful the deals contained in begging letters may have been, the philosophy of the "little boost" was not an idle fantasy indulged by shiftless, vicious, "good-for-nothing" people. The writers were making a vernacular stab at political economy. Bitter experience had proved to them that only sentimental capital could sustain the capitalist market and those who spent their lives in the thick of it. The problem of failure was not the fall of drunken shirkers but of "clean, quiet, virtuous, domestic citizen[s]." Epistolary beggars hunted for bargains that would transform and redeem them. Once investigated, appraised, and pronounced both valuable and verifiable on sentimental terms, they could close the deal and they would no longer be beggars or failures. A favor would be neither charity nor enslavement, but rather a liberating deal between equals in a sentimentalized market. That most beggars did not receive the favors they appealed for does not diminish the weight of their complex vision of a sentimental market and the enduring obligations among its free traders—a vision evidently maintained by thousands of ordinary folk long after economists, philosophers, and millionaires were converted to the religion of rationality. In John D. Rockefeller's words, "rational, sane, modern, progressive administration was necessary to success." Big business, he added, was "here to stay.

Like Brother Jonathan in 1819, Uncle Sam found himself a broken-down loser in Judge *magazine's cartoon after the panic of 1893. (*"A Terrible Shrinkage," *Judge.* Author's collection.)

Individualism has gone, never to return." The kind of solitary striving that the writers of begging letters ached to resume had purportedly become obsolete. But to forgotten men and their wives, leveraging sentimental capital to buy back manly self-respect was a transaction that could tip the balance between failure and freedom.[38]

In the culture of "intense individualism" that emerged after the Civil War, success and failure—not slavery and freedom—became the quintessential American axis. Few understood this better than Emma K. Tourgée, "a true, loving woman" who appealed to John D. Rockefeller for a substantial loan in 1890. She offered as collateral the life insurance policy she had kept up on her husband, "a proud sensitive man, battling with ill-health and ill fortune" and "the inability to retrieve himself." She explained, "without his knowledge I have seen his creditors and learn that for $25,000,

I can settle with them all—and by removing this weight, make my husband a free man once more." Rockefeller passed, and her plan failed. Her husband, Albion W. Tourgée, was a carpetbagger judge and author during Reconstruction and a civil rights lawyer. In 1896, he argued—and lost—the famous segregation case *Plessy v. Ferguson* in the U.S. Supreme Court. In 1898, Tourgée wrote an autobiographical novella. "There is no crime the world will not forgive sooner than failure," he mused in the first chapter of *The Man Who Outlived Himself*, the tale of a bankrupt who contracts amnesia and forgets his own life story. "Who was I? I was sure I had been somebody, and ought still to be somebody," the character asks, "but who? who? who was I?"[39]

The Road to Nowhere

"To what do you ascribe your failure in life?" the *Chicago Tribune* asked its vast readership on New Year's Eve 1890, during the season of annual inventories and resolutions. This was a hard-bitten reporter's question that could not have been imagined, let alone asked, at the beginning of the nineteenth century. In 1800, failure was a word that consumed businesses or fortunes but not entire lives. By 1890, millions understood the *Tribune's* question. "Much of interest has been written about those who have battled successfully with the world," read a small notice in bold type that invited replies from "the unfortunates who are so much more numerous." Respondents besieged the paper, and on the first two Sundays of the New Year it printed large batches of letters—"a chorus of wails from the slough of despond." The paper framed the letters in direct counterpoint to the celebrity interviews that were hackneyed even then; instead of asking how a tycoon made his first thousand, the journal would give "an Army of Unfortunates" a "chance to tell what was their stumbling block." The confidential discussions in the begging letter had gone public.[40]

Everything about this "STORY OF REAR GUARD," as the *Tribune's* headline put it, bespoke nearly a century of change in the meanings and jurisdictions of failure. Letters arrived from women and men, clerks and financiers, young and old, to whom failure meant dissatisfaction as much as disaster. Readers scribbled old plotlines about being ruined by "too much honesty," "a desire for fine living," or "lack of ability for making humbug." They also penned modern gothics about being swallowed by "the almighty monster, Monopoly." Some spouted the latest psychological jargon, having fallen by "one's own egotism" or "because I was the round stick in the square hole." A young woman cited "lack of beauty" that condemned her "to suffer wallflowerdom." The *Tribune* suspended its rule against anonymous correspondence and published the unsigned majority over clever monikers devised, most likely, by smart-aleck newsmen: "A Fool," "A. V. Ictim," "A. F. Aultfinder," "A Dead Failure," "A Frank Chump." Some apparently signed their real names, such as J. W. Radner, whose note read simply, "I ascribe my failure in life to the well-known fact that I have not succeeded."

Radner's tautology embraced a profound change of meaning: failure was not just for bankrupts and drunkards anymore. Chumps and fools made good copy because the reading public had come to understand failure as a broad category of identity, not simply as the financial ruin of an entrepreneur. The *Tribune's* query—"To what do you ascribe your failure in life?"—went straight to this point, asking not about economic endeavor but about life in toto, not about tragedy but about trajectory. In this context, Radner's tautology made perfect sense: no great calamity need transpire for his life to be a failure. One might languish in stasis, simply never succeeding. One who answered the call had "always been at 'sixes and sevens.'" At age forty-five, he felt "dwarfed in the monotony of office life and moss-grown in the north bedroom of a boarding-house, ever chafing against these fetters." Here was the familiar debt slave in new digs, confined not in a damp, dark prison but in a dull, dead office. More than ever, failure was a name for the loss of freedom, but both of these American watchwords had taken on new meanings defined by the dread of stasis and stagnation, a moss-grown existence. "A Frank Chump" understood this, writing bitterly, "I have become a fixture in an office with persons whom I don't know and never care to learn." Neither charity nor bankrupt law could redeem dull, routine obscurity, a fate now shared by millions.

Ironically, when the *Tribune* invited "the silent unfortunates" to speak, many realized that they had come to know a sort of failure that was difficult to articulate. One respondent—appropriately, a frustrated novelist—considered his own life a "significant story" but not a coherent one. Autobiography could not convey his failure; he imparted "simply isolated incidents. . . . Here and there a solitary fact, portentous, vital, epochal." A woman unhappy as a schoolteacher sighed, "Often I am tempted to write 'failure' and then lay down my pen forever." It was as if their stories had disintegrated with their dreams. They walked neither the road to success nor the road to ruin, but rather the road to nowhere.

Who would have predicted this at the beginning of the century? During the panic of 1819, New York merchant John Pintard had called for "not a reformation, but a complete revolution." The American plague of restless ambition had begotten "numerous failurs," he wrote. "A new race must arise on the broken fortunes of the present, who different[ly] educated may be content to plod & earn an honest living." However many of Pintard's posterity were "content to plod," they did not necessarily elude failure. Seventy-five years later, in the wake of the panic of 1893, editor Edward Bok condemned Americans as altogether too content. "The average young man in business to-day," he scolded, "is nothing more nor less than a plodder—a mere automatic machine." Bok and Pintard bracketed the greatest change in the American idea of failure, from the era of the debtor's prison to that of the time clock. Both understood failure as a loss of freedom; but by the turn of the twentieth century, the culprit was not insolvency, but inertia; not ambition, but averageness. A half-century before Bok, Herman Melville had warned of Bartlebys toiling away "silently, palely, mechanically," while *Hunt's Merchants' Magazine* criticized

After a half-century of one-on-one confrontations in commercial il-
lustrations, American losers and winners finally met as categories of
identity—"the 'couldn't-do-it' and the 'can-do-it' men"—in this
1908 advertising spread for International Correspondence Schools.
(N. W. Ayer Advertising Agency Collection, Archives Center, National Museum of American History, Smithsonian Institution.)

"second rate men, your slaves of tape and routine . . . keeping up
their monotonous jog-trot forever." By 1884, a best-selling success manual advised, "Better to be dead than to live without an
aim. Better never to have been born than merely to exist and live
a calm, plodding, listless life." The contented plodder of 1819
became the dull plodder of 1893. "Let him die," Edward Bok
sneered, "and his position can be filled in twenty-four hours."
Such a man shot himself to death in a Washington, D.C., hotel
room in 1911. The young manager left one note for his wife and
another for his employer, the Standard Oil Company, to whom
he confessed, "I suppose I am a failure, and this is the only end
that I can see before me." Such men failed by being expendable,
replaceable, interchangeable—or, in a common expression, "dull
plodders with never a story to tell."[41]

Why did it mean failure to have no story to tell—or to have a story so erratic as to be nearly untellable? Even Mark Twain had to abandon a novel called *The Autobiography of a Damned Fool*, based on his elder brother Orion's hapless career as a lawyer, politician, inventor, land speculator, author, proofreader, and chicken farmer. After giving up on *Damned Fool*, Samuel Clemens cruelly suggested that Orion himself write a memoir and call it *Confessions of a Life That Was a Failure*. Ironically, the novelist himself was an intrepid investor who famously went bankrupt in 1894, having sunk $190,000 into a typesetting machine whose 18,000 parts never quite meshed. To get out of debt, he let Henry H. Rogers (a founder of Standard Oil) manage his finances, and he also wrote *Following the Equator* (1897). Mark Twain had often penned his literary adventures in the red ink of Samuel Clemens's financial misadventures, writing because he needed the money. Running short in 1891, he considered letting Tom Sawyer and Huckleberry Finn grow up and meet again at age sixty in a new novel. "They talk of old times," he wrote in his notebook; "both are desolate, life has been a failure, all that was lovable, all that was beautiful is under the mold." Think of it: the all-American boys growing into all-American losers. Tom, the reckless speculator? Huck, the generous fool? Perhaps the story seemed as unworkable as *The Autobiography of a Damned Fool*, and Twain let the boys rest in peace. "There was never yet an uninteresting life," he insisted in 1905. "Inside of the dullest exterior there is a drama, a comedy, and a tragedy."[42]

Failure had become modern, a low hum rather than a loud crash. It meant a fragmented life, not necessarily a shattered one. Anyone could be a failure if that identity reflected utter stagnation instead of outright misfortune. By the time Mark Twain imagined Tom and Huck fading away "under the mold," the American idea of failure centered on problems recognizably our own: aimlessness, routine, stress, conformity, loss of individuality, the dead-end job, the disgrace of being "merely" average. Losers plodded their lives away in offices, factories, and boardrooms—in another country from the almshouses, chancery courts, and mercantile exchanges of old. Back there, back then, at least failure had not sounded dull. Speculators "exploded." Investors "panicked." Merchants "broke." But plodders? They seldom made the papers. "HIS LAST TRIP; Suicide of C. Wilmer Fulsom, the Well Known Traveling Man," announced a death in Ohio in 1892. This salesman shot himself a week after coming home from the road; "he seemed to be affected with melancholy, and would at times appear a little wandering." Wilmer Fulsom would be missed; "he was of a genial, sunny disposition, and universally liked." In 1897, an unemployed Brooklyn button salesman exited less gracefully, gassing himself to death after two botched attempts with razors and poison. His obituary ran beneath the headline "SUCCEEDED AT LAST."[43]

Epilogue:
Attention Must Be Paid

f he had actually lived, Willy Loman would have been born around 1886. As a boy, he saw hard times after the panic of 1893. The family is in a covered wagon, Dakota bound, and the father is carving and peddling wooden flutes along the way. That was Willy's first memory: the wagon and the flute. Though adversity may have driven the Lomans west, to a small boy the journey felt like an adventure. When Willy grew up, he stayed on the road as a traveling salesman. He did what was expected of a man, and he acquired what a man was supposed to have. Willy had a sense of humor and the gift of gab, he was well liked and handy with tools, he kept his job for thirty-five years (even through the Great Depression), he paid off a house and filled it with modern appliances, he owned a Chevrolet, he brought home his paycheck and his wife, Linda, did not need an outside job, and he had two handsome sons, one of whom got a football scholarship to college. Willy lived the American Dream. But the sound of 1893 never left him: the breathy tenor of the flute and the jangling bass of the wagon, a dissonance of panic and hope in the deep ruts that pointed toward the sunset.[1]

Panic and adventure make a typically American duet: now harmonic, now discordant, this Song of Myself is the anthem of an always ambitious but always anxious nation. This was the legacy of the nineteenth century: failure as an imputed deficiency of self. Of all the tunes of bygone days, this is the one Americans still sing to ourselves and each other. It is the song of Willy Loman, who never lived except as a doomed man of sixty-three in Arthur Miller's 1949 tragedy, *Death of a Salesman*. Revived on Broadway for its golden anniversary in the last year of the twentieth century, the play remains the most visceral portrait of the success that is failure.[2]

Critics still ask why Willy's death hurts audiences so deeply. The obvious reason echoes Walt Whitman's explanation of human contradictions: "I am large, I contain multitudes." Willy stands in for myriad American family men whose lives went awry. My paternal grandfather was what people used to call a drunkard; he drifted from Indiana to Nebraska to California, bootlegging and doing odd jobs between sprees. My other grandfather was an immigrant boy whose parents made him quit school to work in the brickyards. During the Depression, after a stint as a traveling salesman, he borrowed $5, made a mattress, sold it, and made another. He got along in his trade, barely, for thirty-five years. He joked that he graduated from "the school of hard knocks," but he felt uneducated and inadequate. His wife sometimes heard him sobbing in the night. Before he died of a heart attack in middle age, my mother quietly paid his taxes to save the only home he ever owned. Decades later, my grandmother told me about his sense of failure. She paused for a very long time before she said, "He was a darn good man."[3]

I never knew either of these men, but we all know them. A half-century later, Arthur Miller still receives letters from strangers who express "gratitude, for the play's stating what they have felt. A few refer to suicides in their own families," he says; sons write to him about fathers, and wives write about husbands. During the years I worked on this book, people often confided family secrets to me. A fellow researcher divulged her father's suicide after an adequate but undramatic career. "My father was Willy Loman," she said; "he did well but thought he should have done better." Her father shot himself when his Ivy League class reunion questionnaire came in the mail, to avoid itemizing his losses. Advance publicity for this book prompted a Colorado man to write to me, saying, "For lack of greed, ruthlessness, extreme aggression, charisma, & other required US 'qualities,' I am doomed to . . . wake in terror every night."[4]

These stories, like Willy's, reflected an emerging "culture of personality" in twentieth-century America. "The go-ahead man buys Kuppenheimer Clothes," declared a 1911 advertisement, restyling a nineteenth-century motto for the Arrow Collar generation. By the 1920s, character traits (honesty and thrift, for example) gave way to personality traits (style and assertiveness, say) as tickets to success. This process began much earlier (recall the interest in "magnetism" and "adapting one's self" in the 1850s), but the cult of personality ripened in the twentieth century. Willy believed in the promise of America, "that a man can end with diamonds here on the basis of being liked!" And why not? By 1925, Temple University founder Russell Conwell had barnstormed six thousand nights giving his motivational talk "Acres of Diamonds." The age of Horatio Alger yielded to the age of Dale Carnegie; self-help programs promised that a winning personality would influence people and ensure success.[5]

Someone coined a new phrase for this promise: "the American Dream." What sounds like an ancient creed was first heard in daily speech in the years after the 1929 stock market crash. Our worst national failure spawned our best national byword of success. James Truslow Adams defined "the *American dream*" in 1931, in his popular one-volume history *The Epic of America*. "It is not a dream of motor cars and high wages merely," he wrote, "but a

Stoop-shouldered and turning his back in shame, the loser of 1910 had "that 'square peg in the round hole' feeling." Psychological testing had been a familiar part of the American experience since 1890, when Ellis Island officers began using spatial puzzles to weed out the unfit. ("Are You a Misfit?" N. W. Ayer Advertising Agency Records, Archives Center, National Museum of American History, Smithsonian Institution.)

dream of a social order in which each man and each woman shall be able to attain to the fullest stature of which they are innately capable, and be recognized by others for what they are." Achievement and identity were one and the same; and yet, more Americans were down and out. Broadway produced a family drama called *American Dream* in 1933, a year when unemployment hit 24.9 percent, 19,859 businesses failed, and 4,004 banks closed. Did anyone still believe that "faults in our mental make-up" explained *Why Men Fail?* That title graced a 1928 volume of papers by leading psychiatrists (including Karl A. Menninger), who attributed failures to "a wrong attitude toward life" associated with "certain types of personality." Critic H. L. Mencken stated the diagnosis more bluntly. The typical American was "vexed, at one and the same time, by delusions of grandeur and an inferiority complex," Mencken wrote; "failure is a succession of unmaskings."[6]

In this sense, the Great Depression was a great unmasking that many found unbearable. The headlines of 1929 quickly entered the folklore of American failure: "LOSER IN STREET CHOOSES SUICIDE," "Another 'Stock Market Suicide,'" "G. E. CUTLER DIES IN WALL ST. LEAP," "ST. LOUIS BROKER SUICIDE OVER CRASH." In the 1930s, economic losers found that even in the hardest times, "hard times" remained a poor excuse for failing. "Everybody, more or less, blamed himself for his delinquency or lack of talent or bad luck," a psychiatrist later recalled of his middle-class patients. "There was an acceptance that it was your own fault," he told interviewer Studs Terkel, "a kind of shame about your own personal failure." Many poorer citizens expressed their shame by scribbling private notes to public officials. "Letters from the Forgotten Man" to President Franklin D. Roosevelt and other New Dealers echoed the begging letters of the Gilded Age—minus the naïve hope that little people might seek help from "the Duponts, Rockefellers, Morgans, and their kind," as a New York wife put it. In 1934, a fifty-five-year-old Massachusetts man begged FDR for a personal loan, saying that suicide was not an option because his nine grandsons "would never live down the disgrace" and adding, "I would not wish at the cost of my life that any one should know I wrote you this letter." When failure became a matter of life and death, everybody knew. In 1937, a Pennsylvania man's "body was found in a carbon-monoxide filled automobile," a local newspaper reported; "Reilly left a note saying he had been 'a failure in life.'"[7]

A collective eulogy to such casualties, Miller's play burned the contours of the doomed striver into our imagination. The covers of *Playbill* and paperback editions of *Death of a Salesman* culminated a century of artists' renderings of failure. Evoking the correspondence-school advertisements of the 1910s, Willy Loman was a man stuck on a treadmill, his shape so recognizable that the artist no longer needed to draw the machine. We see Willy from behind, a familiar silhouette, bent from years of lugging those heavy valises. He has no face because he has every face. Even more than household names like John D. Rockefeller or Bill Gates, who embody what some people hope will happen to them someday, the anonymity of one who fails makes him truly the American everyman. He personifies what really has happened to us or to people we know and love in spite of their flaws.

Miller explained this in a devastating monologue spoken by Linda Loman. "I don't say he's a great man. Willy Loman never made a lot of money. His name was never in the paper. He's not the finest character that ever lived. But he's a human being, and a terrible thing is happening to him. So attention must be paid. Attention, attention must be finally paid to such a person." Her words are passive and awkward, as if her thoughts can hardly be expressed in the American language. Linda's point is Miller's: master plots of blame cannot explain why failure blots out identity. She challenges her sons to see beyond platitudes: "And you tell me he has no character? The man who never worked a day but for your benefit? When does he get the medal for that?"[8]

By paying attention, we can learn a great deal about our culture and about ourselves from the stories of Americans who failed. Reviewing the book *The Life Stories of Undistinguished Americans*

Joseph Hirsch's drawing of Willy Loman evoked a long tradition of failure as broken manhood, perhaps suggesting the fate of the proud peddler daguerreotyped a century earlier. (Playbill, 17 October 1949. Author's collection; photo by Ken Andreyo. PLAYBILL® used by permission.)

(1906), reform journalist Rebecca Harding Davis quoted Horace Greeley to the effect that "if any ignorant man—a man whose life had been entirely commonplace—would write an absolutely truthful account of it, with not a single concealment or apology, the story would have a power and value which no novelist that ever lived could give to it." People who failed did write their own stories, for practical and emotional reasons. True, some concealed and apologized and denied the master plots. But they also internalized mythic and moral explanations of what happened to them. Their stories show how we turned into what self-help quacks say we are: people who "beat ourselves up."[9]

We do this because a century and a half ago we embraced business as the dominant model for our outer and inner lives. Ours is an ideology of achieved identity; obligatory striving is its method, and failure and success are its outcomes. We reckon our incomes once a year but audit ourselves daily, by standards of long-forgotten origin. Who thinks of the old counting house when we "take stock" of how we "spend" our lives, take "credit" for our gains, or try not to end up "third rate" or "good for nothing"? Someday, we hope, "the bottom line" will show that we "amount to something." By this kind of talk we "balance" our whole lives, not just our accounts. Willy Loman speaks this way. Choosing suicide to launch his sons with insurance money, he asks, "Does it take more guts to stand here the rest of my life ringing up a zero?" He insists that a man is not a piece of fruit to be eaten and the peel discarded, but he does not see that a man is not a cash register.[10]

By the end of the nineteenth century, this ideology was fully formed in American culture. Perhaps this explains why failure inspired so many more bards in the twentieth century than earlier, when few besides Whitman sang "vivas to those who've fail'd." Arguably, those who've fail'd are the central figures in our modern literature, from the moral dilemmas of Bartleby and Huckleberry Finn to Jay Gatsby's "huge incoherent failure of a house" and Harry Angstrom's suburban stagnation in John Updike's *Rabbit* novels. "My characters are all failures," Updike remarked in 1992. Critic Terrence Rafferty assessed failed characters, books, and writers (in particular, Ralph Ellison and his 1952 novel *Invisible Man*) and observed, "failure is a kind of truth, too, and the aura of mortality, of inevitable defeat, somehow enriches them. We have no aesthetic of failure; perhaps we should."[11]

But we do have an aesthetic of failure, a mark of stagnation more than financial crisis, and it was largely complete by 1900. This aesthetic preserves entrepreneurial models of individualism in the corporate age even as it stigmatizes team players for being mere cogs. We see its origins when twentieth-century literary characters mouth the words of their real-life ancestors. Sinclair Lewis's George F. Babbitt, the definitive booster and consumer of the 1920s, judged himself by the hundred-year-old language of the age of go-ahead. On the last page of *Babbitt,* he confessed to his son, "I don't know's I've accomplished anything except just get along." On the stage, Tennessee Williams created a rare female icon of failure in *A Streetcar Named Desire;* Blanche DuBois's most famous line, "I have always depended on the kindness of strangers," could have been snipped directly from a Gilded Age begging letter. We understand such characters because they embody our aesthetic of failure, mourning lost souls more than lost fortunes. Eugene O'Neill portrayed wasted lives at their bleakest in *The Iceman Cometh* and *Long Day's Journey into Night;* a reviewer of Broadway's 1999 *Iceman* revival observed, "Our masterpieces of serious drama are dramas of failure."[12]

So are our masterpieces of humor. Charlie Chaplin and Buster Keaton created wandering losers, and later Woody Allen and Rodney Dangerfield portrayed beleaguered neurotics. A blockhead named Charlie Brown treed kites and pitched home-run balls on the comic pages for fifty years. "I didn't realize how many Charlie Browns there were in the world," Charles Schultz said of the character's popularity. "I thought I was the only one." Schultz created neither the first nor the last cartoon loser. From 1913 into the 1940s, Arthur R. Momand's strip in the *New York World* contributed its title to the American language: *Keeping Up with the Joneses.* Dagwood Bumstead epitomized the man in a rut, the late-for-work-clobber-the-postman-lose-that-raise fellow who runs the same rat race for decades without getting anywhere. More recently, Art and Chip Sansom have drawn a popular strip called *The Born Loser.* Scott Adams's phenomenally popular *Dilbert* sympathizes with a little guy trapped in an office cubicle.[13]

Lovable losers and corporate cogs epitomized a redemptive strain in the aesthetic of stagnant or aimless failure. By the 1950s, sociologists and historians such as David Riesman, C. Wright Mills, William H. Whyte, and Vance Packard confirmed the social and psychological costs of striving and competitiveness.

Riesman found many citizens "lacking the 'nerve of failure'" (as opposed to "a failure of nerve"). He explained, "The 'nerve of failure' is the courage to face aloneness and the possibility of defeat in one's personal life or one's work without being morally destroyed." Instead of this courage, American culture usually fed people corny affirmations. Tony Randall, an actor who made a career out of playing little men of large dignity, spoke for the lonely crowd of "organization men" in the 1957 film of George Axelrod's play *Will Success Spoil Rock Hunter?* This screwball satire of corporate advertising climaxed with an earnest monologue from Randall: "All my life, I've fought against being a failure, and I didn't have sense enough to know that I'm not a failure. I'm the largest success there is. I'm an average guy, and all us average guys are successes. We run the works—not the guy behind the big desk. He's knocking himself out trying to figure out how to please *us*—please you and me and all the other usses like us. Who do they try to sell with advertising? Nobody but us. Who gives a television series a good Trendex? We do. Who elects the presidents? Nobody but us. You understand what I'm trying to tell you?" When Bartleby the Scrivener broke his hundred-year silence, he said that attention, attention must be paid.[14]

In fact, from the 1950s onward, losers have occupied something of a market niche, especially in popular music. The Hit Parade gave voice to new masses of born losers. Frankie Brown's "Born to Lose" became a standard covered by everyone from Ray Price to Ray Charles, Ella Fitzgerald, Shirley Bassey, the Everly Brothers, Dean Martin, Tom Jones, Jerry Lee Lewis, and Johnny Cash. Frank Sinatra crooned, "Here's to the Losers." The Beatles made the charts with "I'm a Loser," Janis Joplin belted out "Women Is Losers," and Paul Revere and the Raiders tried "I'm a Loser Too." Typically understated, the Grateful Dead sang simply, "Loser." Ray Price's "Better Class of Losers," Don Gibson's "A Born Loser," Leslie Gore's "I Don't Wanna Be a Loser," Tom Petty's "Even the Losers," Judy Collins's "Hard Lovin' Loser," the Little

Like the early blues standard "Nobody Knows You When You're Down and Out," written by Ida Cox and immortalized by Bessie Smith, "Song of the Failure" (1928) grew so popular in the early Depression years that Vernon Dalhart (a Texan who turned from opera to hillbilly ballads) recorded it for at least nine labels, including Victor and Paramount. (Author's collection.)

River Band's "Lonesome Loser," and Willie Nelson's "The Loser's Song" all aimed at what seemed a growing market segment. Country music could not exist without failure, as singers regret lost loves, lost jobs, lost mamas, and lost trucks. No wonder a new generation of begging-letter writers sought out early country stars like the Carter Family and Hank Williams. "When you get to be a success," Williams said in 1951, "folks have a habit of writing you and telling you their troubles. . . . I dunno, I reckon they think I'm something like the Red Cross."[15]

The folk revival of the 1950s and 1960s peddled more than old-time remedies for the blues. The music of the civil rights and antiwar movements exorcised the organization man by taking failure as a badge of protest and pride. Songwriter Malvina Reynolds is best remembered for a caustic ditty popularized by Pete Seeger, "Little Boxes," a sing-song attack on tract housing and mindless conformity. Later, in a 1965 blues, Reynolds suggested that rebellion was as much a rejection of the man in the gray flannel suit (immortalized in Sloane Wilson's novel of the same name) as it was an embrace of sex, drugs, and rock-and-roll:

> *I don't mind failing in this world,*
> *I don't mind failing in this world,*
> *Don't mind wearing the ragged britches*
> *'Cause those who succeed are the sons of bitches,*
> *I don't mind failing in this world.*[16]

This reversal of definitions had precursors in nineteenth-century worries about men who were "too honest" to succeed among cutthroats, in the tramp cultures of the turn of the century, and in the anticapitalist dust-bowl ballads of Woody Guthrie.[17]

With the possible exceptions of Guthrie and John Steinbeck, no American prophet since Thoreau or Whitman engaged the dilemmas of failure more intensely than Bob Dylan. "For the loser now / will be later to win," he rasped in 1964, "For the times they are a-changin'." Scruffy and colloquial, Dylan veered away from both the intellectual urban hipster of beat culture and the well-scrubbed, pompadoured rebel of James Dean's Hollywood. Instead, the stylized "loser chic" that made Dylan a mass-market superstar descended from earthier iconoclasts—Thoreau, Whitman, Guthrie, Steinbeck. Our prophets have always been loners and drifters who contained multitudes by cataloguing the accumulation of words, images, goods, occupations, misadventures, and identities that frame the commonest lives. As Whitman put it, "Through angers, losses, ambition, ignorance, ennui, what you are picks its way."[18]

Like Whitman's, Dylan's catalogues of America were dizzying and electric. In his 1965 hit "Subterranean Homesick Blues," Dylan rushed to take in the passing scene all at once:

> *Get jailed, jump bail*
> *Join the army, if you fail*
> *Look out kid*
> *You're gonna get hit.*[19]

In the poetry of his lyrics, Dylan wielded the American aesthetic of failure as a potent source of social critique and alternative identity. In songs like "Desolation Row" and "Love Minus Zero/No Limit" he explored—just as Whitman and Woody Guthrie had done—what it was like to live in a chaos of words and plots and names that were the stuff of identity:

> *In the dime stores and bus stations,*
> *People talk of situations;*
> *Read books, repeat quotations,*
> *Draw conclusions on the wall.*
>
> *Some speak of the future;*
> *My love she speaks softly;*
> *She knows there's no success like failure,*
> *And that failure's no success at all.*[20]

Dylan claimed failure as the only remaining moral identity, the only true success. His critique was less a call to nonconformity than a warning about the moral and spiritual costs of striving. Accelerated life made some folks losers by definition—laggards in the race of life. "You lose yourself, you reappear," he sang, "You suddenly find you got nothing to fear." Janis Joplin sang it better in 1970, in a lyric by Kris Kristofferson—"Freedom's just another word for nothing left to lose." If failure had long meant lost or diminished freedom, the rebels of the 1960s reclaimed and redefined it. The same logic inspired Thoreau's errand into the wilderness: "If a man does not keep pace with his companions, perhaps it is because he hears a different drummer."[21]

As we use this phrase today, "different drummer" encourages (or at least tolerates) diversity; it also enables us to dismiss our prophets as mere eccentrics, curious or cool as the case may be. We would rather pay to ignore the advice of therapists and self-help books than freely accept what Thoreau advised after the panic of 1857. "The merchants and banks are suspending and failing all the country over, but not the sand-banks, solid and warm, and streaked with bloody blackberry vines," he wrote. "Invest, I say, in these country banks. Let your capital be simplicity and contentment."[22]

Our enduring discontent inspired darker analyses of achieved identity; from Max Weber and Sigmund Freud to Karl Polanyi and Norman O. Brown we learned that our impulses to strive, acquire, and achieve are not innate but rather are social. Many of the twentieth century's great thinkers agreed that money represents an effort to make value immortal and thus hold death at bay. "Money," John Kenneth Galbraith observed in *The Age of Uncertainty*, "ranks with love as man's greatest source of joy. And with death as his greatest source of anxiety." It is not often that poets, psychoanalysts, sociologists, and economists give the same advice: we fail because we have not learned to die.[23]

For all our modern advances, many of us still live much as nineteenth-century losers did—in perpetual debt. From 1986 to 1996, personal nonmortgage debt nearly doubled in the United States to an average $12,000 per household, and by the late 1990s record numbers of bankruptcies (a million per year) drew a range of responses quite similar to those of the nineteenth century. A popular television game show, *Debt*, gave perky contestants a chance to wipe out large credit card bills, but this kind of entertainment competed with familiar master plots of extravagance and moral responsibility. "Bankruptcy has become in many instances a device of convenience," federal judge Edith Jones said. "People are financing life styles that are beyond their means." By

In the opening sequence of D. A. Pennebaker's film Don't Look
Back *(1965), Bob Dylan performed "Subterranean Homesick
Blues," his rapid-fire recipe for achieving or avoiding modern
"Suckcess."* (By permission of Pennebaker-Hegedus Films and Special Rider
Music.)

tightening bankruptcy laws, Iowa senator Charles Grassley said,
"people will realize that they have to take personal responsibility
for the money they spend." Congressman George W. Gekas was
"bored to tears" by claims that credit card companies lured the
poor into debt. Editorials lamented that the stigma of failure was
gone; but as in antebellum America, others disagreed. A bankruptcy lawyer vouched that most of his clients were not "deadbeats or scoundrels. They are hard-working citizens who have
fallen on hard times, often caused by ill-health or unemployment." Another agreed, saying, "Most people agonize over the
decision to file and are deeply embarrassed."[24]

   Claims about failure without shame are today heard most often
in high technology fields, where the potential for astronomical

profits makes failure a risk worth taking. The erstwhile watchword of California's Silicon Valley, "start-up," was nothing more than a modern revision of the antebellum slogan "Go Ahead!" In this climate, going bust is virtually a business credential. "Americans generally don't mind failure so long as it's spectacular," Louis Menand observed in 2000. "If your Honda Civic is repossessed, you are a deadbeat; if you blow $28 million, you have bought a ticket to the big time. You are, after all, a person who managed to get his or her hands on $28 million (whereas getting one's hands on a Civic is widely thought to be no big trick)." This may well be, but it is not an innovation of Silicon Valley. In April 1848, *Hunt's Merchants' Magazine* noted that smart fellows learned "to fail at the right time; not for a few paltry dollars, which are rigorously taken from you, but a good slapping sum at once; enough to strike your creditors with reverence for your greatness, and respect for your misfortunes." The trouble with such claims is that shame, then and now, is not so easily banished. Nicholas Hall, an author and counselor in Silicon Valley, reports that shameless failure as a tool of innovation "might be the overriding mentality, but when the entrepreneur is going through [failure], all that philosophy flies out the window."[25]

Ideologies of shame and blame appear to have changed little since Joseph Hornor's dilemma of 1819. Today, however, the logic of "the reason, *in the man*" extends not only to white males but to all citizens, shaping opinion and policy not only about bankruptcy but also about poverty, unemployment, welfare, affirmative action, and education. In 1997, University of Texas law professor Lino Graglia provoked controversy when he suggested that Latino and African-American students were not academically competitive because they are raised in cultures where "failure is not looked upon with disgrace." Affirmative action only worsened this problem, according to U.S. Commissioner on Civil Rights Peter N. Kirsanow. After being appointed by George W. Bush, Kirsanow said he favored higher expectations over entitlements that imposed "loserhood on blacks." Meanwhile, controversial studies like *The Bell Curve: Intelligence and Class Structure in American Life* (1995) by Richard J. Herrnstein and Charles Murray have offered purportedly scientific evidence for the existence of born losers. As always, the perennial doctrine of "a reason, *in the man*" continues to inspire both calls for accountability *and* claims of immutability.[26]

So, take your pick: by nature or nurture, some people *are* losers—just as some others *are* winners. "There is this idea now in this country," retorts essayist Fran Lebowitz, "that all people who succeed, succeed on their own, and all people who fail, fail on their own, whereas neither is true." She adds, "Americans almost universally believe that poor people created their poor circumstances, i.e., their own misfortune. Whereas middle-class and rich people have misfortune befall them." She's right; but these are nineteenth-century myths, not something new.[27]

Contemporary worries about credit and surveillance also echo nineteenth-century ideas. Postal and electronic mailboxes brim with warnings that mistaken credit reports can ruin your life, and heaven help anyone who argues with a computer. "Do you know what your Credit Report says about you?" Chase Bank wrote to me recently. *"Are you sure that this very private and personal information on your Credit Report is complete? Is it correct? . . . [I]t is one of the most important documents in your life."* A century ago, credit and collection agencies developed elaborate information codes and hired detectives; today they hunt deadbeats with computer software that assesses up to 500 characteristics of a given individual. In 1848, Ohio merchant John Beardsley challenged the credit reporter's power over his success or failure. By 2000, surveillance was a ubiquitous part of our lives, from the supermarket to the automatic teller machine.[28]

The most chilling manifestation of the American aesthetic of failure at the end of the twentieth century—and of related dilemmas of identity, morals, and even surveillance—was seen in our educational system. School shootings at Columbine High in Littleton, Colorado, and elsewhere exposed the fact that even children and teenagers were caught up in the culture of success and failure. Highly publicized incidents of school gun violence offered deadly proof of how the meaning of failure had changed over two hundred years, from the quaint-sounding notion of "breaking in business" to an ominous identity based more in personality than in character or achievement.

Ironically, contemporary students grew up on mass culture's most sentimental portraits of failure. Television dosed them regularly with *The Wizard of Oz*, wherein Ray Bolger's scarecrow moans, "Oh, I'm a failure, because I haven't got a brain." Frank Capra's *It's a Wonderful Life*, a 1947 Christmas film starring James Stewart, likewise enjoyed a relentless revival in the 1980s and 1990s. George Bailey is a beloved plodder on the verge of bankruptcy in the small town of Bedford Falls, but all ends well with a message from an angel: "No man is a failure who has friends!" But what if your friends are losers, too? Today we speak an adolescent language of exclusion; contemporary synonyms for failure include nerd, dork, dweeb, geek, wimp, freak, jerk, slacker, weirdo, and even fag. "Loser," however, remains the epithet of choice. This is neither the "looser forlorn" of nineteenth-century business nor striver George of Bedford Falls, but rather a misfit or outcast—as in a 1994 hit by the alternative musician Beck, who sings the refrain, "I'm a loser baby, so why don't you kill me?"[29]

At the beginning of a new century, the loser—signified by your right thumb and index finger held up to your forehead—remains a figure at once vulnerable and menacing. Columbine survivors told the press that other students regarded the two shooters as "losers": they dressed oddly and listened to strange music. "This is a pretty preppie, conservative school," said one young woman. "Kids wear Abercrombie, Tommy Hilfiger, American Eagle." This bespoke an American tradition older than shopping mall culture. In 1859, few were surprised that repeated business failures preceded the violence of old John Brown (whose fantasy of universal equality was prima facie evidence of his madness). Today, media interviews with neighbors and criminologists reassure us that loners and losers commit our culture's most horrible crimes, from the shootings of Medgar Evers and John F. Kennedy in 1963, to the Oklahoma City bombing in 1995, to the career of "Unabomber" Theodore Kaczynski, to shoot-outs in post offices and countless murders and rapes. Expert advice after the school shootings centered on tightening security with metal detectors and other means of surveillance, along with "profiling" techniques to identify losers before their rage kills.[30]

Over the past two hundred years in the United States, the image of failure has shifted, from the overambitious bankrupt to the underambitious plodder. Throughout our history, the loser bears material witness to the American dream gone wrong. We know him through a rhetoric that withstood even the September 2001 collapse of the World Trade Centers, targeted by terrorists as symbols of American wealth. The ensuing swell of patriotism made every victim an American hero, but a hierarchy of loss emerged while the dead were still being excavated. Forensic teams identifying the bodies often resorted to genetic testing, but relief administrators calculating the economic value of their lives upheld an older standard. Just as in any wrongful death settlement, explained the *New York Times*, survivors would collect differing amounts of money determined in part by "whether the victims were rising stars or complacent plodders." Sorting national heroes into winners and losers makes for grim work indeed, but apparently it must be done.[31]

A century and a half after Ralph Waldo Emerson surveyed the panic of 1837 and wrote that "the land stinks with suicide," it is hard not to wonder why talk of failure so often leads to talk of death. In 1940, when a famous Wall Street speculator shot and killed himself, he left this note for his wife: "I am not worthy of your love. I am a failure." Arthur Miller dramatized this deadly logic, and in a 1999 interview he explained why failure means oblivion. "The whole idea of people failing with us is that they can no longer be loved," he said. "People who succeed are loved because they exude some magical formula for fending off destruction, fending off death. It's the most brutal way of looking at life that one can imagine, because it discards anyone who does not measure up. It wants to destroy them." No wonder we have forgotten the American history of failure and the lives it ruined. "You are beyond the blessing of God," Miller concludes. "It's a moral condemnation that goes on. You don't want to be near this failure."[32]

We are not invited to Willy Loman's funeral, but in the brief "Requiem" that ends the play, the characters gather to look at his grave. Even if the tombstone were not imaginary, the audience would not be in a position to see the epitaph for a man who never lived. To paraphrase Linda Loman, a small man can write his own epitaph just as well as a great man. No philosopher since Benjamin Franklin has given us more maxims of success and failure than Willy Loman. "Be liked and you will never want." "A man is not a piece of fruit!" "I am not a dime a dozen!" The most fitting epitaph might have been lines from Wallace Stevens's poem "Men Made Out of Words," published in 1947, two years before Willy's requiem opened on Broadway:

We compose these propositions, torn by dreams,

By the terrible incantations of defeats
And by the fear that defeats and dreams are one.[33]

The losers among us, people who bear failure as an identity, embody the American fear that our fondest hopes and our worst nightmares may be one and the same. How is it plausible that a fifteen-year-old student could be a loser, defined fundamentally yet with his whole life ahead; or Willy Loman, the homeowner, hard worker, husband, father, and seller of the American Dream? These things are possible because that dream—the dream that equates freedom with success—could neither exist nor endure without failure. We need the loser—the word and the person—to sort out our own defeats and dreams. "Let us be thankful for the fools," Mark Twain wrote with typically dark humor in 1897. "But for them the rest of us could not succeed." Of all the paradoxes of failure in America, surely this is the darkest. Long ago, we saw through old fables of rags to riches; it is still fun to dream, but we know that we are partaking of a cultural myth.[34] But if we do not quite believe in that kind of success, our faith in the myths of failure is unshaken. We are merrily cynical about whether the average tycoon really tugged on those bootstraps, but we still believe with deadly seriousness that the reasons for failure are usually individual—*"in the man."* Failure is not the dark side of the American Dream; it is the foundation of it. The American Dream gives each of us the chance to be a born loser.

Notes

Acknowledgments

Index

Notes

Abbreviations

AAS   American Antiquarian Society, Worcester, Mass.
HBS   Harvard Business School, Harvard University, Boston, Mass.
HML   Hagley Museum and Library, Wilmington, Del.
HMM   *Hunt's Merchants' Magazine*
LC   Manuscript Division, Library of Congress, Washington, D.C.
NARA   National Archives and Records Administration, Washington, D.C.
NYHS   New-York Historical Society, New York, N.Y.
NYPL   New York Public Library, New York, N.Y.
NYT   *New York Times*
RFA   Rockefeller Family Archives, Rockefeller Archive Center,
         Pocantico Hills, Sleepy Hollow, N.Y.
RISA   Rhode Island State Archives, Providence, R.I.
VHS   Virginia Historical Society, Richmond, Va.

Prologue

1. Robert D. Richardson, Jr., *Henry Thoreau: A Life of the Mind* (Berkeley: University of California Press, 1986), 389. Walter Harding, *The Days of Henry Thoreau: A Biography* (New York: Dover, 1982 [orig. 1965]), 466–468. Kenneth Walter Cameron, *Emerson, Thoreau, and Concord in Early Newspapers* (Hartford: Transcendental Books, 1958), 16, 146, 318–320.
2. [Ralph Waldo Emerson], "Thoreau," *Atlantic Monthly* 10 (August 1862), 239–249, esp. 248. Joel Myerson, "Emerson's 'Thoreau': A New Edition from Manuscript," in *Studies in the American Renaissance: 1979*, ed. Joel Myerson (Boston: Twayne Publishers, 1979), 53. *The Heart of Emerson's Journals*, ed. Bliss Perry (Boston: Houghton Mifflin, 1926), 256. Louisa May Alcott to Alfred Whitman, 11 May [1862], in *The Selected Letters of Louisa May Alcott*, ed. Joel Myerson and Daniel Shealy (Boston: Little, Brown, 1987), 74–75. Robert Sattelmeyer, "'When He Became My Enemy': Emerson and Thoreau, 1848–49," *New England Quarterly* 62 (1989): 187–204. Thoreau to Henry Williams, Jr., 30 September 1847, in Harding, *Days of Henry Thoreau*, 185–186.
3. Among many early lexicons, see Caleb Alexander, *The Columbian Dictionary of the English Language; in which Many New Words, peculiar to the United States, and many words of general use not found in any other English Dictionary are inserted* . . . (Boston: Thomas and Andrews, 1800), 196.

Henry D. Thoreau, *Walden*, ed. J. Lyndon Shanley (Princeton: Princeton University Press, 1971), 8.

4. Daniel Walker Howe, *The Political Culture of the American Whigs* (Chicago: University of Chicago Press, 1979), ch. 5. Gary J. Kornblith, "Self-Made Men: The Development of Middling-Class Consciousness in New England," *Massachusetts Review* (Summer–Autumn 1985): 461–474.

5. Augustus Thomas to Thomas A. Jenckes, Closter, Bergen County, N.J., 18 May 1866, box 32, folder "May 16–31, 1866," Thomas A. Jenckes Papers, Manuscript Division, Library of Congress. Julia Culbertson to John D. Rockefeller, Sr., Chambersburg, Pa., 2 March 1892, box 10, folder 75, Office Correspondence series, John D. Rockefeller Papers (Record Group 1), Rockefeller Family Archives, Rockefeller Archive Center, Pocantico Hills, Sleepy Hollow, N.Y. (hereafter RFA).

6. "Why They Failed: A Budget of Frank Confessions from Men and Women Who Missed Success," *Success* 1 (November 1898): 24. "The Fear of Failure," *The Cosmopolitan* 35 (June 1903): 233. "Are You Working Like a Horse?" (advertisement for International Correspondence Schools), *Success* 7 (March 1904): 217. Booker T. Washington, "Education Will Solve the Race Problem: A Reply," *North American Review* 171 (August 1900): 221–233, esp. 226. "It Is Easy to Be a 'Nobody,'" *Success* 5 (November 1902): 673.

7. Max Weber, *The Protestant Ethic and the Spirit of Capitalism*, trans. Talcott Parsons (New York: Charles Scribner's Sons, 1958), 54.

8. Henry D. Thoreau, *Journal, Volume 1: 1837–1844*, ed. John C. Broderick et al. (Princeton: Princeton University Press, 1981), 107 (11 February 1840). Weber, *Protestant Ethic*, 72.

9. William Graham Sumner, "The Forgotten Man," in *The Forgotten Man and Other Essays*, ed. Albert Galloway Keller (Freeport, N.Y.: Books for Libraries Press, 1969 [orig. 1918]), 465–495, esp. 480, 475–476, 493. Franklin D. Roosevelt, Radio address, 7 April 1932, in *The Public Papers and Addresses of Franklin D. Roosevelt, with a Special Introduction and Explanatory Notes by President Roosevelt* (New York: Random House, 1938), 1:625. Leo Durocher, *Nice Guys Finish Last* (New York: Simon and Schuster, 1975).

10. *Proceedings of the citizens of Boston favorable to a revision of the laws in relation to debtor and creditor . . .* [Boston: Putnam and Hunt, 1829], 2. Joel Porte, *Representative Man: Ralph Waldo Emerson in His Time* (New York: Oxford University Press, 1979), 249. Ralph Waldo Emerson, *The Journals of Ralph Waldo Emerson*, ed. Edward Waldo Emerson and Waldo Emerson Forbes (Boston: Houghton Mifflin, 1909–1914), 20 and 21 May 1837, 4:217–218. C[ornelius] M[athews], "The Unrest of the Age," *Arcturus* 1, no. 3 (February 1841): 133–137, esp. 133.

11. Diary of Edward Neufville Tailer, Jr., vol. 12, 13 July 1855, New-York Historical Society, New York, N.Y. (hereafter NYHS). Peyton Harrison to father, 7 July 1831, Albemarle, Va., Virginia Historical Society, Richmond, Va. (hereafter VHS). "Suicide.—John Buhring," *New York Commercial Adver-*

tiser, 11 April 1837. "The Louisiana Advertiser Says," *Niles' National Register,* 14 October 1837. "Remarkable Suicides," *The New-Yorker* 8 (7 December 1839): 180–181. "Suicide," *The New-Yorker* 9 (12 September 1840): 415. Diary of Henry Van Der Lyn, 14 August 1846, vol. 6, p. 116, NYHS. Philip Hone, *The Diary of Philip Hone, 1828–1851,* ed. Allan Nevins (New York: Dodd, Mead and Co., 1936), 259. Charles P. Kindleberger, *Manias, Panics, and Crashes: A History of Financial Crises* (New York: Basic Books, 1989), 105–107.

12. "Statistics of the 'Uniform System of Bankruptcy' of 1841," *Hunt's Merchants' Magazine* 16 (April 1847): 414 (hereafter *HMM*). See also "Statistics as to Failures from Dec. 25, 1857, to Dec. 1858," *HMM* 40 (February 1859): 204–205; and "Number of Failures in the United States in January, 1861," *HMM* 44 (March 1861): 327–328. Peter J. Coleman, *Debtors and Creditors in America: Insolvency, Imprisonment for Debt, and Bankruptcy, 1607–1900* (Madison: State Historical Society of Wisconsin, 1974), 287–288. Peter R. Decker, *Fortunes and Failures: White-Collar Mobility in Nineteenth-Century San Francisco* (Cambridge, Mass.: Harvard University Press, 1978), 92. Clyde Griffen and Sally Griffen, *Natives and Newcomers: The Ordering of Opportunity in Mid-Nineteenth-Century Poughkeepsie* (Cambridge, Mass.: Harvard University Press, 1978), 104, 110. Cindy Sondik Aron, *Ladies and Gentlemen of the Civil Service: Middle-Class Workers in Victorian America* (New York: Oxford University Press, 1987), 25–27.

13. Thoreau, *Walden,* 32–33. Robert Louis Stevenson, "Henry David Thoreau: His Character and Opinions" (1880) in *Familiar Studies of Men and Books,* 3rd ed. (London: Chatto and Windus, 1888), 129–171, esp. 137. [Asa Greene], *The Perils of Pearl Street, Including a Taste of the Dangers of Wall Street, by a Late Merchant* (New-York: Published by Betts and Anstice, and Peter Hill, 1834), 7. Henry A. S. Dearborn, "Address before an Agricultural Meeting of the Legislature," 28 February 1840, excerpted in "The Chances of Success in Mercantile Life," *HMM* 15 (November 1846): 475–477. Diary of Samuel C. Morton, 23 December 1842, vol. 8 (5th extant vol.), Hagley Museum and Library, Wilmington, Del. (hereafter HML). U.S. Congress, House Committee on the Judiciary, *Report to Accompany H. R. 16,* 27th Cong., 1st sess., 1841, H. Rept. 5, p. 8. Thomas Wentworth Higginson, "Conscience in the Counting Room, or the True Interests of the Merchant," *HMM* 28 (January 1853): 19–40, esp. 27. George Fitzhugh, *Sociology for the South, or the Failure of Free Society* (Richmond: A. Morris, 1854), 239. Russell H. Conwell, *Acres of Diamonds: How Men and Women May Become Rich . . .* (Philadelphia: Miller-Megee Co., 1889), 77. Joseph C. Carter, *The "Acres of Diamonds" Man* (Philadelphia: University of Pennsylvania Press, 1981), 634. "Do Ninety-Five out of Every Hundred Business Men Fail?" *Success* 8 (March 1905): 210. "Why Business Men Fail," *System* 13 (April 1908): 342.

14. Success studies range from Irvin Wyllie, *The Self-Made Man in America* (New York: Free Press, 1966 [1954]) to the gender analysis in Judy Hilkey,

Character Is Capital: Success Manuals and Manhood in Gilded Age America (Chapel Hill: University of North Carolina Press, 1997). Benjamin Franklin, *The Autobiography of Benjamin Franklin*, ed. Leonard W. Labaree et al. (New Haven: Yale University Press, 1964), 9–19. Michael Burlingame, *The Inner World of Abraham Lincoln* (Urbana: University of Illinois Press, 1994), 4. Samuel Smiles, *Self-Help: With Illustrations of Character, Conduct, and Perseverance*, rev. ed. (Chicago: Belford, Clarke, and Co., 1881 [1859]), vi. George Humphrey quoted in Stephen J. Whitfield, *The Culture of the Cold War*, 2nd ed. (Baltimore: Johns Hopkins University Press, 1996), 71. Alfred D. Chandler, Jr., "Commentary on Gray and Salsbury," in *Proceedings of the Business History Conference*, ed. Herman E. Krooss ([Bloomington]: Division of Research, School of Business, Indiana University, 1975), 192.

15. Joyce Appleby, *Inheriting the Revolution: The First Generation of Americans* (Cambridge, Mass.: Harvard University Press, 2000), 22. For more extended discussion of the historiographical, archival, and theoretical foundations of *Born Losers*, see Scott A. Sandage, "Deadbeats, Drunkards, and Dreamers: A Cultural History of Failure in the United States, 1819–1893" (Ph.D. diss., Rutgers University, 1995).

16. "A Sermon upon Failing," *Boston Miscellany of Literature and Fashion* 1, no. 6 ([June] 1842): 245–247, esp. 246.

17. Charles Sellers, *The Market Revolution: Jacksonian America, 1815–1846* (New York: Oxford University Press, 1991). Melvyn Stokes and Stephen Conway, eds., *The Market Revolution in America: Social, Political, and Religious Expressions, 1800–1880* (Charlottesville: University Press of Virginia, 1996). Thomas L. Haskell and Richard F. Teichgraeber III, eds., *The Culture of the Market: Historical Essays* (Cambridge: Cambridge University Press, 1993). David Leverenz, *Manhood and the American Renaissance* (Ithaca: Cornell University Press, 1989). E. Anthony Rotundo, *American Manhood: Transformations in Masculinity from the Revolution to the Modern Era* (New York: Basic Books, 1993), esp. 178–185. Toby L. Ditz, "Shipwrecked; or, Masculinity Imperiled: Mercantile Representations of Failure and the Gendered Self in Eighteenth-Century Philadelphia," *Journal of American History* 81 (June 1994): 51–81. Louis Galambos, "What Makes Us Think We Can Put Business Back into American History?" *Business and Economic History*, 2nd ser., 20 (1991): 1–11. Kenneth Lipartito, "Culture and the Practice of Business History," *Business and Economic History*, 2nd ser., 24 (1995): 1–41. Studies of aspects of failure include Martha Banta, *Failure and Success in America: A Literary Debate* (Princeton: Princeton University Press, 1978); James Ciment, "In Light of Failure: Bankruptcy, Insolvency and Financial Failure in New York City, 1790–1860," (Ph.D. diss., City University of New York, 1992); Barbara Allen Mathews, "'Forgive Us Our Debts': Bankruptcy and Insolvency in America, 1763–1841" (Ph.D. diss., Brown University, 1994); Edward J. Balleisen, *Navigating Failure: Bankruptcy and Commercial Society in Antebellum America* (Chapel Hill: University of North Carolina Press,

2001); and Bruce H. Mann, *Republic of Debtors: Bankruptcy in the Age of American Independence* (Cambridge, Mass.: Harvard University Press, 2002).

18. Perry Miller, *The New England Mind: From Colony to Province* (Cambridge, Mass.: Belknap Press of Harvard University Press, 1981 [1953]), 40, 51. Thomas Prince, *The Pious Cry to the Lord for Help When the Godly and Faithful Fail among Them: A Sermon . . .* (Boston: Printed for T. Rand in Cornhil[l], 1746), 16.

19. Alexander, *Columbian Dictionary*, 196. "Extract of a Letter from Manchester to a Gentleman in Philadelphia, May 4," *Pennsylvania Gazette*, 3 July 1793. William Cooper Howells, *Recollections of Life in Ohio from 1813 to 1840* (Gainesville, Fla.: Scholars' Facsimiles and Reprints, 1963 [1895]), 83. "Letters on the Eastern States," *North American Review* 11 (July 1820): 68–103, esp. 80.

20. "The Pioneer," *The Free Enquirer* (26 June 1830): 283. Rensselaer Bentley, *The Pictorial Definer; Containing the Most Important Words in the English Language Familiarly Defined . . .* (New York: C. Shepard and Co., 1852); *Noah Webster's First Edition of an American Dictionary of the English Language*, 6th ed. (San Francisco: Foundation for American Christian Education, 1989), n.p.; Noah Webster, *An American Dictionary of the English Language*, ed. Chauncey A. Goodrich (Springfield, Mass: George and Charles Merriam, 1855), 432–433; Noah Webster, *An Explanatory and Pronouncing Dictionary of the English Language, with Synonyms*, ed. William G. Webster and Chauncey A. Goodrich (New York: Mason Brothers, 1857), 133; *The Merchants' and Bankers' Almanac for 1861* (New-York: J. Smith Homans, Jr., 1861), 188.

21. Joel Porte, ed., *Emerson in His Journals* (Cambridge, Mass.: Harvard University Press, 1982), 324. Nathaniel Hawthorne, *The House of the Seven Gables* (Columbus: Ohio State University Press, 1974), 157–158. [Herman Melville], "The Happy Failure: A Story of the River Hudson," *Harper's New Monthly Magazine* 9 (July 1854): 196–199. Abraham Lincoln, "Fragment on Stephen A. Douglas" [December 1856?], *The Collected Works of Abraham Lincoln*, ed. Roy P. Basler (New Brunswick: Rutgers University Press, 1953), 2:382–383 (unless otherwise noted, emphasis in original). Henry David Thoreau, "Life without Principle," in *The Writings of Henry David Thoreau* (Boston: Houghton Mifflin and Co., 1906), 4:455–482, esp. 460. Walt Whitman, *Complete Poetry and Collected Prose*, ed. Justin Kaplan (New York: Library of America, 1982), 44; Whitman later revised this passage of "Song of Myself" as a separate poem, "To those who've fail'd, in aspiration vast" (ibid., 613).

22. Louis P. Masur, "'Age of the First Person Singular': The Vocabulary of the Self in New England, 1780–1850," *Journal of American Studies* 25 (1991): 189–211. Wai-chee Dimock, *Melville and the Poetics of Individualism* (Princeton: Princeton University Press, 1989), ch. 6. Richard Rabinowitz, *The Spiritual Self in Everyday Life: The Transformation of Personal Religious Experience in*

Nineteenth-Century New England (Boston: Northeastern University Press, 1989). Richardson, *Henry Thoreau,* 332, 388. Thoreau, "Life without Principle," 457. Bradley P. Dean, "Reconstructions of Thoreau's Early 'Life without Principle' Lecture," in *Studies in the American Renaissance, 1987,* ed. Joel Myerson (Charlottesville: University Press of Virginia, 1987), 285–364.

23. Thoreau, "Life without Principle," 458, 461, 463. [Henry D. Thoreau], *The Journal of Henry D. Thoreau,* ed. Bradford Torrey and Francis H. Allen (New York: Dover Publications, 1962 [1906]), 2:1735 (29 November 1860). Richardson, *Henry Thoreau,* 332.

24. "Have Merchants Too Much Business to Read?" *HMM* 32 (May 1855): 649–650. William H. Siles, ed., "Quiet Desperation: A Personal View of the Panic of 1837," *New York History* (January 1986): 89–92. Credit report (1853–1857) of Asa L. Shipman, New York, vol. 369, p. 518, R. G. Dun & Co. Collection, Baker Library, Harvard Business School, Harvard University, Boston, Mass. (hereafter HBS; also, unless otherwise noted, all credit reports cited are from this collection).

25. Alexis de Tocqueville, *Democracy in America,* trans. Henry Reeve, rev. Francis Bowen, ed. Phillips Bradley (New York: Knopf, 1949), 2:155, 243–244. Richard L. Bushman, "'This New Man': Dependence and Independence, 1776," in *Uprooted Americans: Essays to Honor Oscar Handlin,* ed. Richard L. Bushman, et al. (Boston: Little, Brown and Co., 1979), 97–124. Rowland Berthoff, "Independence and Attachment, Virtue and Interest: From Republican Citizen to Free Enterpriser, 1787–1837," in ibid., 77–96. Joseph Kett, *Rites of Passage: Adolescence in America, 1790 to the Present* (New York: Basic Books, 1977), 94, 107. The classic work on such anxieties in modern America is Barbara Ehrenreich, *Fear of Falling: The Inner Life of the Middle Class* (New York: Pantheon, 1989). Andrew Delbanco, *The Death of Satan: How Americans Have Lost the Sense of Evil* (New York: Farrar, Straus and Giroux, 1995), 105–106.

26. James M[inor] Holladay, "On the love of Wealth & Preeminence," 26 May 1835, VHS.

27. James M[inor] Holladay, "On Happiness," n.d., VHS.

28. Diary of C[hauncey] W. Moore, entries dated 22–24 December 1842, vol. 1, pp. 6–9, Rare Book and Manuscript Collection, New York Public Library, New York, N.Y. (hereafter NYPL).

29. Ibid., 6 March–29 April 1843, vol. 1, pp. 54–85. Credit reports (1847–1888) of Chauncey W. Moore and John T. Moore, New York, vol. 197, pp. 19, 100G; vol. 204, pp. 701D, 726, 800ZZ; and vol. 375, p. 200A.71. Job 33:29–30.

30. Moore credit report, vol. 197, p. 19.

31. Ibid., vol. 204, pp. 701D, 726.

32. Trifle and the Editor [Warren Tilton], *The Trifleton Papers* (Boston: Whittemore, Niles and Hall, 1856), excerpted in "Mercantile Failures," *HMM* 35 (October 1856): 519–520.

33. D. C. Colesworthy, "A Man Who Has Failed," *HMM* 20 (January 1849):

120. P[hineas] T. Barnum, *The Life of P. T. Barnum, Written by Himself* (New York: Redfield, 1855). Barnum, *Struggles and Triumphs: or, Forty Years' Recollections of P. T. Barnum* (Hartford: J. B. Burr, 1869). Benjamin Wood, *The Successful Man of Business,* 2nd ed. (New York: Brentano's, 1899), 173–174. J. L. Nichols, *The Business Guide; or, Safe Methods of Business,* rev. ed. (Naperville, Ill.: J. L. Nichols and Co., 1901 [orig. 1886]), 18.

34. Orson S. Fowler, *Self-Culture and Perfection of Character* (1868), quoted in Masur, "Age of the First Person Singular," 203.

35. W. E. B. Du Bois, *Black Reconstruction in America, 1860–1880* (New York: Atheneum, 1992 [1935]), 182–183. J. W. Bomgardner to John D. Rockefeller, Sr., Atchison, Kan., 19 November 1890, box 4, folder 34, RFA.

36. Thoreau, *Journal,* 1:133 (20 June 1840). Thoreau, "Life without Principle," 477. Harding, *Days of Henry Thoreau,* 469.

37. Harding, *Days of Henry Thoreau,* 340–341. Thoreau, *Walden,* 326.

1. Going Bust in the Age of Go-Ahead

1. The first American publication of the folktale about the sky falling was [John Greene Chandler], *Remarkable Story of Chicken Little* (Boston: T. H. Carter & Co., 1840). Among many examples of images of panics, see "Scene in the Gold Room, New York City, on 'Black Friday,'" in Charles P. Kindleberger, *Manias, Panics, and Crashes: A History of Financial Crises* (New York: Basic Books, 1989), title page. Philippe Borgeaud, *The Cult of Pan in Ancient Greece,* trans. Kathleen Atlass and James Redfield (Chicago: University of Chicago Press, 1988). "The Panic," *Harper's Weekly,* 7 November 1857, 708.

2. [Frederick Jackson] *A Week in Wall Street: By One Who Knows* (New-York: Published for the Booksellers, 1841), 130. Thomas G. Cary, "Causes of Failure among Men in Business," *HMM* 15 (September 1846): 260.

3. Diary of Frederick E. Westbrook, 2 July 1842, pp. 165–166, Rare Book and Manuscript Collection, NYPL.

4. Thomas Emerson to "Friend Waller," Windsor, Vt., 6 November 1838, in [Letters], [Windsor, Vt.: n.p., 1839?], n.p., Goldsmith Kress Collection, reel 2857, Baker Library, HBS. Diary of Samuel B. Willeford, 31 August 1838, 24 September 1838, 17 October 1838, and 23 February 1839, VHS (I have silently omitted a repeated word in the first quotation). Daniel W. Crofts, "Southhampton County Diarists in the Civil War Era," *Virginia Magazine of History and Biography* 98 (October 1990): 537–612, esp. 544–545.

5. John Russell Bartlett, *Dictionary of Americanisms: A Glossary of Words and Phrases, Usually Regarded as Peculiar to the United States* (New York: Bartlett and Welford, 1848); 2nd ed. (1859); Bartlett, *Dictionary of Americanisms: A Glossary of Words and Phrases Usually Regarded as Peculiar to the United States,* 4th ed. (Boston: Little, Brown and Co., 1877). Diary of Henry Van Der Lyn, 30 November 1844, vol. 5, p. 411, NYHS. Diary of Edward Neufville Tailer, Jr., 30 December 1854, vol. 12, n.p., NYHS. Report of

Cowles, Sickles and Co., 25 June 1855, Ohio, vol. 78, p. 25; and report of George A. Ryan, 18 January 1856, Virginia, vol. 29, p. 31; both in R. G. Dun and Co. Collection, HBS. Van Der Lyn diary, 16 February 1834, vol. 4, p. 44; 30 November 1844, vol. 5, p. 411.

6. Joseph S. Ropes to "My dear Uncle" [Hardy Ropes], St. Petersburg, Russia, 30 August/11 September 1839, folder 2–6 Ropes 1839, Ropes Family Papers, HBS. Ropes to "My dear Grandparents" [Mr. and Mrs. Samuel Ropes], St. Petersburg, Russia, 19 September/1 October 1840, folder 2–7 Ropes 1840, HBS. Harriet Ropes Cabot, "The Early Years of William Ropes & Company in St. Petersburg," *American Neptune* 23 (April 1963): 131–139.

7. *The Crockett Almanac* (Nashville, Tenn: [B. Harding], 1839). Philip Hone, *The Diary of Philip Hone, 1821–1851,* ed. Allan Nevins (New York: Dodd, Mead, 1936), 261. "Influence of Commerce upon Language," *HMM* 24 (February 1851): 174–180, esp. 178. "American Enterprise," *New York Times* (hereafter *NYT*), 29 January 1855.

8. Two essential studies of such legal and moral dilemmas are Edward J. Balleisen, *Navigating Failure: Bankruptcy and Commercial Society in Antebellum America* (Chapel Hill: University of North Carolina Press, 2001); and Bruce Mann, *Republic of Debtors: Bankruptcy in the Age of American Independence* (Cambridge, Mass.: Harvard University Press, 2002). "The Financial Crisis," *New Englander and Yale Review* 15 (November 1857): 701–715, esp. 702. Ropes to "My dear Grandparents," 19 September/1 October 1840.

9. Hon. Joseph Hopkinson, "Lecture on Commercial Integrity," *HMM* 1 (November 1839): 377–390, esp. 381–382.

10. Joseph Schumpeter, "Comments on a Plan for the Study of Entrepreneurship," in *Joseph A. Schumpeter: The Economics and Sociology of Capitalism,* ed. Richard Swedberg (Princeton: Princeton University Press, 1991), 406–428. James T. Kloppenberg, "The Virtues of Liberalism: Christianity, Republicanism, and Ethics in Early American Political Discourse," *Journal of American History* 74 (June 1987): 9–33. Ralph Waldo Emerson, "Wealth," in *The Complete Works of Ralph Waldo Emerson,* ed. Edward Waldo Emerson, vol. 6, *The Conduct of Life* (Boston: Houghton Mifflin, 1903–1904), 125. Cousin "R. Waldo Emerson" appears in Diary of Hardy Ropes, 11 March 1829, Ropes Family Papers, HBS.

11. Letterbook of Joseph P. Hornor, HML. Charles Sellers, *The Market Revolution: Jacksonian America, 1815–1846* (New York: Oxford University Press, 1991), 131–132. Christopher Clark, "The Consequences of the Market Revolution in the American North," in *The Market Revolution in America: Social, Political, and Religious Expressions, 1800–1880* ed. Melvyn Stokes and Stephen Conway (Charlottesville: University Press of Virginia, 1996), 23–42, esp. 37–38. Richard R. John, *Spreading the News: The American Postal System from Franklin to Morse* (Cambridge, Mass.: Harvard University Press, 1995).

12. New Jerseyan quoted in Sellers, *Market Revolution,* 137. Peter Bowdoin

to Joseph Prentis, 21 February 1824, Prentis Family Papers, Alderman Library, University of Virginia, quoted in Jan Lewis, *The Pursuit of Happiness: Family and Values in Jefferson's Virginia* (Cambridge: Cambridge University Press, 1983), 136. "Hard Times" (ca. 1775–1810), broadsides collection, American Antiquarian Society, Worcester, Mass. (hereafter AAS).

13. Murray N. Rothbard, *The Panic of 1819: Reactions and Policies* (New York: Columbia University Press, 1962), v. Sarah Alice Kidd, "The Search for Moral Order: The Panic of 1819 and the Culture of the Early American Republic" (Ph.D. diss., University of Missouri–Columbia, 2002). *Niles' Weekly Register,* 9 January 1819, quoted in Samuel Rezneck, "The Depression of 1819–1822: A Social History," *American Historical Review* 39 (October 1933): 28–47, esp. 30.

14. Joseph Hornor to Mssrs. Wm. C. Poultney and Co., April 28, 1819, HML.

15. Ibid. *Speech of Mr. [John] Sergeant, in the House of Representatives, March 7th, 1822, on the Bill to Establish an Uniform System of Bankruptcy throughout the United States* [Washington City: D. Rapine, 1822], 3–4. Marcellus Smith to John Preston, Richmond, 16 September 1819, Preston Family Papers, VHS.

16. Mann, *Republic of Debtors,* 45–46. Balleisen, *Navigating Failure,* pt. 1. Barbara Allen Mathews, "'Forgive Us Our Debts': Bankruptcy and Insolvency in America, 1763–1841" (Ph.D. diss., Brown University, 1994). Peter J. Coleman, *Debtors and Creditors in America: Insolvency, Imprisonment for Debt, and Bankruptcy, 1607–1900* (Madison: State Historical Society of Wisconsin, 1974), 18–19, 31–36.

17. Balleisen, *Navigating Failure,* ch. 3. "Still More of Mr. Barnum's Affairs," *NYT,* 8 April 1856. Norma Basch, *In the Eyes of the Law: Women, Marriage, and Property in Nineteenth-Century New York* (Ithaca: Cornell University Press, 1982). "Petticoats" in credit reports of David McAlexander (1852–1854), Virginia, vol. 29, p. 35. Samuel Rezneck, "The Social History of an American Depression, 1837–1843," *American Historical Review* 40 (July 1935): 662–687, esp. 664. J[oshua Marsden] Van Cott, "A General Bankrupt Law," *HMM* 4 (January 1841): 22–35, esp. 33.

18. Westbrook diary, 29 January 1840, pp. 38–40; 2 July 1842, p. 166.

19. Daniel T. Rodgers, *The Work Ethic in Industrial America, 1850–1920* (Chicago: University of Chicago Press, 1978), ch. 1. E. Anthony Rotundo, *American Manhood: Transformations in Masculinity from the Revolution to the Modern Era* (New York: Basic Books, 1993), 13, 302n11. Henry J. Galpin, *Annals of Oxford* (Oxford, N.Y.: H. J. Galpin, 1906), 393. Van Der Lyn diary, 30 August 1843, vol. 5, p. 366; n.d. [1846], vol. 6, p. 127; 28 February 1838, vol. 5, p. 168.

20. "Imprisonment for Debt," *Debtors' Journal* 1 (24 February 1821): 94. John Carter transcript, "Declarations of Indebtedness and Examinations of the Poor," folder 4, box 1, Worcester County Court Records, AAS. Diary of Henry J. Hill, 12 June 1846, vol. 4, p. 14, AAS. "Shylock's Year, or 1840 with

No Bankrupt Law" (New York: John C. White, 1840), in *American Political Prints, 1766–1876,* ed. Bernard F. Reilly (Boston: G. K. Hall, 1991), entry 1840–65. Matt. 18:23–35 (King James Version).

21. Van Der Lyn diary, 17 Oct 1831, vol. 1, p. 273.

22. Joseph Hornor to Daniel Sterling, Esq., 8 August 1819. U.S. Census, 1820, Philadelphia, Philadelphia County, p. 25 (reel M33-108, image 29); and U.S. Census, 1830, Philadelphia, Philadelphia County, p. 57 (reel M19-159, image 119), National Archives and Records Administration, Washington, D.C. (hereafter NARA).

23. Rep. Thomas R. Mitchell, *Annals of Congress,* 17th Cong., 1st sess., 12 February 1822, p. 1021. Rep. Thomas Montgomery, ibid., 8 February 1822, pp. 969–970. Rep. Rollin C. Mallary, ibid., 7 February 1822, pp. 958–960. "Address of the Carrier of the Commercial Advertiser to his Patrons, New-York, January 1st 1820," [New York: 1819], broadsides collection, AAS.

24. "The Honorable Debtor and Enterprising Merchant," *HMM* 20 (June 1849): 687–688. Rep. William S. Archer, *Annals of Congress,* 17th Cong., 1st sess., 14 February, 1822, p. 1051.

25. *Speech of Mr. Sergeant,* 20. U.S. Congress, House Committee on the Judiciary, *Report to Accompany H.R. 16,* 27th Cong., 1st sess., 1841, H. Rept. 5, p. 5.

26. "The Carrier's Address to the Patrons of the New-York Evening Post, for the Year 1820," *New-York Evening Post,* 1 January 1820 [New York, 1819], broadsides collection, AAS.

27. Joseph Hornor to Mssrs. Felix J. Gibson and Co., 22 July 1819. Hornor to John Hollenback, 5 October 1819. Hornor to Daniel Sterling, 8 August 1819. Hornor to Abbot Green, 5 October 1819.

28. Hornor to Hollenback. On the advent of more formal debt relationships, see Bruce H. Mann, *Neighbors and Strangers: Law and Community in Early Connecticut* (Chapel Hill: University of North Carolina Press, 1987).

29. Hornor to John Selkirk, 21 July 1821. Hornor to James Whitehouse, 23 July 1821. *City Directories of the United States through 1860: A Collection of Microfiche* (New Haven: Research Publications [1966]), esp. 1100:3, 1108:1, 1110:1, and 1116:1.

30. "To My Sister Rebecca H. Coates," 2 August 1821, Joseph P. Hornor commonplace book, vol. 2, pp. 137–138, Historical Society of Pennsylvania, Philadelphia, Pa.

31. Robert V. Remini, *Henry Clay: Statesman for the Union* (New York: W. W. Norton, 1991), 3. Irvin G. Wyllie, *The Self-Made Man in America: The Myth of Rags to Riches* (New York: Free Press, 1954), 9–10. "Self-Made Men," *Daguerreotype* 2 (5 February 1848): 15. Daniel Walker Howe, *Making the American Self: Jonathan Edwards to Abraham Lincoln* (Cambridge, Mass.: Harvard University Press, 1997), 136–137.

32. John Pintard, 18 May 1819, in *Letters from John Pintard to His Daughter, Eliza Noel Pintard Davidson* (New York: New-York Historical Society,

1940), 1:193–194. "Chances of Success in Mercantile Life," *HMM* 15 (November 1846): 475–477.

33. Robert V. Remini, *Andrew Jackson and the Bank War: A Study in the Growth of Presidential Power* (New York: W. W. Norton and Co., 1967), 113. Rep. Samuel Beardsley quoted in Arthur Schlesinger, Jr., *The Age of Jackson* (Boston: Little, Brown and Co., 1953 [1945]), 108. Martin Van Buren, inaugural address, in *Senate Journal,* 25th Cong., special sess., 4 March 1837, 358–365, esp. 364. Diary of James Morris Whiton, April 1837, pp. 123–124, HBS.

34. B. W. Barnard, "The Use of Private Tokens for Money in the United States," *Quarterly Journal of Economics* 31 (August 1917): 600–634, esp. 612. Russell Rulau, *Standard Catalog of Hard Times Tokens, 1832–1844,* 9th ed. (Iola, Wis.: Krause Publications, 2001), 18–42, 185–211. George W. Bethune, "Leisure—Its Uses and Abuses," *HMM* 1 (November 1839): 399–407, esp. 402.

35. Joshua Marsden Van Cott, "General Bankrupt Law," *HMM* 4 (January 1841): 22–55, esp. 31–33. J[ohn] N. Bellows, "Morals of Trade, Number Four," *HMM* 6 (March 1842): 252–256.

36. Henry Ward Beecher, "The Benefits and Evils of Commerce," *HMM* 24 (February 1851): 147–156, esp. 154. William Howard Van Doren, *Mercantile Morals; or Thoughts for Young Men Entering Mercantile Life* (New York: Charles Scribner, 1852), 49. Thomas Wentworth Higginson, "Conscience in the Counting Room, or the True Interests of the Merchant," *HMM* 28 (January 1853): 19–40, esp. 27. [James Corley], *The Race for Wealth: Considered in a Series of Letters: Written, to Each Other, by a Brother and Sister* (New York: Authors' Publishing Co., 1878), 9.

37. *Niles' National Register,* 7 October 1837, p. 90. Rulau, *Standard Catalog,* 20. [Henry W. Bellows], "The Influence of the Trading Spirit upon the Social and Moral Life of America," *American Whig Review: A Whig Journal of Politics, Literature, Art, and Science,* 1 (January 1845): 94–98; repr. in *Antebellum American Culture: An Interpretive Anthology,* ed. David Brion Davis (University Park: Pennsylvania State University Press, 1979), 106.

2. A Reason in the Man

1. Diary of Jonathan Henry Hill, 1 November 1841, vol. 1, p. 109; 23 January to 28 February 1846, vol. 3, pp. 44–85; and 12 September 1846, vol. 4, p. 125, AAS.

2. Hill diary, 5 November 1845, vol. 2, pp. 141–142; 30 December 1845, vol. 3, p. 13.

3. *Journals and Miscellaneous Notebooks of Ralph Waldo Emerson,* ed. William H. Gilman and J. E. Parsons (Cambridge, Mass.: Belknap Press of Harvard University Press, 1970), 8:295.

4. William Charvat, "American Romanticism and the Depression of 1837," in *The Profession of Authorship in America, 1800–1870: The Papers of William Charvat,* ed. Matthew J. Bruccoli ([Columbus]: Ohio State University

Press, 1968), 49–67. Thomas G. Cary, "Causes of Failure among Men in Business," *HMM* 15 (September 1846): 261.

5. Diary of Charles William Dabney, 7 January 1838,VHS. Hill diary, 1 October 1841, vol. 1, p. 77.

6. Jan Lewis, *The Pursuit of Happiness: Family and Values in Jefferson's Virginia* (Cambridge: Cambridge University Press, 1983), 54–59, 214–229. Susan Juster, "'In a Different Voice': Male and Female Narratives of Religious Conversion in Post-Revolutionary America," *American Quarterly* 41 (March 1989): 34–62. Timothy Whittemore to Henry Whittemore, New York, 9 August 1832, Box 1, Whittemore Family Papers, NYPL. Henry Van Der Lyn to John A. Sidell, Esq., 18 February 1839, transcribed in diary of Henry Van Der Lyn, vol. 4, p. 226; "Spring of 1835," vol. 4, p. 102; 21 October 1837, vol. 5, p. 150; 30 December 1838, vol. 5, p. 253; NYHS.

7. Hill diary, 25 and 26 August 1846, vol. 4, pp. 105–107. "Life of a Clerk," *HMM* 5 (December 1841): 536–540, esp. 539.

8. Hill diary, 26 August 1846. His friend was likely Henry S. Wheaton; see "Messenger's Notice," *Worcester (Mass.) Daily Spy,* 1 September 1846; and "Insolvents in Massachusetts," *Monthly Law Reporter* (November 1846): 288.

9. Hill diary, 15 August 1841, vol. 1, p. 30–31. Mary Howitt, *Strive and Thrive: A Tale* (Boston: James Munroe and Co., 1840). Howitt is perhaps best known for her verse "The Spider and the Fly." "The Wives and Daughters of Merchants," *HMM* 31 (October 1854): 522. "What is Extravagance?" *HMM* 41 (October 1859): 525. Jeanne Boydston, *Home and Work: Housework, Wages, and the Ideology of Labor in the Early Republic* (New York: Oxford University Press, 1990), 117.

10. "Morals in Trade," *HMM* 19 (October 1848): 454–455.

11. Van Der Lyn diary, 15 April 1827, vol. 1, n.p. Charles Russell to Sarah Gilbert, 1 December 1837, Charles Russell Papers, "General Correspondence, 1837–1840," Massachusetts Historical Society, Boston. Diary of Caroline Barrett White, 30 September 1857, vol. 7, n.p., AAS.

12. Van Der Lyn diary, 27 May 1827, vol. 1, pp. 43–44; March 1838, vol. 4, p. 195. Van Der Lyn to Sidell.

13. [Thomas Kensett], "Brother Jonathans Soliloquy on the Times" [1819], Political Cartoons Collection, AAS. The image has been dated as early as 1812; see Frank Weitenkampf, *Political Caricature in the United States* (New York: Arno Press, 1971 [1953]), 16; and Winfred Morgan, *An American Icon: Brother Jonathan and American Identity* (Newark: University of Delaware Press, 1988), 69–70, 171.

14. Richard Hofstadter, *The American Political Tradition and the Men Who Made It* (New York: Vintage, 1989 [1948]), 67. Rep. Lemuel Sawyer, *Annals of Congress,* 17th Cong., 1st sess., 12 February 1822, p. 1091.

15. Corvin [pseud.?], "The Bankrupt," *Debtors' Journal,* 23 September 1820: 16. Van Der Lyn diary, 14 April 1853, vol. 7.

16. Van Der Lyn diary, March 1855, vol. 7, p. 234. "The Sock Seller of the Poydras Market, New Orleans," *HMM* 26 (June 1852): 776–777. "Mutations of a Merchant's Life: the New Orleans Sockseller," in *Cyclopædia of Commercial and Business Anecdotes,* ed. Frazar Kirkland (New York: D. Appleton, 1864), 129–130. James M[inor] Holladay, "On Happiness" [1835–1836], VHS.

17. Milton Buckingham Cushing to Hon. Caleb Cushing, 15 April [1841], box 146, Caleb Cushing Papers, Manuscript Division, LC.

18. On squatters, see Allan Kulikoff, *The Agrarian Origins of American Capitalism* (Charlottesville: University Press of Virginia, 1992), 77–90. On log cabin symbolism, see Harry L. Watson, *Liberty and Power: The Politics of Jacksonian America* (New York: Hill and Wang, 1990), 215, 224.

19. Milton Buckingham Cushing to Hon. Caleb Cushing, 15 April [1841].

20. "The Golden Age, or How to Restore Public Credit" [n.p., 1837]; and [Edward Clay] "The Times" (New York: H. R. Robinson, 1837), Political Cartoons Collection, AAS. David M. Henkin, *City Reading: Written Words and Public Spaces in Antebellum New York* (New York: Columbia University Press, 1999), 162. Clay's cartoon paraphrased Jackson; for the president's exact words, see Arthur Schlesinger, Jr., *The Age of Jackson* (Boston: Little, Brown and Co., 1953 [1945]), 121n12. On patronage jobs, see Cindy Sondik Aron, *Ladies and Gentlemen of the Civil Service: Middle-Class Workers in Victorian America* (New York: Oxford University Press, 1995), ch. 5; and Richard R. John, *Spreading the News: The American Postal System from Franklin to Morse* (Cambridge, Mass.: Harvard University Press, 1995), ch. 4.

21. Ralph J. Roske and Charles Van Doren, *Lincoln's Commando: The Biography of Commander William B. Cushing, U.S. Navy* (Annapolis: Naval Institute Press, 1957), 32–42.

22. "Bankruptcy—Banking," *HMM* 21 (November 1849): 513–518, esp. 514.

23. Glenn Hendler, *Public Sentiments: Structures of Feeling in Nineteenth-Century American Literature* (Chapel Hill: University of North Carolina Press, 2001). Joseph P. Hornor to John Hollenback, 5 October 1819, Hornor letterbook, HML. Rep. Cadwallader D. Colden, *Annals of Congress,* 17th Cong., 1st sess., 12 February 1822, p. 1003. Stephen Girard, *The Merchants' Sketch Book and Guide to New-York City . . . Particularly Intended for the Merchant Visiting New York* (New-York: n.p., 1845), 43. "Ups and Downs in Life," *Cist's Advertiser,* clipping pasted into Van Der Lyn diary, 30 March 1845, vol. 6, p. 83, repr. in Charles Cist, *The Cincinnati Miscellany, Volumes I and II* ([New York]: Arno Press, 1971 [orig. 1845]), 159.

24. Hill diary, 17 October 1845, vol. 2, pp. 119–120. "An Instance of Commercial Integrity," *HMM* 11 (September 1844): 292. "Morality for Merchants," *HMM* 12 (April 1845): 351–356, esp. 354. "Anecdotes of Bankruptcy," *HMM* 18 (April 1848): 455–456. "An Example of Mercantile Honesty," *HMM* 11 (November 1844): 481. "An Honest Merchant," *HMM* 24 (April 1851): 515.

25. Hill diary, 15 July 1846, vol. 4, p. 53; 28 December 1847, vol. 6, p. 14. On

Chapin, see Franklin P. Rice, ed., *The Worcester of Eighteen Hundred and Ninety-Eight: Fifty Years a City* (Worcester: F. S. Blanchard and Co., 1899), 20, 580–581. Hill was still clerking in his last extant diary, January 1849.

26. Hill diary, 28 December 1847; 13 March 1848, vol. 7, p. 88; 11 September 1848, vol. 7, p. 47; 24 December 1847, vol. 6, p. 10; 10 September 1846, vol. 4, p. 122.

27. Hill diary, 16 December 1846, vol. 5, p. 42; 1 July 1848, vol. 6, p. 178; 4 August 1848, vol. 7, p. 16; 28 August 1841, vol. 1, n.p.; 29–30 January 1848, vol. 7, p. 49; 6 January 1849, vol. 7, p. 136; 16–17 February 1848, vol. 7, pp. 64–65; 12 March 1846, vol. 3, p. 99; 13 November 1845, vol. 2, p. 153.

28. Herman Melville, "Bartleby, the Scrivener: A Story of Wall-Street," *Putnum's Monthly Magazine* (November 1853): 546–557, esp. 549, 550; and (December 1853): 609–615. Hill diary, 30 September 1845, vol. 2, p. 103. Richard Olney, "Memoir of Benjamin F. Thomas, LL. D.," *Proceedings*, Massachusetts Historical Society, 2nd. ser., 14 (October 1900): 297–302. Benjamin F. Thomas, *Lemuel Shaw: Chief Justice of the Supreme Judicial Court of Massachusetts* (Cambridge, Mass.: John Wilson and Son, 1885). Hershel Parker, *Herman Melville: A Biography, Volume 1, 1819–1851* (Baltimore: Johns Hopkins University Press, 1996), 305–311.

29. Morton J. Horwitz, *The Transformation of American Law, 1780–1860* (Cambridge, Mass.: Harvard University Press, 1977), 160–210, esp. 209. Leonard W. Levy, *The Law of the Commonwealth and Chief Justice Shaw* (Cambridge, Mass: Harvard University Press, 1957). Thomas L. Haskell, "Capitalism and the Origins of Humanitarian Sensibility," in *The Antislavery Debate: Capitalism and Abolitionism as a Problem in Historical Interpretation*, ed. Thomas Bender (Berkeley: University of California Press, 1992), 107–199.

30. Melville, "Bartleby," 551. My argument here follows Brook Thomas, "The Legal Fictions of Herman Melville and Lemuel Shaw," *Critical Inquiry* 11 (September 1984): 24–51; and John Stark, "Melville, Lemuel Shaw, and 'Bartleby,'" in *Bartleby the Inscrutable: A Collection of Commentary on Herman Melville's Tale "Bartleby the Scrivener,"* ed. M. Thomas Inge (Hamden, Conn.: Archon Books, 1979), 166–173.

31. Hill diary, 5 and 10 October 1841, vol. 1, pp. 83, 87; 30 September 1845, vol. 2, p. 103; 6–7 October 1845, vol. 2, p. 108–112; 4 December 1846, vol. 5, p. 29. Hill discusses the slavery case on 5 October 1841, and he follows the 1845 rape trial in vol. 2, pp. 91–109. The defendant's change of plea (to guilty), Hill remarked, "must save his victim much pain, which she must otherwise have endured in giving in her testimony." Hill diary, 16 October 1845, vol. 2, pp. 118–119.

32. Lon Fuller, *Legal Fictions* (Stanford: Stanford University Press, 1967), 51–58; cited in Norma Basch, *In the Eyes of the Law: Women, Marriage, and Property in Nineteenth-Century New York* (Ithaca: Cornell University Press, 1982), 42–43, 49. Lawrence M. Friedman, *A History of American Law* (New York: Simon and Schuster, 1973), 18–19. "Resolutions of the Legislature of

New Hampshire, in favor of The repeal of the Distribution and Bankrupt laws . . . ," 13 January 1842, vol. 415, 27th Cong., 2nd sess., Doc. 70.

33. Joseph P. Hornor to Mssrs. Wm. C. Poultney and Co., 28 April 1819, Hornor letterbook, HML. Brook Thomas, *American Literary Realism and the Failed Promise of Contract* (Berkeley: University of California Press, 1997).

34. Alexis de Tocqueville, *Democracy in America*, trans. Henry Reeve and Francis Bowen, ed. Phillips Bradley (New York: Knopf, 1945), 2:155. Credit reports (1858–1859) of James B. McLelland, Virginia, vol. 29, pp. 31, 33, 54.

35. Hill diary, 29 January 1848, vol. 7, pp. 47–48; 29 May 1848, vol. 7, p. 150. Waichee Dimock, *Melville and the Poetics of Individualism* (Princeton: Princeton University Press, 1989).

36. Hill diary, 16 April 1846, vol. 3, p. 135; 2 August 1848, vol. 7, pp. 14–15; 9–10 January 1849, vol. 7, pp. 137–138.

37. *Proceedings of the Worcester Society of Antiquity for the Year 1890*, 35 (Worcester, Mass.: Published by the Society, 1891): 163–166. "Death of J. Henry Hill, One of the Oldest and Foremost Members of the Worcester Bar," and "A Young Man of the 1840s sees Worcester and life: Diaries of Jonathan Henry Hill, father of Dr. George H. Hill, when he came to Worcester as a young Law student," undated clippings, AAS.

3. We Are All Speculators

1. "Dead Letter," in John Russell Bartlett, *Dictionary of Americanisms: A Glossary of Words and Phrases, Usually Regarded as Peculiar to the United States* (New York: Bartlett and Welford, 1848), 203. "A Day in the Dead Letter Office," *United States Democratic Review* 19 (December 1846): 446–450. John Flagg to Charles Flagg, Dunstable [N.H.], 26 January 1825, Bowers-Flagg Family Papers, box 1, folder 6, AAS. Diary of Samuel C. Morton, 23 December 1842, vol. 8, HML. Diary of Jonathan Henry Hill, 1 October 1841, vol. 1, p. 77; 25 February 1846, vol. 3, pp. 81–82; 29 January 1848, vol. 7, pp. 47–48, AAS.

2. John Pintard, 18 May 1819, in *Letters from John Pintard to His Daughter, Eliza Noel Pintard Davidson* (New York: New-York Historical Society, 1940), 1:193–194. Diary of Henry Van Der Lyn, 16 May 1849, vol. 6, p. 289, NYHS. "Excerpts for Business Men: or, Thoughts and Observations on Business," *HMM* 21 (August 1849): 250, reprinted from *Acton; or, The Circle of Life* . . . (New-York: D. Appleton and Co., 1849), 42–43. "Incidents in the Life of Hiram Hill," 4 March 1852, September 1855, Manuscript Library, Rhode Island Historical Society, Providence. U.S. Census, 1860, Providence, Providence County, R.I., p. 90 (reel M653-1208, image 259), NARA. On Hill, see Gary J. Kornblith, "Self-Made Men: The Development of Middling-Class Consciousness in New England," *Massachusetts Review* 26 (Summer–Autumn 1985): 461–474, esp. 471–472.

3. "An Address on Success in Business, Delivered Before the Students of Packard's Bryant & Stratton New York Business College by Hon. Horace Greeley . . . " (New York: S. S. Packard, [1867]), 8–9. Thomas Brothers, *The United States of North America as They Are* (London: Longman, 1840), 71. "The Financial Crisis," *New Englander and Yale Review* 15 (November 1857): 701–715, esp. 706.

4. Roxana Wall, Malone City, N.Y., 18 May 1834; ibid., Ohio City, Ohio, 30 July 1839; Thomas Wall, Ohio City, Ohio, 30 July 1839; Wall Family Papers, AAS. Caleb A. Wall, *Reminiscences of Worcester . . .* (Worcester, Mass.: Tyler and Seagrave, 1877). U.S. Census, 1850, Whitestown, Oneida County, N.Y., p. 65 (reel M432–564, image 131), NARA.

5. Edgar Allan Poe, "The Business Man" (1840), in *The Collected Works of Edgar Allan Poe: Tales and Sketches, 1831–1842,* ed. Thomas Ollive Mabbott et al. (Cambridge, Mass.: Belknap Press of Harvard University Press, 1978), 481–491, esp. 481, 486. *How to Do Business: A Pocket Manual of Practical Affairs and Guide to Success in Life . . .* (New York: Fowler and Wells, 1857), 1, 9–10. William Jennings Bryan, "Cross of Gold Speech, July 8, 1896," in *Great Issues in American History, Vol. III: From Reconstruction to the Present Day, 1864–1981,* ed. Richard Hofstadter, rev. ed. (New York: Vintage, 1982), 158–165, esp. 160. Henry Hill diary, 17 January 1848, vol. 6, p. 34.

6. "Wealth," in *Complete Works of Ralph Waldo Emerson,* ed. Edward Waldo Emerson (Boston: Houghton Mifflin, 1903–1904), 6:83–127, esp. 100. Douglass C. North, *The Economic Growth of the United States, 1790–1860* (New York: W. W. Norton, 1966), 179–184, 199. Jackson Lears, *Something for Nothing: Luck in America* (New York: Viking, 2003), 129–136, 140–145.

7. C. C. Hazewell, "Mercantile Failures," *Boston Chronicle,* repr. in *HMM* 34 (May 1856): 645–646. Neil Harris, *Humbug: The Art of P. T. Barnum* (Boston: Little, Brown, 1973). "Sympathy for Barnum," *NYT,* 25 April 1856. "Persecutions of Barnum," *NYT,* 15 May 1856. "Barnum and His Connecticut Creditors," *NYT,* 9 July 1856. "News of the Day," *NYT,* 3 September 1857. P. T. Barnum to Messrs. Curtis and Scribner, New York, 19 May 1856; copy in Sandage's possession, courtesy of David Schulson Autographs, Inc., New York, N.Y.

8. *Barnum's American Museum Illustrated: A Pictorial Guide . . .* [New York? 1850], p. 6. "Lessons of Barnum's Life," *NYT,* 16 December 1854.

9. "Barnumization" in "The New York Crystal Palace Association," *Scientific American* (9 June 1855): 309. *How to Get Money: Or, Eleven Ways of Making a Fortune* (Boston: I. R. Butts, 1850), 51. I. R. Butts, *The Creditor's and Debtor's Assistant, or the Mode of Collecting Debts* (Boston: I. R. Butts, 1849). "Money-Getting—Causes of Failure in Business," *HMM* 35 (December 1856): 774–775. Credit report (1849) of Chas. Dupler, Ohio, vol. 78, p. 92.

10. "New-York City Police Intelligence: Capture of Another Confidence Man," *NYT,* 2 September 1856. "Mr. Barnum in the Insolvent Court in Connecticut," *NYT,* 5 September 1856. "The Last Confidence Game—The

Suicide Dodge," *Cincinnati Gazette,* repr. in *NYT,* 28 April 1859. James W. Cook, *The Arts of Deception: Playing with Fraud in the Age of Barnum* (Cambridge, Mass.: Harvard University Press, 2001). *The Expediency of a Uniform Bankrupt Law* (New York: n.p., 1840), 17. B. F. Foster, *The Merchant's Manual* (Boston: Perkins and Marvin, 1838), 32. Foster taught bookkeeping and penmanship as keys to success. Ray Nash, "Benjamin Franklin Foster," in *Calligraphy and Paleography: Essays Presented to Alfred Fairbank on His 70th Birthday,* ed. A. S. Osley (New York: October House, 1966), 155–168.

11. "A Confidence Man at Cincinnati (From the *Cincinnati Inquirer,* July 15)," *NYT,* 20 July 1859. [Asa Greene], *The Perils of Pearl Street, Including a Taste of the Dangers of Wall Street* (New-York: Betts and Anstice, and Peter Hill, 1834), 187. "Mr. Jones's Experiences with Peter Funk," in Frazar Kirkland [R. M. Devens], *Cyclopædia of Commercial and Business Anecdotes . . .* (New York: D. Appleton and Co., 1864), 1:213. Credit report (1861) of Christopher Mollen, Ohio, vol. 40, p. 203. Credit report (1854) of James H. Reed, Ohio, vol. 78, p. 134. Credit reports (1852–1881) of Phineas T. Barnum, Connecticut, vol. 2, pp. 45, 83, and New York, vol. 376, pp. 389, 384, 522, and 595. Some entries confused Barnum with his half-brother, Philo Fairchild Barnum, or their cousin, U.S. senator William Henry Barnum.

12. Karen Halttunen, *Confidence Men and Painted Women: A Study of Middle-Class Culture in America, 1830–1870* (New Haven: Yale University Press, 1982). "The Morality of Trade," *NYT,* 10 August 1852. "Flunkies," in Bartlett, *Dictionary of Americanisms,* 146–147.

13. "Mercantile Manners," *HMM* 4 (May 1841): 452. "Magnetism in Trade," *Philadelphia Merchant,* repr. in *HMM* 33 (November 1855): 647. "Editor's Easy Chair," *Harper's New Monthly Magazine* 19 (August 1859): 410–415, esp. 412. "Mercantile Honesty," *Dry Goods Reporter,* repr. in *HMM* 22 (June 1850): 693–694. Michael Zuckerman, "The Selling of the Self: From Franklin to Barnum," in *Almost Chosen People: Oblique Biographies in the American Grain* (Berkeley: University of California Press, 1993), 145–174.

14. Peyton Harrison to Randolph Harrison, 10 April 1824, and to "My Dear Mother," 24 May 1823, Harrison Papers, VHS. Comfort Avery Adams to Hon. Elisha Whittlesey, 28 November 1848, Whittlesey Papers, Western Reserve Historical Society, Cleveland, Ohio. "Incidents in the Life of Hiram Hill," 22 June 1852. Credit reports (1850–1876) of Hiram Hill, Rhode Island, vol. 9, p. 145.

15. "Honesty in Mercantile Life," *HMM* 26 (June 1852): 776. Joseph Hornor to Mssrs. Wm C. Poultney & Co., 28 April 1819, Letterbook of Joseph P. Hornor, HML. Diary of Frederick E. Westbrook, 2 July 1842, pp. 165–166, Rare Book and Manuscript Collection, NYPL. Nathaniel D. Goodell to Asahel Goodell, 26 December 1854, quoted in Christopher Clark, "Household Economy, Market Exchange, and the Rise of Capitalism in the Connecticut Valley, 1800–1860," *Journal of Social History* 13 (Winter 1979): 169–189, esp. 182.

16. "Getting Along Slowly," *HMM* 35 (September 1856): 393. "Mr. Barnum in the Insolvent Court in Connecticut," *NYT,* 5 September 1856.

17. Daniel Vickers, "Competency and Competition: Economic Culture in Early America," *William and Mary Quarterly,* 3d ser., 47 (1990): 3–29. William Dean Howells, "Introduction," in William Cooper Howells, *Recollections of Life in Ohio from 1813 to 1840* (Gainesville, Fla.: Scholars' Facsimiles and Reprints, 1963 [1895]), v.

18. "The Freaks of Fortune and Their Lesson," *Harper's New Monthly Magazine* 17 (August 1858): 344–349. A. H. Saxon, *P. T. Barnum: The Legend and the Man* (New York: Columbia University Press, 1989), 201–202, 417. "The Art of Money-Getting," in P. T. Barnum, *Dollars and Sense; or, How to Get On—The Whole Secret in a Nutshell* (New York: Henry S. Allen, 1890), 65.

19. Michael Burlingame, *The Inner World of Abraham Lincoln* (Urbana: University of Illinois Press, 1994), 248, 252. Saxon, *P. T. Barnum,* 134–137. "Sucker," in Bartlett, *Dictionary of Americanisms,* 343–344. Sheldon H. Harris, "Abraham Lincoln Stumps a Yankee Audience," *New England Quarterly* 38 (June 1965): 227–233. Abraham Lincoln to "Dear Brother" [John D. Johnston], 4 November 1851, in *The Collected Works of Abraham Lincoln,* ed. Roy P. Basler (New Brunswick, N.J.: Rutgers University Press, 1953), 2:111–112. "Editor's Drawer," *Harper's New Monthly Magazine* 5 (October 1852): 707. Henry Villard, "Reflections of Lincoln," *Atlantic Monthly* 93 (February 1904): 165–174.

20. David Leverenz, *Manhood and the American Renaissance* (Ithaca: Cornell University Press, 1989), ch. 3. Joseph S. Ropes to "My dear Uncle" [Hardy Ropes], St. Petersburg, Russia, 30 August/11 September 1839, folder 2–6, Ropes Family Papers, Baker Library, HBS. Diary of Edward Neufville Tailer, Jr., 15 August 1850, vol. 8, NYHS. "American Enterprise," *NYT,* 29 January 1855. "Brazil," *Scientific American* 3 (5 August 1848): 366. "Things Lost Forever," *Scientific American* 4 (11 August 1849): 370. "Fresnel's Light-House Reflectors," *Scientific American* 7 (26 June 1852): 325.

21. "Financial and Commercial Review," *United States Democratic Review* 29 (October 1851): 370–371. Credit report of M. Rosenbaum & Co., 1851, New York Trade Agency Reports, p. 16, NYHS. Credit report (1845) of Hugh Alexander, Pennsylvania, vol. 131, p. 50. Credit report (1859) of Detrick & Parr, Pennsylvania, vol. 131, p. 24. "McKinnon's Atlantic and Trans-Atlantic Sketches," *Living Age* 34 (7 August 1852): 269–270. George W. Light, *Keep Cool, Go Ahead, and a Few Other Poems* (Boston: G. W. Light, 1853), 35.

22. Bartlett, *Dictionary of Americanisms,* 157. John Russell Bartlett, *Dictionary of Americanisms: A Glossary of Words and Phrases Usually Regarded as Peculiar to the United States,* 2nd ed. (Boston: Little, Brown, 1859), 171. "Herman Melville's Whale," *London Spectator,* repr. in *International Magazine* 4 (December 1851): 602–604. E. Minold, "Go Ahead Polka," (Louisville: Peters, Webb, and Co., 1850); Jas. E. Magruder, "Few Days, or, Go-Ahead Quick Step" (Baltimore: James E. Boswell, 1854); and H. B. Hart, "Go Ahead Galop" (New York: Ditson and Co., 1871); Music Division, Library of Con-

gress. "The True Spirit of American Politics," *London Spectator,* repr. in *Living Age* 34 (4 September 1852): 475. "Women's Emancipation," *Harper's New Monthly Magazine* 3 (August 1851): 424. "Zip Coon on the Go-Ahead Principle," [Boston: Leonard Deming, n.d.], Rare Book and Special Collections, Library of Congress. Eric Lott, *Love and Theft: Blackface Minstrelsy and the American Working Class* (New York: Oxford University Press, 1993), 23, 107, 132–134.

23. Hill diary, 19 January 1847, vol. 5, pp. 79–80. "Activity is Not Always Energy," *HMM* 35 (September 1856): 381–382. "Energy in Business," *HMM* 29 (December 1853): 775. "Excitement the Stimulus of Business," *HMM* 42 (July 1860): 135–136. Ben Barker-Benfield, "The Spermatic Economy: A Nineteenth-Century View of Sexuality," in *The American Family in Social-Historical Perspective,* ed. Michael Gordon (New York: St. Martin's Press, 1973), 338–372.

24. Lydia Maria Child to Louisa Loring, 29 April 1847, quoted in Carolyn L. Karcher, *The First Woman in the Republic: A Cultural Biography of Lydia Maria Child* (Durham: Duke University Press, 1994), 265–266.

25. John Flagg to Charles Flagg, 16 January 1825, Bowers-Flagg Family Papers, box 1, folder 6, AAS. Thomas Wall, 30 July 1839. Anonymous, "Mr. President & Gentlemen of the Society" [mss. temperance speech], Peyton Family Papers, September 1829, VHS. Rep. Thomas Montgomery, *Annals of Congress,* 17th Cong., 1st sess., 1822, p. 970. J. Van Cott, "A General Bankrupt Law," *HMM* (May 1841): 34–35.

26. "New Books of the Month," *United States Democratic Review* 11 (July 1842): 106–107. Michael Chevalier, *Society, Manners and Politics in the United States: Being a Series of Letters on North America,* trans. from 3rd Paris ed. (Boston: Weeks, Jordan, and Co., 1839), 298, 305, 309.

27. Roger Whitman, *The Rise and Fall of a Frontier Entrepreneur: Benjamin Rathbun, "Master Builder and Architect,"* ed. Scott Eberle and David A. Gerber (Syracuse: Syracuse University Press and Buffalo and Erie County Historical Society, 1996), 95, 108. *Memorial of a Number of Citizens of Oneida County, New York, Remonstrating Against the Passage of Any Retrospective Bankrupt Law,* 26th Cong., 2nd sess., Senate Doc. 176 (Washington, D.C.: Printed by Blair and Rives, 1841). Henry D. Thoreau, 7 December 1838, *Journal, Volume 1: 1837–1844,* ed. John C. Broderick et al. (Princeton: Princeton University Press, 1981), 58.

28. "The Atmospheric Railway," *Littell's Living Age* 4 (4 January 1845): 43. "Speech on the Bank of the United States, Delivered in the House of Representatives, February 22, 1819," in *Select Speeches of John Sergeant of Pennsylvania* (Philadelphia: E. L. Carey and A. Hart, 1832), 120–184, esp. 164. James Flint, *Flint's Letters from America, 1818–1820* (Cleveland: A. H. Clark, 1904 [1822]), 219–220. Whitman, *Rise and Fall,* 100. Edward Chancellor, *Devil Take the Hindmost: A History of Financial Speculation* (New York: Farrar, Straus, and Giroux, 1999), chs. 4–5. Foster, *Merchant's Manual,* 32; repr. with identical text as *The Clerk's Guide, or Commercial Instructor . . . ,*

2nd ed. (Boston: Henry Perkins, 1840). Harry L. Watson, *Liberty and Power: The Politics of Jacksonian America* (New York: Hill and Wang, 1990), 160.

29. Van Der Lyn diary, vol. 4, p. 148. "The Downfall of Speculation," *The New-Yorker* (12 October 1839): 57. Edwin T. Freedley, *A Practical Treatise on Business: or How to Get, Save, Spend, Give, Lend, and Bequeath Money: With an Inquiry into the Chances of Success and Causes of Failure in Business* (Philadelphia: Lippincott, Grambo and Co., 1853), 165–167, 171, 259–260.

30. On speculating farmers, see Allan Kulikoff, *The Agrarian Origins of American Capitalism* (Charlottesville: University Press of Virginia, 1992), 87. Alexis de Tocqueville, *Democracy in America*, trans. George Lawrence, ed. J. P. Mayer and Max Lerner (New York: Harper and Row, 1966), 622; contemporary discussion of this passage is in Van Cott, "General Bankrupt Law," 24. R[ichard] Hildreth, *Banks, Banking, and Paper Currencies* (Boston: Whipple and Damrell, 1840), 159–160. "Snow's Voyage of the Prince Albert," *Littel's Living Age* 28 (1 March 1851): 421.

31. *Wall Street Journal* quoted in "Speculation," *HMM* 24 (June 1851): 781–782. Joseph G. Baldwin, *The Flush Times of Alabama and Mississippi: A Series of Sketches*, ed. James H. Justus (Baton Rouge: Louisiana State University Press, 1987 [1853]), xix; quoted in Andrew Delbanco, *The Death of Satan: How Americans Have Lost the Sense of Evil* (New York: Farrar, Straus and Giroux, 1995), 100. "'Nothing Venture, Nothing Have,' the Maxim of the Speculator and the Merchant," *HMM* 30 (April 1854): 517.

32. Jeanne M. Boydston, *Home and Work: Housework, Wages, and the Ideology of Labor in the Early Republic* (New York: Oxford University Press, 1990), 67–68. "The Habits of a Man of Business," *HMM* 8 (April 1843): 389–390. James W. Alexander et al. *The Man of Business, Considered in His Various Relations* (New-York: Anson D. F. Randolph, 1857). Entries on George Reeves, E[lijah] W. Morgan Credit Ledger, n.p., Bentley Historical Library, University of Michigan, Ann Arbor. *Newburyport (Mass.) Herald*, 16 April 1856, quoted in Stephan Thernstrom, *Poverty and Progress: Social Mobility in a Nineteenth Century City* (New York: Atheneum, 1969), 63.

33. George Forgie, *Patricide in the House Divided: A Psychological Interpretation of Lincoln and His Age* (New York: W. W. Norton, 1977). *A Philadelphia Perspective: The Diary of Sidney George Fisher Covering the Years 1834–1871*, ed. Nicholas B. Wainright (Philadelphia: Historical Society of Pennsylvania, 1967), 279. James L. Huston, *The Panic of 1857 and the Coming of the Civil War* (Baton Rouge: Louisiana State University Press, 1987).

34. *Philadephia Perspective*, 279. C. H. Ludington to George Ludington, New York, 12 October 1857, box 15, "Banking" series, Warshaw Collection of Business Americana, National Museum of American History, Smithsonian Institution. "The Poetry of the Trade—A Song of the Street," *Evening Post*, repr. *HMM* 37 (November 1857): 641.

35. Nelson W. Aldrich, Jr., *Old Money: The Mythology of America's Upper Class*

(New York: Knopf, 1988), 57; quoted in Delbanco, *Death of Satan*, 103. Henry Taylor, *Notes from Life in Seven Essays* (Boston: Ticknor, Reed, and Fields, 1853); quoted in Freedley, *Practical Treatise*, 21, 238. Stephen H. Tyng, "Men of Business: Their Perplexities and Temptations," in Alexander, *Man of Business*, 4–5. Thomas Low Nichols, *Forty Years of American Life, 1821–1861* (New York: Stackpole Sons, 1937 [1864]), 194–195.

36. "Editorial Notes," *Putnam's Monthly* 8 (December 1856): 663. "A Farewell to the Quarters," *Harper's Illustrated Weekly*, 27 February 1857: 130.

37. "Editor's Table: Cheerfulness," *Harper's New Monthly Magazine* 16 (December 1857): 120–125. "Editor's Table: Panics and Investments," *Harper's New Monthly Magazine* 16 (April 1858): 693–698.

38. Diary of Albion W. Clark, December 1858, vol. 4, pp. 62–63, Rare Book and Manuscript Collection, NYPL.

39. U.S. Census, 1850, Atkinson, Piscataquis County, Maine, p. 301 (reel M593-556); U.S. Census, 1860, Atkinson, Piscataquis County, Maine, p. 764 (reel M654-433), NARA. Pvt. Albion W. Clark, company M., First Maine Cavalry, Compiled Military Service Records (reel M543-4), NARA. "Financial and Commercial Review," 370–371. Clark diary, 6 April 1863 and 13 May 1865, vol. 3; and January 1867, 1 June 1867, 25 June 1867, 23 July 1867, 31 August 1867, and 31 December 1867, vol. 4.

40. Mark Twain, *Mark Twain's Autobiography*, ed. Albert Bigelow Paine (New York: Harper and Bros., 1924), 2:94. Walt Wolfram and Donna Christian, "On the Application of Sociolinguistic Information: Test Evaluation and Dialect Differences in Appalachia," in *Standards and Dialects in English*, ed. Timothy Shopen and Joseph M. Williams (Cambridge, Mass.: Winthrop Publishers, 1980), 177–212. U.S. Census, 1870, Orneville, Piscataquis County, Maine, p. 146 (reel M593-556, image 292); U.S. Census, 1880, Auburn, Androscoggin County, Maine, p. 69A (reel T9-475, image 131), NARA.

4. Central Intelligence Agency, since 1841

1. Henry D. Thoreau to Ralph Waldo Emerson, 23 May 1843, in *The Correspondence of Henry David Thoreau*, ed. Walter Harding and Carl Bode (New York: New York University Press, 1958), 107–108. Thoreau to Emerson, 7 August 1843, in ibid., 133–134. Thoreau to Sophia Thoreau, 22 May 1843, in ibid., 105–106. Harmon Smith, "Henry Thoreau and Emerson's 'Noble Youths,'" *Concord Saunterer* 17 (December 1984): 4–12. James D. Norris, *R. G. Dun & Co., 1841–1900: The Development of Credit-Reporting in the Nineteenth Century* (Westport, Conn.: Greenwood Press, 1978).

2. My interpretation of credit agencies and surveillance draws on Michel Foucault, *Discipline and Punish: The Birth of the Prison*, 2nd ed., trans. Alan Sheridan (New York: Vintage, 1995 [1977]), 23–27, 170–194. For a sociological argument, see Barry Cohen, "Marketing Trust: Credit Reporting and Credit Rating in the Nineteenth-Century United States," unpublished es-

say, June 1999, copy in Sandage's possession. For a study of how R. G. Dun & Co. assessed risk in Springfield, Illinois, see Rowena Olegario, "Credit and Business Culture: The American Experience in the Nineteenth Century" (Ph.D. diss., Harvard University, 1998). Bertram Wyatt-Brown, *Lewis Tappan and the Evangelical War against Slavery* (Cleveland, Ohio: Press of Case Western Reserve University, 1969), 40n74, 301. Credit reports (1848–1858) of J. H. Tyler, Pennsylvania, vol. 31, p. 73; credit reports (1848–1875) of Dyott & Kent, Pennsylvania, vol. 31, p. 115; credit reports (1858–1867) of A. P. Shaver, New York, vol. 513, pp. 398, 16, 17.

3. "(Private and Confidential.) To the Directors of the Bank of the United States), Philadelphia, June 28, 1819," broadsides collection, AAS. Sen. Daniel Webster, *Register of Debates in Congress*, 23rd Cong., 1st sess., 18 March 1834, pp. 985–996. Robert T. Bicknell, *Counterfeit Detector and Bank Note List* (Philadelphia: M. T. Miller, 1832–1866).

4. Roy Anderson Foulke, *The Sinews of American Commerce: Published by Dun & Bradstreet, Inc., on the Occasion of Its 100th Anniversary, 1841–1941* (New York: Dun & Bradstreet, 1941), 290–291. *The Mercantile Agency: Its Claims upon the Favor and Support of the Community: Commendatory Letters* (New York: Dun, Barlow and Co. [1871]), 14.

5. Credit reports (1850–1881) of John Cummins, South Carolina, vol. 6, p. 106 ["John Commings"]; vol. 7, pp. 326, 410, 422; and vol. 8, p. 151.

6. Philip Gleason, "Identifying Identity: A Semantic History," *Journal of American History* 69 (March 1983): 910–931. Nick Mansfield, *Subjectivity: Theories of the Self from Freud to Haraway* (New York: New York University Press, 2000), chs. 1–4, 11. Credit reports (1857–1859) of Henry J. Hall, New York, vol. 476, p. 379. U.S. Bureau of the Census, *Historical Statistics of the United States, Colonial Times to 1970* (1975; repr., White Plains, N.Y.: Kraus International Publications, 1989), 1:8.

7. "The Art of Making Money Plenty in Every Man's Pocket," (New-York: S. Wood, 1811), AAS. Bryan F. LeBeau, *Currier & Ives: America Imagined* (Washington, D.C.: Smithsonian Institution Press, 2001), 37–39. Benjamin Franklin, *The Autobiography of Benjamin Franklin*, ed. Leonard W. Labaree et al. (New Haven: Yale University Press, 1964), 125–126.

8. *Benjamin Franklin: Writings*, ed. J. A. Leo Lemay (New York: Library of America, 1987), 1205. Franklin, *Autobiography*, 27–39, 116. Michael Warner, *The Letters of the Republic: Publication and the Public Sphere in Eighteenth-Century America* (Cambridge, Mass.: Harvard University Press, 1990), 75. Jared Sparks, *The Life of Benjamin Franklin, Containing the Autobiography, with Notes and a Continuation* (Boston: C. Tappan, 1842). Lewis Tappan Journal, 18 December 1819, quoted in Lawrence J. Friedman, "Confidence and Pertinacity in Evangelical Abolitionism: Lewis Tappan's Circle," *American Quarterly* 31 (Spring 1979): 81–106, esp. 91.

9. Toby L. Ditz, "Shipwrecked; or, Masculinity Imperiled: Mercantile Representations of Failure and the Gendered Self in Eighteenth-Century Phila-

delphia," *Journal of American History* 81 (June 1994): 51–81. "John Wayles
Rates His Neighbours," ed. John M. Hemphill II, *Virginia Magazine
of History and Biography* 66 (July 1958): 302–306. *Franklin: Writings*, 1298.
Steven C. Bullock, "A Mumper among the Gentle: Tom Bell, Colonial
Confidence Man," *William and Mary Quarterly*, 3rd ser., 55 (April 1998):
231–258.

10. Thomas Emerson to "Mssrs. Waller & Emerson," 3 April 1838, in [*Letters*] (Windsor, Vt.: n.p., 1839?), n.p. Jonas Prentiss to Henry Whittemore, Andover [Mass.], 23 December 1839; Whittemore to Prentiss, n.p., 10 February 1840; William Peirce, Andover, Mass., 10 December 1840, "A Statement of the effects, debts due and debts owed by Jonas W. Prentiss"; Whittemore to Prentiss, 17 December 1840; Prentiss to Whittemore, 22 February 1841; box 2, Whittemore Family Papers, Rare Books and Manuscript Collection, NYPL.

11. R. W. Hidy, "Credit Rating before Dun & Bradstreet," *Bulletin of the Business Historical Society* 13 (December 1939): 81–88. Comfort Avery Adams to Willis Triplett, Peoria, Ill., 11 October 1849, in Comfort Avery Adams Correspondence, 1837–1852, AAS. Richard R. John, *Spreading the News: The American Postal System from Franklin to Morse* (Cambridge, Mass.: Harvard University Press, 1996), 143–149.

12. *"In Bankruptcy": A Complete List . . .* (New York: Thomas Snowden, 1842). *The Fressall and Paynix Detective: Being a Black List for "Texas"* (United States of North America: Fressnix and Payall, 1867). Diary of Jonathan Henry Hill, 25 August 1846, vol. 4, p. 105, AAS. [Frederick Jackson] *A Week in Wall Street: By One Who Knows* (New-York: Published for the Booksellers, 1841), 5, 13.

13. "The Spy System," *Chicago American*, repr. in *New York Commercial Advertiser*, 10 April 1837, 2.

14. John M. Havas, "Commerce and Calvinism: The *Journal of Commerce*, 1827–1865," *Journalism Quarterly* 38 (Winter 1961): 84–86. "Paper Halting Daily Operations," *NYT*, 14 April 2000.

15. Lewis Tappan, *The Life of Arthur Tappan* (Westport, Conn.: Negro Universities Press, 1970 [1871]), 91–104, 173–176, 203–224, 250–252, 264–265, 280. Wyatt-Brown, *Lewis Tappan*, 30–31, 174–175, 226–227. Edward Neville Vose, *Seventy-Five Years of the Mercantile Agency, R. G. Dun & Co., 1841–1916* (Brooklyn, N.Y.: R. G. Dun & Co., 1916), 295–299.

16. On "the Christian self-made man," see Friedman, "Confidence and Pertinacity in Evangelical Abolitionism," esp. 91–92. Tappan, *Life of Arthur Tappan*, 317–337, 345–346. Wyatt-Brown, *Lewis Tappan*, 206–213, 229. The dualistic origins and aims of Tappan's agency paralleled Thomas L. Haskell's thesis in "Capitalism and the Origins of Humanitarian Sensibility," in *The Antislavery Debate: Capitalism and Abolitionism as a Problem in Historical Interpretation*, ed. Thomas Bender (Berkeley: University of California Press, 1992), 107–199, esp. III.

17. Wyatt-Brown, *Lewis Tappan*, 230–232. Ann Fabian, *Card Sharps and Bucket Shops: Gambling in Nineteenth-Century America*, 2nd ed. (New York: Routledge, 1999 [1990]), 85, 98, 101–104.

18. "Mercantile Agency," *New-York City and Co-Partnership Directory, for 1843 and 1844, in Two Parts* (New-York: John Doggett, Jr., [1843]), n.p.

19. Credit reports (1846–1854) of Charles Collins, Ohio, vol. 78, p. 129.

20. Credit reports (1845–1848) of J. B. N. Gould, Massachusetts, vol. 104, p. 545. Credit reports (1857–1868) of T. R. Mattox, Alabama, vol. 12, p. 117. Credit reports (1854–1856) of Alexander W. Bateman, Alabama, vol. 12, p. 97.

21. Wyatt-Brown, *Lewis Tappan*, 230–232, 236–237.

22. Floyd Rinhart and Marion Rinhart, *The American Daguerreotype* (Athens: University of Georgia Press, 1981), 36–38, 48, 95–98. Bruno [pseud.], "Picture Pausings, No. II," *Christian Watchman* 27 (15 May 1846): 77. Carleton Mabee, *The American Leonardo: A Life of Samuel F. B. Morse* (New York: Alfred A. Knopf, 1943), 231–234, 242–243. Madeleine B. Stern, *Heads and Headlines: The Phrenological Fowlers* (Norman: University of Oklahoma Press, 1971), 21–25.

23. Rinhart and Rinhart, *American Daguerreotype*, 53–54, 135–136, 383, 392. Stern, *Heads and Headlines*, 109.

24. My understanding of surveillance draws upon John Tagg, *The Burden of Representation: Essays on Photographies and Histories* (Amherst: University of Massachusetts Press, 1988), chs. 2–3; and Jonathan Crary, *Techniques of the Observer: On Vision and Modernity in the Nineteenth Century* (Cambridge, Mass.: MIT Press, 1990), chs. 1, 4. "Written Descriptions, from Daguerreotypes," *American Phrenological Journal* 24 (July 1856): 1–2. "The Daguerreotype," *New-York Observer* 22, no. 18 (1844). "The Mercantile Agency," *HMM* 24 (January 1851): 46–53, esp. 49.

25. Alan Trachtenberg, *Reading American Photographs: Images as History, Mathew Brady to Walker Evans* (New York: Hill and Wang, 1989), 28–29, 52–60. A Retired Merchant, *Opportunities for Industry and the Safe Investment of Capital; or, A Thousand Chances to Make Money* (Philadelphia: J. B. Lippincott and Co., 1859), 15. "The Pencil of Nature, a New Discovery," *Corsair* 1 (13 April 1839): 70–72. Ronald G. Walters, *American Reformers, 1815–1860* (New York: Hill and Wang, 1978), 161. Alan Trachtenberg, "Mirror in the Marketplace: American Responses to the Daguerreotype, 1839–1851," in *The Daguerreotype: A Sesquicentennial Celebration*, ed. John Wood (Iowa City: University of Iowa Press, 1989), 62. "Commercial Agencies," repr. from *The Independent* in *HMM* 35 (August 1856): 260. "Objects and Results of the Mercantile Agency," *Mercantile Agency Annual for 1873* (New York: Dun, Barlow and Co., n.d.), 27.

26. Noah Webster, *An American Dictionary of the English Language*, ed. Chauncey A. Goodrich (Springfield, Mass.: George and Charles Merriam, 1848), 192. Daniel T. Rodgers, *The Work Ethic in Industrial America, 1850–1920* (Chicago: University of Chicago Press, 1978), 37, 250n12. John

Ashworth, *Slavery, Capitalism, and Politics in the Antebellum Republic, Vol. 1: Commerce and Compromise, 1820–1850* (Cambridge: Cambridge University Press, 1995), ch. 2. Howard P. Chudacoff, "Success and Security: The Meaning of Social Mobility in America," *Reviews in American History* 10 (December 1982): 101–112.

27. Brooks Johnson, "The Progress of Civilization: The American Occupational Daguerreotype," in *America and the Daguerreotype*, ed. John Wood (Iowa City: University of Iowa Press, 1991), 109–117. Josiah M. Graves, "A Phrenological Chart: Presenting a Synopsis of . . . the Phrenological Character of [A. V. Champney]" (Hartford: Hurlbut and Williams, 1839), AAS.

28. Walt Whitman, ["A Song for Occupations"] (1855) in *Complete Poetry and Prose*, ed. Justin Kaplan (New York: Library of America, 1982), 89–99, esp. 89. David Reynolds, *Walt Whitman's America: A Cultural Biography* (New York: Knopf, 1995), pp. 210, 236–251. Whitman, "Broadway Sights" and "One Wicked Impulse!" in *Complete Poetry and Prose*, 701, 1084, 1291. Fowlers and Wells became Fowler and Wells when Orson Fowler left the firm in 1855.

29. Whitman, ["A Song for Occupations,"] 95–96, 98.

30. Whitman, "A Song for Occupations" (1881), in *Complete Poetry and Prose*, 355–362, esp. 358, 360, 357, 361. Walt Whitman, "Poem of the Daily Work of the Workmen and Workwomen of These States," in *Leaves of Grass* (New York: Fowler & Wells, 1856), 23.

31. Walt Whitman, "Starting from Paumonok," in *Complete Poetry and Prose*, 176–188, esp. 182. Kaplan, "A Note on the Texts," in ibid., 1352–1354. Credit reports (1846–1864) of Charles W. Freeland & Co., Massachusetts, vol. 104, p. 532. Walt Whitman, "Song of the Open Road," in *Complete Poetry and Prose*, 297–307, esp. 297. Credit reports (1843–1852) of Rufus D. Dunbar, Massachusetts, vol. 104, p. 535. Credit report (1860) of Harvey Holden, New York, vol. 513, p. 395.

32. Whitman, "Song of the Open Road," 306; "To a Historian," 167; "Song of Myself," 188–247, esp. 214; all in *Complete Poetry and Prose*.

33. Rinhart and Rinhart, *American Daguerreotype*, 114–115. Vose, *Seventy-Five Years of the Mercantile Agency*, 296. "The Mercantile Agency," 46. Joseph W. Errant, *The Law Relating to Mercantile Agencies* (Philadelphia: T. & J. W. Johnson and Co., 1889), 3–4.

34. "Financial and Commercial Review," *United States Democratic Review* 29 (October 1851): 370–371. Diary of Edward Neufville Tailer, Jr., 25 April 1857, vol. 12, NYHS. On Tailer, see Allan Stanley Horlick, *Country Boys and Merchant Princes: The Social Control of Young Men in New York* (Lewisburg, Pa.: Bucknell University Press, 1975), ch. 5. "Commercial Croakers," *HMM* 34 (May 1856): 638–640. Foulke, *Sinews of American Commerce*, 294–299.

35. "Agreement to Dissolve and Terminate Copartnership Under the Firm Name of Dix & Edwards . . . ," 25 April 1857, folder 206, Series 2, Papers of Dix, Edwards & Co., Houghton Library, Harvard University. Herman

Melville, *The Confidence-Man: His Masquerade* (Evanston, Ill.: Northwestern University Press, 1984), 27, 119, 133, 248, 249. Tailer diary, 22 September 1853, vol. 11. Foulke, *Sinews of American Commerce*, 297–298. *The Mercantile Agency's Reference Book . . . , Vol. 3* (New York: Dun, Boyd and Co., 1861) (with brass lock), AAS.

36. Tailer diary, 22 September 1853, vol. 11; 3 November 1854, vol. 12. Credit reports (1854) of F. E. Radcliff [*sic*] & Co., New York, vol. 199, pp. 273, 300.

37. Tailer diary, vols. 1–13, esp. 1 September 1853, vol. 11; 22 October 1854, vol. 12; 30 July 1855, vol. 12; and 18 March 1860, vol. 13.

38. Tailer diary, 15 August 1850, vol. 8; 27 January 1853, vol. 10; 20 July 1855, vol. 12. On self-improvement, see 17 April 1849, vol. 5; undated [pp. 1–2], vol. 7; 18 October 1849, vol. 7; 19 May 1854, vol. 11; and 20 July 1855, vol. 12. On Tailer and phrenology, see Horlick, *Country Boys and Merchant Princes*, 131.

39. Credit reports (1853–1879) of Edward N. Tailer, New York, vol. 199, p. 276; vol. 203, pp. 700N, 700QQ, 700.A88; vol. 204, pp. 800.A112, 800.A127, 800.A167.

40. Tailer diary, 19 September 1857, 2 December 1857, both in vol. 12. "Edward Neufville Tailer," in *America's Successful Men of Affairs: An Encyclopedia of Contemporaneous Biography* (New York: New York Tribune, 1895–1896), 1:639–640. "Edward N. Tailer Dead: Retired Merchant Was Member of an Old New York Family," *NYT*, 16 February 1917. "An Old New Yorker," *NYT*, 18 February 1917.

41. Edward Pessen, "The Egalitarian Myth and American Social Reality: Wealth, Mobility, and Equality in the 'Era of the Common Man,'" *American Historical Review* 76 (October 1971): 989–1034.

42. Tailer diary, 5 May, 7 May, 18 May, 9 June, 26 August, 2 September, 12 September, and 26 December 1857, all in vol. 12.

43. Tailer diary, 7 May 1857. Michel Foucault, *The Archaeology of Knowledge*, trans. A. M. Sheridan Smith (New York: Pantheon, 1982), 126–131.

44. *America's Successful Men*, 640. "Nathan Lane and Co." label, in Tailer diary, vol. 13. Foulke, *Sinews of American Commerce*, 374–375. James H. Madison, "The Evolution of Commercial Credit Reporting Agencies in Nineteenth-Century America," *Business History Review* 48 (1974): 167n9. Clark W. Bryan, *Credit: Its Meaning and Moment* (New York: Bradstreet Press, 1883). "The Red Book," trade card (Cincinnati: Furniture Commercial Agency Co., n.d.); "International Mercantile Agency," letterhead and bookmark, circa 1903; "Red Book Company," ratings key, n.d.; "Bradstreet's deluxe bindings," trade card, n.d.; R. G. Dun & Co. letterhead, circa 1889; all in boxes 1–2, "Mercantile," Warshaw Collection, Smithsonian Institution.

5. The Big Red Book of Third-Rate Men

1. Peter Brooks, *Reading for the Plot: Design and Intention in Narrative* (New York: Alfred A. Knopf, 1984), preface, ch. 1. Hayden White, *The Content of the Form: Narrative Discourse and Historical Representation* (Baltimore:

Johns Hopkins University Press, 1987), ch. 1. Harry Franco [Charles F. Briggs], *Bankrupt Stories* (New York: John Allen, 1843). Ann Fabian, *The Unvarnished Truth: Personal Narratives in Nineteenth-Century America* (Berkeley: University of California Press, 2000), ch. 1. Credit reports (1868–1879) of John Cain, Vermont, vol. 20, p. 118. Reports (1857–1876) of A. L. Griffin, New York, vol. 80, p. 327. Report (1851) of Z. H. Kitchen, New York Trade Agency Reports, p. 8, NYHS.

2. Theodore M. Porter, *The Rise of Statistical Thinking, 1820–1900* (Princeton, N.J.: Princeton University Press, 1986). Reports (1848–1857) of Henry Misroon, South Carolina, vol. 6, p. 71. Reports (1844–1855) of George W. Shurrigan, Ohio, vol. 78, pp. 93, 105. Reports (1852–1858) of Thomas White, Jr., Pennsylvania, vol. 131, p. 57. Reports (1852–1857) of N. H. Calkins, New York, vol. 513, p. 399. Reports (1849) of Bigelow & Coes, Massachusetts, vol. 104, p. 533. Report (1852) of W. H. Tilford, Alabama, vol. 12, p. 208.

3. "FIRE! From the *Boston Daily Advertiser*, Nov. 5," repr. in *Adams Centinel*, 18 November 1820. W. P. Towles & Bro., Baltimore, *Middle States Reports for 1876* (New York: U.S. Mercantile Reporting Co., 1876), 29. Report (1857–1870) of Alexander Baker, New Jersey, vol. 50, p. 314. Reports (1849–1860) of John McQuade, New York, vol. 476, p. 393. Report (1874) of Alex Hamilton, New Jersey, vol. 50, p. 141. Reports (1847–1865) of Theodore B. Guy, South Carolina, vol. 6, p. 40, and vol. 7, p. 342. Reports (1845–1848) of J. B. N. Gould, Massachusetts, vol. 104, p. 545. Reports (1850–1861) of John P. Sunderland, New Jersey, vol. 50, pp. 78, 87, 130. Reports (1849–1876) of H. V. N. DeHart, New Jersey, vol. 50, pp. 73, 164, 365. Reports (1853–1875) of G. W. Calkins, Ohio, vol. 40, p. 298. Report (1852) of Alfred Kell[e]y, Ohio, vol. 40, p. 297. Reports (1854–1858) of George W. Hardcastle, Georgia, vol. 28, p. 31. Reports (1854) of W. H. May & Co., Georgia, vol. 28, p. 31.

4. Reports (1857–1868) of T. R. Mattox, Alabama, vol. 12, pp. 108, 117. "The Philosophy of Statistics," *NYT*, 7 April 1853. Patricia Cline Cohen, *A Calculating People: The Spread of Numeracy in Early America* (New York: Routledge, 1999 [1982]), 150–151, 205–226. Arthur H. Cole, "Conspectus for a History of Economic and Business Literature," *Journal of Economic History* 17 (September 1957): 333–388, esp. 357–358, 377. Reports (1869–1875) of O'Brien & Cahill, Pennsylvania, vol. 131, p. 151. Reports (1857–1866) of Daniel D. Keyes, Massachusetts, vol. 104, p. 547. Reports (1843–1848) of H. N. Drew, New York, vol. 47, p. 181. Reports (1852–1856) of Edmund W. Clark, New York, vol. 47, p. 123. Reports (1881–1883) of M. G. Browne, Illinois, vol. 44, p. 344. Report (1863) of John Cain, Vermont, vol. 19, p. 164. Reports (1846–1854) of S. H. Parvin & Co., Ohio, vol. 81, p. 146. Report (1862) of James S. Weatherby, Ohio, vol. 81, p. 122.

5. "Egg," in J. E. Lighter, ed., *Random House Historical Dictionary of American Slang* (New York: Random House, 1994), 697. Arthur H. Cole, "Agricultural Crazes: A Neglected Chapter in American Economic History," *American Economic Review* 16 (December 1926): 622–639. "The Oonoscope,"

Scientific American 14 (27 November 1858): 96. "A Word to the Rural Districts," *NYT,* 10 May 1852. Credit report (1853) of Charles A. Floyd, Virginia, vol. 29, p. 38. Alan H. Strahler, "Forests of the Fairfax Line," *Annals of the Association of American Geographers* 62 (December 1972): 664–684, esp. 666–668. Report (1857) of W. C. Gatewood, South Carolina, vol. 6, p. 69. Report (1851) of William H. DeGroot, New York Trade Agency Reports, p. 37. Reports (1848–1876) of Hiram Hill, Rhode Island, vol. 9, p. 145; this is the same Hiram Hill whose self-doubts during the early 1850s are discussed in Chapter 3. Reports (1861–1882) of George Morse, New York, vol. 513, p. 395. Reports (1848–1859) of Frederick Hollister, New York, vol. 476, p. 390.

6. Reports (1843–1861) of Alden Thayer, Massachusetts, vol. 104, p. 529. Reports (1845–1857) of Joseph Randolph, New Jersey, vol. 50, p. 99. Reports (1845–1883) of A. P. Winslow, Ohio, vol. 40, pp. 291, 186; vol. 41, pp. 188. Reports (1843–1852) of Rufus Dunbar, Massachusetts, vol. 104, p. 535. Reports (1845–1848) of Gould & Braman, Massachusetts, vol. 104, p. 545. Reports (1848–1871) of M. B. Dyott, Pennsylvania, vol. 131, pp. 115, 125, 284BB, 284CC, 285a77; vol. 134, p. 621. Reports (1847–1851) of Cyrus Bliss, Massachusetts, vol. 104, p. 568. Reports (1847–1860) of Frederick Myerle, Pennsylvania, vol. 131, p. 22. Reports (1843–1857) of Hugh Alexander, Pennsylvania, vol. 131, p. 50. Reports (1848–1856) of Clark Watson & Co., New York, vol. 365, p. 166. Reports (1847–1854) of Alfred Edwards & Co., New York, vol. 197, p. 9.

7. "A 1," *The Compact Edition of the Oxford English Dictionary: Complete Text Reproduced Micrograpically* (Oxford: Oxford University Press, 1971), 1:1. "First rate, first-rate, *phr., a. (adv.),* and *n.,*" ibid., 1:1008. "Second-rate, *a.* and *n.,*" ibid., 2:2701. Reports (1853–1855) of W. & S. Phipps & Co., New York, vol. 199, p. 268. For many A1 reports, see Pennsylvania, vol. 131, p. 70. Report of Amasa Gibson, E. W. Morgan credit ledger (1861–1862), Bentley Historical Library, University of Michigan, Ann Arbor. Reports (1848–1857) of T. J. Kerr, South Carolina, vol. 6, p. 71.

8. Frederick L. Coolidge, *Statistics: A Gentle Introduction* (London: Sage Publications, 2001), 18–19. John Allen Paulos, *Once upon a Number: The Hidden Mathematical Logic of Stories* (New York: Basic Books, 1999), esp. chs. 1, 4. Reports (1849–1854) of Acker & Harris, New York, vol. 197, p. 64. Reports (1857–1858) of W. B. Ufford, New York, vol. 47, p. 179. Reports (1860–1871) of John R. Ross, New Jersey, vol. 50, p. 87.

9. Reports (1844–1846) of Wm. H. Brisbane, Ohio, vol. 81, p. 87. "Stick to Some One Pursuit," *HMM* 33 (November 1855): 648.

10. Arthur C. Danto, *Narration and Knowledge* (New York: Columbia University Press, 1985), esp. chap. 7.

11. Diary of William Henry Brisbane, 1 January 1841, vol. 1, n.p.; and 6 November 1844, vol. 2, n.p.; reel 1, W. H. Brisbane Papers, Archives Division, State Historical Society of Wisconsin, Madison. Lawrence S. Rowland, Alexan-

der Moore, and George C. Rogers Jr., *The History of Beaufort County, South Carolina, 1514–1861* (Columbia: University of South Carolina Press, 1996), 1:417. "William Henry Brisbane," in *Appleton's Cyclopaedia of American Biography*, ed. James Grant Wilson and John Fiske (New York: D. Appleton and Co., 1887), 1:378. Eduardo Haviland Hillman, "The Brisbanes," *South Carolina Historical and Genealogical Magazine* 14 (July and October 1913): 115–133, 175–197.

12. Brisbane diary, 24 April 1841, vol 1, n.p., reel 1. John Niven, *Salmon P. Chase: A Biography* (New York: Oxford University Press, 1995), 68, 213–214.

13. Wallace Alcorn, "Rev. William Henry Brisbane, M. D. (1806–1878): A South Carolina Baptist Enigma," "A Bibliographical Essay: Abundant, But Inadequate, Published Sources," and "A Bibliography of Brisbane Writings," *Journal of the South Carolina Baptist Historical Society* 25 (November 1999): 10–28. *History of Iowa County, Wisconsin* (Chicago: Western Historical Co., 1881), 781–790, 930–931.

14. Edith M. Dabbs, *Sea Island Diary: A History of St. Helena Island* (Spartenburg, S.C.: Reprint Co., 1983), 163–164, 169–171. Thomas Wentworth Higginson, *The Complete Civil War Journal and Selected Letters of Thomas Wentworth Higginson*, ed. Christopher Looby (Chicago: University of Chicago Press, 1999), 76. Brisbane House, or Stone House Farm, Arena, Wisc., site no. 90001458, National Register of Historic Places.

15. Reports (1844–1872) of Solomon Andrews, New Jersey, vol. 50, pp. 179, 188.

16. "Solomon Andrews, M. D., of Perth Amboy," in William C. McGinnis, *The History of Perth Amboy, N.J., 1651–1959* (Perth Amboy: American Pub. Co., 1959), 2:18–25. "Solomon Andrews' clam shell lock," U.S. Senate 33A-H16.1, RG 46 (Records of the Committee on Post Office and Civil Service and Related Committees), NARA.

17. "Local Intelligence: Aerial Navigation. The Aereon Invented by Dr. Andrews, of New Jersey," *NYT,* 11 June 1865. "Aerial Navigation," *NYT,* 29 September 1865. "Ascent and Return of the Aereon," *NYT,* 26 May 1866. "Philosophy in the Clouds," *Harper's Illustrated Weekly,* 2 June 1866: 350. Solomon Andrews, *The Aereon, or Flying-Ship, Invented by Solomon Andrews* (New York: John F. Trow & Co., 1866). John Toland, *Ships in the Sky: The Story of the Great Dirigibles* (New York: Henry Holt, 1957), 13–24, 26, 40. Tom D. Crouch, *The Eagle Aloft: Two Centuries of the Balloon in America* (Washington, D.C.: Smithsonian Institution Press, 1983), 323–330.

18. "The Mercantile Agency," *HMM* 24 (January 1851): 46–53, esp. 46. Reports of Solomon Andrews. Reports (1869–1877) of William E. Jones, Ohio, vol. 41, p. 389. Reports (1847–1856) of Swift & Co., Georgia, vol. 28, p. 11. Reports (1860–1861) of John B. Conover, New Jersey, vol. 50, p. 142.

19. "The Mercantile Agency," 48, 49–50.

20. Karl Marx, "Commodities and Money," from *Kapital,* vol. 1, in *The Marx-Engels Reader,* 2nd ed., ed. Robert C. Tucker (New York: W. W. Norton and Co., 1978), 302–336. "The Mercantile Agency," 47. Henry D. Thoreau,

Journal, Volume 4: 1851–1852, ed. Robert Sattelmeyer et al. (Princeton, N.J.: Princeton University Press, 1992), 181 (13 November 1851).

21. Reports (1858–1876) of James Wirick, Illinois, vol. 114, p. 189. Jonathan A. Glickstein, *American Exceptionalism, American Anxiety: Wages, Competition, and Degraded Labor in the Antebellum United States* (Charlottesville: University of Virginia Press, 2002). On character, see Burton J. Bledstein, *The Culture of Professionalism: The Middle Class and the Development of Higher Education in America* (New York: W. W. Norton and Co., 1976), ch. 4.

22. Reports (1851–1870) of James DeGray, New York, vol. 197, p. 66. Reports of Acker & Harris. Reports (1847–1857) of Alfred Fassitt & Co., Pennsylvania, vol. 131, p. 181. Reports of Daniel D. Keyes. Report (1847) of Joseph Lippmann, Georgia, vol. 28, p. 10. Reports (1854–1858) of Isaac Marchant, Ohio, vol. 78, p. 42.

23. Reports (1854–1880) of Robert L. Brown, Virginia, vol. 29, pp. 40, 33. Alexander Brown [son of Robert L. Brown], *The Cabells and Their Kin: A Memorial Volume of History, Biography, and Genealogy* (Richmond, Va.: Garrett and Massie, 1939), 466–467. Letters of Robert L. Brown and Margaret Cabell Brown, Brown Family Papers, VHS.

24. Reports of Robert L. Brown.

25. Report (1854) of James H. Reed, Ohio, vol. 78, p. 134.

26. On Tappan's "moral regulation," see Christopher Clark, *The Roots of Rural Capitalism: Western Massachusetts, 1780–1860* (Ithaca: Cornell University Press, 1990), esp. 215–220, 225, 263. The classic works on these themes are David J. Rothman, *The Discovery of the Asylum: Social Order and Disorder in the New Republic*, rev. ed. (Boston: Little, Brown and Co., 1990); and Michel Foucault, *Discipline and Punish: The Birth of the Prison*, 2nd ed., trans. Alan Sheridan (New York: Vintage, 1995 [1977]), 200–228. Lewis Tappan to Lewis Tappan Stoddard, February 6, 1843, quoted in Bertram Wyatt-Brown, *Lewis Tappan and the Evangelical War against Slavery* (Cleveland, Ohio: Press of Case Western Reserve University, 1969), 232, 245n27. Report (1852) of Joseph Sargeant, Ohio, vol. 40, p. 285. Reports (1844–1846) of Stone & Swain, Massachusetts, vol. 105, p. 551. Reports (1861–1863) of Fred Wood, New York, vol. 513, pp. 394, 397. Reports (1852–1854) of David McAlexander, Virgina, vol. 29, p. 35. Reports (1852–1854) of Avaritt McVay & Henry M. Bodiford, Alabama, vol. 12, p. 99.

27. Reports (1845–1859) of William Manning, New Jersey, vol. 50, p. 295. U.S. Census, 1850, Woodbridge, Middlesex County, New Jersey, p. 35 (reel M432-455, image 70), NARA.

28. Reports (1870) of R. H. Hitchborn (Scofield & Hitchborn), Ohio, vol. 41, p. 361. Report (1848) of Joseph Masseth, New York, vol. 476, p. 393. Reports (1846–1853) of William E. Mumford, Alabama, vol. 12, p. 98. Reports of Alexander Baker. Reports of Robert L. Brown. Reports (1867–1883) of George F. Peckham, New York, vol. 513, pp. 396, 229, 237, 238.

29. Reports (1847–1865) of Theodore B. Guy, South Carolina, vol. 6, p. 40, and vol. 7, p. 342.

30. Reports (1845–1853) of Isaac Thorne, New Jersey, vol. 50, p. 268.

31. Reports (1847–1875) of Willard E. Allen, Massachusetts, vol. 104, pp. 544, 768, 641. Reports (1855–1860) of J. N. Phelps, Virginia, vol. 29, p. 41, and vol. 9, p. 110.

32. Report (1860) of Corbin Thompson, Book 2, p. 557; R. G. Dun St. Louis Branch Office Collection, University Archives, Pius XII Library, St. Louis University, St. Louis, Mo. Reports (1867–1878) of Lewis W. Spencer, New Jersey, vol. 50, p. 166. Report (1859) of J. M. Woodson, Virginia, vol. 29, p. 60.

33. Reports (1852–1860) of Richard H. Coleman, Virginia, vol. 29, p. 29. Reports of (1847–1861) of Eno, Bulen, & Valentine, New York, vol. 197, pp. 16, 65; vol. 203, p. 676. Report (1860) of M. Cox, New York, vol. 513, p. 395. Reports of Gould & Braman. Reports (1858–1879) of A. S. Gregory, Minnesota, vol. 19, pp. 41, 75, 158.4, 249. Reports (1859–1869) of S. & J. Featherstone, Ohio, vol. 40, p. 201. Reports of A. P. Winslow. Reports (1858–1867) of A. B. Shaver, New York, vol. 513, pp. 398, 16, 17.

34. Reports (1841–1852) of Thomas L. King, Ohio, vol. 178, p. 122. Reports (1876–1879) of J. Estabrook, New York, vol. 47, p. 178. On the links between speculating and storytelling in this context, see Ann Fabian, "Speculation on Distress: The Popular Discourse of the Panics of 1837 and 1857," *Yale Journal of Criticism* 3 (Spring 1989): 127–142. Carol Nackenoff examines speculation and commodified selves in *The Fictional Republic: Horatio Alger and American Political Discourse* (New York: Oxford University Press, 1994), esp. 136, 208; Nackenoff, in turn, draws on Walter Benn Michaels, *The Gold Standard and the Logic of Naturalism: American Literature at the Turn of the Century* (Berkeley: University of California Press, 1987).

35. Reports (1850–1855) of George White, Ohio, vol. 81, p. 200. Reports (1844–1869) of Joseph P. Hall, Virginia, vol. 29, p. 21. Reports (1864–1865) of Hugh Smith and Bernard Smyth [*sic*], Illinois, vol. 9, pp. 238L, 238N, 244B. Reports (1854–1862) of Alfred Tafel & Fred[eric]k Vogeler, Ohio, vol. 81, p. 181.

36. Report (1848) of Willcox & Bennett, New York, vol. 47, p. 178. Reports (1844–1857) of William Remington, Pennsylvania, vol. 131, p. 56. Reports of Alfred Edwards & Co. Reports of W. & S. Phipps & Co.

37. "The Mercantile Agency," 53. Edwin T. Freedley, *A Practical Treatise on Business: or How to Get, Save, Spend, Give, Lend, and Bequeath Money . . .* (Philadelphia: Lippincott, Grambo & Co., 1853), 130. "Commercial Agencies," repr. from *The Independent* in *HMM* 35 (August 1856): 260. On reporters' biases, see Gerald Tulchinsky, "'Said to Be an Honest Jew': The R. G. Dun Credit Reports and Jewish Business Activity in Mid-Nineteenth-Century Montreal," *Urban History/revue d'histoire urbaine* 18 (February 1990): 200–209.

38. Reports (1855) of Collins & Stanford, Alabama, vol. 12, p. 98. Reports of Rufus Dunbar. Reports (1868–1872) of J. J. Corlett, Ohio, vol. 43, p. 124. Report (1860) of James Y. Hart, Book 5, p. 290, St. Louis Branch Collection. Reports of Hugh Smith and Bernard Smyth [sic].

39. Report (1855) of Cowles, Sickles & Co., Ohio, vol. 78, p. 25.

40. Reports (1852–1856) of Edmund W. Clark. Reports (1847–1858) of Ashbury Kent, Ohio, vol. 79, p. 160. Report (1858) of [Thos.] Smyth & Bro., Illinois, vol. 9, p. 238B. "Of General Interest," *Decatur (Illinois) Daily Republican*, 6 May 1885, repr. from *New York Tribune*. Many newspapers carried this filler item in Spring 1885, which later appeared in a best-selling anthology, Alexander K. McClure, *Lincoln's Yarns and Stories: A Complete Collection of the Funny and Witty Anecdotes that made Abraham Lincoln Famous as America's Greatest Story Teller* (Chicago: John C. Winston Co., [1900]), 295–296. Many newspapers used the item again in 1897–98, 1914, 1922–1924, 1929, 1941–42, 1948–1951, 1960, and 1969; for example, "Graham Tells Story of Lincoln's Answer to Credit Inquiry," *Decatur Review*, 28 July 1929. See also P. M. Zall, ed., *Abe Lincoln Laughing: Humorous Anecdotes from Original Sources by and about Abraham Lincoln* (Berkeley: University of California Press, 1982), 116–117.

41. Carl Sandburg, *Abraham Lincoln: The Prairie Years* (New York: Scribner's, 1926), 2:78; adjudged "spurious" in *Collected Works of Abraham Lincoln*, ed. Roy P. Basler (New Brunswick, N.J.: Rutgers University Press), 8:590. Edward Neville Vose, *Seventy-Five Years of the Mercantile Agency, R. G. Dun & Co., 1841–1916* (Brooklyn, N.Y.: R. G. Dun, 1916), 36–37. Roy Anderson Foulke, *The Sinews of American Commerce: Published by Dun & Bradstreet, Inc., on the Occasion of Its 100th Anniversary, 1841–1941* (New York: Dun & Bradstreet, 1941), 350–351.

42. Reports (1857–?) of Abraham Lincoln, Illinois, vol. 198, p. 163 [partially expunged]. Wendell Phillips quoted in Kenneth M. Stampp, *The Era of Reconstruction, 1865–1877* (New York: Vintage, 1967), 44. For entries on Lincoln's reliability as an informant ("No. 1 for you. One of the best [debt] coll[ecto]rs in the Co[unty]") ca. 1847–1860, see Illinois "Lawyer's Book," vol. 2, p. 287. At my request, the Paper Laboratory of the Straus Center for Conservation at Harvard's Fogg Art Museum examined vol. 198, p. 163, on 26 April 2000. Ultraviolet and infrared scans showed "that the area had been systematically abraded" to remove text. Laura Linard (Director of Historical Collections, Baker Library, HBS) to Scott A. Sandage, 3 August 2000.

6. Misinformation and Its Discontents

1. Eula Shorey and Cara Cook, *Bridgton, Maine, 1768–1968* (Bridgton, Me.: Bridgton Historical Society, 1968), 80–81, 95, 103, 122, 128–131, 135–136, 450, 585. George A. Riley, "A History of Tanning in the State of Maine," master's thesis, Tufts College, 1935, 116–124. Credit reports (1854–1886) of Hor-

ace Billings, Maine, vol. 3, p. 201; and vol. 14, p. 155; Massachusetts, vol. 68, pp. 287, 419, 500P, 500Z/12; and vol. 86, p. 24.

2. Credit reports quoted in *Horace Billings v. Edward Russell and Edwin F. Waters, 18 Monthly Law Reporter,* 699–702. [Richard Henry Dana, Jr.,] "Brief," n.d., and "Evidence," n.d., both in case file 1462, "Billings vs. Russell et al." (1856), AAS. I discovered Dana's lost files (1,500 cases, 1840–1878) in the attic of the Worcester Courthouse in 1994; they have since been moved to AAS.

3. *Billings v. Russell,* 700. Richard Henry Dana, Jr., *Two Years before the Mast: A Personal Narrative of Life at Sea* (New York: Modern Library, 2001 [1840]). Billings report, 20 December 1854, Maine, vol. 3, p. 201.

4. *Billings v. Russell,* 699–702. Dana, "Brief." Edward Neville Vose, *Seventy-Five Years of the Mercantile Agency, R. G. Dun & Co.* (Brooklyn, N.Y.: R. G. Dun & Co., 1916), 81.

5. James R. Beniger, *The Control Revolution: Technological and Economic Origins of the Information Society* (Cambridge, Mass.: Harvard University Press, 1986), 257. Alfred D. Chandler and James Cortada, eds., *A Nation Transformed by Information: How Information Has Shaped the United States from Colonial Times to the Present* (New York: Oxford University Press, 2000). Mark Poster, *Information Subject* (New York: Routledge, 2001), 1–45.

6. U.S. Circuit Court, Southern District of New York, *Lewis Tappan, ads. John Beardsley and Horace Beardsley, Bill of Exceptions,* 16–20, 26–27. This printed document is in *Lewis Tappan, Plaintiff in Error, vs. John Beardsley and Horace Beardsley,* case 5330, Appellate Case Files, Records of the Supreme Court of the United States, RG 267, NARA. "Mercantile Agencies," *NYT,* 7 November 1851.

7. "Information," *The Compact Edition of the Oxford English Dictionary: Complete Text Reproduced Micrographically* (Oxford: Oxford University Press, 1971), 1:1432. "Mercantile Agency," *The New-York City and Co-Partnership Directory, for 1843 and 1844, in Two Parts* (New-York: John Doggett, Jr., [1843]), n.p. Lewis Tappan to Lewis Tappan Stoddard, 6 February 1843, quoted in Bertram Wyatt-Brown, *Lewis Tappan and the Evangelical War against Slavery* (Cleveland, Ohio: The Press of Case Western Reserve University, 1969), 232, 245n27.

8. Asa G. Bunker to W. A. Cleveland's Mercantile Agency, 7 May 1845, in unlabeled letterbook, folder 22, Bunker Family Papers, Nantucket Historical Association, Nantucket, Mass.; Bunker's letterbook contains both his notes on local men and copies of his dispatches to Cleveland. Circular flyer, W[arren] A. Cleveland's Mercantile Agency, 1 July 1846, folder 8, box 1, "Mercantile," Warshaw Collection of Business Americana, Smithsonian Institution. Roy Anderson Foulke, *The Sinews of American Commerce: Published by Dun & Bradstreet, Inc., on the Occasion of its 100th Anniversary, 1841–1941* (New York: Dun & Bradstreet, 1941), 297–298. "The Mercantile Agency," *HMM* 24 (January 1851): 46–53, esp. 48. [Dun, Barlow & Co.], *The*

Mercantile Agency: Its Claims upon the Favor and Support of the Community: Commendatory Letters (New York: Dun, Barlow & Co. et al. [1871]), 14. Thomas Haigh, "Inventing Information Systems: The Systems Men and the Computer, 1950–1968," *Business History Review* 75 (Spring 2001): 15–61. "The Basis of Prosperity," *HMM* 42 (April 1860): 516–517.

9. Peter J. Coleman, *Debtors and Creditors in America: Insolvency, Imprisonment for Debt, and Bankruptcy, 1607–1900* (Madison: State Historical Society of Wisconsin, 1974), 283–285. "Bureaucracy," in Max Weber, *From Max Weber: Essays in Sociology,* trans. and ed. H. H. Gerth and C. Wright Mills (New York: Oxford University Press, 1958 [1946]), 196–244, esp. 197. Colin Gordon, "The Soul of a Citizen: Max Weber and Michel Foucault on Rationality and Government," in Scott Lash and Sam Whimster, eds., *Max Weber, Rationality, and Modernity* (London: Allen and Unwin, 1986), 293–316. Wyatt-Brown, *Lewis Tappan,* 232. "The Mercantile Agency System," *Banker's Magazine and Statistical Review* 7 (January 1858): 545–549. Thomas Francis Meagher [Charles F. Maynard], *The Commercial Agency "System" of the United States and Canada Exposed: Is the Secret Inquisition a Curse or a Benefit?* (New York, 1876), 170. For a useful critique of R. G. Dun & Co. as an information system, see Bruce G. Carruthers and Barry Cohen, "Predicting Failure but Failing to Predict: A Sociology of Knowledge of Credit Rating in Post-Bellum America" (paper presented at the Annual Meeting of the American Sociological Association, 2001), draft in Sandage's possession; and Barry Cohen, "Constructing an Uncertain Economy: Credit Reporting and Insurance Rating in the Nineteenth Century United States," (Ph.D. diss., Northwestern University, in progress).

10. Walter J. Ong, *Orality and Literacy: The Technologizing of the Word* (London: Methuen, 1982), chs. 4–6. Reports (1853–1855) of W. & S. Phipps & Co., New York, vol. 199, p. 268. Report (1856) of J. C. Scott, Alabama, vol. 12, p. 158. Report (1848) of Willcox & Bennett, New York, vol. 47, p. 178.

11. Caroline Boalt Strutton and Charlotte Wooster Boalt, *The Old Homes of Norwalk: A Narrative of Old Lace and Lavender* (Norwalk, Ohio: Privately printed, 1938), n.p. Joseph Lee Boyle, *"Fire Cake and Water": The Connecticut Infantry at Valley Forge* (Baltimore, Md.: Clearfield, 1999), iv–xi, 14. Isaac H. Beardsley, *Genealogical History of the Beardsley-Lee Family in America* (Denver: John Dove, 1902), 124–125. Nellie Judson Beardsley Holt, *Beardsley Genealogy: The Family of William Beardsley, One of the First Settlers of Stratford, Connecticut* (West Hartford, Conn., 1951), 68–69. Bryce Metcalf, *Original Members and Other Officers Eligible to the Society of the Cincinnati, 1783–1938* (Strasburg, Va.: Shenandoah Publishing, 1938), 48, 70.

12. *Huron Reflector,* 19 December 1848. *Beardsley et al. v. Tappan,* 2 Federal Cases 1183–87 (1851). *Lewis Tappan, Plff. in Err., v. John Beardsley et al.,* 10 U.S. Reports (Wallace) 427–436 (1871); 77 Supreme Court Reports (Williams), 974–976 (1871). *Reports of the Four Leading Cases against the Mercantile Agency for Slander and Libel* (New York: Dun, Barlow & Co., 1873).

Lewis Tappan, Plaintiff in Error, vs. John Beardsley and Horace Beardsley (no. 437), *Records and Briefs of the Supreme Court of the United States* (Wilmington, Del., n.d.), part 2 (1861–1870), vol. 154, microfilm edition (hereafter cited as *Records and Briefs*).

13. *Huron Reflector,* 27 November 1832, 5 August 1835, 18 August 1835, 15 September 1835, 24 August 1841, 7 September 1841, 29 September 1841, 1 October 1844, 11 March 1845, 4 November 1845, 27 January 1848, and 18 May 1847. Strutton and Boalt, *Old Homes of Norwalk,* n.p. "Subscriber's Book" of St. Paul's Episcopal Church, Firelands Historical Society, Norwalk, Ohio.

14. Reports (1845–1878) of John and Horace Beardsley, Ohio, vol. 101, pp. 316, 317, 250, 270, 271, 250.10, 372.

15. Ibid., 316. *Lewis Tappan, Bill of Exceptions,* 2–4, 10–11, 14–15, 47.

16. *Lewis Tappan, Bill of Exceptions,* pp. 24, 35–36. Several New York wholesalers testified that because of agency reports, they canceled or refused orders from the Beardsley brothers. *Lewis Tappan, Bill of Exceptions,* 24, 47.

17. Diary of Lewis Tappan, 16 December 1851, reel 2 (Journals and Notebooks, Box 2A), Tappan Papers, Manuscript Division, Library of Congress. "Ogden Hoffman," in *Appleton's Cyclopaedia of American Biography,* ed. James Grant Wilson and John Fiske (New York: D. Appleton and Co., 1887), 3:227. "Francis Brockholst Cutting," in ibid., 2:49. "Benjamin Franklin Butler," in ibid., 1:476–477. "Samuel Rossiter Betts," in ibid., 1:253. "Charles O'Conor," in *Memorial and Biographical Record and Compendium of Biography . . .* (Chicago: George A. Ogle and Co., 1899), 187–188.

18. *Four Leading Cases,* 9–10, 211, 236–237. *Lewis Tappan, Bill of Exceptions,* 29–30, 44–46, 48–52, 57, 96. The U.S. Supreme Court extended privilege to libel and slander cases in *White v. Nichols, et al.,* 3 Howard 266 (1845), but mercantile agencies were not specifically protected until *Trussell v. Scarlett, trading as R. G. Dun & Co.,* 18 Federal Reporter 214–220 (1882).

19. *Lewis Tappan, Bill of Exceptions,* 12. "Mercantile Agencies," *NYT,* 29 October 1851, 7 November 1851. *Lewis Tappan, Bill of Exceptions,* 13, 35–36.

20. *Lewis Tappan, Bill of Exceptions,* 16, 32–35. Loose correspondence regarding R. H. Hitchborn (1870), Ohio, vol. 41, p. 361; R. M. Adam Co. (1877), South Carolina, vol. 6; Irvin & Co. (1879), Maryland, vol. 14.; J. D. Sauerberg (1880), Maryland, vol. 14; and David Jankau (1883), Ohio, vol. 45.

21. *Lewis Tappan, Bill of Exceptions,* 36. Reports (1856) of P. T. Barnum, New York, vol. 376, p. 389. Reports of R. H. Hitchborn. Foulke, *Sinews of American Commerce,* 311–312. Reports of John and Horace Beardsley.

22. The copyist misdated two entries as 1858 instead of 1848, apparently being used to writing in the new decade. Cross-references (necessary when reports filled one page and continued on another) show that the first Beardsley entries were on the missing page 359. After starting the recopying on page 316, the file continues on page 317 but then jumps backward, to page 250. Mismatched cross-references indicate that the recopying occurred between the dates reported on page 317: 22 May 1850 to 6 July 1852.

23. *Lewis Tappan, Bill of Exceptions,* 22–23. Another judge had previously denied the agency's motion to dismiss over variance in wording. 2 Federal Cases 1181–83 (1850). *Four Leading Cases,* 207. The agency's 1870 Supreme Court brief purportedly quoted directly from the ledger, yet rendered two variants of the Beardsley report, neither of which matched the 1851 trial text nor the extant page 316. *Records and Briefs,* 2, 9.

24. *Billings v. Russell,* 700. *Lewis Tappan, Bill of Exceptions,* 26, 34–35.

25. *Lewis Tappan, Bill of Exceptions,* 36, 88–90. "United States Court. Before Hon. Judge Betts. Novel and Exciting Scene in Court," *New York Herald,* 12 December 1851. "U.S. Circuit Court. Before Judge Betts. *Beardsley & Beardsley vs. Tappan,*" *NYT,* 10 December 1851. "The Imprisoned Witness," *Evening Post,* 24 December 1851. Lewis Tappan, "The Late Libel Suit," *NYT,* 25 December 1851. Vose, *Seventy-Five Years of the Mercantile Agency,* 48–52.

26. Linda Kerber et al., "Forum—Beyond Roles, Beyond Spheres: Thinking about Gender in the Early Republic," *William and Mary Quarterly* 3d ser., 46 (1989): 565–588. Bishop Morris, "Loquacity," *Ladies' Repository* 2 (September 1842): 278–279.

27. "Mercantile Agency," *New-York City and Co-Partnership Directory.* "The Mercantile Agency," *HMM* 24 (January 1851): 49. George F. Foster, *New York Naked* (New York: R. M. DeWitt, [1853]), 119–120. "Commercial Agencies," reprinted from the *New York Independent* in *HMM* 35 (August 1856): 260.

28. *Lewis Tappan, Bill of Exceptions,* 34–35, 51, 67, 70, 81.

29. Ibid., 66–71, 76.

30. Ibid., 42–43, 72–77, 84–86. On Cornelia Mason, see Henry R. Timman, *Just Like Old Times* (Norwalk, Ohio: privately printed, 1982–1989), 1:71 and 5:99.

31. *Lewis Tappan, Bill of Exceptions,* 73–74, 79–81. Elizabeth Pleck, "Wife-Beating in Nineteenth-Century America," *Victimology: An International Journal* 4 (1979): 60–74.

32. *Lewis Tappan, Bill of Exceptions,* 73.

33. Ibid., 70, 77–79. Timman, *Just Like Old Times,* 5:114. William W. Williams, *History of Ashtabula County, Ohio* (Philadelphia: Williams Bros., 1878), 30. Clark Waggoner, *History of the City of Toledo and Lucas County, Ohio* (New York: Munsell and Co., 1888), 346, 463, 515, 523.

34. Carroll Smith-Rosenberg, "The Hysterical Woman: Sex Roles and Role Conflict in Nineteenth-Century America," in *Disorderly Conduct: Visions of Gender in Victorian America* (New York: Oxford University Press, 1985), 197–216.

35. *Lewis Tappan, Bill of Exceptions,* 93–97. *Beardsley et al. v. Tappan,* 2 Federal Cases 1186.

36. "Heavy Damages," *NYT,* 19 December 1851. "Heavy Damages," *Brooklyn Eagle,* 19 December 1851. "H. Beardsley & Co. *vs.* L. Tappan," reprinted from *New-York Dry Goods Reporter* in *Norwalk Experiment,* 13 January 1852.

"A Righteous Verdict—$10,000 Damages!" *Norwalk Experiment,* 23 December 1851.

37. Tappan diary, 18 December 1851. Lewis Tappan to Jairus Kennan, 10 January 1852 and 29 January 1852, Tappan Papers, vol. 7, pp. 478, 483–484.

38. *Lewis Tappan, Bill of Exceptions,* 68–71. *In re Lewis Tappan et al.,* 7 Monthly Law Reporter 517 (1854). "Mercantile Agencies–Evidence–Rights of Witnesses," *NYT,* 15 July 1854. "Norwalk, Its Men, Women and Girls," *Firelands Pioneer* 20 (1918): 2109–10. Timman, *Just Like Old Times,* 5:10, 2:135. *Huron Reflector,* 2 June 1840, 25 August 1840, 5 January 1841, 20 July 1841, 24 August 1841, 28 September 1841, 15 September 1842, 6 September 1842, 3 November 1845, 29 September 1846, 18 May 1847, and 4 February 1851. George F. Kennan, *An American Kennan Family, 1744–1913* (n.p.: G. F. Kennan, 1996), 62–63. I. T. Frary, *Early Homes of Ohio* (Richmond, Va.: Garrett and Massie, 1936), 292, 295. Thomas Lathrop Kennan, *Genealogy of the Kennan Family* (Milwaukee: Cannon Printing Co., 1907), 32–33, 44–45, 57–58, 76–81.

39. Tappan to Kennan, 29 January 1852.

40. Edwin T. Freedley, *A Practical Treatise on Business* (Philadelphia: Lippincott, Grambo & Co., 1853), 130–131.

41. *Beardsley et al. v. Tappan,* 2 Federal Cases 1187 (1867). *Four Leading Cases,* 234. "Law of Mercantile Agencies," *NYT,* 15 October 1867. "Overdoing the Dead—Beecher on Tappan," *Brooklyn Eagle,* 25 June 1873. "The Law's Delays," *Brooklyn Eagle,* 16 December 1870. See also "The Courts," *New York Herald,* 15 December 1870.

42. *Four Leading Cases,* 234, 240, 249–250, 255, 258–260. Michel Foucault, *Power/Knowledge: Selected Interviews and Other Writings, 1972–1977,* ed. and trans. Colin Gordon (New York: Pantheon, 1980), 130–133.

43. *Tappan v. Beardsley,* 77 Supreme Court Reports, 974. Frederick J. Blue, *Salmon P. Chase: A Life in Politics* (Kent, Ohio: Kent State University Press, 1987), 56–57, 62, 245. Lewis Tappan to Chase & Ball, Esq., 3 March 1842; Salmon P. Chase to Lewis Tappan, 10 March 1842, Salmon P. Chase Papers, series I, reel 5, Manuscript Division, Library of Congress. *Commonwealth v. Stacey,* 8 Philadelphia Reports, 617–622, esp. 621 (1871).

44. Meagher, *The Commercial Agency "System"... Exposed,* 25. *Trussell v. Scarlett,* 219; *Ladd v. Oxnard,* 75 Federal Reporter 703 (1896). For all suits against mercantile agencies, see 32 American Digest 2049–52; and 15 American Digest, 2d dec. ed., 1206–11. "Is It Robbery to Steal Information?" in *The Mercantile Agency Annual for 1873* (New York: Dun, Barlow & Co., [1872]), 199. "Traits of Trade—Laudable and Iniquitous; Chapter V: About Credit," *HMM* 29 (July 1853): 50–54, esp. 51.

45. Henry R. Timman to Scott A. Sandage, 13 November 1994 and 15 January 1995. Henry E. Young (2002 owner of Beardsley's home), "History of This House," n.d., unpublished paper in Sandage's possession. Mary Beardsley obituary, *Norwalk Reflector,* 30 August 1881. "Death of Horace Beardsley," *Norwalk Weekly Reflector,* 13 July 1886. Strutton and Boalt, *Old Homes of*

Norwalk, n.p. "Funeral of John Beardsley," *Norwalk Chronicle*, 7 April 1887. "Norwalk, Its Men, Women and Girls," *Firelands Pioneer* (1918): 2109–10. *Beardsley v. Beardsley*, filed 20 October 1855, granted 4 March 1856, Common Pleas Court Chancery Record, vol. 8, p. 421; John Beardsley and Phila Ann Frayer, 14 September 1865, Marriage Record, vol. 1, p. 485; Huron County Probate Court, Norwalk, Ohio. Among the puzzles in the Beardsleys' private life are indications that Phila and John had two daughters, one born a month before he filed for divorce from Mary in 1855, and the second born in 1859—six years before John and Phila had a respectable wedding in her father's parlor, performed by a Baptist clergyman!

46. Mary-Lou E. Florian, "A Holistic Interpretation of the Deterioration of Vegetable Tanned Leather," *Leather Conservation News* 2 (Fall 1985): 147.

47. Beardsley reports, Ohio, vol. 101, pp. 271, 250.10, 372. *Mercantile Agency: Commendatory Letters*, 15–16. Will of John Beardsley (29 January 1881) probated 11 June 1887, Will Record, vol. 5, p. 111–114, Huron County Probate Court, Norwalk, Ohio.

48. Jairus Kennan obituary, *Huron Reflector*, 19 June 1872. Thomas Lathrop Kennan, *Genealogy*, 45. George F. Kennan, *An American Family: The Kennans, The First Three Generations* (New York: W. W. Norton, 2000), 15–18, 108–111. X [George F. Kennan], "The Sources of Soviet Conduct," *Foreign Affairs* 25 (July 1947): 566–582. George F. Kennan to Scott A. Sandage, 4 March 2002.

49. Samuel D. Warren and Louis D. Brandeis, "The Right to Privacy," *Harvard Law Review* 4 (15 December 1890): 193–220. P. R. Earling, *Whom to Trust: A Practical Treatise on Mercantile Credits* (Chicago: Rand, McNally and Co., 1890), 302–303; Earling was a longtime reporter for the agency of L. Gould and Co., Chicago. David J. Seipp, *The Right to Privacy in American History* (Cambridge, Mass.: Harvard University Center for Information and Policy Research, 1978). James D. Norris, *R. G. Dun & Co., 1841–1900: The Development of Credit-Reporting in the Nineteenth Century* (Westport, Conn: Greenwood Press, 1978), 125–128.

50. Henry D. Thoreau, 28 April 1841, *Journal, Volume 1: 1837–1844*, ed. Elizabeth Hall Witherell et al. (Princeton: Princeton University Press, 1981), 305. Leonard N. Neufeldt, "Thoreau in His Journal," in *The Cambridge Companion to Henry David Thoreau*, ed. Joel Myerson (Cambridge: Cambridge University Press, 1995), 107–123. Thoreau, undated entry [1842–1844], in *Journal: Volume 2: 1842–1848*, ed. Robert Sattelmeyer (Princeton: Princeton University Press, 1984), 87.

51. Stephen B. Oates, *To Purge This Land with Blood: A Biography of John Brown* (New York: Harper and Row, 1979), 33–39, 44–58, 64–72. Wyatt-Brown, *Lewis Tappan*, 332–333. Reports (1848–1850) of John Brown, Massachusetts, vol. 40, p. 246. Henry D. Thoreau, "A Plea for Captain John Brown," in *Reform Papers*, ed. Wendell Glick (Princeton: Princeton University Press, 1978), 111–138, esp. 119, 135.

7. The War for Ambition

1. *Congressional Globe,* 38th Cong., 1st sess., 2636–38, 1 June 1864. Eric Foner, "The Meaning of Freedom in the Age of Emancipation," *Journal of American History* 81 (September 1994): 435–460. For a more detailed political and legislative history of Jenckes's bill, see Scott A. Sandage, "Deadbeats, Drunkards, and Dreamers: A Cultural History of Failure in the United States, 1819–1893" (Ph.D. diss., Rutgers University, 1995), chs. 2–3.

2. U.S. Constitution, art. I, sec. 8. Bankruptcy Act of 4 April 1800, 2 Stat. 19; repealed by the Act of 19 December 1803, 2 Stat. 248. Bankruptcy Act of 19 August 1841, 5 Stat. 440; repealed by the Act of 3 March 1843, 5 Stat. 614. William W. Crosskey, *Politics and the Constitution in the History of the United States* (Chicago: University of Chicago Press, 1953), 1:487–493. "Proceedings of Congress," *New York Evening Post,* 1 June 1864. "House of Representatives," *NYT,* 2 June 1864.

3. J. DeWitt Sheldon to Thomas A. Jenckes, New York, N.Y., 6 June 1864, box 26, folder 141–210, letter 211, Thomas A. Jenckes Papers, LC (unless otherwise noted, all letters cited are in this collection). J. T. Alden to Jenckes, Cincinnati, Ohio, 19 December 1864, box 28, folder "Dec 1864–Jan 1865 1–60," letter 5. "Thomas Allen Jenckes," in *Appleton's Cyclopaedia of American Biography,* ed. James Grant Wilson and John Fiske (New York: D. Appleton, 1887), 3:425–426. *In Memoriam: Thomas Allen Jenckes, Born November 2, 1818, Died November 4, 1875* [Providence, R.I.: n.p., 1876]. Jenckes to Abraham Lincoln, 11 September 1862, Series 1, Abraham Lincoln Papers, LC.

4. Herbert Sloan, *Principle and Interest: Thomas Jefferson and the Problem of Debt* (New York: Oxford University Press, 1995), 23, 98. Thomas Jefferson to John Wayles Eppes, 24 June 1813, ser. 1, Jefferson Papers, LC. *The Papers of Benjamin Franklin,* ed. Leonard W. Labaree (New Haven: Yale University Press, 1963), 7:348–349. Sir Thomas Culpeper, *A Discourse Shewing the Many Advantages Which will Accrue to This Kingdom by the Abatement of Usury . . .* (London: Printed by T. Leach for C. Wilkinson, 1668), 7, 19. Gary B. Nash, "Slaves and Slaveowners in Colonial Philadelphia," *William and Mary Quarterly,* 3d ser., 30 (April 1973): 223–256. Evarts B. Greene and Virginia D. Harrington, *American Population before the Federal Census of 1790* (New York: Columbia University Press, 1932), 22, 63, 66–67, 102. Alan Watson, *Rome of the XII Tables: Persons and Property* (Princeton: Princeton University Press, 1977), ch. 9. Bernard Bailyn, *The Ideological Origins of the American Revolution* (Cambridge, Mass.: Belknap Press of Harvard University Press, 1967), 234–246. "Their Negroes" quoted in Bruce H. Mann, *Republic of Debtors: Bankruptcy in the Age of American Independence* (Cambridge, Mass.: Harvard University Press, 2002), 137; see also 55–56, 109–146. John Adams to Edward Biddle[?], 12 December 1774, in Paul H. Smith, ed.,

Letters of Delegates to Congress (Washington, D.C.: Library of Congress, 1976), 1:265–267. "General Orders," 1 March 1778, in *The Writings of George Washington*, ed. John C. Fitzpatrick (Washington, D.C.: Government Printing Office, 1934), 11:8–12.

5. "Jenks, Prince," Military Index, Rhode Island State Archives, Providence, R.I. (hereafter RISA). *Massachusetts Soldiers and Sailors in the War of Revolution* (Boston: Wright and Potter, 1890), 8:741. *Census of the Inhabitants of the Colony of Rhode Island and Providence Plantations . . . 1774*, ed. John Russell Bartlett (Lambertville, N.J.: Hunterdon House, 1984 [1858]), 45, 107, 233. *Records of the State of Rhode Island and Providence Plantations in New England*, ed. Bartlett (Providence: Alfred Anthony, 1864), 580–582. Lorenzo J. Greene, "Some Observations on the Black Regiment of Rhode Island in the American Revolution," *Journal of Negro History* 37 (April 1952): 142–172. Allison Albee, "The Defenses at Pine's Bridge," *Westchester Historian* 37 (1961): 15–21, 54–59. Col. Jeremiah Olney to the Honorable Speaker, February sess. [1783], in *Petitions to the General Assembly of Rhode Island*, 24:37, RISA. *Report from the Secretary of War . . . in Relation to the Pension Establishment of the United States: Rhode Island* (Washington, D.C.: Duff Green, 1835), 795. U.S. Bureau of the Census, *Heads of Families at the First Census of the United States Taken in the Year 1790: Rhode Island* (Washington: Government Printing Office, 1908), 33. *Thomas Jefferson: Writings*, ed. Merrill D. Petersen (New York: Library of America, 1984), 492–496, esp. 494.

6. Amy Dru Stanley, *From Bondage to Contract: Wage Labor, Marriage, and the Market in the Age of Slave Emancipation* (Cambridge: Cambridge University Press, 1998), ch. 1. "Petition of Thomas Tate" [1786], in *Petitions*, vol. 23, p. 61, RISA. "Jenks Family," in *History of Providence County*, ed. Richard M. Bayles (New York: W. W. Preston, 1891), 2:119–126. "Joseph Jenks" and "Thomas Allen Jenckes," in *Dictionary of American Biography*, ed. Dumas Malone (New York: Scribner's Sons, 1961 [1932]), 5:40–42. Jay Coughtry, *The Notorious Triangle: Rhode Island and the African Slave Trade, 1700–1807* (Philadelphia: Temple University Press, 1981), 10–11, 257, 266, 268, 270, 279.

7. Orlando Patterson, *Slavery and Social Death: A Comparative Study* (Cambridge, Mass.: Harvard University Press, 1982), esp. 9–10, 86, 124–126. Barbara E. Lacey, "Visual Images of Blacks in Early American Imprints," *William and Mary Quarterly*, 3rd ser., 53 (January 1996): 137–180. On *Forlorn Hope*, see Mann, *Republic of Debtors*, frontis., 110, 139–140. Jack McLaughlin, ed., *To His Excellency Thomas Jefferson: Letters to a President* (New York: Norton, 1991), ch. 5. William Dunn to Jefferson, Bedford County, Va., 9 October 1807, ser. 1, Jefferson Papers. Roger R. Ransom, *Conflict and Compromise: The Political Economy of Slavery, Emancipation, and the Civil War* (Cambridge: Cambridge University Press, 1989), 45–48, 75. The 1807 law ending the slave trade took effect in 1808.

8. Kenneth L. Sokoloff, "The Evolution of Suffrage Institutions in the New World: A Preliminary Look," in *Crony Capitalism and Economic Growth in*

Latin America: Theory and Evidence, ed. Stephen Haber (Stanford: Hoover Institution Press, 2002), 75–107, esp. 84. Alex Keyssar, *The Right to Vote: The Contested History of Democracy in the United States* (New York: Basic Books, 2001), 7, 24. *Federal Circular,* 10 August 1812 [Boston: n.p., 1812], and *To the Legislators. Gentlemen of the Senate, and Gentlemen of the House of Representatives* (Boston: s.n., 1812?); broadsides collection, AAS. *Speech of Mr. [John] Sergeant, in the House of Representatives. March 7th, 1822. On the Bill to Establish an Uniform System of Bankruptcy Throughout the United States* [Washington City: D. Rapine, 1822], 22, 25. For a pathbreaking study of women's cases under the Act of 1800, see Karen Gross, Marie Stefanini Newman, and Denise Campbell, "Ladies in Red: Learning from America's First Female Bankrupts," *American Journal of Legal History* 40 (January 1996): 1–40.

9. David R. Roediger, *The Wages of Whiteness: Race and the Making of the American Working Class* (New York: Verso, 1991), 65–68, 73. Daniel T. Rodgers, *The Work Ethic in Industrial America, 1850–1920* (Chicago: University of Chicago Press, 1978), 30–33, 34, 57, 167, 168. *Memorial of a Committee of the Citizens of Philadelphia, in Favor of the Passage of a Law to Establish an Uniform System of Bankruptcy,* 9 January 1821 (Washington: Gales and Seaton, 1821), 6.

10. Mann, *Republic of Debtors,* 139–145. *The Patriot; or, People's Companion: Consisting of Five Essays on the Laws and Politics of Our Country . . .* (Hudson, N.Y.: Stoddard, 1828), 11. *Sturges v. Crowninshield* 17 U.S. 122 (1819). *Ogden v. Saunders* 25 U.S. 213 (1827). Edward White, *The Marshall Court and Cultural Change, 1815–1835,* abr. ed. (New York: Oxford University Press, 1991), 628–655. Sen. Asher Robbins, *Register of Debates in Congress,* 19th Cong., 2nd sess., 29 January 1827, 170.

11. *Memorial of the Citizens of Charleston, Praying the Establishment of an Uniform System of Bankruptcy, Feb. 8, 1822,* 17th Cong., 1st sess., House Doc. 65 (Washington, D.C.: Gales and Seaton, 1822). Sen. John Randolph, *Register of Debates,* 19th Cong., 1st sess., 4 March 1826, 676. Sen. Littleton Tazewell, *Register of Debates,* 19th Cong., 2nd sess., 27 January 1827, 96. William M. Wiecek, "'Old Times There Are Not Forgotten': The Distinctiveness of the Southern Constitutional Experience," in *An Uncertain Tradition: Constitutionalism and the History of the South,* ed. Kermit L. Hall and James W. Ely, Jr. (Athens: University of Georgia Press, 1989), 159–197. Joseph Story, *Commentaries on the Constitution of the United States* (Durham, N.C.: Carolina Academic Press, 1987 [1833]), 386. *Papers of Daniel Webster: Speeches and Formal Writings, Vol. 2, 1834–1852,* ed. Charles M. Wiltse and Alan R. Berolzheimer (Hanover, N.H.: University Press of New England, 1988), 309–239, esp. 327. Morris Weisman, "Story and Webster—and the Bankruptcy Act of 1841," *Commercial Law Journal* (January 1941): 4–8, 26.

12. Robert V. Remini, *Andrew Jackson: The Course of American Empire, 1767–1821* (Baltimore: Johns Hopkins University Press, 1998), 89–90. Harry Watson, *Liberty and Power: The Politics of Jacksonian America* (New York: Hill

and Wang, 1990), 39. "Political Portraits with Pen and Pencil (No. 1) Thomas Hart Benton," *United States Democratic Review* 1 (October 1837): 83–90. Act of 19 August 1841, 5 Stats. 440, repealed 3 March 1843, 5 Stats. 614. *Speech of Hon. Thomas H. Benton, of Missouri, on his motion to postpone the operation of the Bankrupt Act, Delivered in the United States Senate, December 27, 1841* [Washington, D.C.: n.p., 1841]. For a full analysis of the 1841 law, see Edward J. Balleisen, *Navigating Failure: Bankruptcy and Commercial Society in Antebellum America* (Chapel Hill: University of North Carolina Press, 2001), ch. 4. For Balleisen's careful analysis of the slavery metaphor in the 1840s, see 15, 122, 165–167, 204, 205, and 247nn3,5.

13. "Dear Sir," in *Miscellaneous Works of Henry C. Carey* (Philadelphia: Henry Carey Baird, [1872]), 3. George Fitzhugh, *Sociology for the South: or, the Failure of Free Society* (Richmond, Va.: A. Morris, 1854), 237–238.

14. *Congressional Globe*, 38th Cong., 1st sess., June 3, 1864, p. 2724. "The Bankrupt Bill," *NYT*, 22 January 1865. William G. Boardman to Jenckes, Albany, N.Y., 24 May 1866, box 32, folder "May 15–31, 1866," letter not numbered. R. G. Dun annual circular, 2 January 1865, Jenckes Papers, box 28, folder "Dec 1864 121–181," document 155. "Number of Failures in the United States in January, 1861," *HMM* 44 (March 1861): 327–328. Charles Warren, *Bankruptcy in United States History* (New York: Da Capo Press, 1972 [1935]), 97, 101–109. Rep. Owen Lovejoy, *Congressional Globe*, 37th Cong., 3rd sess., 7 January 1863, p. 224. "A Bankrupt Law," *Independent*, 7 April 1864. Louis Filler, "Liberalism, Anti-Slavery, and the Founders of the *Independent*," *New England Quarterly* 27 (September 1954): 291–306. A. L. Mann to Abraham Lincoln, 14 April 1864, Ser. 1, Lincoln Papers, LC. Harry E. Pratt, "Lincoln and Bankruptcy Law," *Illinois Bar Journal* 31 (January 1943): 201–206. Abraham Lincoln to Horace Greeley, 9 July 1864, in Abraham Lincoln, *The Collected Works of Abraham Lincoln*, ed. Roy P. Basler (New Brunswick: Rutgers University Press, 1953, 1974, 1990), 7:435–436; and Lincoln to Greeley, 9 August 1864, 7:489–490.

15. Thomas P. Remington to Abraham Lincoln, Philadelphia, Pa., 18 November 1863, Ser. 1, Lincoln Papers, LC. T[homas] P. Remington to Jenckes, 17 May 1864, box 26, folder 71–140, letter 109. George L. Cannon to Thomas A. Jenckes, New York, N. Y., 5 February 1864, box 25, folder 71–130, letter 127.

16. The myth persists that President Ulysses S. Grant coined the term "lobbyists" in the 1870s to describe politicos who pestered him at the Willard Hotel, but the term actually became popular in the 1850s. See "Preparations for Congress," *NYT*, 15 November 1856; and "Patent Extensions and Lobbyists in Congress," *Scientific American* 13 (30 January 1858): 165. John McKillop to Jenckes, New York, 28 May 1864, box 26, folder 1–70, letter 5. *Patten's New Haven City Directory* (New Haven: J. M. Patten, 1846), 45, 114. "House Warming and Ventilating Warerooms," *NYT*, 22 March 1854. "For Councilman—George L. Cannon," *NYT*, 21 November 1861. "Political," *NYT*, 2

December 1861. "For Councilmen," *NYT,* 18 December 1861. U.S. Census, 1860, New York, New York County, N.Y., p. 34 (reel M653-796, image 34), NARA. Reports (1857–1866) of George L. Cannon, New York, vol. 321, p. 613, and vol. 322, p. 800G. Cannon to Jenckes, 5 February 1864.

17. "A Meeting of the National Bankrupt Association," *NYT,* 9 March 1864. Michael Batterberry, *On the Town in New York: The Landmark History of Eating, Drinking, and Entertainments from the American Revolution to the Food Revolution* (New York: Routledge, 1998), 71–75. "At Delmonico's Restaurant," *Scientific American,* new ser. 7 (16 August 1862): 101. *Evening Post,* 27 May 1864. Cannon to Jenckes, 24 May 1864. William Cullen Bryant to Frances F. Bryant, 11 November and 14 December 1859, in William Cullen Bryant, *Letters of William Cullen Bryant,* ed. William C. Bryant II and Thomas G. Voss (New York: Fordham University Press, 1984), 4:124, 131. Cannon to Jenckes, 16 April 1864, box 26, folder 576–625, letter 622; and 4 June 1864, box 26, folder 141–210, letter 144. "A Plea for a National Bankrupt Act," *NYT,* 5 June 1864.

18. Anonymous to Jenckes, New York, N.Y., 3 June 1864, box 26, folder 71–140, letter 132. Cannon to Jenckes, 21 February 1865, box 27, folder 61–119, letter 80; 22 March 1864, box 25, folder 381–440, letter 390; 24 May 1864, box 26, folder 71–140, letter 122; 4 June 1864, box 26, folder 141–210, letter 144; 8 June 1864, box 26, folder 141–210, letter 191; 9 June 1864, box 26, folder 141–210, letter 192; 11 June 1864, box 26, folder 141–210, letter 197; 14 June 1864, box 26, folder 141–210, letter 180; and 15 December 1864, box 28, folder "Dec. 1864—61–120," letter 107. On Garfield, see *Congressional Globe,* 38th Cong., 1st sess., 4 June 1864, pp. 2741–43; "House of Representatives," *NYT,* 5 June 1864; and "Congress," *NYT,* 6 June 1864. On this and other bribery schemes, see Sandage, "Deadbeats, Drunkards, and Dreamers," 178–182.

19. C. Hillborn to Jenckes, Philadelphia, Pa., 2 June 1864, box 26, folder 71–140, letter 131. Anonymous to Jenckes, New York, N.Y., 23 February 1867, box 33. Name illegible [R. H. Stingen?] to Jenckes, St. Louis, 28 February 1866, box 31, folder 1–60, letter 78. Civil War–era bankrupts' blend of civic activism, fraternity, and entrepreneurship nicely complements Dana D. Nelson's arguments in *National Manhood: Capitalist Citizenship and the Imagined Fraternity of White Men* (Raleigh, N.C.: Duke University Press, 1998). E. Anthony Rotundo, "Body and Soul: Changing Ideals of American Middle-Class Manhood, 1770–1920," *Journal of Social History* 16 (1983): 23–38, esp. 24–25. Isaac W. Potts to Jenckes, Philadelphia, Pa., 19 February 1864, box 25, folder 191–260, letter 234.

20. A. Granger to Jenckes, New York, 20 February 1866, box 31, folder 61–130, letter 63. *Congressional Globe,* 38th Cong., 1st sess., 1 June 1864, p. 2637. A newspaper item in Jenckes's files included the sentence "Some writer truly observes that hopeless insolvency is commercial death." See unidentified clipping by "J. F. B.," box 30, folder 1–48, document 27B. On discourses of slavery and idleness, see Saidiya V. Hartman, *Scenes of Subjection:*

Terror, Slavery, and Self-Making in Nineteenth-Century America (New York: Oxford University Press, 1997), ch. 5. Stanley, *From Bondage to Contract*, 13–17.

21. Lott Frost to Jenckes, Albany, N.Y., 28 September 1864, box 27, folder 351–420, letter 414. Hartman, *Scenes of Subjection*, ch. 4. David Brion Davis, "The Emancipation Moment," in *Lincoln, the War President: The Gettysburg Lectures*, ed. Gabor S. Boritt (New York: Oxford University Press, 1992), 63–88. In another context, I have written about the persistence of the "emancipation moment" into the twentieth century. See Scott A. Sandage, "A Marble House Divided: The Lincoln Memorial, the Civil Rights Movement, and the Politics of Memory, 1939–1963," *Journal of American History* 80 (June 1993): 135–167, esp. 148–151. John S. Matthews to Jenckes, Paineville, Ohio, 22 May 1866, box 32, folder "May 1–15, 1866," letter not numbered. Joseph Peck to Jenckes, Washington, D.C., 18 May 1866, box 32, folder "May 1–15, 1866," letter not numbered. [Stingen?] to Jenckes.

22. [Stingen?] to Jenckes. Cannon to Jenckes, 22 March 1864 and 24 May 1864. Frost to Jenckes. William G. Boardman to Jenckes, Albany, N.Y., 27 June 1864, box 26, folder 141–210, letter 224.

23. *Congressional Globe*, 38th Cong., 1st sess., 9 June 1864, p. 2835; and ibid., 38th Cong., 2nd sess., 13 December 1864, p. 24. W. P. Henderson to Jenckes, Chicago, 13 December 1864, box 28, folder "Dec. 1864 61–120," letter 105. Mason Lowance, *House Divided: The Antebellum Slavery Debates in America, 1776–1865* (Princeton: Princeton University Press, 2003), ch. 3. William M. Wiecek, "The Statutory Law of Slavery and Race in the Thirteen Mainland Colonies of British America," *William and Mary Quarterly*, 3rd ser. (April 1977): 258–280, esp. 274. "Wilson Chinn, a Branded Slave from Louisiana," (New York: Kimball and Co., 1863), Prints and Photographs Division, Library of Congress. Bell Irvin Wiley, *The Life of Johnny Reb: The Common Soldier of the Confederacy* (Indianapolis: Bobbs-Merrill Co., 1943), 227. David Madden, ed., *Beyond the Battlefield: The Ordinary Life and Extraordinary Times of the Civil War Soldier* (New York: Simon and Schuster, 2000), 204–205. William C. DeHart, *Observations on Military Law and the Constitution and Practice of Courts Martial* (New York: Wiley and Halsted, 1859), 196–197. Congress abolished military branding and tattooing on 6 June 1872; see 17 Stat. 261. "Sentence of a U.S. Soldier," *Adams Sentinel* (Gettysburg, Pa.), 25 July 1859. "Flogging in the Army," *Raleigh Weekly Standard*, 28 January 1863. "Branded and Imprisoned," *NYT*, 21 July 1865. Thomas P. Lowry, *Don't Shoot That Boy! Abraham Lincoln and Military Justice* (Mason City, Iowa: Savas Publishing, 1999); my thanks to the author and to Beverly Lowry for sharing "W" cases found during their research. Court martials of Daniel Callaghan, 1 September 1861, file ii484, box 285; John Shay, 1 January 1862, file kk179, box 345; Barney Boyle, 1 May 1862, file ii974, box 326; Thomas Keller, 1 May 1862, file ii974, box 326; and Samuel Jenkins, 1 March 1863, file mm47, box 907; all in Records of the Office of the Judge Advocate General (Army), Record Group 153, NARA.

24. On the atmosphere in Congress in February 1866, see Eric Foner, *Reconstruction: America's Unfinished Revolution, 1863–1877* (New York: Harper and Row, 1988), 246–251; on Stevens, 299 and passim. See also Michael Les Benedict, *A Compromise of Principle: Congressional Republicans and Reconstruction, 1863–1869* (New York: W. W. Norton and Co., 1974), 36, 152–161. *Congressional Globe*, 38th Cong., 1st sess., Part 1, 14 February 1866, pp. 846–847. Ralph Korngold, *Thaddeus Stevens: A Being Darkly Wise and Rudely Great* (New York: Harcourt, Brace & Co., 1955), 66–67, 138. Stevens himself had been nearly bankrupt in 1842—he owed $90,000—but had stubbornly refused to declare bankruptcy, saying, "I may be forced to take advantage of the bankruptcy laws in the next world, but I will never do so in this." For a good description of Stevens's manner see Noah Brooks, *Washington in Lincoln's Time* (New York: Century Co., 1896), 34; cited in Leonard P. Curry, *Blueprint for Modern America: Nonmilitary Legislation of the First Civil War Congress* (Nashville: Vanderbilt University Press, 1968), 27.

25. Jenckes received 419 letters for the three years from January 1864 to May 1867—131 in 1864, 21 in 1865, 159 in 1866, and 108 in 1867. In the first half of 1866, 149 bankruptcy letters arrived, 36 percent of the total. J. Williamson to Jenckes, Philadelphia, Pa., 16 February 1866, box 31, folder 1–60, letter 12. J. DeWitt Sheldon to Jenckes, New York, N.Y., 19 February 1866, box 31, folder 1–60, letter; see also Henry A. Hantz and Peter Ford to Jenckes, York, Pa., 17 February 1866, box 31, folder 1–60, letter 9.

26. Michael Vorenberg, *Final Freedom: The Civil War, the Abolition of Slavery, and the Thirteenth Amendment* (Cambridge: Cambridge University Press, 2001.)

27. Benedict, *Compromise of Principle*, 155–156. N. G. Curtis to Jenckes, Hamilton, Ohio, 30 March 1866, box 32, folder "March 1866," letter not numbered. John E. Stone to Jenckes, Cincinnati, Ohio, 13 April 1866, box 32, folder "April, 1866," letter not numbered.

28. "A Patriot" [J. M. B.] to Stevens, Norfolk, Va., 19 February 1866, box 3, folder "February 1866," Thaddeus Stevens Papers, LC. James Hume to Thaddeus Stevens, Arcola, Ill., 20 February 1866, box 3, folder "February 1866," Stevens Papers, LC. A. L. Griffen to Jenckes, Buffalo, N.Y., 19 February 1866, box 31, folder 1–60, letter 8. A. Granger to Jenckes, New York, 20 February 1866, box 31, folder 61–130, letter 63.

29. *Congressional Globe*, 39th Cong., 1st sess., Part 2, 28 March 1866, pp. 1696–1700, esp. 1698.

30. Ibid. "Humors of the Day," *Harper's Weekly*, 24 March 1866, p. 190.

31. *Congressional Globe*, 39th Cong., 2nd sess., Part 2, 5 February 1867, pp. 1005–1013, esp. 1008; and ibid., 12 February 1867, pp. 1186–1192, esp. 1186. Foner, *Reconstruction*, 273–274. C. Vann Woodward, *The Burden of Southern History* (Baton Rouge: Louisiana State University Press, 1993 [1960]).

32. *Congressional Globe*, 39th Cong., 1st sess., Part 4, 13 June 1866, p. 3148.

33. Foner, Reconstruction, ch. 6. *Congressional Globe*, 39th Cong., 1st sess., Part 1, 23 January 1866, pp. 376–390, esp. 376.

34. *Congressional Globe,* 39th Cong., 1st sess., Part 1, 23 January 1866, p. 376. Fourteenth Amendment scholars have noted but not analyzed this exchange. See Joseph B. James, *The Framing of the Fourteenth Amendment* (Urbana: University of Illinois Press, 1965), 62; and William E. Nelson, *The Fourteenth Amendment: From Political Principle to Judicial Doctrine* (Cambridge, Mass.: Harvard University Press, 1988), 139, 142. On the amendment's economic design, see Herbert Hovencamp, *Enterprise and American Law, 1836–1937* (Cambridge, Mass.: Harvard University Press, 1991), 93–96.

35. *Congressional Globe,* 39th Cong., 1st sess., Part 1, 23 January 1866, p. 376.

36. Ibid., pp. 376–390, 403–412, 535–538, quotations on 385, 386. Jenckes voted against the revised version of section two, but he supported the Fourteenth Amendment when it passed on 13 June 1866. Ibid., p. 538, and Part 4, p. 3149. Robert Sewell to Jenckes, New York, 26 February 1866, box 31, folder 31–130, letter 69.

37. U.S. Constitution, Fourteenth Amendment, sec. 2. *Congressional Globe,* 39th Cong., 1st sess., Part 1, 23 January 1866, pp. 535–538, esp. 536.

38. Bankrupt Act of 2 March 1867, 14 Stat. 517. *Congressional Globe,* 39th Cong., 2nd sess., Part 3, 2 March 1867, p. 1958. Richard Franklin Bensel, *Yankee Leviathan: The Origins of Central State Authority in America, 1859–1877* (Cambridge: Cambridge University Press, 1991), 313–314, 342. On the revision and repeal of the Act of 1867, see Warren, *Bankruptcy,* 109–122. Warren observes (p. 109) that the act of 1867 was "significant in being the first bill constructed as a permanent piece of legislation and with a view to the interest of the Nation" and in its reflection of liberalized "views of the scope of the Bankruptcy Clause of the Constitution."

39. *Congressional Globe,* 39th Cong., 1st sess., 28 March 1866, pp. 1697, 1699. Charles Fairman argues, "In various connections the Bankruptcy Act was entwined with Reconstruction," revealing "the confusion of governmental functions during the period." Charles Fairman, *Reconstruction and Reunion, 1864–88: Part One* (New York: Macmillan, 1971), 355–365, esp. 364.

40. Bankruptcy case file of George L. Cannon, RG 21, entry 130, case 859, box 191, NARA—New York City Branch. U.S. Census, 1870, New York, New York County, N.Y., p. 496 (reel M593-1010, image 111), NARA. Classified advertisement by "G. Lyman Cannon," *New York Herald,* 18 August 1869. U.S. Census, 1880, Denver, Arapahoe County, Colo., p. 58D (reel T9-87, image 119); and Idaho District (Spanish Bar), Clear Creek County, Colo., p. 142B (reel T9-89, image 111), NARA. "Colorado's Latest Gift," *NYT,* 16 February 1879. "Grub Stakes and Millions," *Harper's New Monthly Magazine* 60 (February 1880): 380–398. "George L. Cannon," in *History of Clear Creek and Boulder Valleys, Colorado* (Chicago: O. L. Baskin and Co., 1880), 499. Thomas B. Corbett, *The Colorado Directory of Mines* (Denver: Rocky Mountain News, 1879), 128, 132, 136, 153, 181, 439. "George L. Cannon," in *Encyclopedia of Biography of Colorado,* ed. William N. Byers (Chicago: Cen-

tury Publishing, 1901), 1: 316. *Ballenger and Richards' Eighteenth Annual Denver City Directory . . . for 1890* (Denver: Ballenger and Richards, 1890). Cannon family interment record, Lot 15, Block 10, Fairmount Cemetery administrative offices, Denver, Colo.

41. Alfred Russell to Jenckes, Tiffin, Seneca Co., Ohio, 7 March 1867. Jas. H. Oliver to Jenckes, Baltimore, Md., 8 March 1867, box 33, folder "March 1-12, 1867," not numbered. Ari Hoogenboom, "Thomas A. Jenckes and Civil Service Reform," *Mississippi Valley Historical Review* 47 (March 1961): 636–658. "A Hint to Congressmen," *NYT,* 9 November 1875. "Thomas A. Jenckes: Some Personal Characteristics of Rhode Island's Dead Citizen," *NYT,* 7 November 1875; repr. from *Providence Journal.*

42. Foner, "The Meaning of Freedom," 454. G[abor] S. Boritt, *Lincoln and the Economics of the American Dream* (Memphis: Memphis State University Press, 1978).

43. Abraham Lincoln, "Speech to One Hundred Sixty-Sixth Ohio Regiment," in *The Collected Works of Abraham Lincoln,* ed. Roy P. Basler (New Brunswick, N.J.: Rutgers University Press, 1953), 7:412. Jim Leeke, ed., *A Hundred Days to Richmond: Ohio's "Hundred Days" Men in the Civil War* (Bloomington: Indiana University Press, 1999), 193–198, 252n1. Noah Brooks, *Lincoln Observed: Civil War Dispatches of Noah Brooks,* ed. Michael Burlingame (Baltimore: Johns Hopkins University Press, 1998), 131–132. Michael Burlingame, ed., *With Lincoln in the White House: Letters, Memoranda, and Other Writings of John G. Nicolay, 1860–1865* (Carbondale: Southern Illinois University Press, 2000), 150–154. Stefan Lorant, *Lincoln: A Picture Story of His Life,* rev. ed. (New York: Bonanza Books, 1975), 222–223. David Herbert Donald, *Lincoln* (New York: Simon and Schuster, 1995), 517–523, 524, 528.

44. Donald, *Lincoln,* 523–530. David W. Blight, *Frederick Douglass' Civil War: Keeping Faith in Jubilee* (Baton Rouge: Louisiana State University Press, 1989), 182–184.

45. "H. W.," *Summit County Beacon,* 9 June 1864; this soldier's letter home describes Lincoln greeting the 164th Ohio Regiment at the White House on 28 May 1864; quoted in Leeke, ed., *Hundred Days,* 193. Walt Whitman, *Memoranda during the War [and] Death of Abraham Lincoln,* ed. Roy P. Basler (Westport, Conn.: Greenwood Press, 1972 [1875–1876]), 22–24.

46. Walter B. Stevens, *A Reporter's Lincoln,* ed. Michael Burlingame (Lincoln: University of Nebraska Press, 1998), 102, 235, 294n33. Richard Hofstadter, "Abraham Lincoln and the Self-Made Myth," in *The American Political Tradition and the Men Who Made It* (New York: Vintage Books, 1989 [1948]), 121–173.

47. Stevens, *Reporter's Lincoln,* 72–73.

48. Michael Burlingame, *The Inner World of Abraham Lincoln* (Urbana: University of Illinois Press, 1994), chap. 8. Lincoln, "Eulogy on Henry Clay" (1852), *Collected Works,* 2:121–132, esp. 121. Lincoln, "Speech at New Haven,

Connecticut" (1860), *Collected Works,* 4:13–30, esp. 24. Lincoln, "Message to Congress in Special Session," 4 July 1861, *Collected Works,* 4:421–441, esp. 438.

49. Lincoln, "Address Delivered at the Dedication of the Cemetery at Gettysburg," *Collected Works,* 7:23.
50. Donald, *Lincoln,* 530–545, 588. Daniel Walker Howe, "Self-Made Men: Abraham Lincoln and Frederick Douglass," chap. 5 in *Making the American Self: Jonathan Edwards to Abraham Lincoln* (Cambridge, Mass.: Harvard University Press, 1997), esp. 147–149.
51. Frederick Douglass, "Self-Made Men: An Address Delivered in Carlisle, Pennsylvania, in March 1893," in *Frederick Douglass Papers: Series One,* ed. John W. Blassingame et al. (New Haven: Yale University Press, 1992), 5:545–575, esp. 550, 566, 571.
52. Ibid., 550, 557. Howe, *Making the American Self,* 153–156.
53. Douglass, "Self-Made Men," 572, 554. Blight, *Frederick Douglass' Civil War,* 203–206, Charles Douglass quoted on 205. Wai-chee Dimock, *Melville and the Poetics of Individualism* (Princeton: Princeton University Press, 1989), 198.
54. Ray Ginger, *Altgeld's America: The Lincoln Ideal versus Changing Realities* (New York: Funk and Wagnalls, 1958), 3–7. Andrew Carnegie, *Triumphant Democracy* (1886), quoted in *Familiar Quotations,* ed. John Bartlett and Justin Kaplan (Boston: Little, Brown and Co., 1992), 525. Douglass, "Self-Made Men," 549.

8. Big Business and Little Men

1. Andrew A. Osborne was a traveling salesman and the U.S. agent for the Gutta Percha Paint Company; see *New Haven City Directory, 1890,* vol. 51 (New Haven: Price, Lee and Co., 1890), 384, 385. A. A. Osborne to John D. Rockefeller, Sr., New Haven, Conn., 11 January 1890; and Osborne to George Rogers, 20 January 1890; both in box 30, folder 231, Office Correspondence series, John D. Rockefeller Papers (Record Group 1), RFA. Unless otherwise noted, all letters cited in this chapter are from this collection.
2. Ellen Ashton, "Life's Ladder," *Lady's World* 3 (May 1843): 156–157; "The Bankrupt's Wife," *Harper's New Monthly Magazine* (February 1868): 362–364. Elaine Frantz Parsons and Dorothy Ross, *Manhood Lost: Fallen Drunkards and Redeeming Women in the Nineteenth Century* (Baltimore: Johns Hopkins University Press, 2003). The definition of sentimental culture is from Nina Baym, *Women's Fiction: A Guide to Novels by and about Women in America, 1820–1870* (Ithaca, N.Y.: Cornell University Press, 1978), 27. I use "sentiment" to refer both to language and imagery that popular literature made available to beggars and to the oppositional value system Baym describes. For a scholarly overview, see Mary Chapman and Glenn Hendler, eds., *Sentimental Men: Masculinity and the Politics of Affect in American Culture* (Berkeley: University of California Press, 1999), 1–16.

On sentiment and rationalization, see Christopher Lasch, *Haven in a Heartless World: The Family Besieged* (New York: Basic Books, 1977); Stephanie Coontz, *The Social Origins of Private Life: A History of American Families, 1600–1900* (London: Verso, 1988), chs. 5–7; and Elizabeth Alice White, "Charitable Calculations: Fancywork, Charity, and the Culture of the Sentimental Market, 1830–1880," in *The Middling Sorts: Explorations in the History of the American Middle Class*, ed. Burton J. Bledstein and Robert D. Johnston (New York: Routledge, 2001), 73–85.

3. P. T. Barnum, *Struggles and Triumphs; or, Sixty Years' Recollections of P. T. Barnum, Including His Golden Rules for Money-Making* (Buffalo: Courier Co., 1889). Mark Twain and Charles Dudley Warner, *The Gilded Age: A Tale of Today* (New York: Oxford University Press, 1996). Samuel Rezneck, "Patterns of Thought and Action in an American Depression, 1882–1886," *American Historical Review* 61 (January 1956): 284–307. Charles Hoffman, *The Depression of the Nineties: An Economic History* (Westport, Conn.: Greenwood Publishing Corp., 1970), chs. 1–2. Andrew Carnegie, "The Bugaboo of Trusts," *North American Review* 148 (February 1889): 141–151, esp. 146. U.S. Bureau of the Census, *Historical Statistics of the United States, Colonial Times to 1970* (1975; repr., White Plains, N.Y.: Kraus International Publications, 1989), 1:135. From 1929 through 1931, references to "the great depression" were few and often referred to past years; for its first appearance in a *New York Times* headline, see "The 1929 Speculation and Today's Troubles; Controversy as to How Far the 'Great Boom' Caused the Great Depression," *NYT*, 1 January 1932. On social mobility in the corporate era, see Howard P. Chudacoff, "Success and Security: The Meaning of Social Mobility in America," *Reviews in American History* 10 (December 1982): 101–112.

4. J. W. Bomgardner to Rockefeller, Atchison, Kan., 19 November 1890, box 4, folder 34. U.S. Census, 1880, Quincy, Adams County, Ill., p. 23 (reel T9-175, image 362), NARA. On Rockefeller's grain ventures, see Ron Chernow, *Titan: The Life of John D. Rockefeller, Sr.* (New York: Random House, 1998), 63–72.

5. Bomgardner to Rockefeller, 1 December 1890. See also Rockefeller to Bomgardner, 25 November 1890, Letterbooks series, microfiche edition, Rockefeller Papers (Record Group 1), RFA. Some of Rockefeller's own replies to begging letters survive, but most were written by staff members. Space and the themes of this chapter preclude their analysis.

6. T. S. Nettleton to Rockefeller, Alma City, Minnesota, 7 March 1889, box 29, folder 224. U.S. Census, 1920, Arlington Heights, Tarrant County, Texas, p. 37B (reel T625-1848, image 285), NARA. Details of Theron Samuel Nettleton's later life come from his sister-in-law's family Bible and other records in the possession (2004) of lateral descendants, Patricia and Dean Pierose of Boise, Idaho.

7. David Leverenz, *Manhood and the American Renaissance* (Ithaca: Cornell

University Press, 1989), 89–90. Stuart M. Blumin, *The Emergence of the Middle Class: Social Experience in the American City, 1760–1900* (Cambridge: Cambridge University Press, 1989), ch. 8. William Mathews, *Getting On in the World; or Hints on Success in Life* (Chicago: S. C. Griggs and Co., 1883 [1872]), 5, 323. Judy Hilkey, *Character Is Capital: Success Manuals and Manhood in Gilded Age America* (Chapel Hill: University of Carolina Press, 1997), 20–21, 78–79. Bomgardner to Rockefeller, 1 December 1890.

8. Mathews, *Getting On in the World*, 5. "Philosophy in Tatters," *Fort Wayne Daily Gazette*, 12 September 1884, repr. from the *Boston Globe*. My understanding of how entrepreneurial patterns and transactions shape masculinity draws on interdisciplinary work on capitalism, contracts, and the economics of selfhood. In addition to Leverenz, cited above, see Wai-chee Dimock, *Empire for Liberty: Melville and the Poetics of Individualism* (Princeton: Princeton University Press, 1989), chs. 1, 6; Gillian Brown, *Domestic Individualism: Imagining Self in Nineteenth-Century America* (Berkeley: University of California Press, 1990), ch. 2; Amy Dru Stanley, "Home Life and the Morality of the Market," in *The Market Revolution in America: Social, Political, and Religious Expressions, 1800–1880*, ed. Melvyn Stokes and Stephen Conway (Charlottesville: University Press of Virginia, 1996), 74–96; and C. B. MacPherson, *The Political Theory of Possessive Individualism: Hobbes to Locke* (New York: Oxford University Press, 1962).

9. Credit reports (1859–1869) of S. and J. Featherstone, Ohio, vol. 40, p. 201. U.S. Census, 1880, Toledo, Lucas County, Ohio, p. 36C (reel T9-1042, image 747), NARA; in 1880, Stephen was a carpenter and Sarah a schoolteacher. Sarah E. Featherstone to Rockefeller, Toledo, Ohio, 9 March 1882, 1 December 1884, 8 December 1884, 18 May 1886. Judith Butler's resonant term, "foreclosure," aptly describes the abjection felt by many men who failed. Judith P. Butler, *Bodies That Matter: On the Discursive Limits of "Sex"* (New York: Routledge, 1993), 2–3, 243n2.

10. George M. Beard, *American Nervousness: Its Causes and Consequences* (New York: G. P. Putnam's Sons, 1881), 115–116, 121–123. T. J. Jackson Lears, *No Place of Grace: Antimodernism and the Transformation of American Culture, 1880–1920* (New York: Pantheon, 1981), 47–58. Gail A. Bederman, *Manliness and Civilization: A Cultural History of Gender and Race in the United States, 1880–1917* (Chicago: University of Chicago Press, 1996), chs. 3–4. Charlotte Perkins Gilman, *The Living of Charlotte Perkins Gilman: An Autobiography* (New York: D. Appleton-Century Co., 1935), 8–9, 84, 91, 110, 176. Ann J. Lane, *To Herland and Beyond: The Life and Work of Charlotte Perkins Gilman* (New York: Pantheon, 1990), 25–29, 212. Charlotte Perkins Gilman, *Charlotte Perkins Gilman: A Nonfiction Reader*, ed. Larry Ceplair (New York: Columbia University Press, 1991), 10. Tom Lutz, *American Nervousness, 1903: An Anecdotal History* (Ithaca: Cornell University Press, 1991), part 1.

11. Beggars mirrored Marx's famous formula for the circulation of capital; they tried to adapt the language of commodity exchange into a sentimental currency that would in turn bring them back to the realm of commodity

exchange. Karl Marx and Friedrich Engels, *The Marx-Engels Reader*, 2nd ed., ed. Robert C. Tucker (New York: W. W. Norton, 1978), 329–336; and see the influential discussion of "symbolic capital" in Pierre Bourdieu, *The Logic of Practice*, trans. Richard Nice (Stanford: Stanford University Press, 1990 [1980]).

12. Lionel Rose, *"Rogues and Vagabonds": Vagrant Underworld in Britain, 1815–1985* (London: Routledge, 1988), ch. 4. M. J. D. Roberts, "Reshaping the Gift Relationship: The London Mendicity Society and the Suppression of Begging in England, 1818–1869," *International Review of Social History* 36 (1991): 201–231. "Demands for information and/or financial assistance," box 7, file 81, the Eleuthera Bradford du Pont Collection (accession 146), HML. "Shameful," *New York Journal of Commerce*, 11 November 1850 [p. 2]. Reynold M. Wik, *Henry Ford and Grass-Roots America* (Ann Arbor: University of Michigan Press, 1972), 212–228. Terry Alford, "'. . . Hoping to Hear from You Soon': The Begging Correspondence of Alexander T. Stewart," *Manuscripts* 40 (Spring 1988): 89–100. Lawrence I. Berkove, "'Nobody Writes to Anybody Except to Ask a Favor': New Correspondence between Mark Twain and Dan De Quille," *Mark Twain Journal* 26 (Spring 1988): 2–19. Berkove cites P. T. Barnum, "My Museum of Letters; An Article by P. T. Barnum Finished Just before His Death," *Salt Lake City Daily Tribune*. Debby Applegate, "Henry Ward Beecher and the 'Great Middle Class': Mass-Marketed Intimacy and Middle-Class Identity," in Bledstein and Johnston, *Middling Sorts*. M. M. Comstock to Rockefeller, Great Barrington, Mass., 1890, box 8, folder 61. Recent scholarship includes Dawn M. Greeley, "Beyond Benevolence: Gender, Class, and the Development of Scientific Charity in New York City, 1882–1935" (Ph.D. diss., SUNY Stony Brook, 1995), chap. 4; Ruth Crocker, "'I Only Ask You Kindly to Divide Some of Your Fortune with Me': Begging Letters and the Transformation of Charity in Late Nineteenth-Century America," *Social Politics* 6 (Summer 1999): 131–160; and Daniel Seth Hack, "The Material Interests of the Victorian Writer" (Ph.D. diss., University of California, Berkeley, 1998). On Rockefeller's mail and on the 1917 fire that apparently destroyed his correspondence between 1894 and 1917, see Chernow, *Titan*, 299–302, 596. James D. Reid to Andrew Carnegie, n.p., 24 May 1886, vol. 13, letterbooks, Papers of Andrew Carnegie, Manuscript Division, Library of Congress, Washington, D.C.; Reid was the author of *The Telegraph in America and Morse Memorial* (New York: Printed for the Author by J. Polhemus, 1886 [1879]).

13. Hilkey, *Character Is Capital*, ch. 7. E. Anthony Rotundo, *American Manhood: Transformations in Masculinity from the Revolution to the Modern Era* (New York: Basic Books, 1993), 178–185. Grover Cleveland, *The Self-Made Man in American Life* (New York: T. Y. Crowell and Co., 1897). James V. Catano, *Ragged Dicks: Masculinity, Steel, and the Rhetoric of the Self-Made Man* (Carbondale: Southern Illinois University Press, 2001). Richard S. Tedlow and Walter Friedman, "Statistical Portraits of American Business

Elites: A Review Essay," *Business History* 45 (October 2003): 89–113. William Dean Howells, *The Rise of Silas Lapham* (New York: Ticknor and Co., 1885; Penguin Books, 1983), 354.

14. J. W. Cleland to Rockefeller, Kansas City, Mo., 23 February 1888, box 7, folder 57. *Missouri State Gazetteer and Business Directory, 1881, Volume 3* (Detroit: R. L. Polk and A. C. Danser, 1881), p. 1112. *Decatur* [Illinois] *Daily Review*, 25 December 1892. Pension file of John W. Cleland (111th Ohio Regiment), Case no. 836808, filed 2 March 1892, Records of the Department of Veterans Affairs, Record Group 15, NARA. "An Advertising Device," *Decatur Herald Dispatch*, 19 December 1896. "Government Sends Check for 48 Cents," *Decatur Daily Review*, 22 July 1908. "J. W. Cleland Falls Dead on Street," *Decatur Review*, 29 April 1912.

15. Credit reports (1864–1879) of Fitch Raymond, Ohio, vol. 41, p. 199; and Ohio, vol. 45, p. 98. U.S. Census, 1880, Cleveland, Cuyahoga County, Ohio, p. 171A (reel T9-1008, image 547), NARA. Fitch Raymond to Rockefeller, Cleveland, Ohio, 23 March 1887, box 32, folder 246.

16. *Six Hundred Dollars a Year: A Wife's Effort at Low Living under High Prices* (New York: R. Worthington, 1882 [orig. 1867]). E[lizabeth] G[ilbert] Martin to Elizabeth Barstow Stoddard, 17 January 1866, box 1, Stoddard Papers, Rare Book and Manuscript Collection, NYPL; she misquotes Emerson's "Let us suck the sweetness of those affections and consuetudes that grow near us" from the essay "Prudence," in *Ralph Waldo Emerson: Essays and Lectures* (New York: Library of America, 1983), 267. E. G. Martin wrote commercially to support her husband, a painter of the Hudson River School; see "Homer Dodge Martin," in *Dictionary of National Biography*, ed. Sir Leslie Stephen and Sir Sidney Lee (London: Oxford University Press, 1959–1960), 12:339–340. Jeanne Boydston, *Home and Work: Housework, Wages, and the Ideology of Labor in the Early Republic* (New York: Oxford University Press, 1990), 138–139, 143–144, 153–158. Wendy Gamber, *The Female Economy: The Millinery and Dressmaking Trades, 1860–1930* (Urbana: University of Illinois Press, 1997). "Female Intellect," *The Living Age*, 24 June 1865, p. 554. Mrs. L. M. Woodbridge to Rockefeller, Hudson, Ohio, 3 May 1880, box 50, folder 369. S. P. Darrah to Rockefeller, Mt. Vernon, N.Y., 2 January 1891, box 77, folder 10. Jane A. Pierce to Rockefeller, Toledo, Ohio, 9 March 1887, box 31, folder 239. Jane M. Johnson to Rockefeller, Syracuse, N.Y., 18 November 1890, box 21, folder 165.

17. M. J. Watson to Rockefeller, Cleveland, Ohio, December 1891, box 48, folder 362. Mary K. Tibbetts to Rockefeller, San Diego, 21 February 1888, box 46, folder 348. Pierce to Rockefeller. Chernow, *Titan*, 113–114, 171–172.

18. Credit report (1851) of Isaac Thorne, New Jersey, vol. 50, p. 268. Credit reports (1848) of John A. Guerin, South Carolina, vol. 6, p. 59. Credit reports of Frederick Myerle (1857), Pennsylvania, vol. 131, p. 22. Credit reports of Mrs. Emma Bruton, in U.S. Mercantile Reporting Co., *Middle States Reports for 1876* (New York: U.S. Mercantile Reporting Co., 1876), 35–36. Mi-

chael Willrich, "Home Slackers: Men, Welfare, and the State in Modern America," *Journal of American History* 82 (September 2000): 460–479. For a case referred to the Charity Organization Society, see Mrs. [Sophia] Vigorito to Mrs. [Laura Spelman] Rockefeller, New York, N.Y., n.d. [January 1894], box 48, folder 356. For the use of credit reports, see G. W. Durgin to Rockefeller, Philadelphia, Pa., 16 February 1886 and R. G. Dun & Co., carbon report on George W. Durgin, 27 February 1886, in box 13, folder 97. David Lyon, *The Electronic Eye: The Rise of Surveillance Society* (St. Paul: University of Minnesota Press, 1994), ch. 2.

19. Allan Nevins, *John D. Rockefeller: The Heroic Age of American Enterprise* (New York: Charles Scribner's Sons, 1940), 1:210–217, 266–273, quotation on 266–267. Thomas N. Walker to Rockefeller, Walkerton, Va., 11 March 1891, box 48, folder 357. Failure became a category of identity through intersections of surveillance and confession. My analysis owes much to Michel Foucault's observation that in modern society, "The obligation to confess is now relayed through so many points, is so deeply ingrained in us, that we no longer perceive it as the effect of a power that constrains us." Michel Foucault, *The History of Sexuality, Volume 1: An Introduction,* trans. Robert Hurley (New York: Vintage Books, 1990 [1978]), 60; see also Michel Foucault, *Discipline and Punish: The Birth of the Prison,* 2nd ed., trans. Alan Sheridan (New York: Vintage, 1995 [1977]), 170–171.

20. Mrs. George E. Coryell to Rockefeller, Monte Vista, Colo., 15 March 1889, box 8, folder 62. Pierce to Rockefeller.

21. M. Louise Segur to Rockefeller, New York, N.Y., 28 December 1882, box 39, folder 296. Emma K. Tourgée to Rockefeller, Mayville, N.Y., 26 September 1890, box 46, folder 349.

22. I attempt to ground the concept of the gaze in the systems of surveillance deployed by credit agencies and bankruptcy laws, as well as in noninstitutional situations wherein people watched, evaluated, and reported on themselves and those closest to them. Current scholarship emphasizes the reflexive, sexual, and psychological essence of the gaze; these elements are clearly present in begging letters but remain unexplored here. Jacques Lacan's formulation "I saw myself seeing myself" implies that we are all being watched and evaluated all the time, by ourselves as well as by solitary and communal others. See Kaja Silverman, *Male Subjectivity at the Margins* (New York: Routledge, 1992), introduction and chap. 3; Lacan is quoted at 407n13.

23. Important interdisciplinary work suggests how literature and money (including credit) became modern modes of assessing and representing value. See Marc Shell, *Money, Language, and Thought: Literary and Philosophic Economies from the Medieval to the Modern Era* (Baltimore: Johns Hopkins University Press, 1982); Viviana A. Zelizer, *The Social Meaning of Money* (New York: Basic Books, 1994); and Michael O'Malley, "Specie and Species: Race and the Money Question in Nineteenth-Century America,"

American Historical Review 99 (April 1994): 369–395. Tourgée to Rockefeller, Mayville, N.Y., 7 October 1890, box 46, folder 349.

24. Samuel Abbott to Rockefeller, Wakefield, Mass., 26 September 1889, box 1, folder 1. On the connections between sentiment, evangelical religion, and the market, see Jane Tompkins, *Sensational Designs: The Cultural Work of American Fiction, 1790–1860* (New York: Oxford University Press, 1985), 133–135, 139–146.

25. John P. Bell to Rockefeller, Owego, N.Y., 7 October 1889, box 3, folder 24. H. Bruce to Rockefeller, New York, N.Y., 27 April 1889, box 5, folder 43.

26. Ella Busick to Rockefeller, Martinsville, Va., 11 November 1886, box 6, folder 47. M. D. Cowan to Rockefeller, Salisbury, N.C., 22 August 1891, box 8, folder 63. Shirley Samuels, ed., *The Culture of Sentiment: Race, Gender, and Sentimentality in Nineteenth-Century America* (New York: Oxford University Press, 1992). Carol Nackenoff, *The Fictional Republic: Horatio Alger and American Political Discourse* (New York: Oxford University Press, 1994), chs. 3–4. Brook Thomas, *American Literary Realism and the Failed Promise of Contract* (Berkeley: University of California Press, 1997).

27. Jewett P. Cain to Rockefeller, Rutland, Vt., 20 March 1890, box 6, folder 48. Mary F. Braddock to Rockefeller, Richfield, Ohio, 12 February 1894, box 5, folder 38. A. A. Dale to Rockefeller, Bellefonte, Pa., 10 December 1890, box 10, folder 77. Jane Tompkins rightly insists that sentimental literature was subtle and sophisticated, notwithstanding "continual and obvious appeals to the reader's emotions and use [of] technical devices that are distinguished by their utter conventionality" (*Sensational Designs*, 125). Inspired by W. H. Auden, Perry Miller explored "the tyranny of form over thought" in *The New England Mind: From Colony to Province* (Cambridge, Mass.: Belknap Press of Harvard University Press, 1981 [1953]), esp. 31–32, 51–52; also see Michael Denning, *Mechanic Accents: Dime Novels and Working-Class Culture in America* (London: Verso, 1987), 74–79 and 223n7. Recent theoretical debates are introduced in Tzvetan Todorov, *Genres in Discourse* (Cambridge: Cambridge University Press, 1990), chs. 2–3.

28. John R. Campbell to Rockefeller, Springfield, Ill., 5 March 1885, box 6, folder 49. See also Mrs. J. A. Ackley to Rockefeller, Cleveland, 6 December, New York, box 1, folder 1.

29. John Burrill to Rockefeller, Brooklyn, N.Y., 8 April 1889, box 6, folder 46. Jennie Burroughs to Rockefeller, Westport, Ind., 12 July 1886, box 6, folder 47. Jürgen Habermas, *The Structural Transformation of the Public Sphere: An Inquiry into a Category of Bourgeois Society,* trans. Thomas Burger, with the assistance of Frederick Lawrence (Cambridge, Mass.: The MIT Press, 1989 [1962]). Habermas defines a letter as "a conversation with one's self addressed to another person" (48–49). Begging letters mimicked the simultaneously vertical and horizontal socioeconomic relations that Habermas attributes to modern capitalism. The transformation of the public sphere involved an axis shift from the vertical relations that defined feudalism,

Habermas explains, to the "far-reaching network of horizontal economic dependencies" that proliferated in early capitalism. Yet the ensuing liberal vision of "only horizontal exchange relationships among individual commodity owners" was an insidious fiction, because competitive capitalism preserved vertical relationships between those who succeeded and those who did not (15, 144, 244). This troublesome nexus meant that epistolary beggars had to acknowledge their *vertical* relationship to the addressee (which authorized the charitable transaction) at the same time they had to assert a *horizontal* relationship (which constituted their worthiness and eligibility to continue striving in the market). Acknowledging a superior, beggars nonetheless claimed a right to approach any stranger as an equal in the market. This double axis underlies my analysis, and I thank Glenn Hendler and Jan Lewis for prompting this explanation.

30. Coryell to Rockefeller.

31. Fred A. Abbott to Rockefeller, Cleveland, Ohio, 30 December 1889, box 1, folder 1. H. B. Alvord to Rockefeller, Jamaica Plains, Mass., 8 March 1894, box 1, folder 5.

32. J. L. Nichols, *The Business Guide; or, Safe Methods of Business* (Naperville, Ill.: J. L. Nichols and Co., 1900 [1886]), 79. Alvord to Rockefeller.

33. Cleland to Rockefeller.

34. William Graham Sumner, *The Forgotten Man and Other Essays*, ed. Albert Galloway Keller (New Haven: Yale University Press, 1918), 465–495, quotations on 475–476, 480. Huldah Gaskill to Rockefeller, Cleveland, Ohio, 9 March 1891, box 16, folder 120.

35. Sumner, *Forgotten Man*, 474–475, 477.

36. Andrew Carnegie, *The Gospel of Wealth and Other Timely Essays*, ed. Edward C. Kirkland (Cambridge, Mass.: Belknap Press of Harvard University Press, 1962), 16–18; the essay originally appeared under the title "Wealth" in two 1889 issues of the *North American Review*. Harold G. Butt to Rockefeller, New York, N.Y., 17 July 1894, box 6, folder 47. Mrs. R. H. Gordon to Rockefeller, Cleveland, 27 September 188-, box 17, folder 130.

37. Frank W. Smith to Rockefeller, Rockford, Ill., 10 February 1888, and Hebron, Wisc., 27 March 1888, box 43, folder 324. Sergeant Frank W. Smith, Company D, 124th Ohio Infantry, was captured at Pickett's Mills, Ga., on 27 May 1864 and imprisoned at Andersonville; see *Official Roster of the Soldiers of the State of Ohio in the War of the Rebellion, 1861–1866* (Akron: Werner Co., 1886–1895), 8:397. J. H. H. Hedges to Rockefeller, New Orleans, La., 26 April 1891, box 19, folder 146. Salman Akhtar, "'Someday . . .' and 'If Only . . .' Fantasies: Pathological Optimism and Inordinate Nostalgia as Related Forms of Idealization," *Journal of the American Psychoanalytic Association* 44, no. 3 (1996): 723–753.

38. Rockefeller quoted in Allan Nevins, *A Study in Power: John D. Rockefeller, Industrialist and Philanthropist* (New York: Scribner's, 1953), 1:402. Howard Horwitz argues that Rockefeller and the trusts fashioned a "new logic of

selfhood" that was not based on individual agency. Howard Horwitz, "The Standard Oil Trust as Emersonian Hero," *Raritan* 4 (Spring 1987): 97–119. On the political economy of the self, see James Livingston, *Pragmatism and the Political Economy of Cultural Revolution, 1850–1940* (Chapel Hill: University of North Carolina Press, 1994), ch. 6 and 368–369.

39. Tourgée to Rockefeller, 26 September 1890. Theodore Gross, *Albion W. Tourgée* (New York: Grossett and Dunlap, 1963). Albion W. Tourgée, *The Man Who Outlived Himself* (New York: Fords, Howard, and Hulbert, 1898), 15, 35–36.

40. "Story of Rear Guard; Wail of Men Who Were Left Behind in the March to Wealth; Why Were You a Failure?" *Chicago Daily Tribune,* 4 January 1891.

41. John Pintard, 18 May 1819, in *Letters from John Pintard to His Daughter, Eliza Noel Pintard Davidson* (New York: Printed for the New-York Historical Society, 1940), vol. 1, pp. 193–194. Edward W. Bok, *The Young Man in Business* (Philadelphia: Curtis Publishing Co., 1894), 4. "Activity is not always energy," *HMM* 35 (September 1856): 381. T. L. Haines, *Worth and Wealth: Or, the Art of Getting, Saving and Using Money* (New York: Standard Publishing, 1884), 55. "Bullet Ends Worries," *Washington Post,* 28 January 1911. "Tramps of the Ocean," *Newark (Ohio) Daily Advocate,* 11 October 1897. "A Plodder Who Might Have Been an Enthusiast," *Indianapolis Sunday Star,* 24 January 1915.

42. Samuel Clemens to William Dean Howells, Elmira, N.Y., 15 September 1879 and 9 October 1879, in Mark Twain, *The Selected Letters of Mark Twain,* ed. Charles Neider (New York: Harper and Row, 1982), 116–118. Justin Kaplan, *Mr. Clemens and Mark Twain: A Biography* (New York: Simon and Schuster, 1966), 233–234, 285, 321–323, 337–338, 383–384. Mark Twain, *Mark Twain's Notebook,* ed. Albert Bigalow Paine (New York: Harper and Bros., 1935), 212; and *Mark Twain's Fables of Man,* ed. John S. Tuckey (Berkeley: University of California Press, 1972), 197. For a reappraisal of Orion Clemens, see Philip Ashley Fanning, *Mark Twain and Orion Clemens: Brothers, Partners, Strangers* (Tuscaloosa: University of Alabama Press, 2003).

43. "His Last Trip; Suicide of C. Wilmer Fulsom, the Well Known Traveling Man," *Portsmouth* [Ohio] *Times,* 6 February 1892. "Succeeded at Last; Kohler's Many Attempts to Commit *Suicide;* Had Been Despondent on Account of Business Troubles—Found Dead in a Room with the Gas Turned On," *Brooklyn Eagle,* 23 April 1897.

Epilogue

1. Arthur Miller, *Death of a Salesman* (New York: Penguin Books, 1984 [1949]), 48–49. For the chronology of Willy's life, see June Schlueter, "Remembering Willy's Past: Introducing Postmodern Concerns through *Death of a Salesman,*" in *Approaches to Teaching Miller's Death of a Salesman,* ed.

Matthew C. Roudané (New York: Modern Language Association, 1995), 142–154.

2. Ben Brantley, "A Dark New Production Illuminates 'Salesman,'" *NYT,* 3 November 1998. Margaret Spillane, "Life of a Salesman," *The Nation* (8 March 1999): 7. Walter Goodman, "Cries of Anguish from the Front Lines of Capitalism," *NYT,* 28 April 1999.

3. *Walt Whitman: Complete Poetry and Collected Prose,* ed. Justin Kaplan (New York: Library of America, 1982), 246.

4. Sandage telephone interview with Arthur Miller, 1 March 1999.

5. "The go-ahead man buys Kuppenheimer Clothes," trade card (Asheville, N.C.: R. B. Zageir, 1911), Advertising Ephemera Collection, Rare Book, Manuscript, and Special Collections Library, Duke University, Raleigh, N.C. Warren Susman, "Personality and the Making of Twentieth-Century Culture," in *Culture as History: The Transformation of American Society in the Twentieth Century* (New York: Pantheon Books, 1984), 271–285. Miller, *Death of a Salesman,* 86. Russell H. Conwell, *Acres of Diamonds* (Philadelphia: Miller-Megee Company, 1889). Donald Meyers, *The Positive Thinkers: Popular Religious Psychology from Mary Baker Eddy to Norman Vincent Peale and Ronald Reagan,* 3rd ed. (Middletown, Conn.: Wesleyan University Press, 1988 [1965]).

6. Jim Cullen, *The American Dream: A Short History of an Idea that Shaped a Nation* (New York: Oxford University Press, 2003), 3–4. James Truslow Adams, *The Epic of America* (Boston: Little, Brown, and Co., 1931), 404. Adams popularized the phrase, but Walter Lippmann had used it first in a syndicated column that warned of the "failure of the American dream"; see Walter Lippmann, "Education and the White-Collar Class," *Vanity Fair* 20 (May 1923): 69. In earlier usage, the phrase appeared in military and imperialist contexts, as in "the American dream of Oriental commerce" (1907), "our American dream that no one would ever attack us" (1916), and "the American dream of a great merchant marine" (1919); see "Japan's Business Activity," *Washington Post,* 31 October 1907; "Why Wilson?" *Sandusky* [Ohio] *Star Journal,* 6 October 1916; and "Naval Reserve Force," *Washington Post,* 15 July 1919. Brooks Atkinson, "Fate of the Idealist: In 'American Dream' George O'Neil Describes the Closing of a Tradition—Poet and Social Economist," *NYT,* 5 March 1933. U.S. Bureau of the Census, *Historical Statistics of the United States, Colonial Times to 1970* (1975; repr., White Plains, N.Y.: Kraus International Publications, 1989), 1:135, 2:912, 1038. Morris Fishbein and William A. White, eds., *Why Men Fail* (New York: The Century Co., 1928). George Jean Nathan and H. L. Mencken, *The American Credo: A Contribution toward the Interpretation of the National Mind,* rev. ed. (New York: Alfred A. Knopf, 1921), 30, 39–40.

7. "Loser in Street Chooses Suicide," *Helena* [Montana] *Independent,* 1 November 1929. "Another 'Stock Market Suicide,'" *Danville* [Virginia] *Bee,* 15 November 1929. "G. E. Cutler Dies in Wall St. Leap," *NYT,* 17 November

1929. "St. Louis Broker Suicide over Crash," *NYT,* 24 November 1929. Notwithstanding these and other known cases, statistically suicides did not rise in 1929; see John Kenneth Galbraith, *The Great Crash, 1929* (Boston: Houghton Mifflin, 1955), 133–137. Studs Terkel, *Hard Times: An Oral History of the Great Depression* (New York: Pantheon, 1970), 80. Robert S. McElvaine, ed., *Down and Out in the Great Depression: Letters from the Forgotten Man* (Chapel Hill: University of North Carolina Press, 1983), 226, 158. "Man Suicides," *Indiana* [Pennsylvania] *Evening Gazette,* 4 December 1937.

8.   Miller, *Death of a Salesman,* 56–57.

9.   "Undistinguished Americans," in *A Rebecca Harding Davis Reader,* ed. Jean Pfaelzer (Pittsburgh: University of Pittsburgh Press, 1995), 458–461. Hamilton Holt, ed., *The Life Stories of Undistinguished Americans* (New York: Routledge, 1989).

10.   Miller, *Death of a Salesman,* 82, 126.

11.   F. Scott Fitzgerald, *The Great Gatsby* (New York: Simon and Schuster, 1995 [1925]), 188. John Updike interviewed on *The Charlie Rose Show,* 22 December 1992, WNYC Television, New York. Terrence Rafferty, "Ralph Ellison's Unfinished Business," *GQ* (July 1999): 45–51, esp. 51.

12.   Sinclair Lewis, *Babbitt* (New York: Signet Classics, 1992 [1922]), 326. Tennessee Williams, *Tennessee Williams: Plays, 1937–1955,* ed. Mel Gussow and Kenneth Holditch (New York: Library of America, 2000), 563. Eugene O'Neill, *Long Day's Journey into Night* (New Haven: Yale University Press, 1956), 166. Matthew Gurewitsch, "A Country of Lesser Giants," *NYT,* 4 April 1999.

13.   Alan Schwartz, "A Fifty-Year Streak in a Game of Failure," *NYT,* 19 December 1999. Daniel B. Schneider, "Envying the Joneses," *NYT,* 15 February 1998.

14.   David Riesman, with Nathan Glazer and Reuel Denney, *The Lonely Crowd: A Study of the Changing American Character* (New Haven: Yale University Press, 1950). C. Wright Mills, *White Collar: The American Middle Classes* (New York: Oxford University Press, 1951). William H. Whyte, *The Organization Man* (New York: Simon and Schuster, 1956). Vance Packard, *The Status Seekers* (New York: D. McKay Co., 1959). David Riesman, *Individualism Reconsidered, and Other Essays* (Glencoe, Ill.: Free Press, 1954), 33, 55. *Will Success Spoil Rock Hunter?* dir. Frank Tashlin, Twentieth Century Fox Home Video, 1996 [1957]. On changing American masculinities in the mid-twentieth century, see Peter G. Filene, *Him/Her/Self: Gender Identities in Modern America,* 3rd ed. (Baltimore: Johns Hopkins University Press, 1998), ch. 6.

15.   Mark Zwonitzer with Charles Hirshberg, *Will You Miss Me When I'm Gone? The Carter Family and Their Legacy in American Music* (New York: Simon and Schuster, 2002), 8. Colin Escott and Kira Florita, *Hank Wil-*

liams: *Snapshots from the Lost Highway* (Cambridge, Mass.: Da Capo Press, 2001), 115.

16. Malvina Reynolds, "I Don't Mind Failing," in *The Muse of Parker Street: More Songs by Malvina Reynolds* (New York: Oak Publications, 1967), 32. Sloane Wilson, *The Man in the Gray Flannel Suit* (New York: Simon and Schuster, 1955).

17. Bryan K. Garman, *A Race of Singers: Whitman's Working Class Hero from Guthrie to Springsteen* (Chapel Hill: University of North Carolina Press, 2000).

18. Bob Dylan, "The Times They Are A-Changin'," on *The Times They Are A-Changin'*, Columbia Records, 1964. Bob Dylan, *Lyrics, 1962–1985* (New York: Knopf, 1998). Greil Marcus, *Invisible Republic: Bob Dylan's Basement Tapes* (New York: Henry Holt, 1997). Whitman, *Complete Poetry*, 377.

19. Bob Dylan, "Subterranean Homesick Blues," on *Bringing It All Back Home*, Columbia Records, 1965.

20. Bob Dylan, "Love Minus Zero/No Limit," on *Bringing It All Back Home*.

21. Bob Dylan, "It's Alright Ma (I'm Only Bleeding)," on *Bringing It All Back Home*. "Me and Bobby McGee," words and music by Kris Kristofferson, on Janis Joplin, *Pearl*, Columbia Records, 1971. Henry D. Thoreau, *Walden*, ed. J. Lyndon Shanley (Princeton: Princeton University Press, 1971), 326.

22. [Henry D. Thoreau], *The Journal of Henry D. Thoreau*, ed. Bradford Torrey and Francis H. Allen (New York: Dover Publications, 1962 [1906]), 2:1205 (14 october 1857).

23. Sigmund Freud, *Civilization and Its Discontents*, trans. and ed. James Strachey (New York: W. W. Norton, 1989 [1961]). Norman O. Brown, *Life against Death: The Psychoanalytic Meaning of History* (Middletown, Conn.: Wesleyan University Press, 1959), 234–304. John Kenneth Galbraith, *The Age of Uncertainty* (Boston: Houghton Mifflin, 1977), 161. Galbraith begins a chapter with these words and notes that the chapter summarizes the arguments of his book *Money: Whence It Came, Where It Went* (Boston: Houghton Mifflin, 1975).

24. David J. Morrow, "The Hit Quiz Show for Those Who Owe," *NYT*, 11 August 1996. Jones and Grassley quoted in Saul Hansell, "Battle Emerging on How to Revise Bankruptcy Law," *NYT*, 19 October 1997. Gekas quoted in Katharine Q. Seelye, "House Approves Legislation to Curb Laws on Bankruptcy," *NYT*, 11 June 1998. Lawyers quoted in Bruce Felton, "Going Bankrupt: The Scarlet 'B' or the Great Escape?" *NYT*, 27 October 1996; and John J. D'Emic, "Bankrupt, but Honest" (letter to the editor), *NYT*, 29 May 1995. Karen Gross, *Failure and Forgiveness: Rebalancing the Bankruptcy System* (New Haven: Yale University Press, 1997).

25. James Surowiecki, "The Financial Page: Where Do Dot-Coms Go When They Die?" *New Yorker* (12 June 2000), 34. Louis Menand, "The Downside of the Upside of the Downside," *New York Times Magazine*, 9 January

2000, 13–14. "Speculating and Failing," *HMM* 2 (April 1848): 347. "I'm a Loser," *New York Times Magazine* (4 June 2000), 38–40.

26. "Professor Provokes Furor over Race Comment," *NYT,* 16 September 1997. Neil A. Lewis, "No Room for Bush's Civil Rights Appointee," *NYT,* 5 February 2002. Darryl Fears, "Disputed Conservative Takes Rights Panel Seat," *Washington Post,* 18 May 2002. Darryl Fears, "GOP's Black Counterweight; Conservative Kirsanow Bucks Civil Rights Establishment," *Washington Post,* 28 October 2002. Richard J. Herrnstein and Charles Murray, *The Bell Curve: Intelligence and Class Structure in American Life* (New York: Free Press, 1995). Joe L. Kincheloe, Shirley R. Steinberg, and Aaron D. Gresson, eds., *Measured Lies: The Bell Curve Examined* (Boston: St. Martin's Press, 1996).

27. "Fran Lebowitz on Money," *Vanity Fair* 60 (July 1997): 94–97, 137–138, esp. 97.

28. Richard Powers, "Losing Our Souls, Bit by Bit," *NYT,* 15 July 1998. Tina Kelley, "When Collection Software Runs, Debtors Can't Hide," *NYT,* 6 May 1999. Gore Vidal, "The War at Home," *Vanity Fair* 61 (November 1998): 96–106, 110–112. Christian Parenti, *The Soft Cage: Surveillance in America from Slave Passes to the War on Terror* (New York: Basic Books, 2003).

29. *The Wizard of Oz,* DVD, directed by Mervyn LeRoy (1939; Burbank, Calif.: Warner Home Video, 1999). *Frank Capra's It's a Wonderful Life,* DVD, directed by Frank Capra (1946; [Los Angeles, Calif.]: Republic Entertainment, 1998). Beck [Hansen], "Loser," on *Mellow Gold,* Uni/Dgc Records, 1994.

30. Reed Massengill, *Portrait of a Racist: The Man Who Killed Medgar Evers?* (New York: St. Martin's Press, 1994). James Barron, "Exit Two Bit Players on a Road to Nowhere," *NYT,* 7 May 1995. Jo Thomas, "A Troubled Man in a Life of Dead Ends, False Starts, and Family Problems," *NYT,* 24 December 1997. "Two Suspected Gunmen Were Seen as Losers by Other Students," *NYT,* 22 April 1999. "Internet Provides an Outlet for Dialogue on Ostracism," *NYT,* 24 April 1999. "The Trouble with Looking for Signs of Trouble," *NYT,* 25 April 1999. Adrian Nicole LeBlanc, "The Outsiders: How the Picked-On Cope—or Don't," *New York Times Magazine,* 22 August 1999, 36–41.

31. Diana B. Henriques, "In Death's Shadow, Valuing Each Life," *NYT,* 30 December 2001. Scott A. Sandage, "The *L* on Your Forehead," in *Whitney Biennial 2004* (exhibition catalog), ed. Chrissie Iles, Shamim M. Momin, and Debra Singer (New York: Harry N. Abrams, 2004), 92–97.

32. [United Press Syndicate], "Jesse Livermore, Speculator, Takes Life in New York; One Time 'Boy Plunger' Shoots Self to Death after Leaving Note Saying, 'I Am a Failure,'" *Oshkosh (Wisconsin) Daily Northwestern,* 29 November 1940. "Jesse Livermore Ends Life in Hotel," *NYT,* 29 November

1940. Arthur Miller quoted in John Lahr, "Making Willy Loman," *The New Yorker*, 25 January 1999, 42–49, esp. 47–48.

33. Miller, *Death of a Salesman*, 33, 82, 132. *Wallace Stevens: Collected Poetry and Prose*, ed. Frank Kermode et al. (New York: Library of America, 1997), 309–310.

34. Mark Twain, *Following the Equator, and Anti-Imperialist Essays*, ed. Shelly Fisher Fishkin (New York: Oxford University Press, 1996 [1897]) 268. Andrew Delbanco, *The Death of Satan: How Americans Have Lost the Sense of Evil* (New York: Farrar, Straus and Giroux, 1995), 105.

Acknowledgments

Like many of this book's worst offenders, I have brazenly enriched myself by failing others. In the decade I spent researching and writing this book, I ran up debts that I knew all along I could never make good. All I can do is list my creditors.

I am long overdue in thanking my writing teachers—first of all, Shirley M. Sandage, my mother—and Dale Harmon, Deadra Stanton, Anne Manley, Helen Klussman, Jack McCabe, Chuck Anderson, David Schaal, Evelyn Haught, David Krohne, David J. Gibson, and T. K. Hunter, whose friendship is as lovingly crafted as her prose.

At Harvard University Press, Joyce Seltzer taught me how to write a book and how to keep the faith. Donna Bouvier's copyediting gave my prose (and me) room to breathe. Thanks also to Rachel Weinstein in the New York office and to Tim Jones and Rose Ann Miller in Cambridge.

Lifelong readers know how much they owe to librarians, but only authors can appreciate how completely dependent we are on them. Helen Davis and Marie Colby first showed me the way. I could not have come this far without the help of scholars employed in libraries, archives, and museums. They aided my research at Alexander Library at Rutgers University and the Law Library at Rutgers Newark; the American Antiquarian Society; Bentley Historical Library at the University of Michigan; the Boston Public Library; Butler Library and the Law Library at Columbia University; the Bridgton, Maine, Historical Society; the Firelands Historical Society in Norwalk, Ohio, and the Norwalk Public Library; Hagley Museum and Library; the Historical Society of Pennsylvania; the Library Company of Philadelphia; the Massachusetts Historical Society; the Missouri Historical Society; the Nantucket Historical Society; the National Archives in Washington, Philadelphia, and New York City; the New-York Historical Society; the New York Public Library; the New York State Archives; the Rhode Island Historical Society; the Rhode Island State Archives; the Rockefeller Archive Center; the Saint Louis University Archives; the Smithsonian Institution; the Thoreau Institute at Walden Woods, Lincoln, Massachusetts; the State

Historical Society of Wisconsin; the United States Military Academy at West Point; the Virginia Historical Society; the Western Reserve Historical Society; and the Worcester County Law Library. Special thanks go to Laura Linard and her staff, especially Nicole Hayes, at Baker Library, Harvard Business School; to Fred Bauman, Clark Evans, Jeff Flannery, Tom Mann, Bruce Martin, John Sellers, and Mary Wolfskill at the Library of Congress; and to Susan Collins, Geraldine Kruglak, and Joan Stein at Carnegie Mellon University.

I incurred more traditional debts through the generosity of the Falk Fellowship Fund in the Humanities and the Faculty Development Fund at Carnegie Mellon University; the Hagley Center for the History of Business, Technology, and Society; the Schlatter fund of the Rutgers Department of History; the Rockefeller Archive Center; the Kate B. and Hall J. Peterson fellowship fund of the American Antiquarian Society; the Albert J. Beveridge and Littleton-Griswold funds of the American Historical Association; the Mellon-Christian fund of the Virginia Historical Society; the National Endowment for the Humanities dissertation grants program and Summer Stipends program; the Smithsonian Institution; the Society of Fellows in the Humanities at Columbia University; and the J. Franklin Jameson Fellowship in American History from the Library of Congress and the American Historical Association. I am especially grateful to my hosts in residential fellowships, including Ellen S. Dunlap, John B. Hench, Roger Horowitz, Marsha Manns, Charlie McGovern, Phil Scranton, Darwin H. Stapleton, Les Vogel, and David Wigdor.

Born Losers began as a 1995 doctoral dissertation at Rutgers University, where I was advised by Jackson Lears, whose intellectual and literary guidance is beyond measure. He has remained my teacher and friend— as have dissertation committee members Jan Lewis and Jim Livingston. Outside advice came from the indefatigable Michael Zuckerman of the University of Pennsylvania. Paul Clemens, John Whiteclay Chambers II, John Gillis, Philip Greven and Helen Greven, and Ginny Yans have continued to shape my career. After leaving Rutgers, I have benefited from informal mentoring by David W. Blight, Michael Burlingame, Joan Cashin, Eric Foner, Carolyn Karcher, Pete Karsten, John Lyne, and Bill McFeely.

Many scholars have shared insights and sources with me, including

Ed Balleisen, Toby Ditz, Ann Fabian, and Bruce Mann—the pioneers of what we now call failure studies. I also thank Alan Berolzheimer, Barry Bienstock, Kate Chavigny, Barry Cohen, Ruth Crocker, Robin Dawes, Benjamin Filene, Dawn Greeley, Daniel Hack, Phyllis Whitman Hunter, Sarah Kidd, Staughton Lynd, Jonathan Mann, Barbara Matthews, John Modell, Phillip Mohr, Rowena Olegario, Mary Panzer, Jim Pearson, Niko Pfund, David Sicilia, Beryl Satter, Katherine V. Snyder, Michael Winship, Susan Yohn, and Carol Zisowitz. Wallace Alcorn shared materials from a forthcoming biography of his ancestor William Henry Brisbane. Austin Meredith made available his unrivalled Thoreau databases from the "Stack of the Artist of Kouroo" project at Brown University. Pleun Bouricius, Christine Lamar, Tom Lowry and Beverly Lowry, Henry R. Timman, Jack Waugaman, and David Yosifon provided useful research materials. John Burke of Ithaca, Nebraska, kindly gave me the use of his rare photograph of Samuel L. Clemens and John T. Raymond. Barbara Bennett of Salisbury, Maryland, shared research on her ancestor, the artist known as Pierre Morand. Patricia Pierose shared materials about her ancestor Theron S. Nettleton. George F. Kennan furnished information and Jack and Alice Kennan sent a photograph of their ancestor Jairus Kennan. Henry E. Young, of Norwalk, Ohio, gave me a tour of his home, once owned by John Beardsley, and provided documentation on its history. I also thank Julie Hiner at Dun & Bradstreet.

The lonely business of research and writing would be unbearable without the friendship and insights of fellow scholars. At Rutgers and since, I have enjoyed the companionship of Jeanne Bowlan and Kathleen Casey, Jennie Brier, Danny Burnstein and Jo Gershman Burnstein, Beth Campbell, Noah Elkin, Grace Hale, Beatrix Hoffman, Paul Israel and Kali Israel, Lisa Kannenberg, Glen Kuecker, Lynn Mahoney and Charlie Ponce de Leon, Jacquelyn Miller and Gordon Miller, Tammy Proctor, Brian Roberts, Martin Summers, Andrea Volpe, and Torun Willits. I also thank Sven Beckert, Alison Clarke, Jon Earle and Leslie Tuttle, Curtis Fox, LeeEllen Friedland and David Taylor, Linda Frost, Jonathan Sterne, Meg Jacobs and Eric Goldberg, and Joshua Wolf Shenk. Martha Dennis Burns has been an especially giving colleague and friend.

Carnegie Mellon University has given me a wonderful community of scholars. Steve Schlossman and Joe Trotter, as department heads, and Joel Tarr and David Miller, as faculty mentors, have been wise and encouraging advisors. Peter Stearns and John Lehoczky have been especially supportive deans. I also thank Paul Hopper, David Hounshell, Tera Hunter, and Dave Kaufer. Mary Lindemann and Michael Miller, Kate Lynch, Indira Nair, and Judith Schacter and Albrecht Funk have given friendship as well as guidance. Nothing could get done without the professional support of Gail Dickey, Dee Clydesdale, Natalie Taylor, Janet Walsh, and Amy Hallas-Wells. Ken Andreyo, Head of Photographic Services, copied many of the images used in this book. I also thank doctoral students Sonya Barclay, James Longhurst, Jason Martinek, John Robertson, and Susan Spellman.

Many people have read and commented on parts of this book, including Elizabeth Blackmar, John L. Brooke, Mary Chapman, Christopher Clark, Matthew Craig, Peter Filene, Walter Friedman, Claudia Golden, Glenn Hendler, Roger Horowitz, Jon Klancher, Karl Kroeber, Angel Kwollek-Folland, Pamela Walker Laird, Ken Lipartito, Charles McCurdy, Sonya Michel, Dan Rodgers, Asif Siddiqi, Herb Sloan, Ronald Walters, Thomas Winter, and Mary Yeager. I also thank the Economic History Seminar at Harvard Business School; and the Nineteenth-Century Forum at the University of Michigan. Despite their collective wisdom, this book's failures and misunderstandings are my fault alone.

Writing about failure has been something of a mind game, for me and everyone who loves me. Through the decade I spent outrunning my topic's self-fulfilling prophesies, I often failed my friends and family—in particular David Jasper, who supported me unfailingly during our fifteen years together. Carol Helstosky and Martin Gloege, Suzanne Kaufman and Bill Sites, Todd Shepard, Christine Skwiot and Larry Gross, and Jim Sullivan have kept me going. Old friends Jennifer Allen Newton and Jamie Newton, Cindy Anderson and Cary Anderson, Beth Reynolds, Kathrin Kana, Jody Hovland and Ron Clark, Linda Hopper, the late Michaela Cohan, Miss Debra Palmer, Linda Hadley, Tom Hier and Bill Myhre, Kristin Neun and Lee Clarke, Reggie Allen and Greg Case, Linda Frost, Jeff Zajac and Maria Mataliano, and Mitch Watkins stayed in touch despite my long silences. New friends Bob Zehmisch, Caroline Acker, Mia Bay, Tina Cherpes and Terri Henson, Kathy Newman, and

Diane Shaw and Kai Guschow kept on giving when I didn't. Mike Witmore and Kellie Robertson, along with Carol Hamilton, provided moral and every other kind of support. Michael Kenin, Carol Roskin, Esther Schlesinger, and especially Wendy Kaufman helped me become a better writer and (I hope) a better person. At every level, nobody helped more than Greg Cherpes.

My family has remained loving and patient through all the shortened visits and missed holidays. I still look up to my shorter and older brother, Chip Sandage. John Sandage and Gregg Blackley have encouraged and comforted me at every turn. Christopher Sandage, Autumn Sandage, Lydia Coleman, and my aunt Joy Swab's large brood always remind me how to have fun. Those who are gone—Margaret Garrity and my grandmother, Flossie M. Farrer—were strong women who showed me what kind of man I could become. Finally, I thank my parents. I owe my love of books and history to my mother, Shirley M. Sandage, whose lifelong activism has made the world (and certainly *my* world) a better place. My father, Richard E. Sandage, Sr., has taught me how to work and how to love. They have never failed me, and to them I owe everything.

Index

Page numbers in italics refer to figures.